Introduction to
COMPUTING SYSTEMS

From Bits and Gates to C and Beyond

Yale N. Patt
University of Texas at Austin

Sanjay J. Patel
University of Illinois at Urbana

The McGraw-Hill Companies, Inc.
Primis Custom Publishing

New York   St. Louis   San Francisco   Auckland   Bogotá
Caracas   Lisbon   London   Madrid   Mexico   Milan   Montreal
New Delhi   Paris   San Juan   Singapore   Sydney   Tokyo   Toronto

McGraw-Hill Higher Education
A Division of The McGraw-Hill Companies

Introduction to Computing Systems
From Bits and Gates to C and Beyond

McGraw-Hill's Primis Custom Series consists of products that are produced from camera-ready copy. Peer review, class testing, and accuracy are primarily the responsibility of the author(s).

1 2 3 4 5 6 7 8 9 0 QSR QSR 9 0 9

ISBN 0-07-237683-X

Cover Design: Kyle A. Zimmerman
Printer/Binder: Quebecor Printing Dubuque, Inc.

Preface to the Preliminary Version

This textbook has evolved from EECS 100, the first computing course for computer science, computer engineering, and electrical engineering majors at the University of Michigan, that Kevin Compton and the first author introduced for the first time Fall term 1995. It has been taught every semester since then.

EECS 100 happened because Computer Science and Engineering faculty had been dissatisfied for many years with the lack of student comprehension of some very basic concepts. For example, students had a lot of trouble with pointer variables. Recursion seemed to be "magic," beyond understanding.

We decided in 1993 that the conventional wisdom of starting with a high level programming language, which was the way we (and most universities were doing it) was flawed. We decided that the reason students were not "getting it" was that they were forced to memorize technical details, when they did not understand the basic underpinnings.

The result is the bottom-up approach taken in this book. We treat (in order) MOS transistors (very briefly, long enough for students to grasp their global switch-level behavior), logic gates, latches, logic structures, (MUX, Decoder, Adder, gated latches), finally culminating in an implementation of memory. From there, we move on to the Von Neumann model of execution, then a simple computer (the LC-2), machine language programming of the LC-2, assembly language programming of the LC-2, the high level language C, recursion, elementary data structures (arrays and linked lists), and finally some basic analysis of some of the algorithms the students encounter throughout the book.

We do not endorse today's popular "information hiding" approach when it comes to learning. Information hiding is a useful productivity enhancement technique AFTER one understands what is going on. But until one gets to that point, we insist that "information hiding" gets in the way of understanding. Thus, we continually build on what has gone before, so that nothing is magic, and everything can be tied to the foundation that has already been laid.

What is in the Book:

The book breaks down into two major segments, (a) the underlying structure of a computer, as manifest in the LC-2, and (b) programming in a high level language, in our case C.

The LC-2.

We start with the underpinnings that are needed to understand the workings of a "real" computer. Chapter 2 introduces the bit and arithmetic and logical operations on bits. Then we begin to build the structure needed to understand the LC-2. Chapter 3 takes the student from MOS transistors, step by step, to a "real" memory. The memory consists of 4 words of 3 bits each, rather than 64 megabytes, but the picture fits on one page (Figure 3.20), and by the time the students get there, they have been exposed to all the elements that make the memory "work." Chapter 4 introduces the Von Neumann execution model, as a lead-in to Chapter 5, the LC-2.

The LC-2 is a 16 bit architecture that includes physical I/O via keyboard and monitor, TRAPs to the operating system for handling service calls, conditional branches on N, Z, and P condition codes, a subroutine call/return mechanism, a minimal set of operate instructions (ADD, AND, and NOT), and various addressing modes for loads and stores (direct, indirect, base+offset, and an immediate mode for loading effective addresses).

Students study the operating system routines (written in LC-2 code) for carrying out physical I/O invoked by TRAP.

Chapter 6 is devoted to Programming Methodology (stepwise refinement) and Debugging, and Chapter 7 is an introduction to assembly language programming. We have developed a Simulator and an Assembler for the LC-2. Actually, we have developed two Simulators, one that runs on NT and one that runs on UNIX. These Simulators can be downloaded by the reader at no charge.

Students use the Simulator to test and debug programs written in LC-2 machine language and in LC-2 Assembler. The Simulator allows on-line debugging (deposit, examine, single-step, set breakpoint, etc.) from almost any workstation. The first program is written in machine language, the second and third in LC-2 assembler.

Assembly Language is taught, not to train expert assembly language programmers. Indeed, if the purpose was to train assembly language programmers, the material would be presented in a senior level course, not in an introductory course for freshmen. Rather, the material is presented in Chapter 7 because it is consistent with the paradigm of the book. In our bottom-up approach, by the time the student reaches Chapter 7, he/she can handle the process of transforming assembly language programs to sequences of 0s and 1s. We go through the process of assembly step-by-step for a very simple LC-2 Assembler. By hand assembling, the student (at a very small additional cost in time) reinforces the important fundamental concept of translation.

It is also the case that assembly language provides a user-friendly notation to describe machine instructions, something that is particularly useful for the second half of the book, Starting in Chapter 11, when we teach the semantics of C statements, it is far easier for the reader to deal with ADD R1,R2,R3 than with 0001001010000011.

Chapter 8 deals with physical input (from a keyboard) and output (to a monitor). Chapter 9 deals with TRAPs to the operating system, and subroutine calls and returns. The first half of the book concludes with Chapter 10, a treatment of stacks and data conversion at the LC-2 level, and a comprehensive example that makes use of both. The example is the simulation of a Hand Calculator, which is implemented by a main program and 11 subroutines.

The language C.

From there, we move on to C. The C programming language occupies the second half of the book. By the time the student gets to C, he/she has an understanding of the layers below. Each time a new construct in C is introduced, the student is shown the LC-2 code that a compiler would produce. We cover the basic constructs of C (variables, operators, control, functions), pointers, recursion, arrays, structures, I/O, complex data structures, C libraries and dynamic allocation.

We have found that pointer variables (Chapter 17) is not at all a problem, since by the time students encounter them, they have a good understanding of what memory is all about, since they have analyzed the logic design of a small memory (Chapter 3). They know the difference, for example, between a memory location's address and the data stored there.

Recursion ceases to be magic since, by the time a student gets to that point, (Chapter 16), he/she has already encountered all the underpinnings. students understand how stacks work at the machine level (Chapter 10), and they understand the call/return mechanism from their LC-2 machine language programming, and the need for linkages between a called program and the return to the caller (Chapter 9). From this foundation, it is not a large step to explain functions by introducing run-time activation records (Chapter 14), with a lot of mystery about argument passing, dynamic declarations, etc. going away. Since a function can call a function, it is one additional small step (certainly no magic involved) for a function to call itself.

Some observations.

Understanding, not memorizing. Since the course builds from the bottom up, we have found that less memorization of seemingly arbitrary rules is required than in traditional programming courses. Students understand that the rules make sense since by the time a topic is taught, the student has an awareness of how that topic is implemented at the levels below it. This approach is good preparation for later courses in design, where understanding of and insights gained from fundamental underpinnings is essential to making the required design tradeoffs.

The student (not the TA) debugs the student's program. We hear complaints from industry all the time about CS graduates not being able to program. Part of the problem is the helpful TA who contributes far too much of the intellectual component of the student's program, so the student never has to really master the art for himself. Our approach is to push the student to do the job without the TA. Part of this comes from the bottom-up approach where memorizing is minimized and the student builds on what he/she already knows. Part of this is the Simulator, which the student uses from day one. The student is taught debugging from the beginning, and is required to use the debugging tools of the Simulator to get his/her programs to work from the very beginning. The combination of the Simulator and the order in which the subject material is taught results in students actually debugging their own programs instead of taking their programs to the TA for help. ...and the too-often result that the TAs end up writing the programs for the students.

Preparation for the future: Cutting through protective layers. In today's real world, professionals who use computers in systems but remain ignorant of what is going on underneath are likely to discover the hard way that the effectiveness of their solutions are impacted adversely by things other than the actual programs they write. This is true for the sophisticated computer programmer as well as the sophisticated engineer.

Serious programmers will write more efficient code if they understand what is going on beyond the statements in their high level language.

Engineers, and not just computer engineers, are having to interact with their computer systems today more and more at the device or pin level. In systems where the computer is being used to sample data from some metering device such as a weather meter or feedback control system, the engineer needs to know more than just how to program in FORTRAN. This is true of mechanical, chemical, and aeronautical engineers today, not just electrical engineers. Consequently, the high level programming language course, where the compiler protects the student from everything "ugly" underneath, does not serve most engineering students well, and certainly does not prepare them for the future.

Rippling effects through the Curriculum. The material of "From Bits and Gates ..." clearly has a rippling effect on what can be taught in subsequent courses. Subsequent programming courses can not only assume the students know the syntax of C but also understand how it relates to the underlying architecture. Consequently, the focus can be on problem solving and more sophisticated data structures. On the hardware side, a similar effect is seen in courses in digital logic design and in computer organization. Students start the logic design course with an appreciation of what the logic circuits they master are good for. In the computer organization course, the starting point is much further along than when students are seeing the term Program Counter for the first time. Feedback from Michigan faculty members in the follow-on courses have noticed substantial improvement in student's comprehension, compared to what they saw before students took EECS 100.

We hope you will enjoy the approach taken in this book. Nonetheless, we are mindful that the current version is preliminary, and both of us welcome your comments on any aspect of it. You can reach us by email at patt@ece.utexas.edu and sjp@crhc.uiuc.edu. We hope you will.

Yale N. Patt Sanjay J. Patel

August 1, 1999

Contents

Chapter 1

Welcome Aboard.

1.1 What we will try to do.

Welcome to "From Bits and Gates to C and Beyond." Our intent is to introduce you over the next 456 pages to the world of computing. As we do so, we have one objective above all others always in mind: to show you very clearly that there is no magic to computing. The computer is a deterministic system – every time we hit it over the head in the same way and in the same place (provided, of course, it was in the same starting condition), we get the same response. The computer is not an electronic genius; on the contrary, if anything, it is an electronic idiot, doing exactly what we tell it to do. It has no mind of its own.

What appears to be a very complex organism is really just a systematically interconnected huge collection of very simple parts. Our job over the rest of this book will be to introduce you to those very simple parts, and step-by-step build the interconnected structure that you know by the name computer. Like a house, we will start at the bottom, construct the foundation first, and then go on to add layers and layers, as we get closer and closer to what most people know as a full-blown computer. Each time we add a layer, we will explain what we are doing, tying the new ideas to the underlying fabric. Our goal is that when we are done, you will be able to write programs in a computer language like C or C++, using the sophisticated features of that language, and understand what is going on underneath, inside the computer.

1.2 How will we get there.

We will start (Chapter 2) by noting that the computer is a piece of electronic equipment, and as such consists of electronic parts interconnected by wires. Every wire in the computer (at every moment in time) is either at a high voltage or a low voltage. We do not differentiate exactly how high. For example, we do not distinguish voltages of 115 volts from voltages of 118 volts. We only care whether there is or whether there is not a large voltage relative to

0 volts. That absence or presence of a large voltage relative to 0 volts we represent as 0 or 1.

We will encode all information as sequences of 0's and 1's. For example, one encoding of the letter "a" that is commonly used is the sequence 01100001. One encoding of the decimal number "35" is the sequence 00100011. We will see how to perform operations on such encoded information.

Once we are comfortable with information represented as codes made up of 0's and 1's and operations (addition, for example) being performed on these representations, we will begin the process of showing how a computer works. In Chapter 3, we will see how the transistors that make up today's microprocessors work. We will further see how those transistors are combined into larger structures that perform operations, like addition, and into structures that allow us to save information for later use. In Chapter 4, we will combine these larger structures into the Von Neumann machine, a basic model that describes how a computer works. In Chapter 5, we will begin to study a simple computer, the LC-2. LC-2 stands for Little Computer 2 – we started with LC-1, but needed a second chance before we got it right! The LC-2 has all the important characteristics of the microprocessors that you may have already heard of, for example, the Intel 8088 which was used in the first IBM PCs back in 1981. ...or the Motorola 68000, which was used in the Macintosh, vintage 1984. ... or the Pentium II, the high performance microprocessor of choice in the PC of 1998. That is, the LC-2 has all the important characteristics of these "real" microprocessors, without being so complicated that it gets in the way of your understanding.

Once we understand how the LC-2 works, the next step is to program it, first in its own language (Chapter 6), then in a language called Assembly Language that is a little bit easier for humans to work with (Chapter 7). Chapter 8 will deal with the problem of getting information into (input) and out of (output) the LC-2. Chapter 9 will cover two sophisticated LC-2 mechanisms, TRAPs and subroutines.

We will conclude our introduction to programming the LC-2 in Chapter 10 by first introducing two important concepts (stacks and data conversion), and then by showing a sophisticated example: an LC-2 program that carries out the work of a Hand Calculator

In the second half of the book (Chapters 11-20), we will turn our attention to a high level programming language, C. We will include many aspects of C that are usually not dealt with in an introductory textbook. In almost all cases, we will tie high level C constructs to the underlying LC-2, so that you will understand what you demand of the computer when you use a particular construct in a C program.

Our treatment of C will start with basic topics such as operators (Chapter 12), control structures (Chapter 13), and functions (Chapter 14). We will then move on to the more advanced topics of debugging C programs (Chapter 15), recursion (Chapter 16), and pointers and arrays (Chapter 17).

We will conclude our introduction to C by examining two very common high-level constructs, Input/Output in C (Chapter 18) and the linked list (Chapter 19).

Finally, we will see (Chapter 20) that not all computer programs use the underlying hardware equally efficiently. We will analyze two common programming techniques (recursion and iteration) and see what the respective benefits and costs of using them are.

1.3 A Computer System

We have used the word computer many times in the preceding paragraphs, and although we did not say so explicitly, we used it to mean the mechanism that does two things: direct the processing of information and perform the actual processing of information. By the word "direct" the processing of information, we mean figuring out which task should get carried out next. By the word "perform" the actual processing, we mean doing the actual additions, multiplications, etc. that are necessary to get the job done. A more precise term for this mechanism is the central processing unit (cpu), or simply THE processor. This textbook is primarily about the processor and the programs that are executed by the processor.

Twenty years ago, the processor was constructed out of eight or ten x inch electronic boards, each containing 50 or more electronic parts known as integrated circuit packages (see figure 1.1). Today, a processor usually consists of a single microprocessor chip, built on a piece of silicon material, measuring little more than an inch square, and containing many millions of transistors (see figure 1.2).

Figure 1.1: A cpu board, vintage 1978

However, when most people use the word "computer," they usually mean more than the processor. They usually mean the collection of parts that in combination form their "computer system" (see figure 1.3). A computer system usually includes, in addition to the processor, a keyboard for typing commands, a mouse for clicking on menu entries, a monitor

Figure 1.2: A microprocessor, vintage 1998

for displaying information that the computer system has produced, a printer for obtaining paper copies of that information, memory for temporarily storing information, disks and CD-ROMs of one sort or another for storing information for a very long time, even after the computer has been turned off, and the collection of programs (the "software") that the user wishes to execute.

Figure 1.3: A Personal Computer

These additional items are useful to help the computer user do his/her job. Without a printer, for example, the user would have to copy by hand what is displayed on the monitor. Without a mouse, the user would have to type each command, rather than simply click on the mouse button.

So, as we begin our journey which focuses on how we get one square inch of silicon to do our bidding, we note that the computer systems we use contain a lot of other components to make our life more comfortable.

1.4 Two Very Important Ideas.

Before we leave this first chapter, there are two very important ideas that we would like you to understand, ideas that are at the core of what computing is all about.

> IDEA 1: All computers (the biggest and the smallest, the fastest and the slowest, the most expensive and the cheapest) are capable of computing exactly the same things if they are given enough time and enough memory. That is, anything a fast computer can do, a slow computer can do, also. The slow computer just does it more slowly. A more expensive computer cannot figure out something that a cheaper computer is unable to figure out as long as the cheap computer can access enough memory. (You may have to go to the store to buy disks whenever it runs out of memory in order to keep increasing memory.) ALL computers are able to do EXACTLY the same things. Some computers can do things faster, but none can do MORE than any other.

> IDEA 2: We describe our problems in English, or some other language spoken by people. Yet the problems are solved by electrons running around inside the computer. It is necessary to transform our problem from the language of humans to the voltages that influence the flow of electrons. This transformation is really a sequence of systematic transformations, developed and improved over the last 50 years, which combine to give the computer the ability to carry out what appears to be some very complicated tasks. In reality, these tasks are simple and straightforward.

The rest of this chapter will be devoted to discussing these two ideas.

1.5 Computers as Universal Computational Devices

It may seem strange that an introductory textbook should begin by describing how computers work. After all, mechanical engineering students begin by studying physics, not how car engines work. Chemical engineering students begin by studying chemistry, not oil refineries. Why should computing students begin by studying computers?

The answer is that computers are different. To learn the fundamental principles of computing, you must study computers or machines that can do what computers can do. The reason for this has to do with the notion that computers are *universal computational devices*. Let's see what that means.

Before modern computers, there were many kinds of calculating machines. Some were *analog machines* – machines that produced an answer by measuring some physical quantity such as distance or voltage. For example, a slide rule is an analog machine that multiplies numbers by sliding one logarithmically graded ruler next to another. The user can read a logarithmic "distance" on the second ruler. Some early analog adding machines worked by dropping weights on a scale. The difficulty with analog machines is that it is very hard to increase their accuracy.

This is why *digital machines*, – machines that perform computations by manipulating a fixed finite set of digits or letters, came to dominate computing. You are familiar with the distinction between analog and digital watches. An analog watch has hour and minute hands (and perhaps a second hand). It gives the time by the positions of its hands (which are really angular measures). Digital watches give the time in digits. You can increase accuracy just by adding more digits. For example, if it is important for you to measure time in hundredths of a second, you can buy a watch that gives a reading like 10:35.16 rather than just 10:35. How would you get an analog watch that would give you an accurate reading to one one hundredth of a second?

When we talk about computers in this book, we will always mean digital machines.

Before modern digital computers, the most common digital machines in the West were adding machines. In other parts of the world another digital machine, the abacus, was common. Digital adding machines were mechanical or electro-mechanical devices that could perform a specific kind of computation: adding integers. There were also digital machines that could multiply integers. There were digital machines that could put a stack of cards with punched names in alphabetical order. The main limitation of all of these machines is that they could do only one specific kind of computation. If you owned only an adding machine and wanted to multiply two integers, you had some pencil and paper work to do.

This is why computers are different. You can tell a computer how to add numbers. You can tell it how to multiply. You can tell it how to alphabetize a list, or perform any computation you like. When you think of a new kind of computation, you do not have to buy or design a new computer. You just give the old computer a new set of instructions (or *program*) to carry out the computation. This is why we say the computer is a *universal computational device*. Computer scientists believe that *anything that can be computed, can be computed by a computer* provided it has enough time and enough memory. When we study computers, we study the fundamentals of all computing. We learn what computation is and what can be computed.

The idea of a universal computational device is due to Alan Turing. Turing proposed in 1937 that all computations could be carried out by a particular kind of machine which is now called a Turing machine. He gave a mathematical description of this kind of machine, but did not actually build one. (Digital computers were not operating until 1946.) Turing was more interested in solving a philosophical problem: defining computation. He began by looking at the kinds of actions that people perform when they compute – making marks on paper, writing symbols according to certain rules when other symbols are present, and so on. He abstracted these actions and specified a mechanism that could carry them out. He gave some examples of the kinds of things that these machines could do. One Turing machine could add two integers; another could multiply two integers.

Figure 1.4 provides what we call "black box" models of Turing machines that add and multiply. In each case, the operation to be performed is described in the box. The data to be operated on is shown as input to the box. The result of the operation is shown as output from the box. A black box model provides no information as to exactly how the operation is performed, and indeed, there are many ways to add or multiply two numbers.

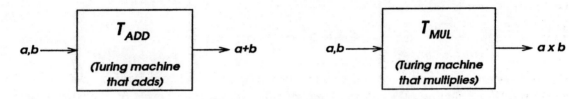

Figure 1.4: "Black box" models of Turing machines

Turing proposed that every computation can be performed by some Turing machine. We call this *Turing's thesis*. Although Turing's thesis has never been proved, there does exist a whole lot of evidence to suggest it is true. We know, for example, that various enhancements one could make to Turing machines do not result in machines that can compute more.

Perhaps the best argument to support Turing's thesis was provided by Turing himself in his original paper. He said that one way to try to construct a machine more powerful than any particular Turing machine was to make a machine U that could simulate *all* Turing machines. You would simply describe to U the particular Turing machine you wanted it to simulate, say a machine to add two integers, give U the input data and U would compute the appropriate output, in this case the sum of the inputs. Turing then showed that there was, in fact, a Turing machine that could do this, so even this attempt to find something that could not be computed by Turing machines failed.

Figure 1.5 further illustrates the point. Suppose you wanted to compute g*(e+f). You would simply provide to U descriptions of the Turing machines to add and to multiply, and the three inputs, e, f, and g. U would do the rest.

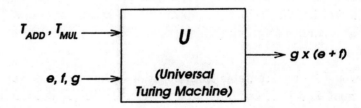

Figure 1.5: Black box model of a Universal Turing Machine

In specifying U, Turing had provided us with a deep insight: he had given us the first description of what computers do. In fact, both a computer (with as much memory as it wants) and a universal Turing machine can compute exactly the same things. In both cases you give the machine a description of a computation and the data it needs, and the machine computes the appropriate answer. Computers and universal Turing machines can compute anything that can be computed because they are *programmable*.

This is the reason that a big or expensive computer cannot do more than a small, cheap computer. More money may buy you a faster computer, a monitor with higher resolution, or a nice sound system. But if you have a small, cheap computer, you already have a universal computational device.

1.6 How do we get the electrons to do the work?

Figure 1.6 shows the process we must go through to get the electrons (which actually do the work) to do our bidding. We call the steps of this process the "Levels of Transformation." As we will see, at each level we have choices. If we ignore any of the levels, our ability to make best use of our computing system can be very adversely affected.

1.6.1 The Statement of the Problem.

We describe the problems we wish to solve with a computer in a "natural language." Natural languages are languages that people speak, like English, French, Japanese, Italian, etc. They have evolved over centuries in accordance with their usage. They are fraught with a lot of things unacceptable for providing instructions to a computer. Most important of these unacceptable attributes is ambiguity. Natural language is filled with ambiguity. To infer the meaning of a sentence, a listener is helped by the tone of voice of the speaker, or at the very least, the context of the sentence,

An example of ambiguity in English is the sentence, "Time flies like an arrow." At least three interpretations are possible, depending on whether (1) one is noticing how fast time passes, (2) one is at a track meet for insects, or (3) one is writing a letter to the Dear Abby of Insectville. In the first case, a metaphor, one is comparing the speed of time passing to the speed of an arrow that has been released. In the second case, one is giving instructions to the timekeeper that he/she do his/her job much like an arrow would. In the third case, one is relating that a particular group of flies (time flies, as opposed to fruit flies) are all in love with the same arrow.

Such ambiguity would be unacceptable in instructions provided to a computer. The computer, electronic idiot that it is, can only do as it is told. To tell it to do something where there are multiple interpretations, would cause the computer to not know which interpretation to follow.

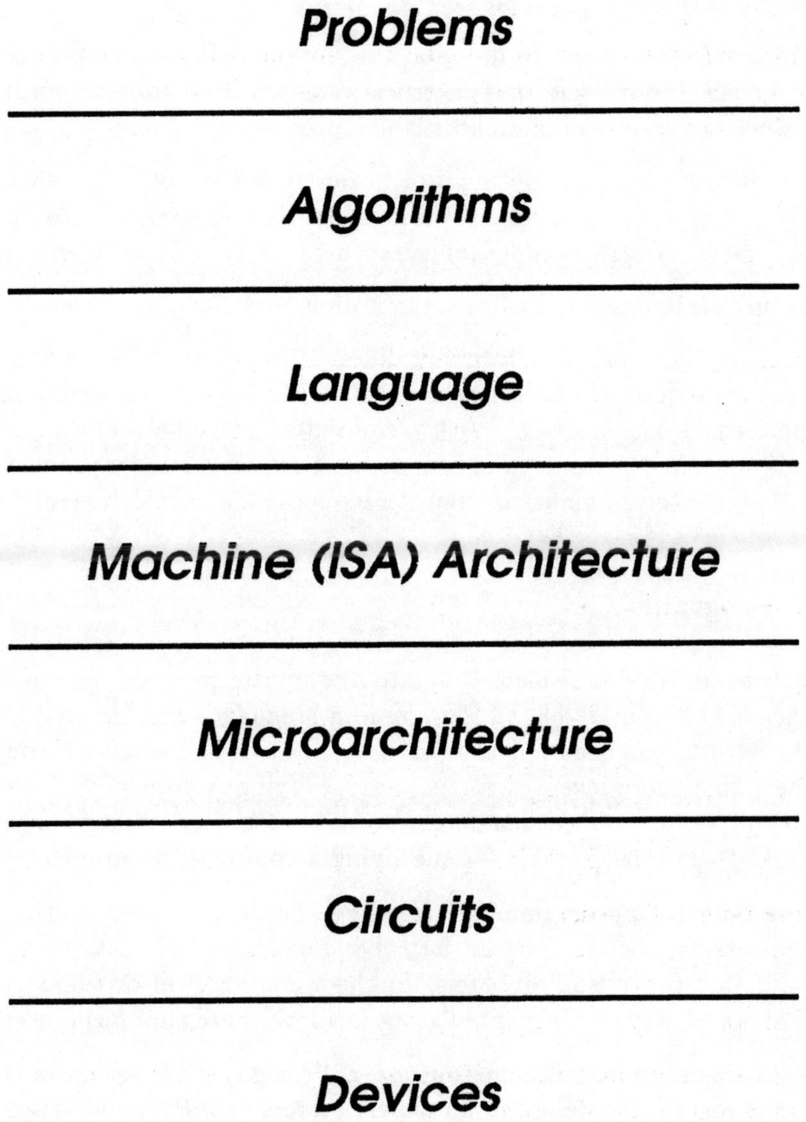

Problems

Algorithms

Language

Machine (ISA) Architecture

Microarchitecture

Circuits

Devices

Figure 1.6: Levels of Transformation

1.6.2   The Algorithm.

The first step in the sequence of transformations is to transform the natural language description of the problem to an algorithm, and in so doing, get rid of the objectional characteristics. An algorithm is a step by step procedure that is guaranteed to terminate, such that each step is precisely stated and can be carried out by the computer. There are terms to describe each of these properties.

We use the term "Definiteness" to describe the notion that each step is precisely stated. A recipe for excellent pancakes that instructs the preparer to "stir until lumpy" lacks definiteness, since the notion of lumpiness is not precise.

We use the term "Effective Computability" to describe the notion that each step can be carried out by a computer. A procedure that instructs the computer to "take the largest prime number" lacks effective computability, since there is no largest prime number.

We use the term "Finiteness" to describe the notion that the procedure terminates.

For every problem, there are usually many different algorithms for solving that problem. One algorithm may require the fewest number of steps. Another algorithm may allow some steps to be performed concurrently. With a computer that allows more than one thing to be done at a time, this can result in lessening the time to solve the problem, even though it is possible that the total number of steps to be performed could be increased.

1.6.3   The Program.

The next step is to transform the algorithm into a computer program, in one of the programming languages that are available. Programming languages are "mechanical languages." That is, unlike natural languages, mechanical languages did not evolve through human discourse. Rather, they were invented for use in specifying a sequence of instructions to a computer. Therefore, mechanical languages do not suffer from failings such as ambiguity that would make them unacceptable for specifying a computer program.

There are more than 1000 programming languages. Some have been designed for use with particular applications, such as Fortran for solving scientific calculations and COBOL for solving business data processing problems. In the second half of this book, we will use C, a language that was designed for manipulating low level hardware structures.

Other languages are useful for still other purposes. Prolog is the language of choice for many applications that require the design of an expert system. LISP was for years the language of choice of a substantial number of people working on problems dealing with Artificial Intelligence. Pascal is a language invented as a vehicle for teaching beginning students how to program.

There are two kinds of programming languages – high level languages and low level languages. High level languages are at a distance (a high level) from the underlying computer. At their best, they are independent of the computer the programs will execute on. We say the language is "machine independent." All the languages mentioned thus far are high level languages. Low level languages are tied to the computer that the programs will execute on. There is generally one such low level language for each computer. That language is called the *assembly language* for that computer.

1.6.4 The ISA.

The next step is to translate the program into the instruction set architecture of the particular computer that will be used to carry out the work of the program. The instruction set architecture (abbreviated ISA) is the complete specification of the interface between programs that have been written and the underlying computer that must carry out the work of those programs.

The ISA specifies the set of instructions the computer can carry out, that is, what operations the computer can perform, and what data is needed by each operation. The term "operand" is used to describe individual data values. The ISA specifies the acceptable representations for operands. The term "data type" is used to describe a legitimate representation for operands such that the computer can perform operations on that representation. The ISA specifies the mechanisms that the computer can use to figure out where the operands are located. The term "addressing modes" is used to describe these mechanisms.

The number of operations, data types, and addressing modes specified by an ISA varies among the different ISAs. Some ISAs have as few as a half dozen operations, while others have as many as several hundred. Some ISAs have only one data type, while others have more than a dozen. Some ISAs have one or two addressing modes, while others have more than 20. The x86 has n operations, m data types, and k addressing modes.

The ISA also specifies the number of unique locations that comprise the computer's memory, and the number of individual 0's and 1's that are contained in each location.

There are many ISAs in use today. The most common example, the one used in the PC, is the x86 ISA, introduced by Intel Corporation in 1979, and currently also manufactured by AMD, National Semiconductor, Texas Instruments, and other companies. Other ISAs are the PowerPC (IBM and Motorola), Alpha (Digital Equipment Corporation), PA-RISC (Hewlett-Packard) and SPARC (SUN Microsystems and HAL).

The translation from a high level language (such as C) to the ISA of the computer the program will have to execute on (such as x86) is usually done by a translating program that is called a "compiler." To translate from a program written in C to the x86 ISA, one would need an "x86 C Compiler." For each high level language and each desired target computer, one must provide a corresponding compiler.

The translation from the unique assembly language of a computer to its ISA is done by means of an "Assembler."

1.6.5   The Microarchitecture.

The next step is to transform the ISA into an implementation. The detailed organization of an implementation is called its microarchitecture. So, for example, the x86 has been implemented by several different microprocessors over the years, each having its own unique microarchitecture. The original implementation was the 8086 in 1979. More recently, in 1998, Intel introduced the Pentium II microprocessor. Digital Equipment Corporation has implemented its Alpha ISA with three different microprocessors, each having its own microarchitecture, the 21064, the 21164, and the 21264.

Each implementation is an opportunity for computer designers to make different tradeoffs between the cost of the microprocessor and the performance that microprocessor will provide. Computer design is always an exercise in tradeoffs, as the designer opts for higher (or lower) performance at greater (or lesser) cost.

The automobile provides a good analogy of the relationship between an ISA and a microarchitecture that implements that ISA. The ISA describes what the driver sees as he/she sits inside the automobile. All automobiles provide the same interface (an ISA different from the ISA for boats and the ISA for airplanes). Of the three pedals on the floor, the middle one is always the brake. The one on the right is the accelerator, and when it is depressed, the car will move faster. The ISA is about basic functionality. All cars can get from point A to point B, can move forward and backward, and can turn to the right and to the left.

The implementation of the ISA is about what goes on under the hood. Here all automobile makes and models are different, depending on what cost/performance tradeoffs the automobile designer made before the car was manufactured. So, some automobiles come with disk brakes, others (in the past, at least) with drums. Some automobiles have eight cylinders, others run on six cylinders, and still others have four. Some are turbo-charged, some are not. In each case, the "microarchitecture" of the specific automobile is a result of the automobile designers' decisions regarding cost and performance.

1.6.6   The Logic Circuit.

The next step is to implement each element of the microarchitecture out of simple logic circuits. Here, also, there are choices, as the logic designer decides how to best make the tradeoffs between cost and performance. So, for example, even for the simple operation of ADDITION, there are several choices of logic circuits to perform this operation at differing speeds and corresponding costs.

1.6.7   The Devices.

Finally, each basic logic circuit is implemented in accordance with the requirements of the particular device technology used. So, CMOS circuits are different from NMOS circuits which are different in turn from gallium arsenide circuits.

1.6.8 Putting it together.

In summary, from the natural language description of a problem to the electrons running around that actually solve the problem, there are many transformations that need to be performed. If we could speak electron, or the electrons could understand English, perhaps we could just walk up to the computer and get the electrons to do our bidding. Since we can't speak "electron" and they can't speak English, the best we can do is this systematic sequence of transformations. At each level of transformation, there are choices as to how to proceed. Our handling of those choices determine the resulting cost and performance of our resulting computer.

In this book, we will describe each of these transformations. We will show how transistors combine to form logic circuits, how logic circuits combine to form the microarchitecture, and how the microarchitecture implements a particular ISA, in our case, the LC-2. We will complete the process by going from the English language description of a problem to a C program that solves the problem, and show how that C program is translated (i.e, compiled) to the ISA of the LC-2.

We hope you will enjoy the ride.

1.7   Exercises.

1.1 Explain, in your own words, the first of the two important ideas stated in Section 1.4.

1.2 Can a higher level programming language instruct a computer to compute more than a lower level programming language?

1.3 What is the difficulty with analog computers that encourages computer designers to use digital designs?

1.4 Say we had a "black box" which takes two numbers as input and outputs their sum. See Figure 1.7(a). Say we had another "box" capable of multiplying two numbers together. See Figure 1.7(b). We can connect these boxes together to calculate $p \times (m + n)$. See Figure 1.7(c).

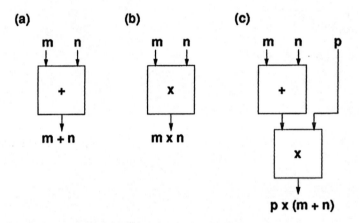

Figure 1.7: "Black boxes" capable of (a) addition, (b) multiplication, (c) a combination of addition and multiplication.

If we had an unlimited number of these boxes, show how to connect them together to calculate:

1. $ax + b$
2. The average of the 4 input numbers w, x, y, and z.
3. $a^2 + 2ab + b^2$
   Can you do this using only 1 add box and 1 multiply box?

1.5 Name one characteristic of natural languages that prevents them from being used as programming languages.

1.6 Write a statement in a natural language and offer two different interpretations of that statement.

1.7 Are natural languages capable of expressing algorithms?

1.8 Name three characteristics of algorithms. Briefly explain each of these three characteristics.

1.9 For each characteristic of an algorithm, give an example of a procedure that does not have the characteristic, and is therefore not an algorithm.

1.10 Are items 1-4 algorithms? If not, what qualities required of algorithms do they lack?

1. Add the first row of the following matrix to another row whose first column contains a non-zero entry. (Reminder: columns run vertically; rows run horizontally).

$$\begin{bmatrix} 1 & 2 & 0 & 4 \\ 0 & 3 & 2 & 4 \\ 2 & 3 & 10 & 22 \\ 12 & 4 & 3 & 4 \end{bmatrix}$$

2. In order to show that there are as many prime numbers as there are natural numbers, match each prime number with a natural number in the following manner. Create pairs of prime and natural numbers by matching the first prime number with 1 (which is the first natural number) and the second prime number with 2, the third with 3 and so forth. If, in the end, it turns out that each prime number can be paired with each natural number, then it is shown that there are as many prime numbers as natural numbers.

3. Suppose you're given two vectors and asked to perform the following operation. Take the first element of the first vector and multiply it by the first element of the second vector. Do the same to the second elements, and so forth. Add all the individual products together to derive the dot product.

4. Lynne and Calvin are trying to decided who will take the dog for a walk. Lynne suggests that they flip a coin and pulls a Quarter out of her pocket. Calvin does not trust Lynne and suspects that the Quarter may be weighted (meaning that it might favor a particular outcome when tossed) and suggests the following procedure to fairly determine who will walk the dog.

   Flip the Quarter twice.

   If the outcome is Heads on the first flip, and Tails on the second, then I will walk the dog

   If the outcome is Tails on the first flip, and Heads on the second, then you will walk the dog

   If both outcomes are tails or both outcomes are heads, then we flip twice again.

   Is Calvin's technique an algorithm?

1.11 Generate an algorithm to search for a particular book title in a library. Explain how this algorithm satisfies the three conditions required of algorithms.

1.12 Suppose we wish to put a set of names in alphabetical order. We call the act of doing so **sorting**. One algorithm that can accomplish that is called the Bubble Sort. We could then program our Bubble Sort algorithm in C, and compile the C program to execute on an x86 ISA. The x86 ISA can be implemented with an Intel Pentium III microarchitecture. Let us call the sequence "Bubble Sort, C program, x86 ISA, Pentium III microarchitecture" one **transformation process**.

Assume we have available four sorting algorithms, and can program in C, C++, Pascal, Fortran and COBOL, and have available compilers that can translate from each of these to either x86 or SPARC, and have available three different microarchitectures for x86 and three different microarchitectures for SPARC.

1. How many transformation processes are possible?
2. Write three examples of transformation processes.
3. How many transformation processes are possible if instead of three different microarchitectures for x86 and three different microarchitectures for SPARC, there were two for x86 and four for SPARC?

1.13 Name at least three things specified by an ISA.

1.14 What is an advantage to programming in a higher level language over a lower level language? What is a disadvantage?

1.15 Briefly describe the difference between the ISA and the Microarchitecture.

1.16 How many ISAs are normally implemented by a single microarchitecture? Conversely, how many microarchitectures could exist for a single ISA?

1.17 List the levels of transformation and name an example for each level.

1.18 Say you go to the store and buy the some word processing software. What form is the software actually in? Is it in a high-level programming language? Is it in assembly language? Is it in the ISA of the computer you'll run it on? Justify your answer.

1.19 Why is an ISA unlikely to change between successive implementations? For example, why would Intel want to make certain that the ISA implemented by the Pentium III is the same as the one implemented by Pentium II? Hint: when you upgrade your computer (or buy one with a newer CPU), do you need to throw out all your old software?

Chapter 2

Bits, Data Types, and Operations.

2.1 Bits and Data Types.

2.1.1 The Bit as the Unit of Information.

We noted in chapter 1 that the computer was organized as a system with several levels of transformation. A problem stated in a natural language such as English is actually solved by the electrons moving around inside the electronics of the computer.

Inside the computer millions of very tiny, very fast devices control the movement of those electrons. These devices react to the presence or absence of voltages in electronic circuits. They could react to the actual voltages, rather than simply to the presence or absence of voltages. However, this would make the control and detection circuits more complex than they need to be. It is much easier to simply detect whether or not a voltage exists between a pair of points in a circuit, than it is to measure exactly what that voltage is.

To understand this, consider any wall outlet in your home. You could measure the exact voltage it is carrying, whether 120 volts or 115 volts, or 118.6 volts, for example. However, the detection circuitry to determine *only* whether there is a voltage (any of the above three will do) or whether there is no voltage is much simpler. Your finger casually inserted into the wall socket, for example, will suffice.

We symbolically represent the presence of a voltage as "1" and the absence of a voltage as "0." We refer to each 0 and each 1 as a "bit," which is a shortened form of "binary digit." Recall the digits you have been using since you were a child – 0,1,2,3,...,9. There are ten of them and they are referred to as "decimal digits." In the case of binary digits, there are two of them: 0 and 1.

To be perfectly precise, it is not really the case that the computer differentiates the *absolute* absence of a voltage (that is, 0) from the *absolute* presence of a voltage (that is, 1). Actually, the electronic circuits in the computer differentiate voltages *close to* 0 from voltages *far from* 0. So, for example, if the computer expects a voltage of 2.9 volts or a voltage of 0 volts (2.9

17

volts signifying 1 and 0 volts signifying 0), then a voltage of 2.6 volts will be taken as a 1 and 0.2 volts will be taken as a 0.

To get useful work done by the computer, it is necessary to be able to identify uniquely a large number of distinct values. The voltage on one wire can represent uniquely one of only two things. One thing can be represented by 0, the other thing can be represented by 1. Thus, to identify uniquely many things, it is necessary to combine multiple bits. For example, if we use 8 bits (corresponding to the voltage present on 8 wires), we can represent one particular value as 01001110, and another value as 11100111. In fact, if we are limited to eight bits, we can differentiate at most only 256 (that is, 2^8) different values. In general, with k bits, we can distinguish at most 2^k distinct items. Each pattern of these k bits is a code; that is, it corresponds to a particular value.

2.1.2   Data types.

There are many ways to represent the same value. For example, the number five can be written as a "5." This is the standard decimal notation that you are used to. The value "five" can also be represented by someone holding up one hand, with all fingers and thumb extended. The person is saying, "The number I wish to communicate can be determined by counting the number of fingers I am showing." A written version of that scheme would be the value 11111. This notation has a name also – "unary." The Romans had yet another notation for "five" – the character "V." We will see momentarily that a fourth notation for "five" is the binary representation 00000101.

It is not enough to simply represent values, we must be able to operate on those values. We say a particular representation is a *data type* if there are operations in the computer that can operate on information that is encoded in that representation. Each ISA has its own set of data types, and its own set of instructions that can operate on those data types. In this book, we will mainly use two data types: *2's complement integers* for representing positive and negative integers that we wish to perform arithmetic on, and *ASCII codes* for representing characters on the keyboard that we wish to input to a computer or display on the computer's monitor. Both data types will be explained shortly.

There are other representations of information that could be used, and indeed that are present in most computers. Recall the "scientific notation" from high school chemistry where you were admonished to represent the decimal number 621 as $6.21 \cdot 10^2$. There are computers that represent numbers in that form, and provide operations that can operate on numbers so represented. That data type is usually called *floating point*. We will show you its representation in Section 2.6.

2.2 Integer Data Types.

2.2.1 Unsigned Integers.

The first representation of information, or data type, that we shall look at is the unsigned integer. Unsigned integers have many uses in a computer. If we wish to perform a task some specific number of times, integers enable us to easily keep track of this number by simply counting how many times we have performed the task "so far." Unsigned integers also provide a means for identifying different locations in the computer, in the same way that house numbers differentiate 129 Main Street from 131 Main Street.

We can represent unsigned integers as strings of binary digits. To do this, we use a positional notation much like the decimal system that you have been using since you were three years old.

You are familiar with the decimal number 329, which also uses positional notation. The "3" is worth much more than the "9," even though the absolute value of "3" standing alone is only worth 1/3 the value of "9" standing alone. This is because, as you know, the "3" stands for 300 $(3 \cdot 10^2)$ due to its *position* in the decimal string 329, while the "9" stands for $9 \cdot 10^0$.

The 2's complement representation works the same way, only the digits used are the binary digits 0 and 1, and the base is "2," rather than "10." So, for example, if we have five bits available to represent our values, the number "6" is represented as 00110, corresponding to

$$0 \cdot 2^4 + 0 \cdot 2^3 + 1 \cdot 2^2 + 1 \cdot 2^1 + 0 \cdot 2^0.$$

With k bits, we can represent in this positional notation exactly 2^k integers, ranging from 0 to $2^k - 1$. In our five-bit example, we can represent the integers from 0 to 31.

2.2.2 Signed Integers.

However, to do useful arithmetic, it is often (although not always) necessary to be able to deal with negative quantities as well as postive. We could take our 2^k distinct representations of k bits and separate them in half, half for positive numbers, and half for negative numbers. In this way, with five bit codes, instead of representing integers from 0 to +31, we could choose to represent positive integers from +1 to +15 and negative integers from -1 to -15. There are 30 such integers. Since 2^5 is 32, we still have two 5-bit codes unassigned. One of them, 00000 we would presumably assign to the value 0, giving us the full range of integer values from -15 to +15. That leaves one more 5-bit code to assign, and there are different ways to do this, as we will see momentarily.

We are still left with the problem of determining what codes to assign to what values. That is, we have 32 codes, but which value should go with which code?

The positive integers are represented in the straightforward positional scheme. Since there are k bits, and we wish to use exactly half of the 2^k codes to represent the integers from 0 to

$2^{k-1} - 1$, all positive integers will have a leading 0 in their representation. In our example (with $k = 5$), the largest positive integer +15 is represented as 01111.

Note that in all three data types shown in Figure 2.1, the representation for 0 and all the positive integers start with a leading 0.

What about the representations for the negative numbers (in our five-bit example, -1 to -15)? The first thought that usually comes to mind is: If a leading 0 signifies a *positive* integer, how about letting a leading 1 signify a *negative* integer? The result is the *Signed-Magnitude* data type shown in Figure 2.1. A second idea (that was actually used on some early computers such as the Control Data Corporation 6600) was the following: Let a negative number be represented by taking the representation of the positive number having the same magnitude, and "flipping all the bits." So, for example, since +5 is represented as 00101, we designate -5 as 11010. This data type is referred to in the computer engineering community as *1's complement*, and is also shown in Figure 2.1.

At this point, you might think that a computer designer could assign any bit pattern to represent any integer he/she wants. And, you would be right! Unfortunately, that could complicate matters when we try to build a logic circuit to add two integers. In fact, the signed-magnitude and 1's complement data types both require unnecessarily cumbersome hardware to do addition. Because computer designers knew what it would take to design a logic circuit to add two integers, they chose representations that simplified that logic circuit. The result is the *2's complement* data type, also shown in Figure 2.1. It is used on just about every computer manufactured today.

2.3   2's Complement Integers.

We saw in Figure 2.1 the representations of the integers from -16 to +15 for the 2's complement data type. Why were the representations chosen that way?

The positive integers, we saw, are represented in the straightforward positional scheme. With 5 bits, we use exactly half of the 2^5 codes to represent the integers from 0 to $2^4 - 1$.

The choice of representations for the negative integers was based, as we said above, on the wish to keep the logic circuits as simple as possible. Almost all computers use the same basic mechanism to do addition. It is called an Arithmetic and Logic Unit, usually known by its acronym ALU. We will get into the actual structure of the ALU in Chapters 3 and 4. What is relevant right now is that an ALU has two inputs and one output. It performs addition by adding the binary bit patterns at its inputs, producing a bit pattern at its output that is the sum of the two input bit patterns.

Representation	Value Represented		
	Signed Mag.	1's Compl.	2's Compl.
00000	0	0	0
00001	1	1	1
00010	2	2	2
00011	3	3	3
00100	4	4	4
00101	5	5	5
00110	6	6	6
00111	7	7	7
01000	8	8	8
01001	9	9	9
01010	10	10	10
01011	11	11	11
01100	12	12	12
01101	13	13	13
01110	14	14	14
01111	15	15	15
10000	-0	-15	-16
10001	-1	-14	-15
10010	-2	-13	-14
10011	-3	-12	-13
10100	-4	-11	-12
10101	-5	-10	-11
10110	-6	-9	-10
10111	-7	-8	-9
11000	-8	-7	-8
11001	-9	-6	-7
11010	-10	-5	-6
11011	-11	-4	-5
11100	-12	-3	-4
11101	-13	-2	-3
11110	-14	-1	-2
11111	-15	-0	-1

Figure 2.1: Three Representation of Signed Integers.

For example, if the ALU processed 5-bit input patterns, and the two inputs were 00110 and 00101, the result (output of the ALU) would be 01011. The addition is shown below.

```
00110
00101
-----
01011
```

Addition of two binary strings is performed in the same way addition of two decimal strings is performed, from right to left, column by column. If the addition in a column generates a carry, the carry is added to the column immediately to its left.

What is particularly relevant is that the binary ALU does not know (and does not care) what the two patterns it is adding represent. It simply adds the two binary patterns. Since the binary ALU only ADDs and does not CARE, it would be a "nice" benefit of our assignment of codes to the integers if it resulted in the ALU doing the right thing.

For starters, it would be nice if, when the ALU adds the representation for an arbitrary integer to the integer of the same magnitude and opposite sign, the sum is 0. That is, if the inputs to the ALU are the representations of A and $-A$, the output of the ALU should be 00000.

To accomplish that, the 2's complement data type specifies the representation for each negative integer so that when the ALU adds it to the representation of the positive integer of the same magnitude, the result will be the representation for 0. For example, since 00101 is the representation of +5, 11011 is chosen as the representation for -5. .

Moreover, as we sequence from representations of -15 to +15, the ALU is adding 00001 to each successive representation.

We can express this mathematically as:

REPRESENTATION (value + 1)   =
    REPRESENTATION (value)   +   REPRESENTATION (1).

This is sufficient to guarantee (as long as we do not get a result larger than +15 or smaller than -16) that the binary ALU will perform addition correctly.

Note in particular, the representations for -1 and 0, that is, 11111 and 00000. When we add 00001 to the representation for -1, we do get 00000 but we also generate a carry. That carry does not influence the result. That is, the correct result of adding 00001 to the representation for -1 is 0, not 100000. Therefore, the carry is ignored. In fact, because the carry obtained by adding 00001 to 11111 is ignored, the carry can *always* be ignored when dealing with 2's complement arithmetic.

Note: A short-cut for figuring out the representation for $-A$, if we know the representation for A is as follows: Flip all the bits of A (the term for "flipping" is *complement*), and add

A to the complement of A, the result is 11111. If we then add 00001 to 11111, the final result is 00000. Thus, the representation for -A can be easily obtained by adding 1 to the complement of A.

For example, if A is +13, its representation is

$$01101.$$

The complement of A is

$$10010.$$

Adding 1 to 10010 gives us

$$10011.$$

The ALU, if presented with bit strings 01101 and 10011, would produce the binary sum 00000,

```
  01101
  10011
  -----
  00000
```

from which we know that the representation for -13 is 10011.

You may have noticed that the addition of 01101 and 10011, in addition to producing 00000, also produces a carry out of the 5-bit ALU. That is, the binary addition of 01101 and 10011 is really 100000. However, as we saw above, in the case of the 2's complement data type, this carry out can be ignored.

At this point, we have identified in our five-bit scheme, 15 positive integers. We have constructed 15 negative integers. We also have a representation for 0. With $k = 5$, we can uniquely identify 32 distinct quantities, and we have accounted for only 31 (15+15+1). The remaining representation is 10000. What value shall we assign to it?

We note that -1 is 11111, -2 is 11110, -3 is 11101, etc. If we continue this, we note that -15 is 10001. Note that as in the case of the positive representations, as we sequence backwards from representations of -1 to -15, the ALU is subtracting 00001 from each successive representation. Thus, it seems to make sense to assign to 10000 the value -16, that is the value one gets by subtracting 00001 from 10001 (the representation for -15).

In Chapter 5 we will specify a computer that we affectionately have named the LC-2 (for little computer 2). The LC-2 operates on 16-bit values. Therefore, the 2's complement integers that can be represented in the LC-2 are the integers from -32768 to +32767.

2.4   Binary-Decimal Conversion.

It is often useful to convert integers between the 2's complement data type and the decimal representation that you have used all your life.

2.4.1   Binary to Decimal Conversion.

We convert from 2's complement to a decimal representation as follows:

For purposes of illustration, we will assume 2's complement representations of 8 bits, corresponding to decimal integer values, from -128 to +127.

Recall that an 8-bit 2's complement number takes the form

$$a_7 \ a_6 \ a_5 \ a_4 \ a_3 \ a_2 \ a_1 \ a_0,$$

where each of the bits a_i is either 0 or 1.

1. Examine the leading bit a_7. If it a 0, the integer is positive, and we can begin evaluating its magnitude. If it is 1, the integer is negative. In that case, we need to first obtain the 2's complement representation of the positive number having the same magnitude.

2. The magnitude is simply

$$a_6 \cdot 2^6 + a_5 \cdot 2^5 + a_4 \cdot 2^4 + a_3 \cdot 2^3 + a_2 \cdot 2^2 + a_1 \cdot 2^1 + a_0 \cdot 2^0.$$

which we can obtain by simply adding the powers of 2 that have coefficients of 1.

3. Finally, if the original number was negative, we affix a minus sign in front. Done!

Example:

Convert the 2's complement integer 11000111 to a decimal integer value.

1. Since the leading binary digit is a 1, the number is negative. We first find the 2's complement representation of the positive number of the same magnitude. This is 00111001.

2. The magnitude can be represented as

$$0 \cdot 2^6 + 1 \cdot 2^5 + 1 \cdot 2^4 + 1 \cdot 2^3 + 0 \cdot 2^2 + 0 \cdot 2^1 + 1 \cdot 2^0.$$

or, $32 + 16 + 8 + 1$.

3. The decimal integer value corresponding to 11000111 is -57.

2.4.2   Decimal to Binary Conversion.

Converting from decimal to 2's complement is a little more complicated. The crux of the method is to note that a positive binary number is odd if the right-most digit is 1, and even if the right-most digit is 0.

Consider again, our generic 8-bit representation:

$$a_7 \cdot 2^7 + a_6 \cdot 2^6 + a_5 \cdot 2^5 + a_4 \cdot 2^4 + a_3 \cdot 2^3 + a_2 \cdot 2^2 + a_1 \cdot 2^1 + a_0 \cdot 2^0.$$

We can illustrate the conversion best by first working through an example.

Suppose we wish to convert the value +105 to a 2's complement binary code. We note that +105 is positive. We first find values for a_i, representing the magnitude 105. Since the value is positive, we will then obtain the 2's complement result by simply appending a_7, which we know is 0.

Our first step is to find values for a_i that satisfies the following:

$$105 = a_6 \cdot 2^6 + a_5 \cdot 2^5 + a_4 \cdot 2^4 + a_3 \cdot 2^3 + a_2 \cdot 2^2 + a_1 \cdot 2^1 + a_0 \cdot 2^0.$$

Since 105 is odd, we know that a_0 is 1. We subtract 1 from both sides of the equation, yielding

$$104 = a_6 \cdot 2^6 + a_5 \cdot 2^5 + a_4 \cdot 2^4 + a_3 \cdot 2^3 + a_2 \cdot 2^2 + a_1 \cdot 2^1.$$

We next divide both sides of the equation by 2, yielding

$$52 = a_6 \cdot 2^5 + a_5 \cdot 2^4 + a_4 \cdot 2^3 + a_3 \cdot 2^2 + a_2 \cdot 2^1 + a_1 \cdot 2^0.$$

We now note that 52 is even, so a_1, the only coefficient not multiplied by a power of 2 must be equal to 0.

We now iterate the process, each time subtracting the right-most digit from both sides of the equation, dividing both sides by 2, and then noting whether the new decimal number on the left side is odd or even. The process produces, in turn:

$$52 = a_6 \cdot 2^5 + a_5 \cdot 2^4 + a_4 \cdot 2^3 + a_3 \cdot 2^2 + a_2 \cdot 2^1.$$

$$26 = a_6 \cdot 2^4 + a_5 \cdot 2^3 + a_4 \cdot 2^2 + a_3 \cdot 2^1 + a_2 \cdot 2^0.$$

Therefore, $a_2 = 0$.

$$13 = a_6 \cdot 2^3 + a_5 \cdot 2^2 + a_4 \cdot 2^1 + a_3 \cdot 2^0.$$

Therefore, $a_3 = 1$.

$$6 = a_6 \cdot 2^2 + a_5 \cdot 2^1 + a_4 \cdot 2^0.$$

Therefore, $a_4 = 0$.

$$3 = a_6 \cdot 2^1 + a_5 \cdot 2^0.$$

Therefore $a_5 = 1$.

$$1 = a_6 \cdot 2^0$$

Therefore, $a_6 = 1$. and we are done. The binary representation is 01101001.

We can summarize the process as follows: If we are given a decimal integer value N, we construct the 2's complement representation as follows:

1. We first obtain the binary representation of the magnitude of N by forming the equation

$$N = a_6 \cdot 2^6 + a_5 \cdot 2^5 + a_4 \cdot 2^4 + a_3 \cdot 2^3 + a_2 \cdot 2^2 + a_1 \cdot 2^1 + a_0 \cdot 2^0.$$

and iterating the following, until the left side of the equation is 0:

a. If N is odd, the right-most bit is 1. If N is even, the right most bit is 0.
b. Subtract 1 or 0 (according to whether N is odd or even) from N, and divide both sides of the equation by 2.

Each iteration produces the value of one coefficient a_i.

2. If the original decimal number was positive, append a leading 0 sign bit, and you are done.

3. If the original decimal number was negative, append a leading 0, and form the negative of this 2's complement representation, and then you are done.

2.5   Operations on bits – Part I: Arithmetic.

2.5.1   Addition and Subtraction.

Arithmetic on 2's complement numbers is very much like the arithmetic on decimal numbers that you have been doing for a long time.

Addition still proceeds from right to left, one digit at a time. At each point, we generate a sum digit and a carry. Instead of generating a carry after "9", since "9" is the largest decimal digit, we generate a carry after "1" since "1" is the largest digit.

Example: Using our five-bit notation, what is 11 + 3?

```
The decimal value 11 is represented as 01011
The decimal value 3 is represented      00011

The sum is                              01110, which is the value 14.
```

Subtraction is simply addition, preceded by taking the negative of the subtrahend first. That is, $A - B$ is simply $A + (-B)$.

Example: What is 14 - 9?

```
The decimal value 14 is represented as  01110
The decimal value 9 is represented      01001

First we form the negative, that is -9: 10111.

Adding 14 to -9, we get                 01110
                                        10111

which results in                        00101, which is the value 5.
```

Note again that the carry out is ignored.

Example: What happens when we add a number to itself (e.g., $x + x$).

Let's assume for this example eight-bit codes, which would allow us to represent integers from -128 to 127. Consider a value for x, the integer 59, represented as 00111011. If we add 59 to itself, we get the code 01110110. Note that the bits have all shifted to the left by one position. Is that a curiosity, or will that happen all the time (as long as the sum $x + x$ is not too large to represent with the available number of bits)?

The number 59 is formed, using our positional notation, as

$$0 \cdot 2^6 + 1 \cdot 2^5 + 1 \cdot 2^4 + 1 \cdot 2^3 + 0 \cdot 2^2 + 1 \cdot 2^1 + 1 \cdot 2^0.$$

The sum $59 + 59$ is $2 \cdot 59$, which, in our representation, is:

$$2 \cdot (0 \cdot 2^6 + 1 \cdot 2^5 + 1 \cdot 2^4 + 1 \cdot 2^3 + 0 \cdot 2^2 + 1 \cdot 2^1 + 1 \cdot 2^0).$$

But that is nothing more than

$$0 \cdot 2^7 + 1 \cdot 2^6 + 1 \cdot 2^5 + 1 \cdot 2^4 + 0 \cdot 2^3 + 1 \cdot 2^2 + 1 \cdot 2^1,$$

which shifts each digit one position to the left. Thus, adding a number to itself (provided there are enough bits to represent the result) is equivalent to shifting the representation one bit position to the left.

2.5.2 Sign-extension.

It is often useful to represent a small number with fewer bits. For example, rather than represent the value 5 as 0000000000000101, there are times when it is useful to allocate only six bits to represent the value 5: 000101. There is little confusion, since we are all used to adding leading zeroes without affecting the value of a number. A check for $456.78 and a check for $0000456.78 are checks having the same face value.

What about negative representations? We obtained the negative representation from its positive counterpart by complementing the positive representation and adding 1. Thus the representation for -5, given that 5 is represented as 000101, is 111011. If 5 is represented as 0000000000000101, then the representation for -5 is 1111111111111011. In the same way that leading 0s do not affect the value of a positive number, leading 1s do not affect the value of a negative number.

In order to add representations of different lengths, it is first necessary to represent them with the same number of bits. For example, suppose we wish to add the number 13 to -5, where 13 is represented as 0000000000001101 and -5 is represented as 111011. If we do not represent the two values with the same number of bits, we have:

```
            0000000000001101
      +               111011
            ----------------
```

When we attempt to perform the addition, what shall we do with the missing bits in the representation for -5? If we take the absence of a bit to be a "0," then we are no longer adding -5 to 13. On the contrary, if we take the absence of bits to be 0s, we have changed the -5 to the number which is represented as 0000000000111011, that is +59. Not surprising, then, our result turns out to be the representation for 72.

However, if we understand that a 6-bit -5 and a 16-bit -5 only differ in the number of meaningless leading 1s, then we first extend the value of -5 to 16-bit before we perform the addition. Thus we have:

```
            0000000000001101
      +     1111111111111011
            ----------------
```

and the result is   0000000000001000, which is +8, as we should expect.

The value of a positive number does not change if we extend the sign bit 0 as many bit positions to the left as desired. Similarly, the value of a negative number does not change its value by extending the sign bit 1 as many bit positions to the left as desired. Since in both cases, it is the sign bit that is extended, we refer to the operation as Sign-EXTension, often abbreviated SEXT. Sign-extension is performed in order to be able to operate on equal sized representations; it does not affect the values of the numbers being represented.

2.5.3 Overflow.

Up to now, we have always insisted that the sum of two integers be small enough to be represented by the available bits. What happens if such is not the case?

You are undoubtedly familiar with the odometer on the front dashboard of your automobile. It keeps track of how many miles your car has been driven – but only up to a point. In the old days, when the odometer registered 99992 and you drove it 100 miles, its new reading became 00092. A brand new car! The problem, as you know, is that the largest value the odometer could store was 99999, so the value 100092 showed up as 00092. The carry out of the ten-thousands digit was lost. (Of course, if you grew up in Boston, the carry out was not lost at all – it was in full display in the rusted chrome all over the car.)

We say the odometer OVERFLOWed. Representing 100092 as 00092 is unacceptable. As more and more cars lasted more than 100000 miles, car makers felt the pressure to add a digit to the odometer. Today, practically all cars overflow at one million miles, rather than one hundred thousand miles.

The odometer provides an example of unsigned arithmetic. The miles you add always positive miles. The odometer reads 000129 and you drive 50 miles. The odometer now reads 000179. Overflow is a carry out of the leading digit.

In the case of signed arithmetic, or more particularly, 2's complement arithmetic, overflow is a little more subtle.

Let's return to our 5-bit 2's complement data type, which allowed us to represent integers from -16 to +15. Suppose we wish to add +9 and +11. Our arithmetic takes the following form:

```
       01001
       01011
       -----
       10100
```

Note that the sum is larger than +15, and therefore too large to represent with our 2's complement scheme. The fact that the number is too large means that the number is larger than 01111, the largest positive number we can represent with a 5-bit 2's complement data type. Note that because our positive result was larger than +15, it generated a carry into the leading bit position. But this bit position is used to indicate the sign of a value. Thus detecting that the result is too large is an easy matter. Since we are adding two positive numbers, the result must be positive. Since the ALU has produced a negative result, something must be wrong. The thing that is wrong is that the sum of the two positive numbers is too large to be represented with the available bits. We say that the result has OVERFLOWed the capacity of the representation.

Suppose instead, we had started with negative numbers, for example, -12 and -6. In this case our arithmetic takes the following form:

```
10100
11010
-----
01110
```

Here, too, the result has overflowed the capacity of the machine, since -12 + -6 equals -18, which is more negative than -16, the negative number with the largest allowable magnitude. The ALU obliges by producing a positive result. Again, this is easy to detect since the sum of two negative numbers can not be positive.

Note that the sum of a negative number and a positive number never presents a problem. Why is that?

2.6   Operations on bits – Part II: Logical operations.

We have seen that it is possible to perform arithmetic (ADD, SUB, for example) on values represented as binary patterns. Another class of operations that it is useful to perform on binary patterns is the set of *logical* operations.

Logical operations operate on logical variables. A logical variable can have one of two values, 0 or 1. The name "logical" is a historical one; it comes from the fact that the two values 0 and 1 can represent the two logical values FALSE and TRUE, but the use of logical operations have traveled far from this original meaning.

There are several basic logic functions, and most ALUs perform all of them.

2.6.1   The AND function.

AND is a binary function. This means it requires two pieces of input data. Said another way, AND requires two source operands. Each source is a logical variable, taking the value 0 or 1. The output of AND is 1 only if both sources have the value 1. Otherwise, the output is 0. We can think of the AND operation as the ALL operation; that is, the output is 1 only if ALL two inputs are 1. Otherwise, the output is 0.

A convenient mechanism for representing the behavior of a logical operation is the *truth table*. A truth table consists of $n+1$ columns and 2^n rows. The first n columns correspond to the n source operands. Since each source operand is a logical variable and can have one of two values, there are 2^n unique sets of values that these source operands can have. Each such set of values (sometimes called an input combination) is represented as one row of the truth table. The final column in the truth table shows the output for each input combination.

In the case of a two-input AND function, the truth table has 2 columns for source operands, and 4 (2^2) rows for unique input combinations.

```
A   B |   AND
------|--------
0   0 |   0
0   1 |   0
1   0 |   0
1   1 |   1
```

We can apply the logical operation AND to two bit patterns of m bits each. This involves applying the operation individually to each corresponding pair of bits in the two source operands. For example, if a and b, shown below, are 16-bit patterns, then c is the AND of a and b.

```
a:   0011101001101001
b:   0101100100100001
     ----------------
c:   0001100000100001
```

2.6.2 The OR function.

OR is also a binary function. It requires two source operands, both of which are logical variables. The output of OR is 1 if any source has the value 1. Only if both sources are 0 is the output 0. We can think of the OR operation as the ANY operation; that is, the output is 1 if ANY of the two inputs are 1.

The truth table for a two-input OR function is shown below.

```
A   B |   OR
------|--------
0   0 |   0
0   1 |   1
1   0 |   1
1   1 |   1
```

In the same way that we applied the logical operation AND to two m-bit patterns, we can apply the OR operation bit-wise to two m-bit patterns. For example, if a and b are as before, then c (shown below) is the OR of a and b.

```
a:   0011101001101001
b:   0101100100100001
     ----------------
c:   0111101101101001
```

Sometimes, the OR operation is referred to as inclusive-OR in order to distinguish it from the exclusive-OR function that we will discuss momentarily.

2.6.3   The NOT function.

NOT is a unary function. This means it operates on only one source operand. It is also known as the *complement* operation. The output is formed by complementing the input. We sometimes say the output is formed by inverting the input. A "1" input results in a "0" output. A "0" input results in a "1" output.

The truth table for the NOT function is shown below.

```
A | NOT
--|----
0 |  1
1 |  0
```

In the same way that we applied the logical operation AND to two m-bit patterns, we can apply the NOT operation bit-wise to one m-bit pattern. If a is as before, then c is the NOT of a.

```
a:   0011101001101001
     ----------------
c:   1100010110010110
```

2.6.4   The Exclusive-OR function.

Exclusive-OR, often abbreviated XOR, is a binary function. It, too, requires two source operands, both of which are logical variables. The output of XOR is 1 if the two sources are different. The output is 0 if the two sources are the same.

The truth table for the XOR function is shown below.

```
A  B | XOR
-----|-------
0  0 |  0
0  1 |  1
1  0 |  1
1  1 |  0
```

In the same way that we applied the logical operation AND to two m-bit patterns, we can apply the XOR operation bit-wise to two m-bit patterns. For example, if a and b are 16-bit patterns as before, then c (shown below) is the XOR of a and b.

```
a:   0011101001101001
b:   0101100100100001
     ----------------
c:   0110001101001000
```

Note the distinction between the truth table for XOR shown here and the truth table for OR shown earlier. In the case of exclusive-OR, if both source operands are 1, the output is 0. That is, the output is 1 if the first operand is 1 but the second operand is not 1 or if the second operand is 1 but the first operand is not 1. The term *exclusive* is used because the output is 1 *only* if one of the two sources is 1. The OR function, on the other hand, produces an output 1 if both sources are 1. Ergo, the name inclusive-OR.

2.6.5   Examples.

The following examples illustrate the use of logical operations to perform useful functions in the computer.

Example:
Consider a complex system made up of eight units that are independently busy or available. This system can be a manufacturing plant where each unit is a particular machine. Or the system could be a taxicab network where each unit is a particular taxicab. In both cases, it is important to identify which units are busy and which are available, so that work can be assigned as it becomes necessary.

One can keep track of these eight units with an 8-bit binary BUSYNESS pattern, where a bit is 1 if the unit is free and 0 if the unit is busy. The bits are labeled, from right to left, from 0 to 7. The BUSYNESS pattern 11000010 corresponds to the situation where only units 7, 6, and 1 are free, and therefore available for work assignment.

Suppose work is assigned to unit 7. We can update our BUSYNESS pattern by performing the logical AND with sources 11000010 and 01111111. The result is the BUSYNESS pattern 01000010.

The second source 01111111 is an example of a *mask*. The purpose of a mask is to differentiate how some bits in a pattern will be handled from how other bits will be handled. In this instance, the mask leaves all bits except the leading bit unchanged. The leading bit is *cleared* (set to 0).

Suppose unit 5 finishes its task and becomes idle. We can reflect that by performing the logical OR with the BUSYNESS pattern and 00100000. The result is 01100010.

Example:
Suppose we have an 8-bit pattern in which the right-most two bits have particular significance. The computer could be asked to do one of four tasks depending on the value stored in the two right-most bits. We could isolate those two bits by ANDing the 8-bit pattern with the mask 00000011. For example, if the pattern is 01010110, the AND of 01010110 and 00000011 is 00000010, which highlights the 2 bits that are relevant, i.e., 10.

Example:
Suppose we wish to know if two patterns are identical. Since the XOR function produces a 0 only if the corresponding pair of bits are identical, two patterns are identical if the output of the XOR are all zeroes.

2.7   Other representations.

Three other representations of information that we will find useful in our work are the Floating Point data type, the ASCII codes and the Hexadecimal notation.

2.7.1   Floating Point Data Type.

Most of the arithmetic we will do in this book will use integer values. For example, the LC-2 will use the 16-bit, 2's complement data type, which provides, in addition to one bit to identify positive or negative, 15 bits to represent the magnitude of the value. With 16 bits used in this way, we can express values between -32,768 and +32,767. We say the *precision* of our value is 15 bits, and the *range* is 2^{15}. As you learned in high school chemistry or physics, sometimes we need to express much larger numbers, but we do not require so many digits of precision. In fact, recall the value $6.023 \cdot 10^{23}$ which you may have been required to memorize back then. The range required to express this value is far greater than the 2^{15} available with 16-bit 2's complement integers. On the other hand, the 15 bits of precision available with 16-bit 2's complement integers is overkill. We need only enough bits to express four significant decimal digits (6023).

The *floating point* data type is the solution to the problem. Instead of using all the bits (except the sign bit) to represent the precision of a value, the floating point data type allocates some of the bits to the range of values (i.e., how big or small) that can be expressed. The rest of the bits (except for the sign bit) are used for precision.

Most ISAs today specify more than one floating point data type. One of them, usually called *float* consists of 32 bits, allocated as follows:

```
1 bit for the sign (positive or negative)
8 bits for the range
23 bits for precision
```

Most computers manufactured today interpret those bits according to the IEEE Standard for Floating Point Arithmetic, as shown in Figure 2.2.

The leading bit is the sign bit: 0 is positive, 1 is negative. The factor -1^s in Figure 2.2 evaluates to +1 if s = 0, and -1 if s = 1.

The next eight bits comprise the exponent field, which determines the range of values that can be expressed. If the exponent field does not contain 00000000 or 11111111, the actual exponent is obtained by treating the contents of the exponent field as an unsigned integer and subtracting 128. For example, if the exponent field contained 00000101, the actual exponent would be -122. If the exponent field contained 10000010, the actual exponent would be +3. Question: What is the largest exponent the IEEE Standard allows for a 32-bit floating point number? What is the smallest exponent the IEEE Standard allows for a 32-bit floating point number?

The remaining 23 bits comprise the fraction field, which provides the significant digits of the value being expressed. If the exponent field does not contain 00000000 or 11111111, the significant digits are determined by starting with a leading 1, followed by a binary point (the binary equivalent of a decimal point), followed by the 23 bits of the fraction field. For example, if the exponent field does not contain 00000000 or 11111111 and the fraction field contains 01110000000000000000000, then the significant digits are evaluated as 1.01110000000000000000000, which is 1 7/16.

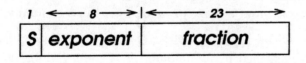

$$N = -1^s \times 1.fraction \times 2^{exponent - 127}, \quad 1 \leqslant exponent \leqslant 254$$

$$N = -1^s \times 0.fraction \times 2^{-126}, \quad exponent = 0$$

Figure 2.2: The Floating Point Data Type

Note that the interpretation of the 32 bits required that the exponent field contained neither 00000000 nor 11111111. The IEEE Standard for Floating Point Arithmetic also specifies how to interpret the 32 bits if the exponent field contains 00000000 or 11111111.

If the exponent field contains 00000000, the exponent is -126, and the significant digits are obtained by starting with a leading 0, followed by a binary point, followed by the 23 bits of the fraction field. This allows very tiny numbers to be represented.

The following four examples illustrate the interpretation of the 32-bit floating point data type according to the rules of the IEEE Standard.

Examples:

0 10000011 00101000000000000000000 is $1.00101 \times 2^4 = 18.5$

1 10000010 00101000000000000000000 is $-1 \times 1.00101 \times 2^3 = -9.25$

0 11111110 11111111111111111111111 is $\sim 2^{128}$

1 00000000 00000000000000000000001 is $\sim -2^{-149}$

A detailed understanding of IEEE Floating Point Arithmetic is well beyond what should be expected in this first course. Indeed, we have not even considered how to interpret the 32 bits if the exponent field contains 11111111. Our purpose in including this section in the textbook is to at least let you know that there is, in addition to 2's complement integers, another very important data type available in almost all ISAs. This data type is called floating point; it allows very large and very tiny numbers to be expressed at the expense of reducing the number of binary digits of precision.

2.7.2 ASCII codes.

An additional representation of information is the standard code that almost all computer equipment manufacturers have agreed to use for transferring character codes between input and output devices and the main computer processing unit. That code is a 7 bit code referred to as ASCII. ASCII stands for American Standard Code for Information Interchange. It (ASCII) greatly simplifies the interface between a keyboard manufactured by one company, a computer made by another company, and a monitor made by a third company.

For our purposes, each 7-bit code will be appended with a leading 0 and stored as an 8-bit code. Each key on the keyboard is identified by its unique ASCII code. So, for example the digit "3" expanded to 8 bits with a leading 0 is 00110011, the digit "2" is 00110010, the lower case "e" is 01100101, and the carriage return is 00001101. The entire set of ASCII codes is listed in Figure F.3 of Appendix F. When you type a key on the keyboard, the corresponding 8-bit code is stored and made available to the computer. Where it is stored and how it gets into the computer is part of the subject matter of Chapter 8. When the computer wants to display on the monitor a particular character, it transfers the ASCII code for that character to the electronics associated with the monitor. That, too, is part of the subject matter of Chapter 8.

2.7.3 Hexadecimal notation.

We have seen that information can be represented as 2's complement integers, or in floating point format, or as an ASCII code. There are other representations also, but we will leave them for another book. However, before we leave this topic, we would like to introduce you to a representation that is used more as a convenience for humans than as a data type to support operations being performed by the computer. This is the *hexadecimal* notation. As we will see, it evolves nicely from the positional binary notation, and is useful for dealing with long strings of binary digits without making errors.

It will be particularly useful in dealing with the LC-2 where 16-bit binary strings will be encountered frequently.

An example of such a binary string is

$$0011110101101110.$$

Let's try an experiment. Cover this page with a sheet of paper, and try to write down the 16-bit string of zeroes and ones. How did you do? Hexadecimal notation is about being able to do this without making mistakes. We shall see how.

In general, a 16-bit binary string takes the form

$$a_{15}\ a_{14}\ a_{13}\ a_{12}\ a_{11}\ a_{10}\ a_9\ a_8\ a_7\ a_6\ a_5\ a_4\ a_3\ a_2\ a_1\ a_0,$$

where each of the bits a_i is either 0 or 1.

If we think of this binary string as an unsigned integer, its value can be computed as:

$$a_{15} \cdot 2^{15} + a_{14} \cdot 2^{14} + a_{13} \cdot 2^{13} + a_{12} \cdot 2^{12} + a_{11} \cdot 2^{11} + a_{10} \cdot 2^{10} + a_9 \cdot 2^9 + a_8 \cdot 2^8 +$$
$$a_7 \cdot 2^7 + a_6 \cdot 2^6 + a_5 \cdot 2^5 + a_4 \cdot 2^4 + a_3 \cdot 2^3 + a_2 \cdot 2^2 + a_1 \cdot 2^1 + a_0 \cdot 2^0.$$

We can factor 2^{12} from the first four terms, 2^8 from the second four terms, 2^4 from the third set of four terms, and 2^0 from the last four terms, yielding:

$$2^{12}[a_{15} \cdot 2^3 + a_{14} \cdot 2^2 + a_{13} \cdot 2^1 + a_{12} \cdot 2^0] + 2^8[a_{11} \cdot 2^3 + a_{10} \cdot 2^2 + a_9 \cdot 2^1 + a_8 \cdot 2^0] + (2.1)$$
$$2^4[a_7 \cdot 2^3 + a_6 \cdot 2^2 + a_5 \cdot 2^1 + a_4 \cdot 2^0] + 2^0[a3 \cdot 2^3 + a_2 \cdot 2^2 + a_1 \cdot 2^1 + a_0 \cdot 2^0](2.2)$$

Note that the largest value inside a set of square brackets is 15, which would be the case if each of the four bits is 1. If we replace what is inside each square bracket by a symbol representing its value (from 0 to 15), and we replace 2^{12} by its equal (16^3), 2^8 by 16^2, 2^4 by 16^1 and 2^0 by 16^0, we have:

$$h_3 \cdot 16^3 + h_2 \cdot 16^2 + h_1 \cdot 16^1 + h_0 \cdot 16^0,$$

where (for example), h_3 is a symbol representing

$$a_{15} \cdot 2^3 + a_{14} \cdot 2^2 + a_{13} \cdot 2^1 + a_{12} \cdot 2^0.$$

Since the symbols must represent values from 0 to 15, we assign symbols to these values as follows: 0, 1, 2, 3, 4, 5, 6, 7, 8, 9, A, B, C, D, E, F. That is, we represent 0000 with the symbol 0, 0001 with the symbol 1, ... 1001 with 9, 1010 with A, 1011 with B, ... 1111 with F.

The resulting notation is the hexadecimal notation, or base-16.

So, for example, if the hex digits E92F represent a 16-bit 2's complement integer, is the value of that integer positive or negative? How do you know?

Now, then, what is this hexadecimal representation good for, anyway? It seems like just another way to represent a number without adding any benefit. Let's return to our little exercise where you tried to write from memory the string

0011110101101110.

If we had first broken the string at 4-bit boundaries

0011   1101   0110   1110

and then converted each 4-bit string to its equivalent hex digit

3   D   6   E,

it would have been no problem to jot down (with the page covered) 3D6E.

In summary, hexadecimal notation is mainly used as a convenience for humans. It can be used to represent binary strings that are integers or floating point numbers or sequences of ASCII codes, or bit vectors. It simply reduces the number of digits by a factor of four, where each digit is in hex (0, 1, 2, ...F) instead of binary (0,1). The usual result is far fewer copying errors due to too many 0s and 1s.

2.8 Exercises.

2.1 Given n bits, how many distinct combinations of the n bits exist?

2.2 There are 26 characters in the English alphabet. What is the least number of bits needed to have a unique bit pattern for each of the 26 characters? What if we need to distinguish between upper and lower case characters? How many bits are needed to distinguish between these 52 characters?

2.3   1. Assume that there are about 400 students in your class. If every student is to be assigned a unique bit pattern, what is the minimum number of bits required to do this?

     2. How many more students can be admitted to the class without requiring additional bits for the unique bit pattern?

2.4 Given n bits, how many unsigned integers can be represented with the n bits? What is the range of these integers?

2.5 Write the representations of 7 and -7 in 1's complement, signed magnitude and 2's complement integers.

2.6 Write the 6-bit 2's complement representation of -32.

2.7 Create a table showing the decimal values of all 4-bit two's complement numbers.

2.8   1. What is the largest positive number one can represent in an 8-bit two's complement code? Write your result in binary and decimal.

     2. What is the greatest magnitude negative number one can represent in 8-bit two's complement code? Write your result in binary and decimal.

     3. What is the largest positive number one can represent in n-bit two's complement code?

     4. What is the greatest magnitude negative number one can represent in n-bit two's complement code?

2.9 Convert the following 2's complement binary numbers to decimal. Explicitly show each step of the conversion algorithm laid out in Section 2.4.1.

    1. 1010

    2. 01011010

    3. 11111110

    4. 0011100111010011

2.10 Convert the following decimal numbers to 8-bit 2's complement binary numbers. Explicitly show each step of the the conversion algorithm laid out in section 2.4.2.

    1. 102

    2. 64

3. 33

4. -128

5. 127

2.11 If the last digit of a 2's complement binary number is 0, then the number is even. If the last two digits of a 2's complement binary number are 00, e.g., the binary number 01100, what does that tell you about the number?

2.12 Adjust the following 2's complement binary numbers to 8-bit 2's complement numbers without changing their values.

1. 1010

2. 011001

3. 1111111000

4. 01

2.13 Add the following binary numbers. Leave your results in binary.

1. 1011 + 0001

2. 0000 + 1010

3. 1100 + 0011

4. 0101 + 0110

5. 1111 + 0001

2.14 Write the results of the following computations both in binary and in decimal.

1. Using standard binary addition, add the 1's complement representation of 7 to the 1's complement representation of −7.

2. Using standard binary addition, add the signed magnitude representation of 7 to the signed magnitude representation of −7.

3. Using standard binary addition, add the 2's complement representation of 7 to the two's complement representation of −7.

2.15 It was demonstrated in this section that shifting a binary number one bit to the left is equivalent to multiplying the number by two. Show in a similar manner what operation is performed when a binary number is shifted one bit to the right.

2.16 Add the following 2's complement binary numbers. Also express the answer in decimal.

1. 01 + 1011

2. 11 + 01010101

3. 0101 + 110

4. 01 + 10

2.17 Add the following unsigned binary numbers. Also express the answer in decimal.

1. $01 + 1011$
2. $11 + 01010101$
3. $0101 + 110$
4. $01 + 10$

2.18 Sign extension does not affect the value of a 2's complement number, correct? Does it affect the value of an unsigned number, a 1's complement number or a signed magnitude number? If it does change the value of a number in one of these data-types, give an example to demonstrate.

2.19 The following binary numbers are two's complement binary numbers. Which of the following operations generate overflow? Justify your answer by translating the operands and results into decimal.

1. $1100 + 0011$
2. $1100 + 0100$
3. $0111 + 0001$
4. $1000 - 0001$
5. $0111 + 1001$

2.20 Describe in English what conditions indicate overflow has occurred when two's complement numbers are added.

2.21 Create two 16-bit two's complement integers such that their sum causes an overflow.

2.22 Describe in English what conditions indicate overflow has occurred when unsigned numbers are added.

2.23 Create two 16-bit unsigned integers such that their sum causes an overflow.

2.24 Why does the sum of a negative 2's complement number and a positive 2's complement number never generate an overflow?

2.25 When is the output of an AND operation equal to 1?

2.26 Fill in the following truth table for a one bit AND operation.

X	Y	X AND Y
0	0	
0	1	
1	0	
1	1	

2.27 Compute the following. Write your results in binary.

1. 01010111 AND 11010111

2. 101 AND 110

3. 11100000 AND 10110100

4. 00011111 AND 10110100

5. (0011 AND 0110) AND 1101

6. 0011 AND (0110 AND 1101)

2.28 When is the output of an OR operation equal to 1?

2.29 Fill in the following truth table for a one bit OR operation.

X	Y	X OR Y
0	0	
0	1	
1	0	
1	1	

2.30 Compute the following,

1. 01010111 OR 11010111

2. 101 OR 110

3. 11100000 OR 10110100

4. 00011111 OR 10110100

5. (0101 OR 1100) OR 1101

6. 0101 OR (1100 OR 1101)

2.31 Compute the following,

1. NOT(1011) OR NOT(1100)

2. NOT(1000 AND (1100 OR 0101))

3. NOT(NOT(1101))

4. (0110 OR 0000) AND 1111

2.32 What is a mask used for?

2.33 Refer to the "machine busy" example in Section 2.6.5 to answer the following questions.

1. What mask value and what operation would one use to indicate that machine 2 is busy?

2. What mask value and what operation would one use to indicate that machines 2 and 6 are no longer busy? (Only one operation here)

3. What mask value and what operation would one use to indicate that all machines are busy?

    4. What mask value and what operation would one use to indicate that no machines are busy?

    5. Develop a procedure to isolate the status bit of machine 2 as the sign bit. For example, if the BUSYNESS pattern is 0101100, then the output of this procedure is 10000000. If the BUSYNESS pattern is 01110011, then the output is 00000000. In general, if the BUSYNESS pattern is: | b7 | b6 | b5 | b4 | b3 | b2 | b1 | b0 | the output is: | b2 | 0 | 0 | 0 | 0 | 0 | 0 | 0 |.
    Hint: What happens when you ADD a bit pattern to itself?

2.34 If n and m are both 4-bit 2's complement numbers, and s is the 4-bit result of adding them together, how can we determine, using only the logical operations described in Section 2.6, if an overflow occurred during the addition? Develop a "procedure" for doing so. The inputs to the procedure are n, m, and s and the output will be a bit pattern of all zeros (0000) if no overflow occurred and 1000 if an overflow did occur.

2.35 If n and m are both 4-bit unsigned numbers, and s is the 4-bit result of adding them together, how can we determine, using only the logical operations described in Section 2.6, if an overflow occurred during the addition? Develop a "procedure" for doing so. The inputs to the procedure are n, m, and s and the output will be a bit pattern of all zeros (0000) if no overflow occurred and 1000 if an overflow did occur.

2.36 Write IEEE Floating Point representation of the following decimal numbers.

    1. 3.75

    2. $-55\frac{23}{64}$

    3. 3.1415927

    4. 64,000

2.37 Write the decimal representation for the following IEEE Floating Point numbers.

    1. 0 10000000 00000000000000000000000

    2. 1 10000011 00010000000000000000000

    3. 0 11111111 00000000000000000000000

    4. 1 10000000 10010000000000000000000

2.38   1. What is the largest exponent the IEEE standard allows for a 32-bit floating point number?

    2. What is the smallest exponent the IEEE standard allows for a 32-bit floating point number?

2.39 A computer scientist wrote a program which adds two numbers. The program's output for 5 + 8 was 'm'. What did the computer scientist do wrong? Include in your answer an example of how 5 + 8 can be 'm'.

2.40 Translate the following ASCII codes into strings of characters by interpreting each group of 8 bits as an ASCII character.

    1. x48656c6c6f21

    2. x68454c4c4f21

    3. x436f6d70757465727321

    4. x4c432d32

2.41 What operation(s) can be used to convert the binary representation for 3 (i.e., 0000 0011) into the ASCII representation for 3 (i.e., 0110 0011)? What about the binary 4 into the ASCII 4? What about any digit?

2.42 Convert the following unsigned binary numbers to hexadecimal.

    1. 1101 0001 1010 1111

    2. 001 1111

    3. 1

    4. 1110 1101 1011 0010

2.43 Convert the following hexadecimal numbers to binary. The prefix, 'x', is used to indicate the numbers are in hexadecimal form.

    1. x10

    2. x801

    3. xF731

    4. x0F1E2D

    5. xBCAD

2.44 Convert the following hexadecimal representations of 2's complement binary numbers to decimal numbers.

    1. xF0

    2. x7FF

    3. x16

    4. x8000

2.45 Convert the following decimal numbers to hexadecimal representations of 2's complement numbers.

    1. 256

    2. 111

    3. 123,456,789

    4. -44

2.46 Perform the following additions. The corresponding 16-bit binary numbers are in two's complement notation. Provide your answers in hexadecimal.

    1. x025B + x26DE

    2. x07D96 + xF0A0

    3. xA397 + xA35D

    4. x7D96 + x7412

    5. What happens when the answers to parts (c) and (d) are added together?

2.47 Perform the following logical operations. Provide your answers in hexadecimal.

    1. x5478 AND xFDEA

    2. xABCD OR x1234

    3. NOT((NOT(xDEFA)) AND (NOT(xFFFF)))

    4. x00FF XOR x325C

2.48 What is the hexadecimal representation of the following numbers.

    1. 25,675

    2. 675.625 (that is, $675\frac{5}{8}$), in the IEEE 754 floating point standard.

    3. The ASCII string: "Hello"

2.49 Consider the following two hexadecimal numbers: x434F4D50 and x55544552. Fill in the table with the appropriately converted values.

	x434F4D5	x55544552
Unsigned Binary		
1's Compliment		
2's Compliment		
IEEE 754 Floating Point		
ASCII String		

2.50 Fill in the truth table for the equations given below. The first line is done as an example.

Q_1 = NOT(A AND B)
Q_2 = NOT(NOT(A) AND NOT(B))

A	B	Q_1	Q_2
0	0	1	0

Express Q_2 another way.

2.51 Fill in the truth table for the equations given below. The first line is done as an example.

$Q_1 = $ NOT(NOT(X) OR (X AND Y AND Z))

$Q_2 = $ NOT((Y OR Z) AND (X AND Y AND Z))

X	Y	Z	Q_1	Q_2
0	0	0	0	1

Chapter 3

Digital Logic Structures.

In Chapter 1, we stated that computers were constructed out of very large numbers of very simple structures. For example, Intel's Pentium II microprocessor, first offered for sale in 1998, is made up of more than 7 million MOS transistors. The Digital Equipment Corporation Alpha 21264 consists of more than 15 million MOS transistors. In this chapter, we will explain how the MOS transistor works (as a logic element), show how these transistors are connected to form logic gates, and then show how logic gates are interconnected to form larger units that are needed to construct a computer. In Chapter 4, we will connect those larger units into a computer.

But first, the transistor.

3.1 The transistor

Most computers today, or rather most microprocessors (which form the core of the corresponding computer) are constructed out of MOS transistors. MOS stands for Metal-oxide Semiconductor. The electrical properties of Metal Oxide Semiconductors are well beyond the scope of what we want to understand in this course. However, it is useful to know that there are two types of MOS transistors: P-type and N-type. They both operate "logically" very similar to the way wall switches works.

Figure 3.1 shows the most basic of electrical circuits: a power supply (in this case, the 120 volts that come into your house), a wall switch, and a lamp (plugged into an outlet in the wall). In order for the lamp to glow, electrons must flow; in order for electrons to flow, there must be a closed circuit from the power supply to the lamp and back to the power supply. The lamp can be turned on and off by simply making or breaking the closed circuit by manipulating the wall switch.

Instead of the wall switch, we could use an N-type or a P-type MOS transistor to make or break the closed circuit. Figure 3.2 shows a schematic rendering of an N-type transistor, (a) by itself, and (b) in a circuit. Note (figure 3.2a) that the transistor has three terminals. If the gate of the transistor is supplied with 2.9 volts, terminals #1 and #2 act like a piece of

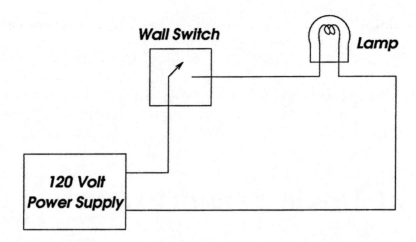

Figure 3.1: A Simple Electric Circuit Showing the Use of a Wall Switch.

wire. We say (in the language of electricity) that we have a *closed circuit* between terminals #1 and #2. If the gate of the transistor is supplied with 0 volts, terminals #1 and #2 act like a broken connection. We say that between terminals #1 and #2, we have an *open circuit.*

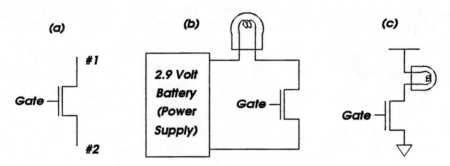

Figure 3.2: The N-type MOS Transistor.

Figure 3.2b shows the N-type transistor in a circuit with a battery and a bulb. When the gate is supplied with 2.9 volts, the transistor acts like a piece of wire, completing the circuit and causing the bulb to glow. When the gate is supplied with 0 volts, the transistor acts like an open, breaking the circuit, and causing the bulb to not glow.

Figure 3.2c is a short-hand notation for describing the circuit of Figure 3.2b. Rather than always show the power supply and the complete circuit, electrical engineers usually show only the terminals of the power supply. The fact that the power supply itself provides the completion of the completed circuit is well understood, and so not usually shown.

The P-type transistor works exactly the opposite of the N-type transistor. Figure 3.3 shows the schematic representation of a P-type transistor. When the gate is supplied with 0 volts, the P-type transistor acts (more or less) like a piece of wire, closing the circuit. When the gate is supplied with 2.9 volts, the P-type transistor acts like an open circuit. Because the P-type and N-type transistors act in this complementary way, we refer to circuits that contain both P-type and N-type transistors as CMOS circuits, for *complementary metal oxide semiconductor.*

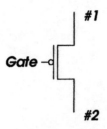

Figure 3.3: A P-type MOS Transistor.

3.2 Logic Gates.

One step up from the transistor is the logic gate. That is, we construct basic logic structures out of individual MOS transistors. In Chapter 2 we studied the behavior of the AND, the OR, and the NOT functions. In this chapter we construct transistor circuits that implement these functions. These circuits are called AND, OR, and NOT gates.

3.2.1 The NOT gate (or, inverter).

Figure 3.4 shows the simplest logic structure that exists in a computer. It is constructed from two MOS transistors, one P-type and one N-type. Figure 3.4a is the schematic representation of that circuit. Figure 3.4b shows the behavior of the circuit if the input is supplied with 0 volts. Note that the P-type transistor conducts and the N-type transistor does not conduct. The output is, therefore connected to 2.9 volts. On the other hand, if the input is supplied with 2.9 volts, the P-type transistor does not conduct, but the N-type transistor does conduct. The output in this case is connected to ground (i.e., 0 volts). The complete behavior of the circuit can be described by means of a table, as shown in Figure 3.4c. If we replace 0 volts by the symbol 0 and 2.9 volts by the symbol 1, we have the truth table (Figure 3.4d) for the complement or NOT function, which we discussed in Chapter 2.

In other words, we have just shown how to construct an electronic circuit that implements the NOT logic function discussed in Chapter 2. We call this circuit a NOT gate, or an *inverter.*

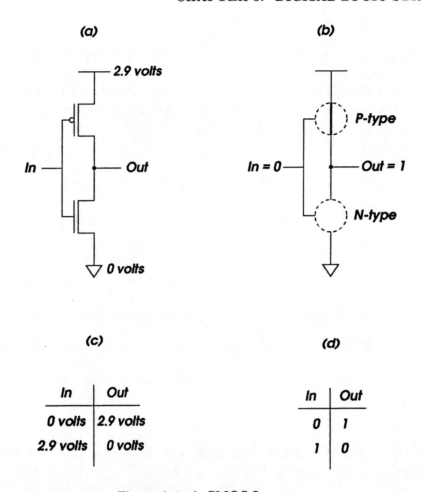

Figure 3.4: A CMOS Inverter.

3.2.2   OR and NOR gates.

First examine Figure 3.5. Figure 3.5a is a schematic containing two P-type and two N-type transistors.

Figure 3.5b shows the behavior of the circuit if A is supplied with 0 volts and B is supplied with 2.9 volts. In this case, the lower of the two P-type transistors produces an open circuit, and the output C is disconnected from the 2.9 volt power supply. However, the left-most N-type transistor acts like a piece of wire, connecting the output C to 0 volts.

Note that if both A and B are supplied with 0 volts, the two P-type transistors conduct, and the output C is connected to 2.9 volts. Note, further, that there is no ambiguity here, since both N-type transistors act as open circuits, and so C is disconnected from ground.

If either A or B is supplied with 2.9 volts, the corresponding P-type transistor results in an open circuit. That is sufficient to break the connection from C to the 2.9 volt source. However, 2.9 volts supplied to the gate of one of the N-type transistors is sufficient to cause that transistor to conduct, resulting in C being connected to ground (i.e., 0 volts).

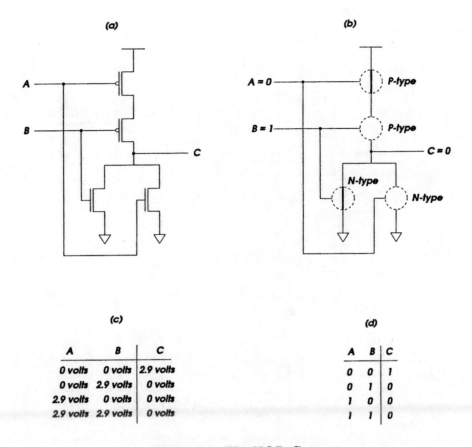

Figure 3.5: The NOR Gate.

Figure 3.5c summarizes the complete behavior of the circuit of Figure 3.5a. It shows the behavior of the circuit for each of the four pairs of voltages that A and B can be supplied with. That is,

```
A = 0 volts,    B = 0 volts
A = 0 volts,    B = 2.9 volts
A = 2.9 volts,  B = 0 volts
A = 2.9 volts,  B = 2.9 volts
```

If we replace the voltages with their logical equivalents, we have the truth table of Figure 3.5d. Note that the output C is exactly the opposite of the logical OR function discussed in Chapter 2. In fact, it is the NOT-OR function, more typically abbreviated as NOR. We refer to the circuit that implements the logical function NOR as a NOR gate.

If we augment the circuit of Figure 3.5a by adding an inverter at the output, as shown in Figure 3.6a, we have at the output D the logical function OR. Figure 3.6a is the circuit for an OR gate. Figure 3.6b describes the behavior of this circuit if the input variable A is set to 0 and the input variable B is set to 1. Figure 3.6c shows the circuit's truth table.

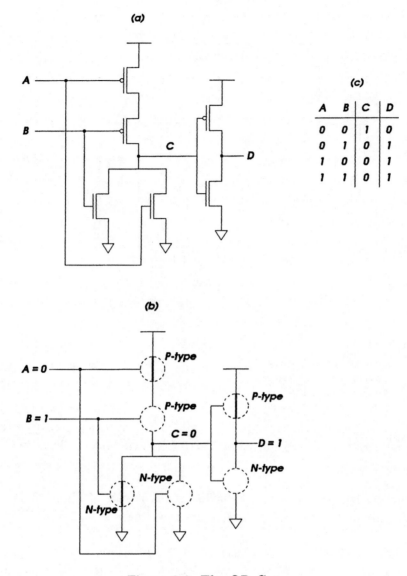

Figure 3.6: The OR Gate.

3.2.3   AND and NAND gates.

Next, we will examine Figure 3.7. Note that if either A or B is supplied with 0 volts, there is a direct connection from C to the 2.9 volt power supply. The fact that C is at 2.9 volts means the N-type transistor whose gate is connected to C provides a path from D to ground. Therefore, if either A or B is supplied with 0 volts, the output D of the circuit of Figure 3.7 is 0 volts.

Again, we note that there is no ambiguity. The fact that at least one of the two inputs A or B is supplied with 0 volts means that at least one of the two N-type transistors whose gates are connected to A or B is an open, and that consequently, C is disconnected from

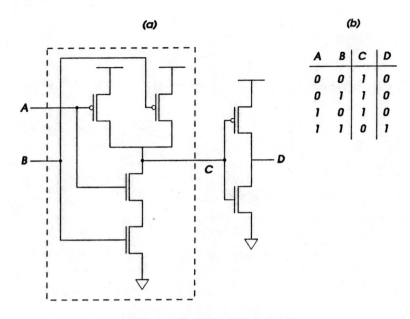

Figure 3.7: The AND Gate.

ground. Furthermore, the fact that C is at 2.9 volts means the P-type transistor whose gate is connected to C is open-circuited. Therefore, D is not connected to 2.9 volts.

On the other hand, if both *A* and *B* are supplied with 2.9 volts, then both of their corresponding P-type transistors are open. However, their corresponding N-type transistors act like pieces of wire, providing a direct connection from C to ground. Because C is at ground, the right-most P-type transistor acts like a closed circuit, forcing D to 2.9 volts.

Figure 3.7b summarizes in truth table form the behavior of the circuit of Figure 3.7a. Note that the circuit is an AND gate. The circuit shown within the dashed lines (i.e., having output C) is a NOT-AND gate, which we generally abbreviate as NAND.

The gates discussed above are very common in digital logic circuits and in digital computers. There are hundreds of thousands of inverters (NOT-gates) in the Pentium II microprocessor. As a convenience, we can represent each of the above gates by standard symbols, as shown in Figure 3.8. The bubble shown in the inverter, NAND and NOR gates signifies the complement (i.e., NOT) function.

From now on, we will not draw circuits showing the individual transistors. Instead, we will use the symbols of Figure 3.8.

3.2.4 DeMorgan's Law.

Note (see Figure 3.9a) that one can complement an input before applying it to a gate. Consider the effect on the two input AND gate if we apply the complements of *A* and *B* as inputs to the gate, and also complement the output of the AND gate. The bubbles at the inputs to the AND gate designate that the inputs *A* and *B* are complemented before they are used as inputs to the AND gate.

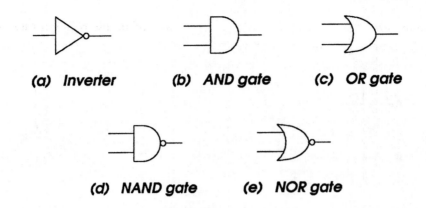

(a) Inverter   (b) AND gate   (c) OR gate

(d) NAND gate   (e) NOR gate

Figure 3.8: Basic Logic Gates.

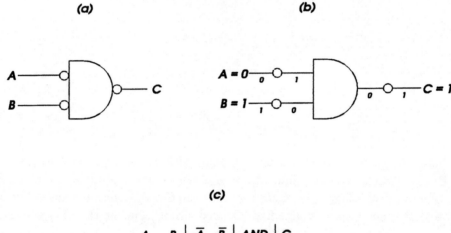

(c)

A	B	$\overline{A}$	$\overline{B}$	AND	C
0	0	1	1	1	0
0	1	1	0	0	1
1	0	0	1	0	1
1	1	0	0	0	1

Figure 3.9: DeMorgan's Law.

Figure 3.9b shows the behavior of this structure for the input combination $A = 0$, $B = 1$. For ease of representation, we have moved the "bubbles" away from the inputs and the output of the AND gate. That way, we can more easily see what happens to each value as it passes through a bubble.

Figure 3.9c summarizes by means of a truth table the behavior of the logic circuit of Figure 3.9a for all four combinations of input values. Note that the NOT of A is represented as $\overline{A}$.

We can describe the behavior of this circuit algebraically:

$$\overline{A} \ AND \ \overline{B} \ = \ A \ OR \ B$$

This equivalence is known as DeMorgan's Law. Is there a similar result if one inverts both inputs to an OR gate, and then inverts the output?

3.2.5 Larger Gates.

Before we leave the topic of logic gates, we should note that the notion of AND, OR, NAND, and NOR gates extends to larger numbers of inputs. One could build a three-input AND gate or a four-input OR gate, for example. An n-input AND gate has an output value of 1 only if ALL the input variables have values of 1. If any of the n inputs has a value of 0, the output of the n-input AND gate is 0. An n-input OR gate has an output value of 1 if ANY of the input variables has a value of 1. That is, an n-input OR gate has an output value of 0 only if ALL n input variables have values of 0.

Figure 3.10 illustrates a three-input AND gate. Figure 3.10a shows its truth table. Figure 3.10b shows the symbol for a three-input AND gate.

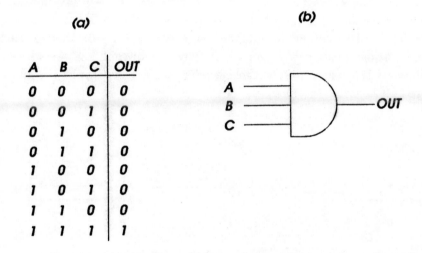

(a)

A	B	C	OUT
0	0	0	0
0	0	1	0
0	1	0	0
0	1	1	0
1	0	0	0
1	0	1	0
1	1	0	0
1	1	1	1

(b)

Figure 3.10: A Three-input AND Gate.

Can you draw a transistor-level circuit for a three-input AND gate? How about a four-input OR gate?

3.3 Combinational logic structures.

Now that we understand the workings of the basic logic gates, the next step is to build some of the logic structures that are important components of the microarchitecture of a computer.

There are fundamentally two kinds of logic structures, those that include the storage of information and those that don't. In sections 3.4 and 3.5, we will deal with structures that store information. In this section, we will deal with those that don't. These structures are sometimes referred to as decision elements. Usually, they are referred to as combinational logic structures, because their outputs are strictly dependent on the combination of input values that are being applied to the structure *right now*. Their outputs are not at all dependent on any past history of information that is stored internally, since no information can be stored internally in a combinational logic circuit.

We will examine a Decoder, a Mux, and a Full Adder.

3.3.1 DECODER

Figure 3.11 shows a logic gate description of a two-input decoder. A decoder has the property that it provides at its output exactly one 1 and all the rest 0s. The one output that is logically 1 is the output corresponding to the input pattern that it is expected to detect. In general, decoders have n inputs and 2^n outputs. We say the output line that detects the input pattern is *asserted*. That is, that output line has the value 1, rather than 0 as is the case for all the other output lines, In Figure 3.11, note that for each of the four possible combinations of inputs A and B, exactly one output has the value 1 at any one time. In Figure 3.11b, the input to the Decoder is 10, resulting in the third output line being asserted.

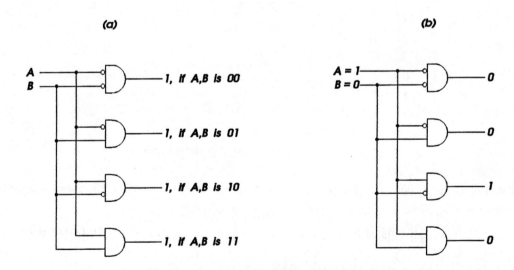

Figure 3.11: A Two-input Decoder.

The decoder is useful in determining how to interpret a bit pattern. We will see in Chapter 5 that the work to be carried out by each instruction in the LC-2 is determined by a four bit pattern, called an opcode, that is part of the instruction. A four-to-16 decoder is a simple combinational logic structure for identifying what work is to be performed by each instruction.

3.3.2 MUX

Figure 3.12a shows a gate level description of a two-input multiplexer, more commonly referred to as a MUX. The function of a MUX is to select one of the inputs and connect it to the output. The select signal (S in Figure 3.12) determines which input is connected to the output.

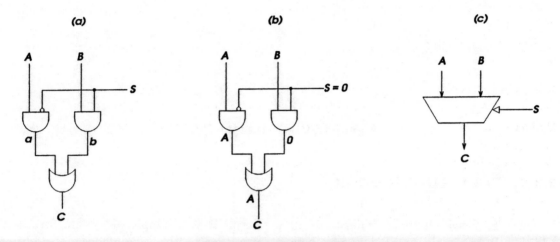

Figure 3.12: A 2-to-1 MUX.

The MUX of Figure 3.12 works as follows: Suppose S=0, as shown in Figure 3.12b. Since the output of an AND gate is 0 unless all inputs are 1, the output of the right-most AND gate is 0. Also, the output of the left-most AND gate is whatever the input A is. That is, if A=0, then the output of the left-most AND gate is 0, and if A=1, then the output is 1. Since the output of the right-most AND gate is 0, it has no effect on the OR gate. Consequently, the output at C is exactly the same as the output of the left-most AND gate. The net result of all this is that if S=0, the output C is identical to the input A.

On the other hand, if $S=1$, it is B that is ANDed with 1, resulting in the output of the OR gate having the value of B.

In summary, the output C is always connected to either the input A or the input B – which one depends on the value of the select line S. We say S selects the source of the MUX (either A or B) to be routed through to the output C.

Figure 3.12c shows the standard representation for a MUX.

In general a MUX consists of 2^n inputs and n select lines. Figure 3.13a shows a gate-level description of a four-input MUX. It requires two select lines. Figure 3.13b shows the standard representation for a four-input MUX.

Can you construct the gate-level representation for an eight-input MUX? How many select lines must you have?

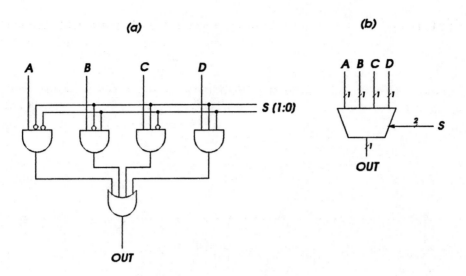

Figure 3.13: A four-input MUX.

3.3.3   FULL ADDER circuit.

In Chapter 2, we discussed binary addition. Recall that a simple algorithm for binary addition is to simply proceed as you have always done in the case of decimal addition, except one gets a carry after 1, rather than after 9.

Figure 3.14 is a truth table that describes the result of binary addition on *one column* of bits within two n-bit operands. At each column, there are three values that must be added: one bit from each of the two operands and the carry from the previous column. We designate three bits as a_i, b_i, and $carry_i$. There are two results, the sum bit (s_i) and the carry over to the next column, $carry_{i+1}$. Note that if only one of the three bits equals 1, we get a sum of 1, and no carry (i.e., $carry_{i+1} = 0$). If two of the three bits equal 1, we get a sum of 0, and a carry of 1. If all three bits equal 1, the sum is 3, which in binary addition corresponds to a sum of 1 and a carry of 1.

a_i	b_i	CARRY$_i$	CARRY$_{i+1}$	s_i
0	0	0	0	0
0	0	1	0	1
0	1	0	0	1
0	1	1	1	0
1	0	0	0	1
1	0	1	1	0
1	1	0	1	0
1	1	1	1	1

Figure 3.14: A Truth Table for a Binary Adder.

Figure 3.15 is the gate level description of the truth table of Figure 3.14. We call a circuit that provides three inputs (a_i, b_i, and $carry_i$) and two outputs (the sum bit (s_i) and the carry over to the next column $carry_{i+1}$) a *Full Adder*.

Note that each input combination (a specific value associated with each of the three input variables) corresponds to a three-input AND gate with the inputs complemented if the corresponding variable is 0. The output of an AND gate is asserted (equals 1) if the corresponding input combination is present. Thus, to implement the logic circuit to perform the carry function, it is only necessary (as shown in Figure 3.15) (1) to construct AND gates that are asserted for each input combination that produces a carry out, and (2) to connect those AND gates as inputs to a single OR gate. The carry out is 1 if at least two of the three bits being added are 1's. That is, the carry out is 1 if the input combination is 011, 101, 110, or 111. Thus, we first construct AND gates that will produce an output 1 for each of these four input combinations. Since the output of an OR gate is 1 if any of its input combinations is 1, we connect these four AND gates as inputs to a single OR gate. The result is that if the input combination produces a carry out, the output of the OR gate will be 1. The logic circuit to perform the sum function is built in a similar way.

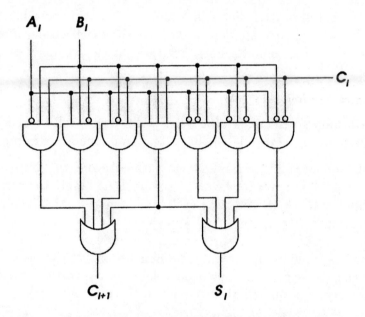

Figure 3.15: Gate Level Description of a Full Adder.

Figure 3.16 illustrates a circuit for adding two 4-bit binary numbers, using four of the full adder circuits of Figure 3.15. Note that the carry out of column i is an input to the addition performed in column i+1.

3.3.4 Logical Completeness.

Before we leave this section, it is worth noting that any arbitrary truth table can be implemented by a logic circuit, provided sufficiently many AND, OR, and NOT gates are

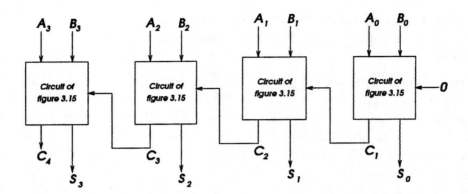

Figure 3.16: A Circuit for Adding Two Four-bit Binary Numbers.

available. We say that the set of gates {AND, OR, NOT} are *logically complete* because we can build a circuit to carry out the specification of any arbitrary truth table without using any other kind of gate. That is, the set of gates {AND, OR, and NOT} is logically complete because a barrel of AND gates, a barrel of OR gates and a barrel of NOT gates are sufficient to build a logic circuit that carries out the specification of any desired truth table. The barrels may have to be big ones, but the point is, we don't need any other kind of gate to do the job.

We can prove this in the following way.

1. Choose any arbitrary specification of a truth table. There will be n input variables, 2^n input combinations, and 2^n entries in the output column, one for each input combination.

2. For each input combination that results in an output 1, construct an AND gate having n inputs. For each input that is a 1 in the input combination, apply the corresponding input directly to the input of the AND gate. For each input that is a 0 in the input combination, invert the input using a NOT gate before applying it to the corresponding input of the AND gate. The output of this AND gate equals 1 exactly when the inputs to the circuit are the corresponding input combination. The number of AND gates constructed in this step is equal to the number of 1s in the output column of the truth table. Note that this is exactly how we constructed the full adder circuit in the previous section.

3. Apply the outputs of each of the AND gates to an input of one (perhaps large) OR gate. The output of that OR gate will exactly carry out the truth table of step 1, as follows:

a. Any input combination of the truth table that results in an output 1 corresponds (by construction in step 2) to an AND gate. The output of that AND gate equals 1. Since the output of that AND gate is an input to the OR gate, the output of the OR gate is likewise 1.

b. Any input combination of the truth table that does not result in an output 1 does not correspond to any AND gate. Since the output of each AND is equal to 1 only if the input combination is the one specified for that AND gate, the outputss of all AND gates equal 0. Since all inputs to the OR gate are 0, the output of the OR gate is 0. Done!

3.4 Basic Storage Elements.

Recall our statement at the beginning of Section 3.3 that there are two kinds of logic structures, those that involve the storage of information and those that don't. We have discussed three examples of those that don't: the Decoder, the MUX and the Adder. Now we are ready to discuss logic structures that do include the storage of information.

3.4.1 The R-S Latch.

A simple example of a storage element is the R-S latch. It can store one bit of information. The R-S latch can be implemented in many ways, the simplest being the one shown in Figure 3.17. Two two-input NAND gates are connected such that the output of each is connected to one of the inputs of the other. The remaining input S and R are normally held at a logic level 1.

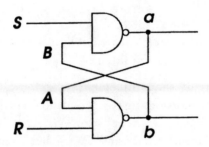

Figure 3.17: An R-S Latch.

The R-S latch works as follows: We start with what we call the quiescent (or quiet) state, where inputs S and R both have logic value 1. We consider first the case where the output a is 1. Since that means the input A equals 1, (and we know the input R equals 1 since we are in the quiescent state), the output b must be 0. That, in turn, means the input B must be 0, which results in the output a equal to 1. As long as the inputs S and R remain 1, the state of the circuit will not change. We say the R-S latch stores the value 1 (the value of the output a).

If, on the other hand, we assume the output a is 0, then the input A must be 0, and the output b must be 1. This in turn results in the input B equal to 1, and combined with the input S equal to 1 (again due to quiescence) results in the output a equal to 0. Again, as long as the inputs S and R remain 1, the state of the circuit will not change. In this case, we say the R-S latch stores the value 0.

The latch can be set to 1 by momentarily setting S to 0, provided we keep the value of R at 1. Similarly, the latch can be set to 0 by momentarily setting R to 0, provided we keep the value of S at 1. We use the term *set* to denote setting a variable to 0 or 1, as in *set to 0* or *set to 1*. In addition, we often use the term *clear* to denote the act of setting a variable to 0.

If we clear S, then a equals 1, which in turn causes A to equal 1. Since R is also 1, the output at b must be 0. This causes B to be 0, which in turn makes a equal 1. If we now return S to 1, it does not affect a, since B is also 0, and only one input to a NAND gate must be 0 in order to guarantee that the output of the NAND gate is 1. Thus the latch continues to store a 1 long after S returns to 1.

In the same way, we can clear the latch (set the latch to 0) by momentarily setting R to 0.

We should also note that in order for the R-S latch to work properly, one must take care that it is never the case that both S and R are allowed to be set to 0 at the same time. If that does happen, the outputs a and b are both 1, and the final state of the latch depends on the electrical properties of the transistors making up the gates and not on the logic being performed. How the electrical properties of the transistors will determine the final state in this case is a subject we will have to leave for a later semester.

3.4.2   The gated D latch.

To be useful, it is necessary to control when a latch is set and when it is cleared. A simple way to accomplish this is with the gated latch.

Figure 3.18 shows a logic circuit that implements a gated D latch. It consists of the R-S latch of Figure 3.17, plus two additional gates that allow the latch to be set to the value of D, but **only** when WE is asserted. WE stands for Write Enable. When WE is not asserted (i.e., when WE equals 0), the outputs S and R are both equal to 1. Since S and R are also inputs to the R-S latch, if they are kept at 1, the value stored in the latch remains unchanged, as we explained above,

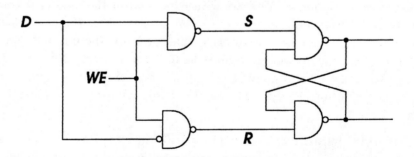

Figure 3.18: A Gated D Latch.

When WE is momentarily asserted (i.e., set to 1), exactly one of the outputs S or R is set to 0, depending on the value of D. If D equals 1, then S is set to 0. If D equals 0, then both inputs to the lower NAND gate are 1, resulting in R being set to 0. i As we saw above, if S is set to 0, the R-S latch is set to 1. If R is set to 0, the R-S latch is set to 0. Thus, the R-S latch is set to 1 or 0 according to whether D is 1 or 0. When WE returns to 0, S and R return to 1, and the value stored in the R-S latch persists.

3.4.3 A Register.

We have already seen in Chapter 2 that it is useful to deal with values consisting of more than 1 bit. In chapter 5, we will introduce the LC-2 computer, where most values are represented by 16 bits. It is useful to be able to store these larger numbers of bits as a self-contained unit. The *register* is a structure that stores a number of bits, taken together as a unit. That number can be as large as is useful or as small as 1. In the LC-2, we will need many 16-bit registers, and also a few one-bit registers. We will see in Figure 3.22, which describes the internal structure of the LC-2, that PC, IR, and MAR are all 16-bit registers, and that N, Z, and P are all one-bit registers.

Figure 3.19 shows a 4-bit register made up of 4 gated D latches. The four-bit value stored in the register is Q_3, Q_2, Q_1, Q_0. The value D_3, D_2, D_1, D_0 can be written into the register when WE is asserted.

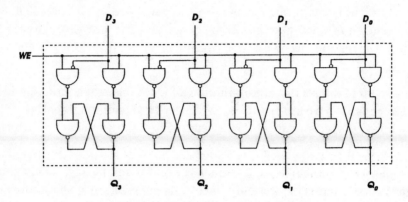

Figure 3.19: A Four-bit Register.

Note: a common shorthand notation to describe a sequence of bits that are numbered as above is Q[3:0]. That is, each bit is assigned its own bit number. The right-most bit is bit[0], and the numbering continues from right to left. If there are n bits, the left-most bit is bit[n-1]. For example, in the following 16-bit pattern,

$$0011101100011110$$

bit[15] is 0, bit[14] is 0, bit[13] is 1, bit[12] is 1, etc.

We can designate a subunit of this pattern with the notation Q[l:r], where *l* is the left-most bit in the sub-unit and *r* is the right-most bit in the sub-unit. We call such a sub-unit a *field*.

In the above 16-bit pattern, if A[15:0] is the entire 16-bit pattern, then, for example:

```
A[15:12] is 0011
A[13:7]  is 1110110
A[2:0]   is 110
A[1:1]   is 1
```

We should also point out that the numbering scheme from right to left is purely arbitrarily. We could have just as easily designated the left-most bit as bit[0] and numbered them from left to right. Indeed, many people do. So, it is not important whether the numbering scheme is left to right or right to left. But it is important that the bit numbering be consistent in a given setting, that is, that it always be done the same way. In our work, we will always number bits from right to left.

3.5   The Concept of Memory.

We now have all the tools we need to describe what is perhaps the most important structure in the electronic digital computer, its *memory*. We will see in Chapter 4 how memory fits into the basic scheme of computer processing, and you will see throughout the rest of the book and indeed the rest of your work with computers how important the concept of memory is to computing.

Memory is made up of a (usually large) number of locations, each uniquely identifiable and each having the capability to store a value. We refer to the unique identifier associated with each memory location as its *address*. We refer to the number of bits of information stored in each location as its *addressibility*.

For example, an advertisement for a personal computer might say, "This computer comes with 16 megabytes of memory." Actually, most ads generally use the abbreviation 16 MB. This statement means, as we will explain momentarily, that the computer system includes 16 million memory locations, each containing one byte of information.

3.5.1   Address Space.

We refer to the total number of uniquely identifiable locations as the memory's *address space*. A 16MB memory, for example, refers to a memory that consists of 16 million uniquely identifiable memory locations.

Actually, the number 16 million is only an approximation, due to the way we identify memory locations. Since everything else in the computer is represented by sequences of 0s and 1s, it should not be surprising that memory locations are identified by binary addresses, as well. With n bits of address, we can uniquely identify 2^n locations. Ten bits provide 1024 locations, which is approximately one thousand. If we have 20 bits to represent each address, we have 2^{20} uniquely identifiable locations, which is approximately one million. Thus "16 mega" really corresponds to the number of uniquely identifiable locations that can be specified with 24 address bits. We say the address space is 2^{24}, which is *exactly* 16,777,216 locations, rather than 16,000,000 that we colloquially refer to it as.

3.5.2 Addressibility.

The number of bits stored in each memory location is the memory's addressibility. A 16 megabyte memory is a memory consisting of 16,777,216 memory locations, each containing one byte (i.e., 8 bits) of storage. Most memories are byte-addressible. The reason is historical; most computers got their start processing data, and one character stroke on the keyboard corresponds to one 8-bit ASCII character, as we learned in Chapter 2. If the memory is byte-addressible, then each ASCII code occupies one location in memory. Uniquely identifying each byte of memory allowed individual bytes of stored information to be changed easily.

Many computers that have been designed specifically to perform large scientific calculations are 64-bit addressible. This is due to the fact that numbers used in scientific calculations are frequently represented as 64 bit floating point quantities. Recall we discussed the floating point data type in Chapter 2. Since scientific calculations are likely to use numbers that require 64 bits to represent them, it is reasonable to design a memory for such a computer that stores one such number in each uniquely identifiable memory location.

3.5.3 A 2^2 by 3 bit Memory.

Figure 3.20 illustrates a memory of size 2^2 by 3 bits. That is, the memory has an address space of four locations, and an addressibility of 3 bits. A memory of size 2^2 requires 2 bits to specify the address. A memory of addressibility 3 stores 3 bits of information in each memory location.

Accesses of memory require decoding the address bits. Note that the Address Decoder takes as input A[1:0] and asserts exactly one of its four outputs, corresponding to the *word line* being addressed. In Figure 3.20, each row of the memory corresponds to a unique 3-bit word; therefore, the term word line. Memory can be read by applying the address A[1:0], which asserts the word line to be read. Note that each of the 12 bits in this memory is ANDed with its word line and then ORed with the corresponding bits of the other words. Since only one word line can be asserted at a time, the output of each *bit line* is the value stored in the corresponding bit of the word line that is asserted.

Figure 3.21 shows the process of reading location 3. The code for 3 is 11. The address A[1:0] = 11 is decoded, and the bottom word line is asserted. Note that the three other decoder outputs are not asserted. That is, they have the value 0. The value stored in location 3 is 101. These three bits are each ANDed with their word line producing the bits 101 which are supplied to the three output OR gates. Note that all other inputs to the OR gates are 0, since they have been produced by ANDing with unasserted word lines. The result is that D[2:0] = 101. That is, the value stored in location 3, is output by the OR gates.

Memory can be written in a similar fashion. The address specified by A[1:0] is presented to the Address Decoder, resulting in the correct word line being asserted. With WE asserted as well, the three bits $D_i[2:0]$ can be written into the three gated latches corresponding to that word line.

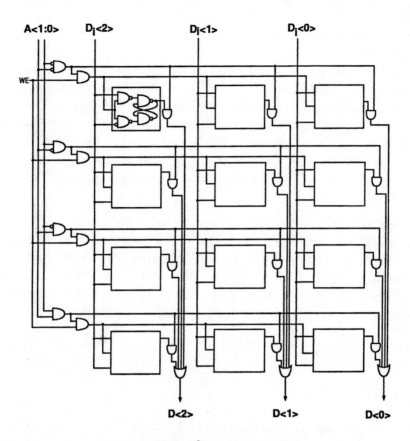

Figure 3.20: A 2^2 by 3 bit Memory.

3.6   The Data Path of the LC-2.

(Preview of Coming Attractions)

In chapter 5, we will specify a computer, which we call the LC-2, and you will have the opportunity to write computer programs to execute on the LC-2. Figure 3.22 is a block diagram of what we call the *Data Path* of the LC-2. The Data Path consists of all the logic structures that combine to process information in the core of the computer. Right now, Figure 3.22 is undoubtedly a little intimidating, and that is not surprising. You are not ready to analyze it yet. That will come in Chapter 5. We have included it here, however, to show you that you are already familiar with many of the basic structures that make up a computer. That is, you already know how many of the elements in the data path work, and furthermore, you know how those elements are constructed from gates. For example, PC, IR, MAR, and MDR are registers and store 16 bits of information, each. Each wire that is labeled with a cross-hatch 16 represents 16 wires, each carrying one bit of information. N, Z, and P are one-bit registers. There are three MUXes, one supplying a 16-bit value to the PC register. In Chapter 5 we will see why these elements must be connected as shown in order to execute the programs written for the LC-2 computer.

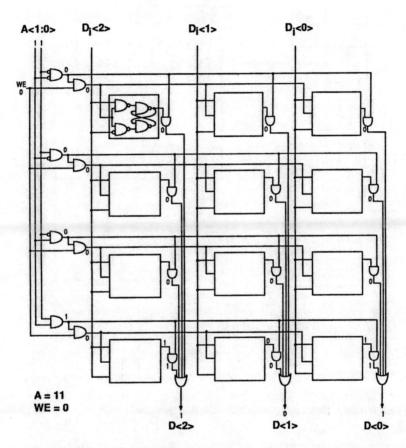

Figure 3.21: Reading location 3 in our 2^2 by 3 bit Memory.

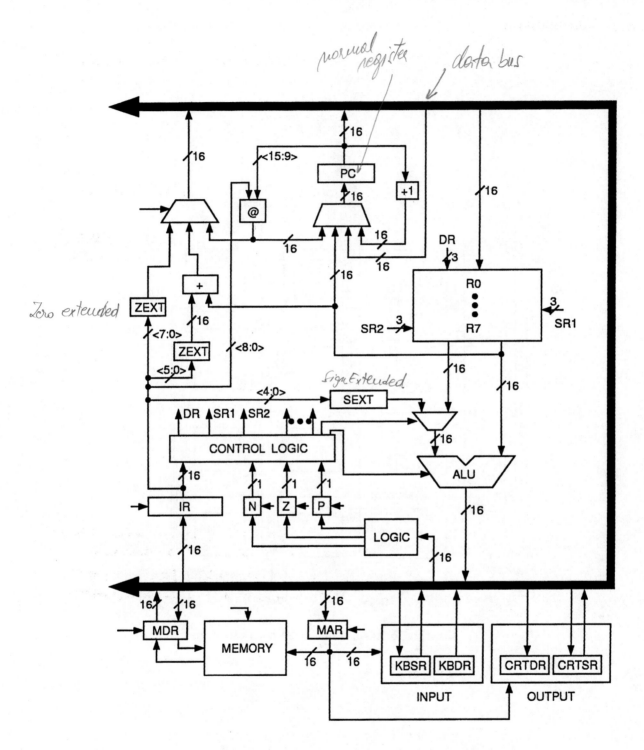

Figure 3.22: The Data Path of the LC-2 Computer.

3.7 Exercises.

3.1 In the table below, write whether each type of transistor will act as an open circuit or a closed circuit.

	n-type	p-type
Gate = 1		
Gate = 0		

3.2 A 2-input AND and a 2-input OR are both examples of 2-input logic functions. How many different 2-input logic functions are possible?

3.3 Following the example of Figure 3.4(b), replace the missing parts in the circuit in Figure 3.23 with either a wire or no wire to give the output OUT a logical value of 0 when the input IN is a logical 1.

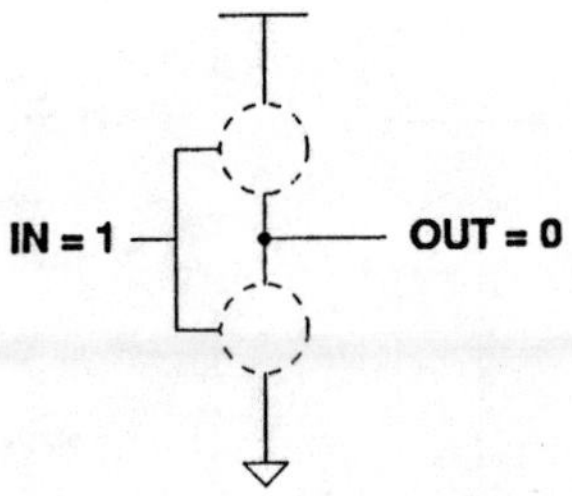

Figure 3.23: Diagram for Problem 3.23.

3.4 Following the example of Figure 3.5(b), replace the missing parts in the circuit in Figure 3.24 with either a wire or no wire to give the output C a logical value of 1.

Other than the one given in the example, list a set of inputs which give the output C a logical value of 0. Replace the missing parts with wires or no wires corresponding to that set of inputs.

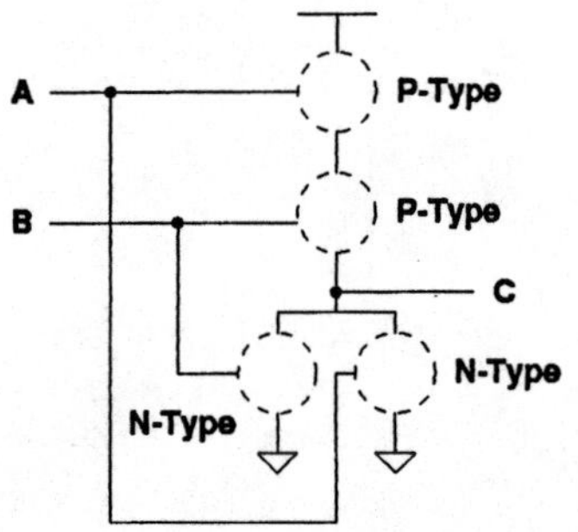

Figure 3.24: Diagram for Problem 4.

3.5 Complete a truth table for the transistor-level circuit in Figure 3.25.

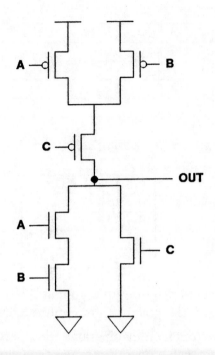

Figure 3.25: Diagram for Problem 5.

3.6 The circuit in Figure 3.26 has a major flaw. Can you identify it? **Hint: evaluate the circuit for all sets of inputs.**

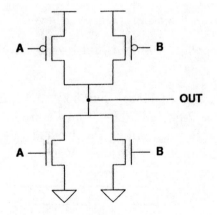

Figure 3.26: Diagram for Problem 6

3.7 Fill in the truth table for the logical expression: NOT(NOT(A) OR NOT(B)). What simpler gate has the same truth table?

A	B	NOT(NOT(A) OR NOT(B))
0	0	
0	1	
1	0	
1	1	

3.8 Fill in the truth table for a 2-input NOR gate.

A	B	A NOR B
0	0	
0	1	
1	0	
1	1	

3.9   1. Draw a transistor-level diagram for a 3-input AND gate and a 3-input OR gate. Do this by extending the designs from Figures 3.6(a) and 3.7(a).

   2. Replace the transistors in your diagrams from part A with either a wire or no wire to reflect the circuit's operation when the following inputs are applied.

   (a) A = 1, B = 0, C = 0

   (b) A = 0, B = 0, C = 0

   (c) A = 1, B = 1, C = 1

3.10 Following the example of Figure 3.11(a), draw the gate level schematic of a 3-input decoder. For each output of this decoder, write the input conditions under which that output will be 1 (again, follow the example of Figure 3.11(a)).

3.11 How many output lines will a 5-input decoder have?

3.12 How many output lines will a 16-input multiplexer have? How many select lines will this multiplexer have?

3.13 If A and B are 4-bit unsigned binary numbers, 0111 and 1011, complete the table obtained when using the 2-bit full adder from Figure 3.15 to calculate the sum, S, of A and B. Check your answer by adding the decimal value of A and B and comparing the sum with S. Are the answers the same? Why or why not?

C_{in}				0
A	0	1	1	1
B	1	0	1	1
S				
C_{out}				

3.14 Given the following truth table generate the gate level circuit that implements this truth table. Follow the algorithm given in Section 3.3.4.

A	B	C	Z
0	0	0	1
0	0	1	0
0	1	0	0
0	1	1	1
1	0	0	0
1	0	1	1
1	1	0	1
1	1	1	0

3.15   1. Given 4 inputs, A, B, C, and D and one output Z, create a truth table for a circuit with at least seven input combinations generating 1's at the output. (How many rows will this truth table have?)

   2. Now that you have a truth table, generate the gate level circuit that implements this truth table following the the algorithm given in steps (2) and (3) in Section 3.3.4.

3.16 Implement the following functions using the logic gate symbols for AND, OR, NOT. The inputs are A, B and the output is F.

   1. F has the value 1 only if A has the value 0 and B has the value 1.

   2. F has the value 1 only if A has the value 1 and B has the value 0.

   3. Use your answers from (a) and (b) to implement a one-bit adder. The truth table for the one bit adder is given below.

A	B	Sum
0	0	0
0	1	1
1	0	1
1	1	0

   4. Is it possible to create a 4-bit adder (a circuit that will correctly add two 4-bit quantities) using only four copies of the logic diagram from (c)? If not, what information is missing? **Hint: When A = 1 and B = 1 , a Sum of 0 is produced. What information is disregarded?**

3.17 Logic circuit 1 in Figure 3.27 has inputs A, B, C. Logic circuit 2 in Figure 3.28 has inputs A and B. Both logic circuits have an output D. There is a fundamental difference between the behavioral characteristics of these two circuits. What is it? **Hint: What happens when the voltage at input A goes from 0 to 1 in both circuits?**

3.18 You know a byte is 8 bits. We call a 4-bit quantity a **nibble.** If a byte addressable memory has a 14-bit address, how many nibbles of storage are in this memory?

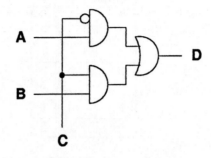

Figure 3.27: Circuit 1 for Problem 17.

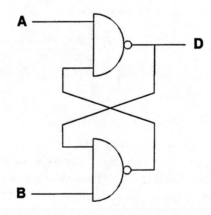

Figure 3.28: Circuit 2 for Problem 17.

3.19   1. Figure 3.29 shows a logic circuit that appears in many of today's processors. Each of the boxes is a full adder circuit. What does the value on the wire X do? That is what is the difference in the output of this circuit if X=0 versus if X=1?

2. Construct a logic diagram which implements A + B or A - B (Adder/Subtracter) based on the value of X. Hint: use the logic diagram from part A as a building block.

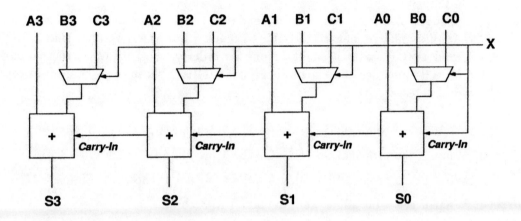

Figure 3.29: Diagram for Problem 19.

3.20 Given the logic circuit in Figure 3.30, fill in the truth table for the output value Z.

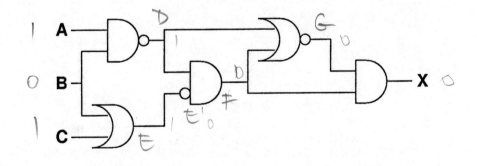

Figure 3.30: Diagram for Problem 20.

A	B	C	Z
0	0	0	
0	0	1	
0	1	0	
0	1	1	
1	0	0	
1	0	1	
1	1	0	
1	1	1	

3.21 Say the speed of a logic structure depends on the largest number of logic gates any of the inputs must propagate through to reach an output. Assume that a NOT, an AND, and an OR gate all count as one gate delay. For example, the propagation delay for a 2-input decoder shown in Figure 3.11 is 2 because some inputs propagate through 2 gates.

1. What is the propagation delay for the 2-input MUX shown in Figure 3.12?

2. What is the propagation delay for the 1-bit full adder in Figure 3.15?

3. What is the propagation delay for the 4-bit adder shown in Figure 3.16?

4. What if the 4-bit adder were extended to 32 bits?

3.22 For this question, refer to Figure 3.31.

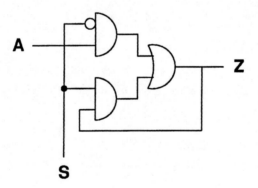

Figure 3.31: Diagram for Problem 22.

1. Describe the output of this logic circuit when the select S is a logical 0. That is, what is the output Z for each value of A?

2. If the select line, S, is switched from a logical 0 to 1, what will the output be?

3. Is this logic circuit a storage element?

3.23 A 16-bit register contains a value. The value x75A2 is written into it. Can the original value be recovered?

3.24 Distinguish between a memory address and the memory's addressability.

3.25 If a computer has 8-byte addressability and needs 3 bits to access a location in memory, what is the total size of memory in bytes?

3.26 Using Figure 3.20, the diagram of the 4-entry, 3-bit memory,

1. To read from the fourth memory location, what must the values of A[1:0], and WE be?

2. To change the number of entries in the memory from 4 to 60, how many total address lines would be needed? What would the addressability of the memory be after this change was made?

3. Suppose the minimum width (in bits) of the Program Counter (the Program Counter is a special register within a CPU and we will discuss it in detail in the next chapter) is the minimum number of bits needed to address all 60 locations in our memory from part (B). How many additional memory locations could be added to this memory without having to alter the width of the Program Counter.

3.27 Given a memory that is addressed by 22 bits and is 3-bit addressable, how many bits of storage does the memory contain?

3.28 Given the following truth table, generate the gate level logic that implements the truth table. From the gate level structure, generate the transistor diagram that implements the gate level structure and verify the truth table.

in_0	in_1	$f(in_0, in_1)$
0	0	1
0	1	0
1	0	1
1	1	1

Chapter 4

The Von Neumann Model.

We are now ready to build on the logic structures that we studied in Chapter 3. We will need both decision elements and storage elements to construct the basic computer model first proposed by John Von Neumann in 1945.

4.1 Basic Components.

Figure 4.1 shows the basic structure proposed by John Von Neumann for processing computer programs. We have taken a little poetic license and added a few of our own minor embellishments to Von Neumann's original diagram.

The Von Neumann model consists of five parts: *memory, a processing unit, input, output, and a control unit*. A computer program consists of a set of instructions, each specifying a well-defined piece of work for the computer to carry out. The *instruction* is the smallest piece of work specified in a computer program. That is, the computer either carries out the work specified by an instruction or it doesn't. The computer does not have the luxury of carrying out a piece of an instruction. The computer program is contained in the computer's memory. The control of the order in which the instructions are carried out is performed by the control unit.

We will describe each of the five parts of the Von Neumann model.

4.1.1 Memory.

Recall that in Chapter 3 we examined a simple 2^2 by 3 bit memory that was constructed out of gates and latches. A more realistic memory for one of today's computer systems is 2^{28} by 8 bits. That is, a typical memory in today's world of computers consists of 2^{28} distinct memory locations, each of which is capable of storing 8 bits of information. We say that such a memory has an *address space* of 2^{28} uniquely identifiable locations, and an *addressibility* of 8 bits. We refer to such a memory as a 256 megabyte memory (abbreviated, 256 MB). The "256 mega" refers to the 2^{28} locations, and the "byte" refers to the 8 bits

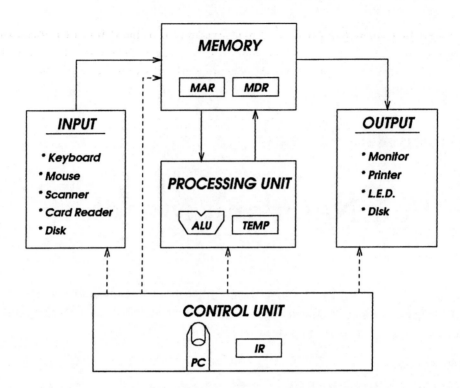

Figure 4.1: The Von Neumann Model, Overall Block Diagram.

stored in each location. The term *byte* is, by definition, the word used to describe 8 bits, much the way "gallon" describes "four quarts."

We note (as we will note again and again) that with k bits, we can represent uniquely 2^k items. Thus, to uniquely identify 2^{28} memory locations, each location must have its own 28 bit *address*.

In Chapter 5, we will begin the complete definition of the instruction set architecture (ISA) of the LC-2 computer. We will see that the memory address space of the LC-2 is 2^{16}, and the addressibility is 16 bits.

Recall from Chapter 3 that we access memory by providing the address from which we wish to read, or to which we wish to write. To read the contents of a memory location, we first place the address of that location in the memory's address register (**MAR**), and then interrogate the computer's memory. The information stored in the location having that address will be provided in the memory's data register (**MDR**). To write (or, store) a value in a memory location, we first write the address of the memory location in the MAR, and the value to be stored in the MDR. We then interrogate the computer's memory with the Write Enable signal asserted. The information contained in the MDR will be written into the memory location whose address is in the MAR.

Before we leave the notion of memory for the moment, let us again emphasize the two characteristics of a memory location: its address and what is stored there. Figure 4.2 shows a representation of a memory consisting of eight locations, Its addresses are shown at the left, numbered in binary from 0 to 7. Each location contains 8 bits of information. Note that we have stored the value 6 in the memory location whose address is 4, and we have stored the value 4 in the memory location whose address is 6. These represent two very different situations.

Finally, an analogy comes to mind: the post office boxes in your local post office. The box number is like the memory location's address. Each box number is unique. The information stored in the memory location is like the letters contained in the post office box. As time goes by, what is contained in the post office box at any particular moment can change. But the box number remains the same. So, too, with each memory location. The value stored in that location can be changed, but the location's memory address remains unchanged.

```
000 ┌──────────────┐
    │              │
001 ├──────────────┤
    │              │
010 ├──────────────┤
    │              │
011 ├──────────────┤
    │              │
100 ├──────────────┤
    │   00000110   │
101 ├──────────────┤
    │              │
110 ├──────────────┤
    │   00000100   │
111 ├──────────────┤
    │              │
    └──────────────┘
```

Figure 4.2: Location 6 contains the value 4, location 4 contains the value 6.

4.1.2 Processing Unit.

The actual processing of information in the computer is carried out by the *processing unit*. The processing unit in a modern computer can consist of many sophisticated complex functional units, each performing one particular operation (divide, square root, etc.). The simplest processing unit, and the one normally thought of when discussing the basic Von Neumann model, is the **ALU**. ALU is the abbreviation for Arithmetic and Logic Unit, so called because it is usually capable of performing basic arithmetic functions (like ADD and SUBTRACT) and basic logic operations (like bit-wise AND, OR, and NOT that we have already studied in Chapter 2). As we will see in Chapter 5, the LC-2 has an ALU which can perform ADD, AND, and NOT operations.

The size of the quantities normally processed by the ALU is often referred to as the *word length* of the computer, and each element is referred to as a *word*. In the LC-2, the ALU processes 16 bit quantities. We say the LC-2 has a word length of 16 bits. Each ISA has its own word length, depending on the intended use of the computer. Most microprocessors today that are used in PCs or workstations have a word length of either 32 bits (as is the case with Intel's Pentium II) or 64 bits (as is the case with Digital Equipment Corporation's Alpha processors and Intel's Merced processor). For some applications, like the microprocessors used in pagers, vcrs and cellular telephones, 8 bits are usually enough. Such microprocessors we say have a word length of 8 bits.

It is almost always the case that a computer provides some small amount of storage very close to the ALU to allow results to be temporarily stored if they will be needed to produce other results in the near future. For example, if a computer is to calculate (A+B)*C, it could store the result of A+B in memory, and then subsequently read it in order to multiply that result by C. However, the time it takes to access memory is long relative to the time it takes to perform the ADD or MULTIPLY. Almost all computers, therefore, have temporary storage for storing the result of A+B in order to avoid the unnecessarily longer access time that would be necessary when it came time to multiply. The most common form of temporary storage is a set of registers, like the register described in Section 3.4.3. Typically, the size of each register is identical to the size of values processed by the ALU, that is, they each contain one word. The LC-2 has eight registers (R0, R1, ...R7), each consisting of 16 bits. The Alpha ISA has 32 registers (R0, R1, ... R31), each containing 64 bits.

4.1.3 Input and Output.

In order for a computer to process information, the information must get into the computer. In order to use the results of that processing, it must be displayed in some fashion outside the computer. Many devices exist for the purposes of input and output. They are generically referred to in computer jargon as *peripherals* because they are in some sense accessories to the processing function. Nonetheless, they are no less important.

In the LC-2 we will have the two most basic of input and output devices. For input, we will use the keyboard, and for output, we will use the monitor.

There are, of course, many other input and output devices present in computer systems today. For input, we have among other things the mouse, digital scanners, and floppy disks. For output, we have among other things printers, LED displays, and disks. In the old days, much input and output was carried out by punched cards. Fortunately, for those who would have to lug boxes of cards around, most of the use of punched cards has disappeared.

4.1.4 Control Unit.

The control unit is like the conductor of an orchestra; it is in charge of making all the other parts play together. As we will see in the next section when we describe the step by step process of executing a computer program, it is the control unit that keeps track of both where we are within the process of executing the program and where we are in the process of executing each instruction.

To keep track of which instruction is being executed, the control unit has an *Instruction Register* to contain that instruction. To keep track of which instruction is to be processed next, the control unit has a register which contains the next instruction's address. For historical reasons, that register is called the *Program Counter* (abbreviated, PC), although a simpler name for it would be the *Instruction Pointer*, since the contents of this register are, in some sense, "pointing" to the next instruction to be processed. Curiously, Intel does in fact call that register the instruction pointer, but the simple elegance of that name has not caught on.

4.1.5   Summary: The LC-2 as an Example of the Von Neumann Model.

In Chapter 5 we will introduce the LC-2, a simple computer that we will study extensively. We have already introduced its data path in Chapter 3 (Figure 3.22). Figure 4.3 shows part of the data path of the LC-2. In fact, we constructed Figure 4.3 by starting with the full data path of the LC-2 (Figure 3.22) and removing all elements that are not essential to showing the presence of the basic components of the Von Neumann model.

Memory consists of the storage elements, along with the MAR for addressing individual locations and the MDR for holding the contents of a memory location on its way to/from the storage.

Input consists of a keyboard and output consists of a monitor. The simplest keyboard requires two registers, a data register (KBDR) for holding the ASCII codes of keys struck, and a status register (KBSR) for maintaining status information about the keys struck. The simplest monitor also requires two registers, one for holding the ASCII code of something to be displayed on the screen (CRTDR), and one for maintaining associated status information (CRTSR). The details of these input and output registers will be discussed in more detail in Chapter 8.

The processing unit consists of a functional unit which can perform arithmetic and logic operations (ALU) and eight registers (R0, ... R8) for storing temporary values that will be needed in the near future as operands for subsequent instructions.

The control unit contains the program counter (PC), instruction register (IR), and the control logic necessary for managing the control of all the activity going on.

4.2   Instruction Processing.

The central idea in the Von Neumann model of computer processing is that the program and data are both stored as sequences of bits in the computer's memory, and the program is executed one instruction at a time under the direction of the control unit.

4.2.1   The Instruction.

The most basic unit of computer processing is the instruction. It is made up of two parts, the *opcode* (what the instruction does) and the *operands* (who it is to do it to). In Chapter 5, we will see that each LC-2 instruction consists of 16 bits (one word), numbered from left to right, bit [15] to bit [0]. Bits [15:12] contain the opcode. This means there are at most 2^4 distinct opcodes. Bits [11:0] are used to figure out where the operands are.

Example: The ADD instruction.

The ADD instruction requires three operands: two source operands (the data that is to be added) and one destination operand (the sum that is to be stored after the addition is performed). We said that the Processing Unit of the LC-2 contained eight registers for purposes of storing data that may be needed later. In fact, the ADD instruction **requires** that the two source operands be contained in these registers, and that the result of the ADD be put into one of these eight registers. Since there are eight registers, three bits are necessary to identify each one. Thus the 16-bit LC-2 ADD instruction has the following form (we say *format*):

15	14	13	12	11	10	9	8	7	6	5	4	3	2	1	0
0	0	0	1	1	1	0	0	1	0	0	0	0	1	1	0
ADD				R6			R2			not used			R6		

The 4-bit opcode for ADD, contained in bits [15:12] is 0001. Bits [11:9] identify the location to be used for storing the result, in this case R6. Bits [8:6] and bits [2:0] identify the registers to be used to obtain the source operands, in this case R2 and R6. Thus the instruction encoded above is interpreted:

> Add the contents of R2 (register 2) to the contents of R6 and store the result back into R6.

Example: The LDR instruction.

The **LDR** instruction requires two operands. **LD** stands for "load," which is computerese for "go to a particular memory location, read the value that is contained there, and store it in one of the registers. The two operands that are required are the value to be read from memory and the destination register that will contain that value after the instruction is processed. The **R** in LDR identifies the mechanism that will be used to calculate the address of the memory location to be read. That mechanism is called the *addressing mode*, and the particular addressing mode identified by the use of the letter **R** is called **BASE+offset**. Thus the 16-bit LC-2 LDR instruction has the following format:

15	14	13	12	11	10	9	8	7	6	5	4	3	2	1	0
0	1	1	0	0	1	0	0	1	1	0	0	0	1	1	0
LD				R2			R3			6					

The 4-bit opcode for LDR is 0110. Bits [11:9] identify the register that will contain the value read from memory after the instruction is executed. Bits [8:0] are used to calculate the address of the location to be read. In particular, since the addressing mode is BASE+offset, the address is computed by adding the value 6 (the binary number contained in bits [5:0]) to the contents of R3 (Bits [8:6]. Thus the instruction encoded above is interpreted:

> Add the contents of R3 to the value 6 to form the address of a memory location.
> Load the contents stored in that memory location into R2.

4.2.2 The Instruction Cycle.

Instructions are processed under the direction of the control unit in a very systematic step-by-step manner. The sequence of steps is called the *instruction cycle*, and each step is referred to as a *phase*. There are basically six phases to the instruction cycle, although many computers have been designed such that not all instructions require all six phases. We will discuss this momentarily.

But first, we will examine the six phases of the instruction cycle:

```
FETCH
DECODE
EVALUATE ADDRESS
FETCH OPERANDS
EXECUTE
STORE RESULT
```

The process is as follows (again refer to Figure 4.3, our simplified version of the LC-2 data path):

FETCH: The FETCH phase obtains the next instruction from memory and loads it into the Instruction Register (IR) of the Control Unit. Recall that a computer program consists of a collection of instructions, that each instruction is represented by a sequence of bits, and that the entire program (in the Von Neumann model) is stored in the computer's memory. In order to carry out the work of the next instruction, we must first identify where it is. The Program Counter (PC) contains the address of the next instruction. Thus the FETCH phase takes multiple steps:

```
First the MAR is loaded with the contents of the PC.

Then the memory is interrogated, which results in the next
instruction being placed by the memory into the MDR.

Then the IR is loaded with the contents of the MDR.
```

We are now ready for the next phase, decoding the instruction. However, when the instruction cycle is complete, and we wish to fetch the next instruction, we would like the PC to contain the address of the next instruction. Therefore, the final step in the FETCH phase is to increment the PC. In that way, at the completion of the execution of this instruction, the FETCH phase of the next instruction will load into IR the contents of the next memory location, provided the execution of the current instruction does not involve changing the value in the PC.

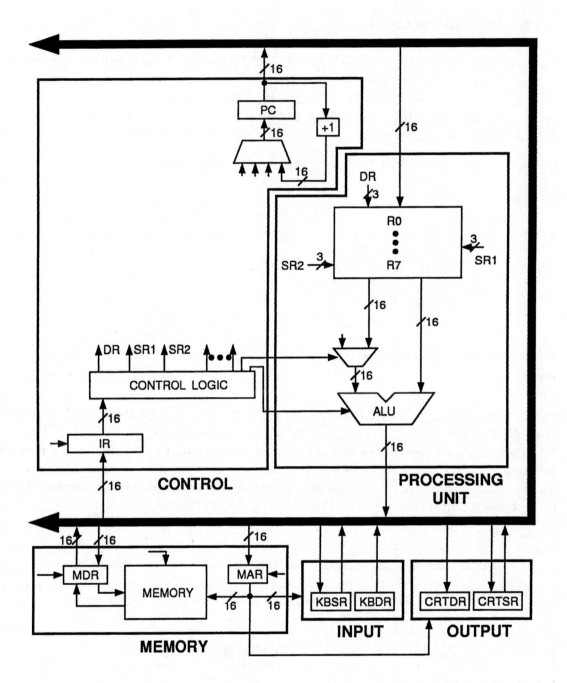

Figure 4.3: The LC-2 as an Example of the Von Neumann Model.

Note that the FETCH phase takes several steps.

Step 1: Load the MAR with the contents of the PC.

Step 2: Interrogate memory, resulting in the instruction being placed in the MDR.

Step 3: Load the IR with the contents of the MDR, and simultaneously increment the PC.

Each of these steps is under the direction of the Control Unit, much like, as we said earlier, the instruments in an orchestra are under the control of a conductor's baton. Each stroke of the conductor's baton corresponds to one *machine cycle*. Step 1 takes one machine cycle. Step 2 could take one machine cycle, or many machine cycles, depending on how long it takes to access the computer's memory. Step 3 takes one machine cycle. In a modern digital computer, a machine cycle takes a very small fraction of a second. Indeed, an 800 MHz Digital Alpha completes 800 million cycles in one second. Said another way, one machine cycle takes 1.25 billionths of a second (1.25 nanoseconds). Recall that the light bulb that is helping you read this text is switching on and off at the rate of 120 times a second. Thus in the time it takes a light bulb to switch on and off once, today's computers can complete 8 million machine cycles!

DECODE: The DECODE phase examines the instruction in order to figure out what the microarchitecture is being asked to do. Recall the decoder we studied in Chapter 3. In the LC-2, a four-to-16 decoder identifies which of the 16 opcodes is to be processed. The corresponding output of the decoder is asserted. Depending on which output of the decoder is asserted (i.e., depending on the opcode), the remaining 12 bits identify what else is needed to process the instruction.

EVALUATE ADDRESS: This phase computes the address of the memory location that will be needed to process the instruction. Recall the example of the LDR instruction above. The LDR instruction causes a value stored in memory to be loaded into a register. In the example above, the address was obtained by adding the value 6 to the contents of R3. This calculation was performed during the EVALUATE ADDRESS phase.

FETCH OPERANDS: This phase obtains the source operands needed to process the instruction. In the LDR example above, this phase took two steps: loading MAR with the address calculated in the EVALUATE ADDRESS phase, and reading memory, which resulted in the source operand being placed in MDR.

In the ADD example above, this phase consisted of obtaining the source operands from R2 and R6.

(In most current microprocessors, this phase (for the ADD instruction) can be done at the same time the instruction is being decoded. Exactly how we can speed up the processing of an instruction in this way is a fascinating subject, but one we are forced to leave for a later course.)

EXECUTE: This phase carries out the execution of the instruction. In the ADD example, this phase consists of the single step of performing the addition in the ALU.

STORE RESULT: The final phase of an instruction's execution. The result is written to its designated destination.

Once the sixth phase (STORE RESULT) has been completed, the Control Unit begins anew the Instruction Cycle, starting from the top with the FETCH phase. Since the PC was updated during the previous instruction cycle, it contains at this point the address of the instruction stored in the next sequential memory location. Thus the next sequential instruction is fetched next. Processing continues in this way until something breaks this sequential flow.

4.2.3 Examples.

Example: *ADD [eax], edx.* This is an example of an Intel x86 instruction that requires all six phases of the instruction cycle. All instructions require the first two phases, FETCH and DECODE. This instruction uses [eax] to calculate the address of a memory location (EVALUATE ADDRESS). The contents of that location are then read (FETCH OPERAND), added to the contents of the edx register (EXECUTE), and the result written into the memory location that originally contained the first source operand (STORE RESULT).

Example: The LC-2 ADD and LDR instructions do not require all six phases. In particular, the ADD instruction does not require an EVALUATE ADDRESS phase. The LDR instruction does not require an EXECUTE phase.

4.3   Changing the Sequence of Execution.

Everything we have said thus far suggests that a computer program is executed in sequence. That is, the first instruction is executed, then the second instruction is executed, followed by the third instruction, etc.

We have identified two types of instructions, the ADD which is an example of an *operate instruction* in that it processes data, and the LDR which is an example of a *data movement instruction* in that it moves data from one place to another. There are other examples of both operate instructions and data movement instructions, as we will discover in Chapter 5 when we study the LC-2.

There is a third type of instruction, the *control instruction*, whose purpose is to change the sequence of instruction execution. For example, there are times, as we shall see, when it is desirable to first execute the first instruction, then the second, then the third, then the first again, the second again, then the third again, then the first for the third time, etc. As we know, each instruction cycle starts with loading the MAR with the PC. Thus, if we wish to change the sequence of instructions executed, we must change the PC between the time it is incremented (during the FETCH phase) of one instruction and the start of the FETCH phase of the next.

Control instructions perform that function by loading the PC during the EXECUTE phase, which wipes out the incremented PC that was loaded during the FETCH phase. The result is that, at the start of the next instruction cycle, when the computer accesses the PC to obtain the address of an instruction to fetch, it will get the address loaded during the previous EXECUTE phase, rather than the next sequential instruction in the computer's program.

Example: Consider the LC-2 instruction JMPR, whose format is shown below. Assume this instruction is stored in memory location x36A2.

15	14	13	12	11	10	9	8	7	6	5	4	3	2	1	0
1	1	0	0	0	0	0	0	1	1	0	0	0	1	1	0
JMPR							R3				6				

The 4-bit opcode for JMPR is 1100. Bits [8:0] are used to calculate the address of the next instruction to be processed. In particular, since the addressing mode is BASE+offset (as was the case with the LDR), the address of the next instruction to be fetched is 6 (the binary number contained in bits [5:0] plus the contents of R3 (Bits [8:6]. Thus the instruction encoded above is interpreted:

Add the contents of R3 to the value 6 to form the address of a memory location. Load that address into the PC (during the EXECUTE phase) so that the next instruction processed will be at the address calculated.

Processing will go on as follows. Let's start at the beginning of the instruction cycle, with PC = x36A2. The FETCH phase results in the IR being loaded with the JMPR instruction and the PC updated to contain the address x36A3. Suppose the contents of R3 at the start of this instruction is x3440. During the EVALUATE ADDRESS phase, 6 is added to x3440, producing x3446. During the EXECUTE phase, the PC is loaded with x3446. Therefore, in the next instruction cycle, the instruction processed will be the one at address x3446, rather than the one at address x36A3.

4.4 Stopping the computer.

From everything we have said, it appears that the computer will continue processing instructions, carrying out the instruction cycle again and again, ad nauseum. Since the computer does not have the capacity to be bored, must this continue until someone pulls the plug and disconnects power to the computer?

Usually, user programs execute under the control of an operating system. UNIX, DOS, WindowsNT are all examples of operating systems. Operating systems are just computer programs themselves. So as far as the computer is concerned, the instruction cycle continues whether a user program is being processed or the operating system is being processed. This is fine as far as user programs are concerned since each user program terminates with a control instruction which changes the PC to again start processing the operating system – often to initiate the execution of another user program.

But what if we actually want to stop this infinite sequence of instruction cycles? Recall our analogy to the conductor's baton, beating at the rate of millions of machine cycles per second. Stopping the instruction sequencing requires stopping the conductor's baton. There is inside the computer, a component that corresponds very closely to the conductor's baton. It is called the CLOCK. The clock defines the machine cycle; it is the element of control that allows the Control Unit to continue on to the next machine cycle, whether that be the next step of the current phase, or the first step of the next phase of the instruction cycle. Stopping the instruction cycle requires stopping the clock.

Figure 4.4 describes the behavior of the clock.

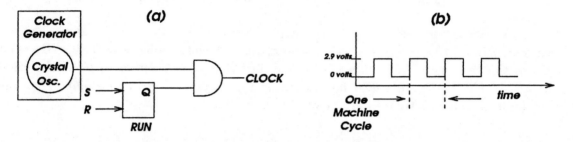

Figure 4.4: The Clock circuit and its Control.

Figure 4.4a shows a block diagram of the clock circuit, consisting primarily of a clock generator and a RUN latch. The clock generator is a crystal oscillator, a piezoelectric device that you may have studied in your physics or chemistry class. For our purposes, the crystal oscillator is a black box (recall our definition of black box in Section 1.4) that produces the oscillating voltage shown in Figure 4.4b. Note the resemblance of that voltage to the conductor's baton. Every machine cycle, the voltage rises to 2.9 volts and then drops back to 0 volts.

If the RUN latch is in the 1 state (i..e, Q = 1),the output of the clock circuit is the same as the output of the clock generator. If the RUN latch is in the 0 state (i.e., Q = 0), the output of the clock circuit is 0.

Thus, stopping the instruction cycle only requires clearing the RUN latch.

Every computer has some mechanism for doing that. In some older machines, it is done by executing a HALT instruction. In the LC-2, as in many other machines, it is done under control of the operating system, as we will see in Chapter 9.

Question: If a HALT instruction can clear the RUN latch, thereby stopping the instruction cycle, what instruction is needed to set the RUN latch, thereby re-initiating the instruction cycle?

4.5 Exercises.

4.1 Name the 5 components of the Von Neumann model. For each component, state its purpose.

4.2 Briefly describe the interface between the Memory and the Processing Unit. That is, describe the method by which the Memory and the Processing Unit communicate.

4.3 What is misleading about the name Program Counter? Why is the name Instruction Pointer more insightful?

4.4 What is the word length of a computer? How does the word length of a computer affect what the computer is able to compute? That is, is it a valid argument, in light of what you learned in Chapter 1, to say that a computer with a larger word size can process more information and therefore is capable of computing more than a computer with a smaller word size?

4.5 The following table represents a small memory. Refer to this table for the following questions.

Address	Data
0000	0001 1110 0100 0011
0001	1111 0000 0010 0101
0010	0110 1111 0000 0001
0011	0000 0000 0000 0000
0100	0000 0000 0110 0101
0101	0100 0101 0110 0111
0110	1111 1110 1101 0011
0111	0000 0110 1101 1001

1. What binary value does location 3 contain? Location 6?

2. The above table shows a diagram of memory similar to Figure 4.2. The binary value within each location can be interpreted in many ways. We have seen that binary values can represent unsigned numbers, 2'complement signed numbers, floating point numbers, etc.

   (a) Interpret location 0 and location 1 as 2's complement integers.

   (b) Interpret location 4 as an ASCII value.

   (c) Interpret location 6 as a floating point number.

   (d) Interpret location 5 as an unsigned value.

3. In the Von Neumann model, the contents of a memory location can also be an instruction. If the binary pattern in location 0 were interpreted as an instruction, what instruction would it be?

4. A binary value can also be interpreted a memory address. Say the value stored in location 5 is a memory address. To which location does it refer? What binary value does that location contain?

4.6 What are the two components of an instruction? What information do these two components contain?

4.7 Suppose a 32-bit instruction takes the following format:

| OPCODE | SR | DR | IMM |

If there are 60 opcodes and 32 registers, what are the maximum and minimum values that the immediate (IMM) can take? Assume IMM is a 2's complement value.

4.8 The FETCH phase of the instruction cycle does two important things. One is that it loads the instruction to be processed next into the IR. What is the other important thing?

4.9 State the phases of the instruction cycle and briefly describe what operations occur in each phase.

4.10 For these instructions, ADD, LD, NOP, write what operations occur in each phase of the instruction cycle.

4.11 Refer to the two instructions given in Example 4.3.2. Say it takes 100 cycles to read from or write to memory and only 1 cycle to read from or write to a register. Calculate the number of cycles it takes for each phase of the instruction cycle for both the x86 instruction "ADD [eax], edx" (this means add the value at the memory address pointed to by the register eax with the contents of register edx and store the results in the memory address pointed to by the register eax) the LC-2 instruction "ADD R6, R2, R6". Assume each phase (if required) takes 1 cycle, unless a memory access is required.

4.12 Refer to the example in Section 4.3 which describes a JMPR instruction stored in location x36A2. Describe the execution of the JMPR instruction if R3 contains x369C.

4.13 If a HALT instruction can clear the RUN latch, thereby stopping the instruction cycle, what instruction is needed to set the RUN latch, thereby re-initiating the instruction cycle?

4.14   1. If a machine cycle is 2 nsec (i.e., 2×10^{-9} seconds), how many machine cycles occur each second?

   2. If the computer requires on the average 8 cycles to process each instruction, and the computer processes instructions one at a time from beginning to end, how many instructions can the computer process in one second?

   3. (Preview of future courses). In today's microprocessors, there are many features added to increase the number of instructions processed each second. One such feature is the computer's equivalent of assembly line. Each phase of the instruction cycle is implemented as one or more separate pieces of logic. Each step in the processing of an instruction picks up where the previous step left off in the previous machine cycle. Using this feature, an instruction can be fetched from

memory every machine cycle and handed off at the end of the machine cycle to the decoder, which performs the decoding function during the next machine cycle while the next instruction is being fetched. Ergo, the assembly line. Assuming instructions are located at sequential addresses in memory, and nothing breaks the sequential flow, how many instructions can the microprocessor execute each second if the assembly line is present. (The assembly line is called a pipeline, which you will encounter in your advanced courses. There are many reasons why the assembly line can not operate at its maximum rate, a topic you will consider at length in some of these courses.)

Chapter 5

The LC-2.

In Chapter 4, we discussed the basic components of a computer – its memory, its processing unit including the associated temporary storage (usually a set of registers), input and output devices, and the control unit that directs the activity of all the units (including itself!). We also studied the six phases of the instruction cycle – FETCH, DECODE, ADDRESS EVALUATION, OPERAND FETCH, EXECUTE, and STORE RESULT. We are now ready to introduce a "real" computer, the LC-2. To be more nearly exact, we are ready to introduce the instruction set architecture (ISA) of the LC-2. We have already teased you with a few facts about the LC-2, and a few of its instructions. Now we are ready for the LC-2 in a more comprehensive way.

Recall (chapter 1) that the ISA is the interface between what the software commands and what the hardware actually carries out. In this chapter and in chapters 8 and 9, we will point out the important features of the ISA of the LC-2. You will need these features to write programs in the LC-2's own language, that is, in the *machine language* of the LC-2.

A complete but terse description of the ISA of the LC-2 is contained in Appendix A. Additional detail and usage of the LC-2 is contained in *The LC-2 Programmer's Reference Manual*, by Matt Postiff.

5.1 The ISA, Overview.

The ISA specifies all the information about the computer that the software has to be aware of. In other words, the ISA specifies everything in the computer that is available to a programmer that he/she can use when he/she writes programs in the computer's own machine language. Thus, the ISA also specifies everything in the computer that is available to someone who wishes to translate programs written in a high level language like C or Pascal or Fortran or COBOL into the machine language of the computer.

The ISA specifies the memory organization, register set, and instruction set, including opcodes, data types and addressing modes.

5.1.1 Memory Organization.

The LC-2 memory has an address space of 2^{16} (i.e., 65,536) locations, and an addressibility of 16 bits. Not all 65,536 addresses are actually used for memory locations, but we will leave that discussion for Chapter 8.

We will see momentarily that it is often useful to think of memory as a sequence of pages, each containing a certain number of memory locations. In the LC-2, the 2^{16} addresses are sliced into 2^7 pages of size 2^9 locations each. Thus, bits [15:9] of an address specify the page number, and bits [8:0] specify the word on the page. Two locations that are on the same page have identical values in bits [15:9].

Since the normal unit of data that is processed in the LC-2 is 16 bits, we refer to 16 bits as one *word* and we say the LC-2 is *word-addressible*.

5.1.2 Registers.

Since it usually takes far more than one machine cycle to obtain data from memory, the LC-2 provides (like almost all computers) additional temporary storage locations that can be accessed in a single machine cycle.

The most common type of temporary storage locations and the one used in the LC-2 is the general purpose register set. Each register in the set is called a general purpose register, abbreviated GPR. Registers have the same property as memory locations in that they are used to store information that can be later retrieved. The number of bits stored in each register is usually one word.

Registers must be uniquely identifiable. The LC-2 specifies eight GPRs, identified by a three-bit register number. They are referred to as R0, R1, ...R7. Recall that the instruction to ADD the contents of R0 to R1 and store the result in R2 is specified as

15	14	13	12	11	10	9	8	7	6	5	4	3	2	1	0
0	0	0	1	0	1	0	0	0	0	0	0	0	0	0	1

$$\underbrace{\qquad}_{\text{ADD}} \quad \underbrace{\qquad}_{\text{R2}} \quad \underbrace{\qquad}_{\text{R0}} \quad \underbrace{\qquad}_{\text{R1}}$$

where the two *sources* of the ADD instruction are in bits [8:6] and bits [2:0]. The *destination* of the ADD result is specified in bits [11:9].

5.1.3 The Instruction Set.

An instruction is made up of two things, its *opcode* (what the instruction is asking the computer to do) and its *operands* (who the computer is expected to do it to). The instruction set of an ISA is defined by its set of opcodes and the *data types* and *addressing modes* that determine the operands.

5.1.4 Opcodes.

Some ISAs have a very large set of opcodes, one for each of a large number of tasks that a program may wish to carry out. Other ISAs have a very small set of opcodes. Some ISAs have specific opcodes to help with processing scientific calculations. For example, the Hewlett-Packard *Precision Architecture* has an instruction that performs a multiply, followed by an add (A * B) + C on three source operands. Other ISAs have instructions that process video images obtained from the world wide web. The Intel x86 ISA added a number of instructions which Intel calls MMX instructions because they eXtend the ISA to assist with MultiMedia applications that use the web. Still other ISAs have specific opcodes to help with handling the tasks of the operating system. For example, the VAX architecture, popular in the 1980s, had an opcode to save all the information pertaining to a program that was running prior to switching to another program. Almost all computers prefer to use a long sequence of instructions to ask the computer to carry out the task of saving all that information. Although that sounds counterintuitive, there is a rationale for it. Unfortunately, the topic will have to wait for a later semester. The decision as to which instructions to include or leave out of an ISA is usually a hotly debated topic in a company.

The LC-2 ISA has 16 instructions, each identified by its unique opcode. The opcode is specified by bits [15:12] of the instruction. There are three different types of instructions, which means three different types of opcodes: *operates*, *data movement*, and *control*. Operate instructions process information. Data movement instructions move information between memory and the registers and between registers/memory and input/output devices. Control instructions change the sequence of instructions that will be executed. That is, they enable the execution of an instruction other than the one that is stored in the next sequential location in memory. Figure 5.1 lists the 16 instructions of the LC-2, the bit encoding [15:12] for each opcode, and the format of each instruction. The use of each of the formats will be further explained in Sections 5.2, 5.3, and 5.4 below.

5.1.5 Data Types.

A data type is a representation of information such that the ISA has opcodes that operate on that representation. There are many ways to represent the same information in computer. That should not surprise us. We, in our daily lives, represent the same information in many different ways as well. For example, a child when asked how old he is, might hold up three fingers, signifying he is three years old. If the child is particularly precocious, he might write the decimal digit **3** to indicate his age. Or, if he is a University of Michigan CS or CE major, he might write 0000000000000011, the 16-bit binary representation for 3. If he is a chemistry major, he might write $3.0 \cdot 10^0$. All four represent the same entity: "three."

If the ISA has an opcode that operates on information represented by a data type, then we say the ISA **supports** that data type.

In Chapter 2, we introduced the only data type supported by the ISA of the LC-2: 2's complement integers.

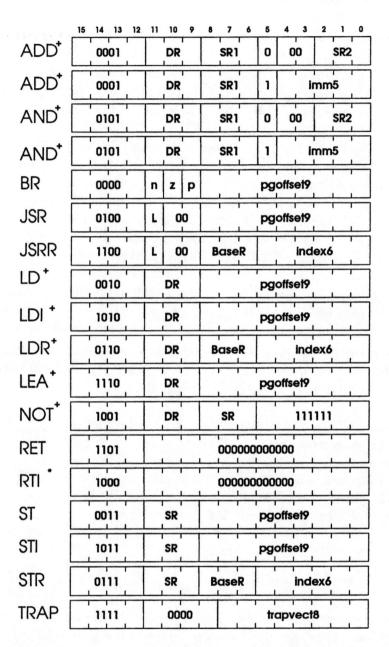

Figure 5.1: Formats of the 16 LC-2 Instructions. (+ indicates instructions that modify condition codes; * indicates that meaning and use of RTI is beyond the scope of this book.)

5.1.6   Addressing Modes.

An addressing mode is a mechanism for specifying where the operand is located. Operands can generally be found in one of three places: in memory, in a register, or as a part of the instruction. If the operand is a part of the instruction, we refer to it as a *literal* or as an *immediate* operand. The term "literal" comes from the fact that the bits of the instruction "literally" form the operand. The term "immediate" comes from the fact that we have the operand immediately, that is, we don't have to look elsewhere for it.

The LC-2 supports five addressing modes: immediate (or literal), register, and three memory addressing modes: *direct*, *indirect*, and *Base+offset*. We will see in Section 5.2 that operate instructions use two addressing modes: register and immediate. We will see in Section 5.3 that data movement instructions use all five addressing modes.

5.1.7 Condition Codes.

One final item will complete our overview of the ISA of the LC-2: condition codes. Most ISAs (the x86 and SPARC, for example) allow the instruction sequencing to change on the basis of a previously generated result. The LC-2 has three single-bit registers that are set (set to 1) or cleared (set to 0) each time one of the eight general purpose registers is written. The three single-bit registers are called N, Z, and P, corresponding to their meaning: negative, zero, and positive. Each time a GPR is written, the N,Z, and P registers are individually set to 0 or 1, corresponding to whether the result written to the GPR is negative, zero or positive. That is, if the result is negative, the N register is set, and Z and P are cleared. If the result is zero, Z is set and N and P are cleared. Finally, if the result is positive, P is set and N and Z are cleared.

Each of the three single-bit registers is referred to as a *condition code* because the condition of that bit can be used by one of the control instructions to change the sequence of instructions that get executed. We will see in Section 5.4 how this is done.

5.2 Operate instructions.

Operate instructions process data. Arithmetic operations (like ADD, SUB, MUL, and DIV) and logical operations (like AND, OR, NOT, XOR) are common examples of operate instructions. The LC-2 has three operate instructions: ADD, AND, and NOT.

The **NOT** instruction is the only operate instruction that performs a *unary* operation, that is, the operation requires one source operand. The NOT instruction bit-wise complements a 16-bit source operand, and stores the result of this operation in a destination. NOT uses the register addressing mode for both its source and destination. Bits [8:6] specify the source register and bits [11:9] specify the destination register. Bits [5:0] must contain all 1s.

If R2 initially contains 0101000011110000, after executing the following instruction

15	14	13	12	11	10	9	8	7	6	5	4	3	2	1	0
1	0	0	1	0	1	1	0	1	0	1	1	1	1	1	1

NOT   R3   R2

R3 will contain 1010111100001111.

The **ADD** and **AND** instructions both perform *binary* operations; they require two 16-bit source operands. The ADD instruction performs a 2's complement addition of its two source operands. The AND instruction performs a bit-wise AND of each pair of bits in its two 16-bit operands. Like the NOT, the ADD and AND use the register addressing mode for one of the source operands and for the destination operand. Bits [8:6] specify the source register and bits [11:9] specify the destination register, that is, where the result will be written.

The second source operand for both ADD and AND can be specified by either register mode or as an immediate operand. Bit [5] determines which is used. If bit [5] is 0, then the second source operand uses a register, and bits [2:0] specify the register. In that case, bits [4:3] are set to 0 to complete the specification of the instruction.

For example, if R4 contains the value 6 and R5 contains the value -18, then after the following instruction is executed

15	14	13	12	11	10	9	8	7	6	5	4	3	2	1	0
0	0	0	1	0	0	1	1	0	0	0	0	0	1	0	1

ADD   R1   R4   R5

R1 will contain the value -12.

If Bit [5] is 1, the second source operand is contained within the instruction. In fact, the second source operand is obtained by sign-extending bits [4:0] to 16 bits before performing the ADD or AND. Note, then, that a 2's complement integer, represented as an immediate operand in an ADD instruction, can only be a value from -16 to +15. Why is that?

Example: What does the instruction shown below do?

15	14	13	12	11	10	9	8	7	6	5	4	3	2	1	0
0	1	0	1	0	1	0	0	1	0	1	0	0	0	0	0

Answer: Register 2 is cleared (i.e., set to all 0's).

Example: What does the following instruction do?

15	14	13	12	11	10	9	8	7	6	5	4	3	2	1	0
0	0	0	1	1	1	0	1	1	0	1	0	0	0	0	1

Answer: Register 6 is incremented (i.e., R6 <— R6 + 1).

Note that a register can be used as a source and also a destination in the same instruction. This is true for all the instructions in the LC-2.

Example: Subtraction.

Recall that the 2's complement of a number can be obtained by complementing a value and adding 1. Therefore, assuming the values A and B are in R0 and R1, the following sequence of instructions performs "A minus B," and writes the result into R2:

Answer:

15	14	13	12	11	10	9	8	7	6	5	4	3	2	1	0	
1	0	0	1	0	0	1	0	0	1	1	1	1	1	1	1	Complement B, in R1
	NOT				R1			R1								

15	14	13	12	11	10	9	8	7	6	5	4	3	2	1	0	
0	0	0	1	0	1	0	0	0	1	1	0	0	0	0	1	Add 1, producing -B
	ADD				R2			R1				1				

15	14	13	12	11	10	9	8	7	6	5	4	3	2	1	0	
0	0	0	1	0	1	0	0	0	0	0	0	0	0	1	0	A + (-B)
	ADD				R2			R0					R2			

5.3   Data movement instructions.

Data movement instructions move information between memory and the registers, and between memory/registers and the input/output devices. We will ignore for now the business of moving information from input devices to registers/memory and from registers/memory to output devices. This will be the major topic of Chapter 8, and an important part of Chapter 9 as well. In this chapter, we will confine ourselves to moving information between memory and the general purposes registers.

The process of moving information from memory to a register is called a *load* and the process of moving information data from a register to memory is called a *store*. In both cases, the location of the source operand remains unchanged. In both cases, the source operand overwrites the value that was in the location of the destination operand, destroying the old value in the process.

The LC-2 contains seven instructions that move information : LD, LDR, LDI, LEA, ST, STR, and STI.

The format of the load and store instruction is as follows:

15	14	13	12	11	10	9	8	7	6	5	4	3	2	1	0
opcode				DR or SR			OPERAND SPECIFIER								

If the instruction is a load, DR refers to the destination register that will contain the value after it is read from memory (at the completion of the instruction cycle). If the instruction is a store, SR refers to the register that contains the value that will be written to memory.

Bits [8:0] contain the *operand specifier*. That is, bits 8:0 encode information that is used to obtain the memory operand. There are four ways to interpret the code in bits [8:0]. They are called *addressing modes*. The opcode specifies how to interpret bits [8:0]. That is, the opcode specifies which addressing mode should be used to obtain the operand from bits [8:0] of the instruction.

5.3.1   Immediate mode.

Immediate mode is used only with LEA. The LEA instruction loads the immediate value formed by concatenating bits [15:9] of the address of the instruction (i.e., PC [15:9]) with bits [8:0] of the instruction. Those 16 bits are loaded into the register specified by bits [11:9]. The instruction (Load Effective Address) is useful to initialize a register with an address on the same page as the instruction. Note that LEA is the **only** load instruction that does not access memory to obtain the information it will load into the DR. If the following instruction is contained in location x4018

15	14	13	12	11	10	9	8	7	6	5	4	3	2	1	0
1	1	1	0	1	0	1	1	1	1	1	1	1	1	0	1

          LEA   R5   x1FD

after execution, R5 will contain x41FD.

5.3.2   Direct mode.

LD and ST specify the *direct mode* addressing mode. Direct mode addressing is so named because the address of the operand is specified in the instruction. Actually, only bits [8:0] of the address is specified in the instruction. Bits [15:9] are implicit. They are identical to bits [15:9] of the address of the instruction. That is, LD and ST can only refer to memory locations on the same page as the instruction using the direct addressing mode.

If the following instruction is located at x3018,

15	14	13	12	11	10	9	8	7	6	5	4	3	2	1	0
0	0	1	0	0	1	0	1	1	0	1	0	1	1	1	1

           LD   R2   x1AF

it will cause the contents of x31AF to be loaded into R2.

5.3.3   Indirect mode.

LDI and STI specify the *indirect mode* addressing mode. An address is first formed exactly the same way as with LD and ST. However, instead of this **being** the address of the operand to be loaded or stored, it **contains** the address of the operand to be loaded or stored. Hence the name *indirect*. Note that the address of the operand can be anywhere in the computer's memory, not just on the same page as the instruction, as is the case for LD and ST.

If the following instruction is in x4A1B, and the contents of x4BCC is x2110,

15	14	13	12	11	10	9	8	7	6	5	4	3	2	1	0
1	0	1	0	0	1	1	1	1	1	0	0	1	1	0	0

          LDI   R3   x1CC

execution of this instruction will result in the contents of x2110 being loaded into R3.

5.3.4 Base+offset mode.

LDR and STR specify the *Base+offset mode* addressing mode. Base+offset mode is so named because the address of the operand is obtained by adding the zero-extended 6-bit offset to the base register. The 6-bit offset is **literally** taken from the instruction, bits [5:0]. The base register is identified by bits [8:6] in the instruction.

Since bits [5:0] consists of 6 bits, and the register specified by bits [8:6] contains 16 bits, the 6 bit quantity must first be expanded to 16 bits before the addition can take place. Base+offset addressing uses the 6-bit value as a positive integer between 0 and 63. Thus, expanding it to 16 bits involves appending 10 leading 0s. Expanding by appending leading 0s is called *zero-extending*.

If R2 contains the 16-bit quantity x2345, the following instruction

15	14	13	12	11	10	9	8	7	6	5	4	3	2	1	0
0	1	1	0	0	0	1	0	0	1	0	1	1	1	0	1
LDR				R1			R2			29					

loads R1 with the contents of x236E

Note that the Base+offset addressing mode also allows the address of the operand to be anywhere in the computer's memory.

5.3.5 An Example.

We conclude our study of addressing modes with a comprehensive example. Assume the contents of memory locations x30F6 through x30FC are as shown in Figure 5.2, and the PC contains x30F6. We will examine the effects of carrying out the instruction cycle seven times.

Address	15	14	13	12	11	10	9	8	7	6	5	4	3	2	1	0
30F6	1	1	1	0	0	0	1	0	1	1	1	1	0	1	0	0
30F7	0	0	0	1	0	1	0	0	0	1	1	0	1	1	1	0
30F8	0	0	1	1	0	1	0	0	1	1	1	1	0	1	0	0
30F9	0	1	0	1	0	1	0	0	1	0	1	0	0	0	0	0
30FA	0	0	0	1	0	1	0	0	1	0	1	0	0	1	0	1
30FB	0	1	1	1	0	1	0	0	0	1	0	0	1	1	1	0
30FC	1	0	1	0	0	1	1	0	1	1	1	1	0	1	0	0

Figure 5.2: Addresssing Mode Example.

Since the PC points initially to location x30F6, that is, since the contents of the PC is the address x30F6, the first instruction to be executed is the one stored in location x30F6.

The opcode 1110 identifies the load effective address instruction (LEA) which loads the register identified by bits [11:9] with the address formed by the high seven bits (i.e., the page number) of the address of the instruction (in this case 0011000) concatenated with bits [8:0] of the instruction (in this case 011110100). Therefore, at the end of execution of this instruction, R1 contains 0011000011110100 (which is x30F4), and the PC contains x30F7.

The second instruction to be executed is the one stored in location x30F7. The opcode 0001 identifies the ADD instruction, which stores in the register identified by bits [11:9] the sum of the contents of the register identified in bits [8:6] added to the sign-extended immediate in bits [4:0] (since bit [5] is 1). At the end of execution, R2 contains the value x3102, and the PC contains x30F8. R1 still contains x30F4.

The third instruction to be executed is the one stored in location x30F8. The opcode 0011 identifies the ST instruction, which stores the contents of the register identified in Bits [11:9] into the memory location whose address is formed using the direct addressing mode. Recall, direct addressing obtains the address by concatenating the high seven bits of the instruction's address (in this case 0011000) and bits [8:0] of the instruction (in this case 011110100). At the end of execution of this instruction, location x30F4 contains the value x3102, and the PC contains x30F9.

At x30F9, we find the opcode 0101, which represents the AND instruction. After execution, R2 contains the value 0, and the PC contains x30FA.

At x30FA, we find the opcode 0001, signifying the ADD instruction. After execution, R2 contains the value 5, and the PC contains x30FB.

At x30FB, we find the opcode 0111, signifying the STR instruction. The STR instruction (like the LDR instruction) uses the Base+offset addressing mode. The memory address is obtained by adding the contents of the register specified by bits [8:6] (the BASE register) to the zero-extended offset contained in Bits [5:0]. The STR instruction stores in that memory location the contents of the register specified by Bits [11:9]. After execution of this instruction, memory location x3102 contains the value 5 (0000000000000101), and the PC contains x30FC.

At x30FC, we find the opcode 1010, signifying the LDI instruction. The LDI instruction (like the STI instruction) uses the indirect addressing mode. The memory address is obtained by first forming an address as is done in the direct addressing mode. That is, the page number (bits [15:9] of the address of the instruction) is concatenated with bits [8:0] of the instruction to form an address. The memory location at that address contains the address of the operand. The LDI instruction loads the value found at that address into the register identified by bits [11:9] of the instruction. After execution, R3 contains the value 5 and the PC contains x30FD.

5.4 Control instructions.

Control instructions change the sequence of the instructions that are executed. Up to now the PC has been incremented in the FETCH phase of the instruction and not changed for the duration of the instruction cycle. Thus, when the next instruction cycle starts, the PC directs the FETCH of the instruction located in the next sequential memory location. We will see momentarily that it is often useful to be able to break that sequence.

The LC-2 has five instructions that enable the sequential flow to be broken: BRx, JMP/JSR, JMPR/JSRR, RET, and TRAP. In this section, we will deal almost exclusively with the most common control instruction, *the conditional branch*, BRx. We will also introduce the TRAP instruction because of its immediate usefulness to getting information into and out of the computer. However, most of the discussion on the TRAP instruction and all of the discussion on JMP/JSR, JMPR/JSRR, and RET we will save for Chapter 9.

5.4.1 Conditional Branches.

The format of the conditional branch instruction (opcode = 1000) is shown below:

15	14	13	12	11	10	9	8	7	6	5	4	3	2	1	0
0	0	0	0	N	Z	P				page offset					

Bits [11], [10], and [9] correspond to the three condition codes discussed in Section 5.2. Recall that in the LC-2 **all** instructions that write values into registers set the three condition codes (i.e., the single-bit registers N,Z,P) in accordance with whether the value written is negative, zero, or positive. These instructions are ADD, AND, NOT, LD, LDI, LDR and LEA.

The condition codes are used by the conditional branch instruction to determine whether to change the instruction flow; that is, whether to depart from the usual sequential execution of instructions that we get as a result of incrementing PC during the FETCH phase of each instruction.

The instruction cycle is as follows: FETCH and DECODE are the same as for all instructions. The PC is incremented during FETCH. The EVALUATE ADDRESS phase is the same as that for LD and ST: The page number (bits [15:9] of the instruction address is concatenated with bits [8:0] of the instruction to form an address.

During the EXECUTE phase, the processor examines the condition codes whose corresponding bits in the instruction are 1. That is, if bit [11] is 1, condition code N is examined. If bit [10] is 1, condition code Z is examined. If bit [9] is 1, condition code P is examined. If any of bits [11:9] are 0, the corresponding condition codes are not examined. If any of the condition codes that are examined are in state 1, then the PC is loaded with the address obtained in the EVALUATE ADDRESS phase. If none of the condition codes which are examined are in state 1, the PC is left unchanged. In that case, in the next instruction cycle the next sequential instruction will be fetched.

For example, if the previous instruction loaded the value 0 into R5, then the current instruction (located at x4027) shown below

15	14	13	12	11	10	9	8	7	6	5	4	3	2	1	0
0	0	0	0	0	1	0	1	0	0	0	0	0	0	0	1

BR   n   z   p   x101

will load the PC with x4101, and the next instruction to be executed will be the one at x4101, rather than the one at x4028.

If all there bits [11:9] are 1, then all three condition codes are examined. In this case, since the last result stored into a register had to be either negative, zero, or positive (there are no other choices), one of the three condition codes must be in state 1. Since all three are examined, the PC is loaded with the address obtained in the EVALUATE ADDRESS phase. We call this an *unconditional branch* since the instruction flow is changed unconditionally, that is, independent of the data that is being processed.

For example, if the following instruction, located at x507B

15	14	13	12	11	10	9	8	7	6	5	4	3	2	1	0
0	0	0	0	1	1	1	0	0	0	0	0	0	0	0	1

BR   n   z   p   x001

is executed, the PC is loaded with x5001.

What happens if all three bits [11:9] in the BR instruction are 0?

5.4.2   An Example.

Suppose we know that the 12 locations x3100 to x310B contain integers, and we wish to compute the sum of these twelve integers.

A flow chart for an algorithm to solve the program is shown in Figure 5.3.

First, as in all algorithms, we must *initialize our variables*. That is, we must set up the initial values of the variables that the computer will use in executing the program that solves the problem. There are three such variables: the address of the next integer to be added (assigned to R1), the running sum (assigned to R4), and the number of integers left to be added (assigned to R2). The three variables are initialized as follows: The address of the first integer to be added is put in R1. R4, which will keep track of the running sum, is initialized to 0. R2, which will keep track of the number of integers left to be added is intialized to 12. Then the process of adding begins.

The program repeats the process of loading into R4 one of the twelve integers, and adding it R3. Each time we perform the ADD, we increment R1 so it will point to (i.e., contain the address of) the next number to be added and decrement R2 so we will know how many additions are still needed. When R2 becomes zero, the Z condition code is set, and therefore we can detect that we are done.

The ten instruction program shown in Figure 5.4 accomplishes the task.

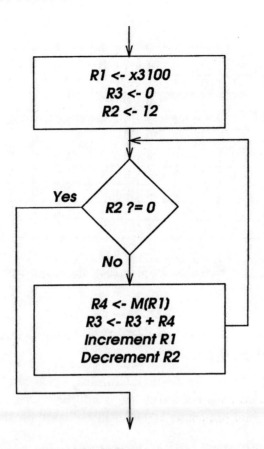

Figure 5.3: An Algorithm for Adding Twelve Integers.

The details of the program execution are as follows: The program starts with PC = x3000. The first instruction (at location x3000) loads R1 with the address x3100 (page number is 0011000 and bits [8:0] is 100000000).

The instruction at x3001 clears R3. R3 will keep track of the running sum, so it must start off with the value zero. As we said above, this is called *initializing* the SUM to zero.

The instructions at x3002 and x3003 set the value of R2 to twelve, the number of integers to be added. R2 will keep track of how many numbers have already been added. This will be done (by the instruction contained in x3008 below) by decrementing R2 after each addition takes place.

The instruction at x3004 is a conditional branch instruction. Note that bit [10] is a 1. That means that the Z condition code will be examined. If it is set, we know R2 must have just been decremented to zero. That means there are no more numbers to be added and we are done. If it is clear, we know we still have work to do and we continue.

The instruction at x3005 loads the contents of x3100 (i.e., the first integer) into R4, and the instruction at x3006 adds it to R3.

The instructions at x3007 and x3008 perform the necessary bookkeeping. The instruction at x3007 increments R1, so R1 will point to the next location in memory containing an

Address	15	14	13	12	11	10	9	8	7	6	5	4	3	2	1	0	
3000	1	1	1	0	0	0	1	1	0	0	0	0	0	0	0	0	R1<- 3100
3001	0	1	0	1	0	1	1	0	1	1	1	0	0	0	0	0	R3 <- 0
3002	0	1	0	1	0	1	0	0	1	0	1	0	0	0	0	0	R2 <- 0
3003	0	0	0	1	0	1	0	0	1	0	1	0	1	1	0	0	R2 <- 12
3004	0	0	0	0	0	1	0	0	0	0	0	0	1	0	1	0	BRz x300A
3005	0	1	1	0	1	0	0	0	0	1	0	0	0	0	0	0	R4 <- M[R1]
3006	0	0	0	1	0	1	1	0	1	1	0	0	0	1	0	0	R3 <- R3+R4
3007	0	0	0	1	0	0	1	0	0	1	1	0	0	0	0	1	R1 <- R1+1
3008	0	0	0	1	0	1	0	0	1	0	1	1	1	1	1	1	R2 <- R2-1
3009	0	0	0	0	1	1	1	0	0	0	0	0	0	1	0	0	BRnzp x3004

Figure 5.4: A Program that Implements the Algorithm of Figure 5.3.

integer to be added (in this case, x3101). The instruction at x3008 decrements R2, which is keeping track of the number of integers still to be added, as we have already explained, and sets the N, Z, and P condition codes.

The instruction at x3009 is an unconditional branch, since bits [11:9] are all 1. It loads the PC with x3004. It also does not affect the condition codes, so the next instruction to be executed (the conditional branch at x3004) will be based on the instruction executed at x3008.

This is worth saying again. The conditional branch instruction at x3004 follows the instruction at x3009, which does not affect condition codes, which in turn follows the instruction at x3008. Thus the conditional branch instruction at x3004 will be based on the condition codes set by the instruction at x3008. The instruction at x3008 sets the condition codes depending on the value produced by decrementing R2. As long as there are still integers to be added, the ADD instruction at x3008 will produce a value greater than zero, and therefore clear the Z condition code. The conditional branch instruction at x3004 examines the Z condition code. As long as Z is clear, the PC will not be affected, and the next instruction cycle will start with an instruction fetch from x3005.

The conditional branch instruction causes the execution sequence to follow: x3000, x3001, x3002, x3003, x3004, x3005, x3006, x3007, x3008, x3009, x3004, x3005, x3006, x3007, x3008, x3009, x3004, x3005, ... until the value in R2 becomes 0. At that point, the conditional branch instruction at x3004 leaves the PC at PC+1, and program continues at x300A with the next activity of the program.

5.4.3 Two Methods for Loop Control.

We use the term *loop* to describe a sequence of instructions that get executed again and again under some controlling mechanism. The example of adding 12 integers contains a loop. Each time the *body* of the loop executes, one more integer is added to the running total and the counter is decremented so we can detect whether there are any more integers left to add. Each time the loop body executes is called one *iteration* of the loop.

There are two common methods for controlling the number of iterations of a loop. One method we just examined: the use of a counter. If we know we wish to execute a loop n times, we simply set a counter to n, then after each execution of the loop, we decrement the counter and check to see if it is zero. It is not zero, we set the PC to the start of the loop, and continue with another iteration.

A second method for controlling the number of executions of a loop is to use a *sentinel*. This method is particularly effective if we do not know ahead of time how many iterations we will want to perform. Each iteration is usually based on processing a value. We append to our sequence of values to be processed a value that we know ahead of time can never occur (i.e., the sentinel). For example, if we are adding a sequence of numbers, a sentinel could be a # or a *, that is, something that is not a number. Our loop test is simply a test for the occurrence of the sentinel. When we find it, we know we are done.

5.4.4 Example: Adding a Column of Numbers, Using a Sentinel.

Suppose in our example of Section 5.4.2, we know the values stored in x3100 to x310B are all positive. Then we could use any negative number as a sentinel. Let's say the sentinel stored at memory address x310C is -1. The resulting flow chart for the program is shown in Figure 5.5 and the resulting program is shown in Figure 5.6.

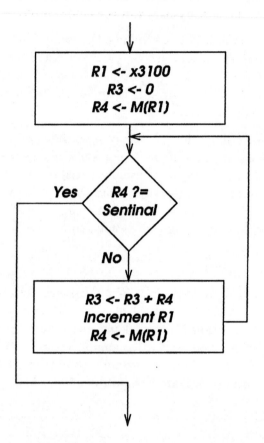

Figure 5.5: An Algorithm Showing the Use of a Sentinel for Loop Control.

Address	15	14	13	12	11	10	9	8	7	6	5	4	3	2	1	0	
x3000	1	1	1	0	0	0	1	1	0	0	0	0	0	0	0	0	R1<- x3100
x3001	0	1	0	1	0	1	1	0	1	1	1	0	0	0	0	0	R3 <- 0
x3002	0	1	1	0	1	0	0	0	0	1	0	0	0	0	0	0	R4 <- M[R1]
x3003	0	0	0	0	1	0	0	0	0	0	0	0	1	0	0	0	BRn x3008
x3004	0	0	0	1	0	1	1	0	1	1	0	0	0	1	0	0	R3 <- R3+R4
x3005	0	0	0	1	0	0	1	0	0	1	1	0	0	0	0	1	R1 <- R1+1
x3006	0	1	1	0	1	0	0	0	0	1	0	0	0	0	0	0	R4 <- M[R1]
x3007	0	0	0	0	1	1	1	0	0	0	0	0	0	0	1	1	BRnzp x3003

Figure 5.6: A Program that Implements the Algorithm of Figure 5.5.

As before the instruction at x3000 loads R1 with the address of the first value to be added, and x3101 initializes R3 (which keeps track of the sum) to zero.

At x3002, we load the contents of the next memory location into R4. If the sentinel is loaded, the N condition code is set.

The conditional branch at x3003 examines the N condition code, and if it is set, sets PC to $3008 and onto the next task at hand. If the N condition code is clear, R4 must contain a valid number to be added. In this case, the number is added to R3 (x3004), R1 is incremented to point to the next memory location (x3005), R4 is loaded with the contents of the next memory location (x3006) and the PC is loaded with x3003 to begin the next iteration (x3007).

5.4.5 The TRAP instruction.

Finally, because it will be useful long before Chapter 9 to get data in and out of the computer, we introduce the TRAP instruction. The TRAP instruction changes the PC to a memory address which is part of the operating system in order for the operating system to perform some task in behalf of the program that is executing. In the language of operating system jargon, we say the TRAP instruction invokes an operating system SERVICE CALL. Bits [7:0] of the TRAP instruction, called the *trapvector*, identifies the service call that the program wishes the operating system to perform. Table A.3 contains the trapvectors for all the service calls that we will use with the LC-2 in this book.

15	14	13	12	11	10	9	8	7	6	5	4	3	2	1	0
1	1	1	1	0	0	0	0				trapvector				

Once the operating system is finished performing the service call, the program counter is set to the address of the instruction following the TRAP instruction and the program continues. In this way, a program can, during its execution, request services from the operating system, and continue processing after each such service is performed. The services we will require for now are

```
* input a character from the keyboard (trapvector = x23),
* output a character to the monitor (trapvector = x21), and
* halt the program (trapvector = x25).
```

Exactly how the LC-2 carries out that interaction between operating system and executing programs is an important topic for Chapter 9.

5.5 Another Example: Counting Occurrences of a Character.

We will finish our introduction to the ISA of the LC-2 with another example program.

We would like to be able to input a character from the keyboard, and then count the number of occurrences of that character in a file. Finally, we would like to display that count on the monitor. We will simplify the problem by assuming that the number of occurrences of any character that we would be interested in is small. That is, there will be at most nine occurrences. This simplification allows us to not have to worry about complex conversion routines between the binary count and the ASCII display on the monitor – a subject we will get into in Chapter 9, but not today.

Figure 5.7 is a flow chart of the algorithm that solves this problem. Note that each step is expressed both in English and also (in parentheses) in terms of an LC-2 implementation.

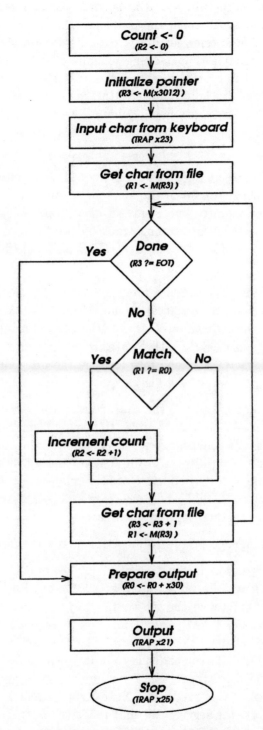

Figure 5.7: An Algorithm to Count Occurrences of a Character.

The first step is (as always) to initialize all the variables. This means providing starting values (called *initial values*) for R0, R1, R2, and R3, the four registers the computer will use to execute program that will solve the problem. R2 will keep track of the number of occurrences; in Figure 5.7, it is referred to as **Count**. It is initialized to zero. R3 will point to the next character in the file that is being examined. We refer to it as **pointer** since it contains the **address** of the location where the next character of the file that we wish to examine resides. The pointer is initialized with the address of the **first** character in the file. R0 will hold the character that is being counted; we will input that character from the keyboard and put it in R0. R1 will hold, in turn, each character that we get from the file being examined.

The next step is to count the number of occurrences of the input character. This is done by processing, in turn, each character in the file being examined, until the file is exhausted. Processing each character requires one iteration of a loop. Recall from Section 5.4 that there are two common methods for keeping track of iterations of a loop. We will use the sentinel method, using the ASCII code for EOT (End of Text) (00000100) as the sentinel.

In each iteration of the loop, the contents of R1 is first compared to the ASCII code for EOT. If yes, the loop is exited, and the program moves on to the final step, displaying on the screen the number of occurrences. If no, there is work to do. R1 (the current character under examination) is compared to R0 (the character input from the Keyboard). If they match, R2 is incremented. In either case, we get the next character, that is R3 is incremented, the next character is loaded into R1, and the program returns to the test that checks for the sentinel at the end of the file.

When the end of the file is reached, all the characters have been examined, and the count is contained as a binary number in R2. In order to display it on the monitor, it is necessary to first convert it to an ASCII code. Since we have assumed the count is less than ten, that is simply putting a leading 0011 in front of the four bit binary representation of the count. Figure F.3 contains a table of ASCII codes. Note the relationship between the binary value of each decimal digit between 0 and 9 and its corresponding ASCII code. Finally, the count is output to the monitor, and the program terminates.

Figure 5.8 is a machine language program that implements the flow chart of Figure 5.7.

First the initialization steps. The instruction at x3000 clears R2 by ANDing it with x0000, the instruction at x3001 loads the value stored in x3012 into R3. Initially, x3012 contains the address of the first character in the file that is to be examined for occurrences of our character. x3002 contains the TRAP instruction, which requests the operating system to perform a service call on behalf of this program. The function requested, as identified by the eight bit trapvector 00100011 (or, x23), is to input a character from the keyboard, and load it into R0. Table A.3 lists trapvectors for all operating system service calls that can be performed in behalf of a user program. Note (from Table A.3) that x23 directs the operating system to perform the service call that reads the next character struck and loads it into R0. The instruction at x3003 loads the character pointed to by R3 into R1.

Then the process of examining characters begins. We start (x3004) by subtracting 4 (the ASCII code for EOT) from R1, and storing it in R4. If the result is zero, the end of the file

Address	15	14	13	12	11	10	9	8	7	6	5	4	3	2	1	0	
x3000	0	1	0	1	0	1	0	0	1	0	1	0	0	0	0	0	R2 <- 0
x3001	0	0	1	0	0	1	1	0	0	0	0	1	0	0	1	0	R3 <- M[x3012]
x3002	1	1	1	1	0	0	0	0	0	0	1	0	0	0	1	1	TRAP x23
x3003	0	1	1	0	0	0	1	0	1	1	0	0	0	0	0	0	R1 <- M[R3]
x3004	0	0	0	1	1	0	0	0	0	1	1	1	1	1	0	0	R4 <- R1-4
x3005	0	0	0	0	0	1	0	0	0	0	0	0	1	1	1	0	BRz x300E
x3006	1	0	0	1	0	0	1	0	0	1	1	1	1	1	1	1	R1 <- NOT R1
x3007	0	0	0	1	0	0	1	0	0	1	1	0	0	0	0	1	R1 <- R1 + 1
x3008	0	0	0	1	0	0	1	0	0	1	0	0	0	0	0	0	R1 <- R1 + R0
x3009	0	0	0	0	1	0	1	0	0	0	0	0	1	0	1	1	BRnp x300B
x300A	0	0	0	1	0	1	0	0	1	0	1	0	0	0	0	1	R2 <- R2 + 1
x300B	0	0	0	1	0	1	1	0	1	1	1	0	0	0	0	1	R3 <- R3 + 1
x300C	0	1	1	0	0	0	1	0	1	1	0	0	0	0	0	0	R1 <- M[R3]
x300D	0	0	0	0	0	0	0	0	0	0	0	1	0	0	0	0	BRnzp x3004
x300E	0	0	1	0	0	0	0	0	0	0	0	1	0	0	1	1	R0 <- M[x3013]
x300F	0	0	0	1	0	0	0	0	0	0	0	0	0	0	1	0	R0 <- R0 + R2
x3010	1	1	1	1	0	0	0	0	0	0	1	0	0	0	0	1	TRAP x21
x3011	1	1	1	1	0	0	0	0	0	0	1	0	0	1	0	1	TRAP x25
x3012	Starting Address of file																
x3013	0	0	0	0	0	0	0	0	0	0	1	1	0	0	0	0	ASCII TEMPL.

Figure 5.8: A Machine Language Program that Implements the Algorithm of Figure 5.7.

has been reached, and it is time to output the count. The instruction at x3005 conditionally branches to x300E, where the process of outputting the count begins.

If R4 is not equal to zero, the character in R1 is legitimate, and must be examined. The sequence of instructions at locations x3006, x3007, and x3008 determine if the contents of R1 and R0 are identical. The sequence of instructions perform the following operation:

$$R0 + (NOT~(R1) + 1)$$

This produces all zeroes only if the bit patterns of R1 and R0 are identical. If the bit patterns are not identical the conditional branch at x3009 branches to x300B, that is, it skips the instruction x300A which increments the counter, R2.

The instruction at x300B increments R3, so it will point to the next character in the file being examined, the instruction at x300C loads that character into R1, and the instruction at x300D unconditionally takes us back to x3004 to start processing that character.

When the sentinel (EOT) is finally detected, the process of outputting the count begins (at x300E). The instruction at x300E loads 0011000 into R0, and the instruction at x300F adds the count to R0. This converts the binary representation of the count (in R2) to the ASCII representation of the count (in R0). The instruction at x3010 invokes a TRAP to the operating system to output the contents of R0 on the monitor. When that is done and the program resumes execution, the instruction at x3011 invokes a TRAP instruction to terminate the program.

5.6   The Data Path Revisited.

Before we leave Chapter 5, let us revisit the data path diagram (Figure 3.22) that we first encountered in Chapter 3. Now we are ready to examine all the structures that are needed to implement the LC-2 ISA. We reproduce this diagram as Figure 5.9. Note at the outset that there are two kinds of arrows in the data path, those with arrowheads filled in, and those with arrowheads not filled in. Filled-in arrowheads designate information that is processed. Unfilled-in arrowheads designate control signals. Control signals emanate from the block labeled Control Logic. The connections from "Control Logic" to most control signals have been left off Figure 5.9 to reduce unnecessary clutter in the diagram.

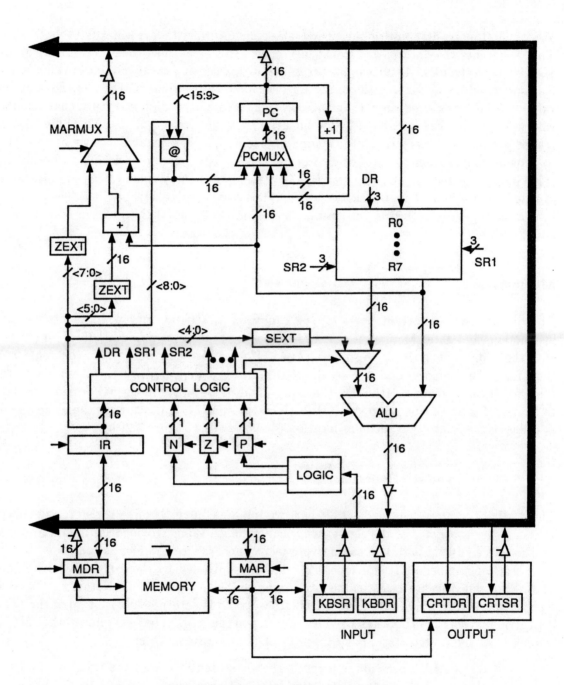

Figure 5.9: The Data Path of the LC-2.

5.6.1   Basic Components of the Data Path.

The Global Bus.

You undoubtedly first notice the heavy black structure with arrowheads at both ends. This represents the data path's global bus. The LC-2 global bus consists of 16 wires and associated electronics. It allows one structure to transfer up to 16 bits of information to another structure by making the necessary electronic connections on the bus. Exactly one value can be transferred on the bus at one time. Note that each structure that supplies values to the bus has a "triangle" just behind its "input arrow" to the bus. This triangle (called a *tri-state device*) allows the computer's control logic to enable exactly one supplier to provide information to the bus at any one time. The structure wishing to obtain the value being supplied can do so by asserting it WE (write enable) signal (recall our discussion of gated latches in Section 3.4.2). Not all computers have a single global bus. The pros and cons of a single global bus is yet another one of those topics that will have to wait for a later course.

Memory.

One of the most important parts of any computer is the memory which contains both instructions and data. Memory is accessed by loading the Memory Address Register (MAR) with the address of the location to be accessed. If a load is being performed, control signals then read the memory, and the result of that read is delivered by the memory to the Memory Data Register (MDR). On the other hand, if a store is being performed, the data to be stored is first loaded into the MDR. Then, the control signals specify the write enable in order to store into that memory location (as you saw in Figure 3.20).

The ALU and the Register File.

The ALU is the processing element. It has two inputs, source 1 from a register, and source 2 from either a register or the sign-extended immediate value provided by the instruction. The registers (R0 through R7) can provide two values, source 1, which is controlled by the 3-bit register number SR1, and source 2, which is controlled by the 3-bit register number SR2. SR1 and SR2 are fields in the LC-2 operate instruction. The selection of a second register operand or a sign-extended immediate operand is determined by bit [5] of the LC-2 instruction. Note the MUX that provides source 2 to the ALU. The select line of that MUX, coming from the control logic, is bit [5] of the LC-2 operate instruction.

The result of an ALU operation is a result that is stored in one of the registers, and the three single-bit condition codes. Note that the ALU can supply 16 bits to the bus, and that value can then be written into the the register specified by the 3-bit register number DR. Also, note that the 16 bits supplied to the bus are also input to logic that determines whether that 16-bit quantity is negative, zero, or positive, and sets the three registers N, Z, and P accordingly.

The PC and the PCMUX.

The PC supplies via the global bus to the MAR the address of the instruction to be fetched at the start of the instruction cycle. The PC, in turn, is supplied via the four-to-one PCMUX, depending on the instruction being executed. During the FETCH phase of the instruction cycle, the PC is incremented and written into the PC. That is shown as the right-most input to the PCMUX.

If the current instruction is a control instruction, then the relevant source of the PCMUX depends on which control instruction is currently being processed. If the current instruction is a conditional branch, and the branch is taken, then the PC is loaded with PC [15:9] (the page number) concatenated with INST [8:0] (the pg9offset). That is shown as the left-most input to PCMUX. The other two inputs to PCMUX are used to obtain the new PC when the TRAP instruction, a RET instruction, or a JSRR instruction is being executed. They will be covered in Chapter 9.

The MARMUX.

As you know, memory is accessed by supplying the address to the MAR. The MARMUX controls which of three sources will supply the MAR with the appropriate address during the execution of a load, a store, or a TRAP instruction. The right-most input to the MARMUX is obtained by concatenating PC [15:9] with INST [8:0] in the same way the address of a conditional branch instruction is generated. This address is used in the case of LD and ST instructions to obtain source and destination addresses of the data to be loaded and stored, respectively. It is also used with LDI and STI instructions to obtain the address of the source or destination address. The left-most input to MARMUX provides the zero-extended trapvector, which is needed to invoke service calls, as will be discussed in further detail in Chapter 9. The middle input to MARMUX provides the zero-extended bits [5:0] of the instruction (index6) to the base register to obtain the address of source data for the LDR instruction and the address of destination data for the STR instruction.

5.6.2 The Instruction Cycle.

We complete our tour of the LC-2 data path by following the flow through an instruction cycle.

Suppose the contents of the PC is x3456 and the contents of location x3456 is 0110011010000100. And suppose the LC-2 has just completed processing the instruction at x3455, which happened to be an ADD instruction.

FETCH.

As you know, the instruction cycle starts with the FETCH phase. That is, the instruction is obtained by accessing memory with the address contained in the PC. In the first cycle, the contents of the PC is loaded via the global bus into the MAR, and the PC is incremented and loaded into the PC. At the end of this cycle, the PC contains x3457. In the next cycle (if memory can provide information in one cycle), the memory is read, and the instruction 0110011010000100 is loaded into the MDR. In the next cycle, the contents of the MDR is loaded into the instruction register (IR), completing the FETCH phase.

DECODE.

In the next cycle the contents of the IR are decoded, resulting in the Control Logic providing the correct control signals (unfilled arrowheads) to control the processing of the rest of this instruction. The opcode is 0110, identifying the LDR instruction. This means that the base+offset addressing mode is to be used to determine the address of data to be loaded into the destination register R3.

EVALUATE ADDRESS.

In the next cycle, the contents of R2 (the base register) and the zero-extended bits [5:0] of the IR are added and supplied via the MARMUX to the MAR. The SR1 field specifies 010, the register to be read to obtain the base address.

OPERAND FETCH.

In the next cycle (or more than one, if memory access takes more than one cycle) the data at that address is loaded into the MDR.

EXECUTE.

The LDR instruction does not require an EXECUTE phase, so this phase takes zero cycles.

STORE RESULT.

In the last cycle, the contents of the MDR are loaded into R3. The DR control field specifies 011, the register to be loaded.

5.7 Exercises.

5.1 Given instructions, ADD, JMP, LEA, NOP tell whether the instructions are operate instructions, data movement instructions or control instructions.

For each instruction, list the addressing modes that can be used with the instruction.

5.2   1. State the page number for each of the following LC-2 memory addresses:

      (a) x12FE

      (b) xA931

      (c) x3110

      (d) x3210

      (e) x3310

      (f) x3610

  2. State the page offset for each of the above LC-2 memory addresses.

5.3 Say we have a memory consisting of 256 locations, and each location contains 16 bits.

  1. How many bits are required for the address?

  2. If we divide this memory into 8 pages, how many bits are required to represent the page number?

  3. How many bits specify the location of a word on the page?

  4. What is the address of the first word on page number 2 (remember page numbering starts with 0)?

  5. What is the address of the last word on the same page?

5.4   1. What is an addressing mode?

  2. Name three places an instruction's operands might be located?

  3. List the five addressing modes of the LC-2 and for each one state where the operand is located (from part 2).

  4. What addressing mode is used by the ADD instruction shown in Section 5.1.2?

5.5 Recall the "machine busy" example from Section 2.6.5. We can use the LC-2 instruction 0101 011 010 1 00001 (AND R3 R2 00001) to determine whether machine 0 is busy or not. If the result of this instruction is 0, then machine 0 is busy.

  1. Now write an instruction that determines whether machine 0 is busy.

  2. Write an instruction that determines whether machines 2 or 3 are busy.

  3. Write an LC-2 instruction that indicates all the machines are no longer busy.

  4. Write an instruction that determines whether machine 13 is busy.
    Is there a problem here?

5.6 What is the largest positive number we can represent literally (i.e., as an IMMEDIATE value) within an LC-2 ADD instruction?

5.7 At location x3E00, we would like to put an instruction that does nothing. Many ISAs actually have an opcode devoted to doing nothing. The instruction is fetched, decoded, and executed. The execution phase is to do nothing! Which of the following three instructions could be used for NOP and have the program still work correctly? What does the ADD instruction do that the others do not do?

   1. 0001 001 001 1 00000

   2. 0000 111 000000001

   3. 0000 000 000000000

5.8 After executing the following LC-2 instruction: ADD R2, R0, R1, we notice that R0[15] equals R1[15], but is different from R2[15]. We are told that R0 and R1 contain UNSIGNED integers (that is, non-negative integers between 0 and 65,535). Under what conditions can we trust the result in R2?

5.9   1. How might one use a single LC-2 instruction to move the value in R2 into R3?

   2. The LC-2 has no subtract instruction. How could one perform the following operation using only three LC-2 instructions:

$$R1 \leftarrow R2 - R3$$

   3. Using only one instruction and without changing the contents of any register, how might one set the condition codes based on the value that resides in R1?

   4. What sequence of LC-2 instructions will cause the condition codes at the end of the sequence to be N=1, Z=1 and P=0?

   5. Write an LC-2 instruction that clears the contents of R2.

   6. Which of parts 1 through 5 is impossible to implement on the LC-2?

5.10 State the contents of R1, R2, R3, and R4 after the program starting at location x3100 halts.

Address	Data
0011 0001 0000 0000	1110 001 100100011
0011 0001 0000 0001	0010 010 100100011
0011 0001 0000 0010	0110 011 010 000001
0011 0001 0000 0011	1010 100 100100011
0011 0001 0000 0100	1111 0000 0010 0101
:	:
:	:
0011 0001 0010 0011	0100 0101 0110 0111
:	:
:	:
0100 0101 0110 0111	1010 1011 1100 1101
0100 0101 0110 0111	1111 1110 1101 0011

5.11 Which addressing mode makes the most sense to use under the following conditions. (There may be more than one correct answer to each of these, therefore justify your answers with some explanation).

1. If you want to load one value from the current page.

2. If you want to load one value form a page other than the current page.

3. If you want to load an array of sequential addresses on the current page.

5.12 How many times does the LC-2 make a read or write request to memory during the processing of the LD instruction? How many times during the processing of the LDI instruction? How many times during the processing of the LEA instruction?

5.13 The LC-2 program counter (PC) contains 16 bits, of which the least significant nine bits [8:0] represent the page offset. If we change the ISA so that bits [6:0] represent the page offset, how many pages will memory consist of?

5.14 If we made the LC-2 memory pages shorter by 384 locations, how many bits would be required for the page offset in the LD instruction?

5.15 What is the maximum number of TRAP service routines that the LC-2 ISA allows? Explain.

5.16 Suppose the following LC-2 program is loaded into memory starting at location x30FF.

30FF	1110001100000001
3100	0110010001000010
3101	1111000000100101
3102	0001010001000001
3103	0001010010000010

If the program is executed, what is the value in register 2 (R2) at the end of execution?

5.17 Write an LC-2 program that compares two numbers in R2 and R3 and puts the larger number in R1. If the numbers are equal then R1 is set equal to zero.

5.18 Your task is to consider the successor to the LC-2. We will add 16 additional instructions to the ISA, and expand the register set from 8 to 16. We would like our machine to have an addressability of 1 byte, and a total memory size of 64 K Bytes. We will keep the size of an instruction at 16 bits. Also, we will encode all new instructions with the same five fields as the original 16 instructions, although it may be necessary to change the size of some of those fields.

1. How many bits do we need in the PC to be able to address all of memory?

2. Assuming we still support page-offset addressing, what is the size in bytes of a page? How many memory locations are on a page? How many pages are there?

3. What is the largest immediate value that can be represented in an arithmetic instruction?

4. If we want 128 different operating system routines to be able to be accessed with a trap instruction and we form the address of each of these routines by shifting the trap vector to the left by 5 bits, what is the minimum amount of memory required by the trap service routines?

5. If, in the new version of the LC-2, we reduced the number of registers from 8 to 4 and did not change any of the opcodes, what is the largest immediate value we could represent in an ADD instruction on this new machine?

5.19 The LC-2 instruction LDR DR, BaseR, Offset can be broken down into the following constituent operations (called "micro-instructions"):

```
MAR ← BaseR + Offset ; set up the memory address
MDR ← Memory[MAR] ; read mem at BaseR + offset
DR ← MDR ; load DR
```

Suppose that the architect of the LC-2 wanted to include an instruction MOVE DR, SR that would copy the memory location with address given by SR and store it into the memory location whose address is in DR.

1. Using regular LC-2 instructions, write code to carry out a MOVE R0, R1 instruction. If necessary, use R2 for temporary storage.

2. List the constituent micro-instructions required to carry out the MOVE instruction.

5.20 1. The LC-2 JMP/JSR instruction does not execute exactly the same if L=0 and if L=1. Why is the case L=0 irrelevant to the LC-2 ISA?

2. Why is this not also true for JMPR/JSRR instruction pair?

5.21 In the example of Section 3.5.5, before the seven instructions are executed, R2 contains the value xAAAA. How many different values are contained in R2 during the execution of the seven instructions? What are they?

5.22 The following table shows a part of the LC-2's memory.

Address	Data
0011 0001 0000 0000	1001 001 001 111111
0011 0001 0000 0001	0001 010 000 000 001
0011 0001 0000 0010	1001 010 010 111111
0011 0001 0000 0011	0000 010 100000000

State what is known about R1 and R0 if the conditional branch redirects control to location x3100.

Chapter 6

Programming.

We are now ready to start developing programs to solve problems with the computer. In this chapter we will attempt to do two things: first, we will develop a methodology for constructing programs, and second, we will develop a methodology for fixing those programs under the likely condition that we did not get it right the first time. There is a long tradition that the errors present in programs are referred to as *bugs*, and the process of removing those errors *debugging*. The opportunity for introducing bugs into a complicated program is so great that it usually takes more time to get the program to work (debugging) than it does to create it in the first place.

6.1 Problem Solving.

6.1.1 Systematic Decomposition.

Recall in Chapter 1 that in order for the electrons to solve a problem, we need to go through several levels of transformation to get from a natural language description of the problem (in our case English, although some of you might prefer Italian, Mandarin, Hindi, or something else) to something the electrons can deal with. Once we have a natural language description of the problem, the next step is to transform the problem statement into an algorithm. That is, the next step is to transform the problem statement into a step-by-step procedure that has the properties of finiteness (it terminates), definiteness (each step is precisely stated), and effective computability (each step can be carried out).

In the late 1960's, Harlan Mills introduced the concept of *Structured Programming* to improve the ability of average programmers to take a complex description of a problem and systematically decompose it into sufficiently smaller manageable units that they could ultimately write a program that executed correctly. The mechanism has alternatively been called *systematic decomposition* because the larger tasks are systematically broken down into smaller ones.

We will find the systematic decomposition model a useful technique for designing computer programs to carry out complex tasks.

6.1.2   The three constructs: Sequential, Conditional, Iterative.

Systematic decomposition is the process of taking a task, i.e., a unit of work (see Figure 6.1a), and breaking it down into smaller units of work such that the collection of smaller units carry out the same task as the one larger unit. The idea is that if one starts with a large complex task, and applies this process step-by-step, one will end up with very small units of work, and consequently one will be able to easily write a program to carry out each of these small units of work. The process is also referred to as *step-wise refinement*, since each step refines one of the tasks that is still too complex into a collection of simpler sub-tasks.

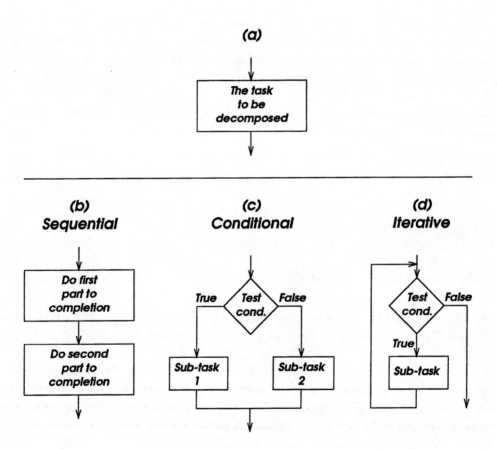

Figure 6.1: The Basic Constructs of Structured Programming.

There are basically three constructs for doing this: *Sequential, Conditional, and Iterative.* The idea is to replace the large unit of work with a construct that correctly decomposes it.

The **Sequential** construct (Figure 6.1b) is the one to use if our task can be broken down into two sub-tasks, one following the other. That is, the computer is to carry out the first sub-task completely, *then* go on and carry out the second sub-task completely—never going back to the first sub-task after starting the second sub-task.

The **Conditional** construct (Figure 6.1c) is the one to use if our task consists of doing one of two sub-tasks but not both, depending on some condition. If the condition is true, the computer is to carry out one sub-task. If the condition is not true, the computer is to carry out a different sub-task. (Either sub-task may be vacuous, that is, it may "do nothing.") Regardless, after the correct sub-task is completed, the program moves onward. The program never goes back and re-tests the condition, for example.

The **Iterative** construct (Figure 6.1d) is the one to use if our task consists of doing a sub-task a number of times, but only as long as some condition is true. If the condition is true, do the sub-task. After the sub-task is finished, go back and test the condition again. As long as the result of the condition tested is true, the program continues to carry out the same sub-task. The first time the test is not true, the program proceeds onward.

Note in Figure 6.1 that whatever the task of Figure 6.1a is, work starts with the arrow into the top of the "box" representing the task, and finishes with the arrow out of the bottom of the box. There is no mention of what goes on *inside* the box representing the task of Figure 6.1a. In each of the three possible decompositions of Figure 6.1a (i.e., Figures 6.1b, 1c, and 1d), there is exactly one entrance into the construct and one exit out of the construct. Thus it is easy to replace any task of the form of Figure 6.1a with whichever of its three decompositions apply. We will see how in the following example.

6.1.3   LC-2 Control Instructions to Implement the Three Constructs.

Before we move on to an example, we illustrate in Figure 6.2 the use of LC-2 control instructions to direct the Program Counter to carry out each of the three decomposition constructs. That is, Figures 6.2b, 6.2c, and 6.2d correspond respectively to the three constructs shown in Figures 6.1b, 6.1c, and 6.1d.

We use the letters A, B, C and D to represent addresses in memory containing LC-2 instructions. A, for example, is used in all three cases to represent the address of the first LC-2 instruction to be executed.

Figure 6.2b illustrates the control flow of the sequential decomposition. Note that no control instructions are needed since the PC is incremented from Address B1 to Address B1+1. The program continues to execute instructions through address D1. It does not return to the first sub-task.

Figure 6.2c illustrates the control flow of the conditional decomposition. First a condition is generated, resulting in the setting of one of the condition codes. This condition is tested by the conditional branch instruction at Address B2. If the condition is true, the PC is set to Address C2, and sub-task 1 is executed. (Note: x corresponds to bits $\langle 8:0 \rangle$ of the address represented by C2.) If the condition is false, the PC (which had been incremented during the FETCH phase of the branch instruction) fetches the instruction at Address B2+1, and

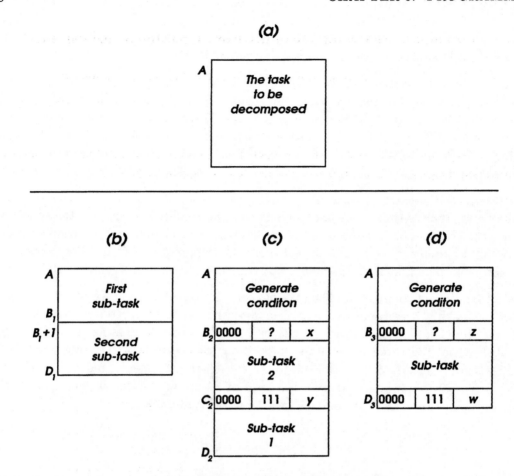

Figure 6.2: Use of LC-2 Control Instructions to Implement Structured Programming.

sub-task 2 is executed. Sub-task 2 terminates in a branch instruction that unconditionally branches to D2+1. (Note: y corresponds to bits $\langle 8 : 0 \rangle$ of the address represented by D2+1.)

Figure 6.2d illustrates the control flow of the iterative decomposition. As in the case of the condition construct, first a condition is generated, a condition code is set, and a conditional branch is executed. In this case the condition bits of the instruction at address B3 are set to cause a conditional branch if the condition generated is false. If the condition is false, the PC is set to address D3+1. (Note: z corresponds to bits $\langle 8 : 0 \rangle$ of the address represented by D3+1.) On the other hand, as long as the condition is true, the PC will be incremented to B3+1 and the sub-task will be executed. The sub-task terminates in an unconditional branch instruction at address D3, which sets the PC to A to again generate and test the condition. (Note: w corresponds to bits [8:0] of address A.)

Now, we are ready to move on to an example.

6.1.4 The Character Count Example from Chapter 5, Revisited.

Recall the example of Section 5.5. The statement of the problem is as follows:

> We wish to count the number of occurrences of a character in a file. The character in question is to be input from the keyboard; the result is to be displayed on the monitor.

The systematic decomposition of this English language statement of the problem to the final LC-2 implementation is shown in Figure 6.3. Figure 6.3a is a brief statement of the problem.

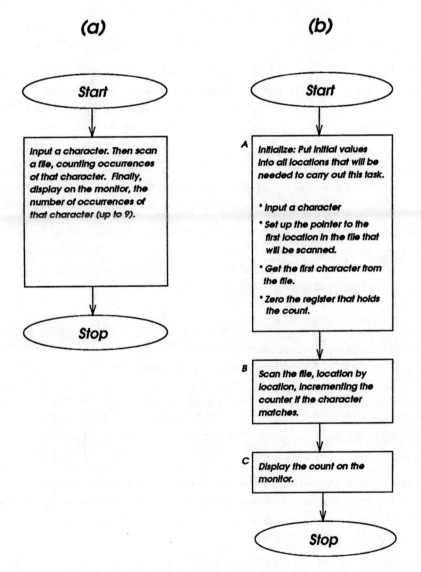

Figure 6.3: Stepwise Refinement of the Character Count Program.

In order to solve the problem, it is always a good idea to first examine exactly what is being asked for, and what is available to help solve the problem. In this case, the statement of the problem says that we will get the character of interest from the keyboard. We will scan all characters in a file, and when we find a match, we will increment a counter. Finally, we will output the result.

We will need places to hold various pieces of information:

```
(1) the character input from the keyboard,
(2) where we are (a pointer) in our scan of the file),
(3) the character in the file which is currently being examined, and
(4) the count of the number of occurrences.
```

We will also need some mechanism for knowing when the file terminates.

The problem decomposes naturally (using the sequential construct) into three parts as shown in Figure 6.3b: (A) initialization, which includes keyboard input of the character to be "counted," (B) the actual process of determining how many occurrences of the character are present in the file, and (C) displaying the count on the monitor.

We have seen the importance of proper initialization in several examples already. Before a computer program can get down to the crux of the problem, it must have the correct initial values. These initial values don't just show up in the GPRs by magic. They get there as a result of the first set of steps in every algorithm: the initialization of its variables.

In this particular algorithm, initialization (as we said in Chapter 5) consists of starting the counter at 0, setting the pointer to the address of the first character in the file to be examined, getting an input character from the keyboard, and getting the first character from the file. Collectively, these four steps comprise the intialization of the algorithm shown in Figure 6.3b as A.

Figure 6.3c decomposes B into an iteration construct, such that as long as there are characters in the file to examine, the loop iterates. B1 shows what gets accomplished each iteration. The character is tested and the count incremented if there is a match. Then the next character is prepared for examination. Recall in Chapter 5 that there are two basic techniques for controlling the number of iterations of a loop, the sentinel method and a counter. This program uses the sentinel method by terminating the file we are examining with an EOT (End of Text) character. The test to see if there are more legitimate characters in the file is a test for the ASCII code for EOT.

Figure 6.3c also shows the initialization step in greater detail. Four LC-2 registers (R0, R1, R2, and R3) have been specified to handle the four requirements of the algorithm: the input character from the keyboard, the current character being tested, the counter, and the pointer to the next character to be tested.

Figure 6.3d decomposes both B1 and C using the sequential construct. In the case of B1, first the current character is tested (B2), and the counter incremented if we have a match, and then the next character is fetched (B3). In the case of C, first the count is prepared for display by converting it from a 2's complement integer to ASCII (C1), and then the actual character output is performed (C2).

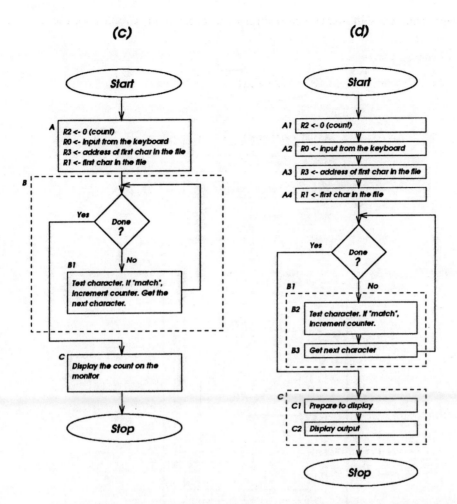

Figure 6.3: Stepwise Refinement of the Character Count Program.

Finally, 3e completes the decomposition, replacing B2 with the elements of the condition construct, and B3 with the sequential construct (first the pointer is incremented, and then the next character to be scanned is loaded).

The last step (and the easy part, actually) is to write the LC-2 code corresponding to each box in Figure 6.3e. Note that Figure 6.3e is essentially identical to Figure 5.7 of Chapter 5 (except now you know where it all came from!).

Before leaving this topic, it is worth pointing out that it is not always possible to understand everything at the outset. When you find that to be the case, it is not a signal to simply throw up your hands and quit. In such cases (which realistically are most cases), you should see if you can make sense of a piece of the problem, and expand from there. Problems are like puzzles, initially they can be opaque, but the more you work at it, the more it yields under your attack. Once you do understand what is given, what is being asked for, and how to proceed, you are ready to return to square one (Figure 6.3a) and re-start the process of systematically decomposing the problem.

(e)

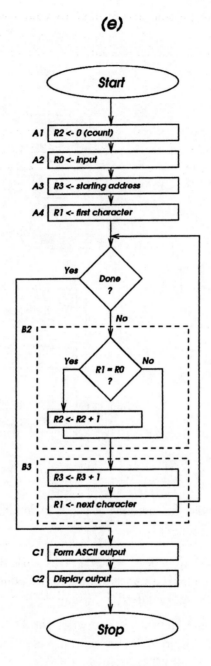

Figure 6.3: Stepwise Refinement of the Character Count Program.

6.2   Debugging.

Debugging a program is pretty much applied common sense. A simple example comes to mind: You are driving to a place you have never visited, and somewhere along the way you made a wrong turn. What do you do now? One common "driving debugging" technique is to wander aimlessly hoping to find your way back. When that doesn't work, and you are finally willing to listen to the person sitting next to you, you turn around and return to some "known" position on the route. Then, using a map (very difficult for some people) you follow the directions provided, periodically comparing where you are (from landmarks you see out the window) with where the map says you should be, until you reach your desired destination.

Debugging is somewhat like that. A logical error in a program can make you take a wrong turn. The simplest way to keep track of where you are as compared to where you want to be is to *trace* the program. This consists of keeping track of the **sequence** of instructions that have been executed, and the **results** produced by each instruction executed. When one examines the sequence of instructions executed, one can detect errors in the control flow of the program. When one compares what each instruction has done to what it is supposed to do, one can detect logical errors in the program. In short, when the behavior of the program as it is executing is different from what it should be doing, you know there is a bug.

A useful technique is to partition the program into parts, often referred to as *modules*, and examine the results that have been computed at the end of each module. In fact, the structured programming approach discussed in Section 6.1 can help you determine where in the program's execution you should examine results. This allows you to systematically get to the point where you are focusing your attention on the instruction or instructions that are causing the problem.

6.2.1 Debugging Operations.

There are many sophisticated debugging tools offered in the marketplace, and undoubtedly you will use many of them in the years ahead. In Chapter 14 we will examine some debugging techniques available through dbx, the debugger for the programming language C. For right now, however, we wish to stay at the level of the machine architecture, and so we will see what we can accomplish with a few very elementary on-line debugging operations. When debugging on-line, the user sits in front of the keyboard and monitor and issues commands to the computer. In our case, this means operating an LC-2 Simulator, using the menu available with the Simulator.

It is important to be able to

```
(1) deposit values in memory and in registers,
(2) execute sequences of a program,
(3) stop the execution when desired, and finally
(4) examine what is in memory and registers.
```

These few simple operations will go a long way toward debugging programs.

Set Values.

It is useful to deposit values in memory and in registers in order to test the execution of a part of a program in isolation, without having to worry about parts of the program that come before it. For example, suppose one module in your program supplies input from a keyboard, and a subsequent module operates on that input. Suppose you want to test the second module before you have finished debugging the first module. If you know that the keyboard input module ends up with an ASCII code in R0, you can test the module that operates on that input by first placing an ASCII code in R0.

Execute sequences.

It is important to be able to execute a sequence of instructions, and then stop execution in order to examine the values that the program has computed. Three simple mechanisms for doing so are usually available for doing this: Run, Step, and Set (and Clear) Breakpoints.

The **Run** command causes the program to execute until something makes it stop. The "something" can either be a HALT instruction, or a Breakpoint (which is explained below). The **Step** command causes the program to execute a fixed number of instructions, and then stop. The on-line user enters the number of instructions he/she wishes the Simulator to execute before it stops. When that number is one, the computer executes one instruction, then stops. Executing one instruction and then stopping is called *single stepping*. It allows the person debugging the program to examine the individual results of every instruction executed.

One can stop execution at a specific known point in a program by setting a *Breakpoint*. Executing the on-line debugging command **Set Breakpoint** consists of adding an address to a list maintained by the Simulator. During the FETCH phase of each instruction simulated, the Simulator compares the PC with the addresses in that list. If there is a match, execution stops. Thus, the effect of setting a breakpoint is to allow execution to proceed until the PC contains the address of the breakpoint. This is useful if one wishes to know what has been computed up to a particular point in the program. One sets a breakpoint at that address in the program, and executes the Run command. The program executes until that point, thereby allowing the on-line user to examine what has been computed up to that point.

Display Values.

Finally, it is useful to examine the results of execution when the Simulator has stopped execution. The Display command allows the on-line user to examine the contents of any memory location or any register.

6.2.2   Example: Debugging a Program by Examining an Execution Trace.

We conclude this chapter with an example, showing how the use of the on-line debugging operations can find errors in a program. Consider the program of Figure 6.4. The goal of the program is to multiply the contents of the two positive numbers contained in R4 and R5. Given the fact that the LC-2 does not have a "multiply" instruction, the program clears R2 (that is, initializes R2 to zero), and then attempts to perform the multiplication by adding R4 to itself a number of times equal to the initial value in R5. Each time an add is performed, R5 is decremented. When R5 = 0, the program terminates.

It sounds like the program should work! Upon execution however, one finds that if R4 is initially 10 and R5 is initially 3, the program produces the value 40. What went wrong?

Figure 6.4b shows a trace of the program, which one can obtain by single-stepping the program. The column labeled PC shows the contents of the PC at the start of each instruction. R2, R4, and R5 show respectively the values in those three registers at the start of each instruction. An examination of the contents of the registers shows that the branch condition codes were set wrong; that is, the conditional branch should take place as long as R5 is positive, not as long as R5 is non-negative, as was done. That caused an extra iteration of the loop, resulting in 10 being added to itself four times, rather than three.

The program can be corrected by simply replacing the instruction at x3203 with

15	14	13	12	11	10	9	8	7	6	5	4	3	2	1	0
0	0	0	0	0	0	1	0	0	0	0	0	0	0	0	1

      BR   n   z   p   x001

Figure 6.4c shows how setting a breakpoint at x3203 could have saved some of the tedium. Instead of examining the results of **each instruction**, a breakpoint at x3203 allows us to examine the results of **each iteration** of the loop. As before, we would see the loop executed four times rather than three, as it should have been.

Address	15	14	13	12	11	10	9	8	7	6	5	4	3	2	1	0
x3200	0	1	0	1	0	1	0	0	1	0	1	0	0	0	0	0
x3201	0	0	0	1	0	1	0	0	1	0	0	0	0	1	0	0
x3202	0	0	0	1	1	0	1	1	0	1	1	1	1	1	1	1
x3203	0	0	0	0	0	1	1	0	0	0	0	0	0	0	0	1
x3204	1	1	1	1	0	0	0	0	0	0	1	0	0	1	0	1

Figure 6.4: (a) An LC-2 Program to Multiply (without a Multiply Instruction)

PC	R2	R4	R5
x3201	0	10	3
x3202	10	10	3
x3203	10	10	2
x3201	10	10	2
x3202	20	10	2
x3203	20	10	1
x3201	20	10	1
x3202	30	10	1
x3203	30	10	0
x3201	30	10	0
x3202	40	10	0
x3203	40	10	-1
x3204	40	10	-1
	40	10	-1

Figure 6.4: (b) A Trace of the Multiply Program

PC	R2	R4	R5
x3203	10	10	2
x3203	20	10	1
x3203	30	10	0
x3203	40	10	-1

Figure 6.4: (c) Tracing with Breakpoints

Figure 6.4: The Use of On-line Debugging to Find Errors in a Program.

6.3   Exercises.

6.1 Can a procedure that is **not** and algorithm be be constructed from the three basic constructs of structured programming? If so, demonstrate through an example.

6.2 The LC-2 has no subtract instruction. If a programmer needed to subtract two numbers he or she would have to write a routine to handle it. Systematically decompose the process of subtracting two integers.

6.3 Write a short LC-2 program that compares two numbers and puts the larger of the two in R1 and the smaller of the two in R2.

6.4 Which of the two algorithms for multiplying two numbers is preferable and why? 88 * 3 = 88 + 88 + 88 OR 3 + 3 + 3 + 3 + ... + 3?

6.5 Use your answers from the last two problems to systematically decompose a routine that efficiently multiplies two integers and places the result in R3.

6.6 What does the following LC-2 program do?

x3000	0011000000000000
x3001	1110000000001110
x3002	1110001000010011
x3003	0101010010100000
x3004	0010010000001101
x3005	0110011000000000
x3006	0110100001000000
x3007	0001011011000100
x3008	0111011000000000
x3009	0001000000100001
x300a	0001001001100001
x300b	0001010010111111
x300c	0000001000000100
x300d	1111000000100101
x300e	0000000000000101
x300f	0000000000000100
x3010	0000000000000011
x3011	0000000000000110
x3012	0000000000000010
x3013	0000000000000100
x3014	0000000000000111
x3015	0000000000000110
x3016	0000000000001000
x3017	0000000000000111
x3018	0000000000000101

6.7 Recall the machine busy example from previous chapters. Suppose memory location x4000 contains an integer between 0 and 15 identifying a particular machine that has just become busy. Suppose further that the value in memory location x4001 tells which machines are busy and which machines are idle. Write an LC-2 machine language program that sets the appropriate bit in x4001 indicating that the machine in x4000 is busy.

For example, if x4000 contains a x0005 and x4001 contains x3101 at the start of execution, 0x4001 should contain x3121 after your program terminates.

6.8 Why is it necessary to initialize R2 in the character counting example in Section 6.1.4? In other words, in what manner might the program behave incorrectly if the R2 ← 0 step were removed from the routine?

6.9 Using the iteration construct, write an LC-2 machine language routine that displays exactly 100 "Z"s on the screen.

6.10 Using the conditional construct, write an LC-2 machine language routine that determines if a number stored in R2 is odd.

6.11 Write an LC-2 machine language routine to increment each of the numbers stored in memory locations A through memory locations B. Assume these locations have already been initialized with meaningful numbers. The values for A and B can be found in memory locations x3100 and x3101.

6.12   1. Write an LC-2 machine language routine which "echoes" the last character typed at the keyboard. If the user types a "R", the program then immediately outputs an "R" on the screen.

   2. Expand the routine from part (a) such that it echoes a line at a time. For example, if the user types:

   The quick brown fox jumps over the lazy dog.

   then the program waits for the user to press the "Enter" key (the ASCII code for which is x0A) and then outputs the same line.

6.13 Notice that we can shift a number to the left by one bit position by adding it to itself. For example when the binary number 0011 is added to itself, the result is 0110. Shifting a number one bit pattern to the right not as easy. Devise a routine in LC-2 machine code to shift the contents of memory location x3100 to the right by one bit.

6.14 Consider the following machine language program:

x3000	0101010010100000
x3001	0001001001111111
x3002	0001001001111111
x3003	0001001001111111
x3004	0000100000000111
x3005	0001010010100001
x3006	0000111000000001
x3007	1111000000100101

What are the possible initial values of R1 which cause the final value in R2 to be 3?

Chapter 7

Assembly Language.

By now, you are probably a little tired of 1s and 0s and keeping track of 0001 meaning ADD and 1001 meaning NOT. Also, wouldn't it be nice if we could refer to a memory location by some meaningful symbolic name instead of memorizing its 16-bit address. And, wouldn't it be nice if we could represent each instruction in some more easily comprehensible way, instead of having to keep track of which bit of the instruction conveys which individual piece of information about the instruction. It turns out that help is on the way.

In this chapter, we introduce Assembly Language, a mechanism that does all that, and more.

7.1 Assembly Language Programming—Moving up a level.

Recall the levels of transformation identified in Figure 1.6 of Chapter 1. Algorithms are transformed into programs described in some mechanical language. This mechanical language can be, as it is in Chapter 5, the machine language of the particular computer we are interacting with. Recall that a program is in a computer's machine language if every instruction in the program is from the ISA of that computer.

On the other hand, the mechanical language can be more user-friendly.

We generally partition mechanical languages into two classes, high-level and low-level. Of the two, high-level languages are much more user-friendly. Examples are C, C++, Fortran, COBOL, Pascal, plus more than a thousand others. Instructions in a high-level language almost (but not quite) resemble statements in a natural language such as English. High-level languages tend to be ISA-independent. That is, once you learn how to program in C (or Fortran or Pascal) for one ISA, it is a small step to write programs in C (or Fortran or Pascal) for another ISA.

Before a program written in a high-level language can be executed, it must be translated into a program in the ISA of the particular computer we are dealing with. It is usually the case that each statement in the high-level language specifies several instructions in the

141

ISA of the computer. In Chapter 10, we will introduce the high-level language C, and in Chapters 11 through 18, we will show the relationship between various statements in C and their corresponding translations in LC-2 code. In this chapter, however, we will only move up a small step from the ISA we dealt with in Chapter 5.

A small step up from the ISA of a machine is that ISA's assembly language. Assembly language is a low-level language. There is no confusing an instruction in a low-level language with a statement in English. Each assembly language instruction usually specifies a single instruction in the ISA. Unlike high-level languages which are usually ISA-independent, low-level languages are very ISA-dependent. In fact, it is usually the case that each ISA has only one assembly language.

The purpose of assembly language is to make the programming process more user-friendly than programming in machine language (i.e., the ISA of the computer we are dealing with), while still providing the programmer with detailed control over the individual instructions that the computer can execute. So, for example, while still retaining control over the detailed instructions the computer is to carry out, we are freed from having to remember what opcode is 0001 and what opcode is 1001, or what is being stored in memory location 0011111100001010 and what is being stored in location 0011111100000101. Assembly languages let us use mnemonic devices for opcodes, such as ADD and NOT, and let us give meaningful symbolic names to memory locations, such as SUM or PRODUCT, rather than use their 16-bit addresses. This makes it easier to differentiate which memory location is keeping track of a SUM and which memory location is keeping track of a PRODUCT.

We will see, starting in Chapter 11, that when we take the larger step of moving up to a higher-level language (like C), programming will be even more user-friendly, but we will relinquish control of exactly which detailed instructions are to be carried out in behalf of a high-level language statement.

7.2 An assembly language program

We will describe LC-2 assembly language by means of an example. The program below multiplies a number by 6 by adding the number to itself six times. For example, if the number is 123, the program computes the product by adding 123+123+123+123+123+123.

```
01      ;
02      ; Program to multiply a number by the constant 6
03      ;
04              .ORIG   x3050
05              LD      R1,SIX
06              LD      R2,NUMBER
07              AND     R3,R3,#0        ; Clear R3. It will contain the product.
08      ;
09      ; The inner loop
0A      ;
0B      AGAIN   ADD     R3,R3,R2
0C              ADD     R1,R1,#-1       ; R1 keep tracks of the iterations
0D              BRp     AGAIN
0E      ;
0F              HALT
10      ;
11      NUMBER  .BLKW   1
12      SIX     .FILL   x0006
13      ;
14              .END
```

The program consists of 20 lines of code. We have added a *line number* to each line of the program in order to be able to refer to individual lines easily. This is a common practice. These line numbers are not part of the program. Nine lines start with a semi-colon, designating that they are strictly for the benefit of the human reader. More on this momentarily. Seven lines (05, 06, 07, 0B, 0C, 0D, and 0F) specify actual instructions to be translated into instructions in the ISA of the LC-2 which will actually be carried out when the program runs. The remaining four lines (04, 11, 12, and 14) contain pseudo-ops, which are messages from the programmer to the translation program to help in the translation process. The translation program is called an *Assembler* (in this case the LC-2 Assembler) and the translation process is called *assembly*.

7.2.1 Instructions.

Instead of an instruction being 16 0s and 1s, as is the case in the LC-2 ISA, an instruction in Assembly Language consists of four parts, as shown below:

LABEL   OPCODE   OPERANDS   ;   COMMENTS

Two of the parts (LABEL and COMMENTS) are optional. More on this momentarily.

Opcodes and Operands.

Two of the parts (OPCODE and OPERANDS) are **mandatory**. An instruction must have an OPCODE (the thing the instruction is to do), and the appropriate number of operands (the things it is supposed to do it to). Not surprisingly, this was exactly what we encountered in Chapter 5 when we studied the LC-2 ISA.

The OPCODE is a symbolic name for the opcode of the corresponding LC-2 instruction. The idea is that it is easier to remember an operation by the symbolic name ADD, AND, or LDR than by the four-bit quantity 0001, 0101, or 0110. Figure 5.1 (also, Figure A.3) lists the OPCODES of the 16 LC-2 instructions. Pages 464 through 479 show the assembly language representations for the 16 LC-2 instructions.

The number of operands depends on the operation being performed. For example, the ADD instruction (line 0B) requires three operands (two sources to obtain the numbers being added, and one destination to designate where the result is to be placed). All three operands must be explicitly identified in the instruction.

AGAIN   ADD   R3,R3,R2

The operands to be added are obtained from register 2 and from register 3. The result is to be placed in register 3. We represent each of the registers 0 through 7 as R0, R2, ..., R7.

The LD instruction (line 06) requires two operands (the memory location from which the value is to be read) and the destination register which is to contain the value after the instruction completes execution. We will see momentarily that memory locations will be given symbolic addresses called *labels*. In this case, the location from which the value is to be read is given the label NUMBER. The destination in which the value is to be loaded into is register 2.

LD   R2, NUMBER

As we discussed in Section 5.1.6, operands may be obtained from registers, from memory, or they may be literal (i.e., immediate) values in the instruction. In the case of register operands, the registers are explicitly represented (such as R2 and R3 in line 0B). In the case of memory operands, the symbolic name of the memory location is explicitly represented (such as NUMBER in line 6 and SIX in line 05). In the case of immediate operands, the actual value is explicitly represented (such as the value 0 in line 07).

AND   R3, R3, #0   ; Clear R3. It will contain the product.

A literal value must contain a symbol identifying the representation base of the number. We use # for decimal, x for hexadecimal, and b for binary. Sometimes there is no ambiguity, such as in the case 3F0A, which is a hex number. Nonetheless, we write it as x3F0A. Sometimes there is ambiguity, such as in the case 1000. x1000 represents the decimal numer 4096, b1000 represents the decimal number 8, and #1000 represents the decimal number 1000.

Labels.

Labels are symbolic names which are used to identify memory locations that are referred to explicitly in the program. There are two reasons for explicitly referring to a memory location.

1. The location contains the target of a branch instruction (for example, AGAIN in line 0B).

2. The location contains a value that is loaded or stored (for example, NUMBER, line 11, and SIX, line 12).

The location AGAIN is specifically referenced by the branch instruction in line 0D.

$$\text{BRp} \qquad \text{AGAIN}$$

If the result of ADD R1,R1,#−1 is positive (as evidenced by the P condition code being set), then the program branches to the location explictly referenced as AGAIN to perform another iteration.

The location NUMBER is specifically referenced by the load instruction in line 06. The contents of the memory location explicitly referenced as NUMBER is loaded into R2.

If a location in the program is not explicitly referenced, then there is no need to give it a label.

Comments.

Comments are messages intended only for human consumption. They have no effect on the translation process, and indeed are not acted on by the LC-2 Assembler. They are identified in the program by semi-colons. A semi-colon signifies that the rest of the line is a comment and is to be ignored by the Assembler. If the semi-colon is the first non-blank character on the line, the entire line is ignored. If the semi-colon follows the operands of an instruction, then only the comment is ignored by the Assembler.

The purpose of comments is to make the program more comprehensible to the human reader. They help explain a non-intuitive aspect of an instruction or a set of instructions. In line 07, the comment "Clear R3; it will contain the product" lets the reader know that the instruction on line 07 is initializing R3 prior to accumulating the product of the two numbers. While the purpose of line 07 may be obvious to the programmer today, it may not be the case two years from now, after the programmer has written an additional 30,000 lines of code and can't remember why he/she wrote AND R3,R3,#0. It may also be the case that two years from now, the programmer no longer works for the company and the company needs to modify the program in response to a product update. If the task is assigned to someone who has never seen the code before, comments go a long way to help comprehension.

It is important that comments provide additional insight and not just restate the obvious. There are two reasons for this. First, comments that restate the obvious are a waste of everyone's time. Second, they tend to obscure the comments that say something important because they add clutter to the program. For example, in line 0C, the comment "Decrement R1" would be a bad idea. It would provide no additional insight into the instruction and it would add clutter to the page.

Another purpose of comments, and also the judicious use of extra blank spaces to a line, is to make the visual presentation of a program easier to understand. So, for example, comments are used to separate pieces of the program from each other to make the program more readable. That is, lines of code that work together to compute a single result are placed on successive lines, while pieces of a program that produce separate results are separated from each other. For example, note that lines 0B through 0D are separated from the rest of the code by lines 0A and 0E. There is nothing on lines 0A and 0E other than the semi-colons.

Extra spaces that are ignored by the assembler provides an opportunity to align elements of a program for easier readability. For example, all the opcodes start in the same column on the page.

7.2.2 Pseudo-ops (assembler directives).

The LC-2 Assembler is a program which takes as input a string of characters representing a computer program written in LC-2 Assembly Language, and translates it into a program in the ISA of the LC-2. Pseudo-ops are helpful to the Assembler in performing that task.

Actually, a more formal name for pseudo-op is *assembler directive*. They are called pseudo-ops because they do not refer to operations that will be performed by the program during execution. Rather, the pseudo-op is strictly a message to the Assembler to help the Assembler in the assembly process. Once the Assembler handles the message, the pseudo-op is discarded. The LC-2 Assembler contains five pseudo-ops: .ORIG, .FILL, .BLKW, .STRINGZ, and .END. All are easily recognizable by the "dot" as their first character.

.ORIG

.ORIG tells the Assembler where to locate the LC-2 program. In line 04, .ORIG x3050 says: start with location x3050. As a result, the LD R1,SIX instruction will be put in x3050.

.END

.END tells the Assembler where the program ends. Any characters that come after .END will not be utilized by the Assembler. Note: .END does not stop the program during execution. In fact, .END does not even exist at execution time. It is simply a delimiter—it marks the end of the source program.

.BLKW

.BLKW tells the Assembler to set aside some number of next sequential locations (i.e., a **BL**oc**K** of **W**ords) in the program. The actual number is the operand of the .BLKW pseudo-op. In line 11, the pseudo-op instructs the Assembler to set aside one location in memory (and also to label it NUMBER, incidentally).

The pseudo-op .BLKW is particularly useful when the actual value of the operand is not yet known. For example, one might want to set aside a location in memory for storing a character input from a keyboard. It will not be until the program is run that we will know the identity of that keystroke.

.FILL

.FILL tells the Assembler to set aside the next location in the program and initialize it with the value of the operand. In line 12, the ninth location in the resultant LC-2 program is initialized to the value x0006.

.STRINGZ

.STRINGZ tells the Assembler to initialize a sequence of $n + 1$ memory locations. The argument is a sequence of n characters, inside double quotation marks. The first **n** words of memory are initialized with the zero-extended ASCII codes of the corresponding characters in the string. The final word of memory is initialized to zero. The last character, x0000, provides a convenient sentinel for processing the string of ASCII codes.

For example, the code fragment

```
          .ORIG     x3010
HELLO     .STRINGZ  "Hello, World!"
```

would result in the Assembler initializing locations x3010 through x3014 to the following values:

```
                    x3010: x0048
                    x3011: x0065
                    x3012: x006C
                    x3013: x006C
                    x3014: x006F
                    x3015: x002C
                    x3016: x0020
                    x3017: x0057
                    x3018: x006F
                    x3019: x0072
                    x301A: x006C
                    x301B: x0064
                    x301C: x0021
                    x301D: x0000
```

7.2.3   Example: The Character Count Example of Section 5.5, Revisited.

Now, we are ready for a complete example. Let's consider again the problem of Section 5.5. We wish to write a program that will take a character that is input from the keyboard and a file, and count the number of occurrences of that character in that file. As before, we first develop the algorithm by constructing the flow chart. Recall that in Section 6.1, we showed how to systematically decompose the problem so as to generate the flow chart of Figure 5.7. In fact, the final step of that process in Chapter 6 is the flow chart of Figure 6.3e, which is essentially identical to Figure 5.7. Next, we use the flow chart to write the actual program. This time, however, we enjoy the luxury of not worrying about 0s and 1s, and instead write the program in LC-2 Assembly Language. The program is shown in Figure 7.1, below:

A few notes regarding this program:

```
01      ;
02      ; Program to count occurrences of a character in a File.
03      ; Character to be input from the keyboard.
04      ; Result to be displayed on the monitor.
05      ; Program only works if no more than 9 occurrences are found.
06      ;
07      ;
08      ; Initialization
09      ;
0A              .ORIG   x3000
0B              AND     R2,R2,#0        ; R2 is counter, initialize to 0
0C              LD      R3,PTR          ; R3 is pointer to characters in file
0D              TRAP    x23             ; R0 gets character input
0E              LDR     R1,R3,#0        ; R1 gets the next character in file
0F      ;
10      ; Test character for end of file
11      ;
13      TEST    ADD     R4,R1,#-4       ; Test for EOT
14              BRZ     OUTPUT          ; If done, prepare the output
15      ;
16      ; Test character for match.  If a match, increment count.
17      ;
18              NOT     R1,R1
19              ADD     R1,R1,R0        ; If match, R1 = xFFFF
1A              NOT     R1,R1           ; If match, R1 = x0000
1B              BRnp    GETCHAR         ; If no match, skip the increment
1C              ADD     R2,R2,#1
1D      ;
1E      ; Get next character from the file
1F      ;
20      GETCHAR ADD     R3,R3,#1        ; Increment the pointer
21              LDR     R1,R3,#0        ; R1 gets the next character to test
22              BR      TEST            ; Get next character from the file
23      ;
24      ; Output the count.
25      ;
26      OUTPUT  LD      R0,ASCII        ; Load the ASCII template for convert
27              ADD     R0,R0,R2        ; Convert binary to ASCII
28              TRAP    x21             ; ASCII code in R0 is displayed
29              TRAP    x25             ; Halt machine
2A      ;
2B      ; Storage for pointer and ASCII template
2C      ;
2D      ASCII   .FILL   x0030
2E      PTR     .FILL   x4000
2F              .END
```

Figure 7.1: The Assembly Language Program to Count Occurrences of a Character.

Three times during this program, assistance in the form of a service call is required of the operating system. In each case, a TRAP instruction is used. TRAP x23 causes a character to be input from the keyboard and placed in R0 (line 0D). TRAP x21 causes the ASCII code in R0 to be displayed on the monitor (line 28). TRAP x25 causes the machine to be halted (line 29). As we said before, we will leave until Chapter 9 the details of how the TRAP instruction is carried out.

The ASCII codes for the decimal digits 0 to 9 (0000 to 1001) are 00110000 to 00111001. The conversion from binary to ASCII is done by simply adding 00110000 to the binary value of the decimal digit. Line 2D shows ASCII initialized to that value (i.e., x0030).

The file that is to be examined starts at address x4000 (see line 2E). Usually, this starting address would not be known to the programmer who is writing this program, since we would want the program to work on files that will become available in the future. That situation will be discussed in Section 7.4 below.

7.3   The Assembly Process

7.3.1   Introduction.

Before an LC-2 assembly language program can be executed, it must first be translated into a machine language program, that is, one in which each instruction is in the LC-2 ISA. It is the job of the LC-2 Assembler to perform that translation.

If you have available an LC-2 Assembler, you can cause it to translate your assembly language program into a machine language program by executing an appropriate command. In the LC-2 Assembler generally available via the web, that command is **assemble** and requires as an argument the file name of your assembly language program. For example, if the file name is solution1.asm, then

```
assemble solution1.asm outfile
```

produces the file outfile, which is in the ISA of the LC-2. It is necessary to check with your local instructor for the correct command line for causing the LC-2 Assembler to produce a file of 0s and 1s in the ISA of the LC-2.

7.3.2   A Two-Pass Process.

In this section, we will see how the Assembler goes through the process of translating an assembly language program into a machine language program. We start with the example of Figure 7.1.

Recall that there is in general a one-to-one correspondence between instructions in the assembly language program and instructions in the final machine language program. The process consists in making that one-to-one translation.

Starting at the top of Figure 7.1, the Assembler sees (line 0A) that the machine language program will start at location x3000. The Assembler can easily transform the first instruction (line 0B) to machine language, that is: 0101010010100000. At this point, we have

x3000: 0101010010100000

The LC-2 Assembler moves on to the next instruction (line 0C). It would next want to translate this line, but would be unable to, since it does not know the meaning of the symbolic address, PTR.

Consequently, the assembly process is done in **two steps,** or two passes, so named because the LC-2 Assembler passes over the whole assembly language program twice, from beginning to end. The objective of the first pass is to identify the actual binary addresses corresponding to the symbolic names (or labels) so that the problem alluded to above (not knowing the 16-bit address corresponding to PTR) is removed. This set of correspondences is known as the Symbol Table. In pass one, we construct the Symbol Table. In pass two, we translate the individual assembly language instructions into their corresponding machine language instructions.

7.3.3 The first pass: Creating the Symbol Table.

For our purposes, the Symbol Table is simply a correspondence of symbolic names with their 16-bit memory addresses. We obtain these correspondences by passing through the assembly language program once, noting which instruction is assigned to which address, and identifying each label with the address of its assigned entry.

Recall that we provide labels in those cases where we have to refer to a location, either because it is the target of a branch instruction or because it contains data that must be loaded or stored. Consequently, if we have not made any programming mistakes, and if we identify all the labels, we will have identified all the symbolic addresses used in the program.

The above paragraph assumes that our entire program exists between our .ORIG and .END pseudo-ops, This is true at the moment. In Section 7.4, we will consider programs that consist of multiple parts, each with its own .ORIG and .END, and where each part is assembled separately.

The first pass starts by noting (line 0A) that the first instruction will be assigned to address x3000. We keep track of the location assigned to each instruction by means of a Location Counter, abbreviated LC. The LC is initialized to the address specified in .ORIG, that is x3000.

The first pass continually increments the LC, and notes whether or not the instruction contains a label. If it does, a Symbol Table entry is made for that label, specifying the current contents of LC as its address. The first pass terminates when the .END instruction is encountered.

The first instruction that has a label is at line 13. Since it is the fifth instruction in the program, and the LC at that point contains x3004, a Symbol Table entry is constructed thus:

Symbol	Address
TEST	x3004

The second instruction that has a label is at line 20. At this point, the LC has been incremented to x300B. Thus a Symbol Table entry is constructed, as follows:

Symbol	Address
GETCHAR	x300B

At the conclusion of the first pass, the Symbol Table has the following entries:

Symbol	Address
TEST	x3004
GETCHAR	x300B
OUTPUT	x300E
ASCII	x3012
PTR	x3013

7.3.4   The second pass: Generating the machine language program.

The second pass consists of going through the assembly language program a second time, this time with the help of the Symbol Table. At each step, the assembly language instruction is translated into a machine language instruction (i.e., in the ISA of the LC-2).

Starting at line 0B, x3000 is set to 0101010010100000, and the LC is incremented to x3001.

This time, when we get to line 0C, we can completely assemble the instruction since we know that PTR corresponds to x3013. The instruction is LD, which has an opcode encoding of 0010. The Destination register (DR) is R3, that is, 011. Since PTR and the contents of LC (i.e., the address of this instruction) are on the same page (that is bits [15:9] are 0011000), LD is a legitimate opcode. The page offset of PTR is 000010011. Putting this all together, x3001 is set to 0010011000010011, and the LC is incremented to x3002.

Note: If the symbolic address of PTR had not been on the same page as the address assigned to the LD instruction, we could not have assembled the instruction. An assembly error would have occurred, preventing the assembly process from completing successfully. Fortunately, PTR is on the same page as x3001, so the instruction assembled correctly.

The second pass continues. At each step, the LC is incremented and the location specified by LC is assigned the translated LC-2 instruction or, in the case of .FILL, the value specified. When the second pass encounters the .END instruction, assembly terminates.

The resulting translated program is shown in Figure 7.2.

Address	Binary
	0011000000000000
x3000	0101010010100000
x3001	0010011000010011
x3002	1111000000100011
x3003	0110001011000000
x3004	0001100001111100
x3005	0000010000001110
x3006	1001001001111111
x3007	0001001001000000
x3008	1001001001111111
x3009	0000110000001011
x300A	0001010010100001
x300B	0001011011100001
x300C	0110001011000000
x300D	0000111000000100
x300E	0010000000010010
x300F	0001000000000010
x3010	1111000000100001
x3011	1111000000100101
x3012	0000000000110000
x3013	0100000000000000

Figure 7.2: The Machine Language Program for the Assembly Language Program of Figure 7.1.

That process was, on a good day, merely tedious. Fortunately, you don't have to do it for a living—the LC-2 Assembler does that. And, since you now know LC-2 assembly language, there is no need to program in machine language any more. Now we can write our programs symbolically in LC-2 assembly language and invoke the LC-2 Assembler to create the machine language versions that can execute on an LC-2 computer.

7.4 Beyond Assembly of a single assembly language program.

Our purpose in this chapter was to take you one step up from the ISA of the computer, introduce assembly language, which although is still quite a large step from C or C++, does in fact save us a good deal of pain. We also showed how a rudimentary two-pass Assembler actually works to translate an assembly language program into the machine language of the LC-2 ISA.

There are many more aspects to sophisticated assembly language programming that go well beyond an introductory course. However, our reason for teaching assembly language is not to deal with its sophistication, but rather to show its innate simplicity. Before we leave this chapter, however, there are a few additional highlights we should explore.

7.4.1 The Executable Image.

When a computer begins execution of a program, the entity being executed is called an executable image. The executable image is created from modules created by you and others. Each module is translated separately into an object file. We have just gone through the process of performing that translation ourselves by mimicing the LC-2 Assembler. Other modules, some written in C perhaps, are translated by the C compiler. Some modules are written by users, and some modules are supplied as library routines by the operating system. Each object file consists of instructions in the ISA of the computer being utilized, along with its associated data. The final step is to *link* all the object modules together into one executable image. It is the executable image that the FETCH, DECODE, ... instruction cycle is applied to.

7.4.2 More than one object file.

It is very common to form an executable image from more than one object file. In fact, in the real world, where most programs invoke libraries provided by the operating system, as well as modules generated by other programmers, it is much more common to have multiple object files than a single one.

A case in point is our example character count program. The program counts the number of occurrences of a character in a file. A typical application can easily have the program as one module and the input data file as another. If this is the case, then the starting address of the file, shown as x4000 in line 2E of Figure 7.1 would not be known when the program was written. If we remove line 2E, then the program of Figure 7.1 will not assemble because there would be no Symbol Table entry for PTR. What can we do?

One solution is to identify PTR as the symbolic name of an address that is not known at the time the program of Figure 7.1 is assembled. We can do that by identifying PTR to the Assembler. A pseudo-op like

```
.EXTERNAL PTR
```

would send a message to the LC-2 Assembler that the absence of a label PTR is not an error in the program. Rather, PTR is a label in some other module that will be translated independently. In fact, in our case, it will be the label of the location of the first character in the file to be examined by our character count program.

With PTR designated .EXTERNAL, the LC-2 will create a Symbol Table entry for PTR, but instead of assigning it an address, it would mark it as belonging to another module.

At *link-time*, when all the modules are combined, the Linker (the program that manages the "combining" process) would use the Symbol Table entry for PTR in another module to complete the translation of the instruction at line 0C in our character count module.

In this way, references by one module to symbolic locations in another module do not present problems. They are resolved by the Linker.

7.5   Exercises.

7.1 An assembly language program contains the following two instructions. The Assembler puts the translated version of the LDI instruction shown below into location x3025 of the object module. After assembly is complete, what is in location x3025?

```
PLACE    .FILL    x45A7
         LDI      R3, PLACE
```

7.2 What is the problem with using the string 'NOP' as a label?

7.3 Create the symbol table entries generated by the assembler when translating the following routine into machine code.

```
              .ORIG    x301C
              ST       R3, SAVE3
              ST       R2, SAVE2
              AND      R2, R2, #0
TEST          IN
              BRz      TEST
              ADD      R1, R0, #-30
              BRn      FINISH
              ADD      R1, R0, #-40
              NOT      R1
              BRn      FINISH
              HALT
FINISH        ADD      R2, R2, #1
              HALT
SAVE3         .FILL    X0000
SAVE2         .FILL    X0000
              .END
```

7.4   1. What does the following program do?

```
            .ORIG   x3000
            LD      R2, ZERO
            LD      R0, M0
            LD      R1, M1
LOOP        BRz     DONE
            ADD     R2, R2, R0
            ADD     R1, R1, -1
            BRnzp   LOOP
DONE        ST      R2, RESULT
            HALT
RESULT      .FILL   x0000
ZERO        .FILL   x0000
M0          .FILL   x0004
M1          .FILL   x0803
            .END
```

2. What value will be contained in RESULT after the program runs to completion?

7.5 Write a program in LC-2 assembly language that counts the number of 1's in the value stored in R0 and stores the result into R1. For example, if R0 contains 0001001101110000, then after the program executes, the result stored in R1 would be 0000 0000 0000 0110.

7.6 What is the purpose of the .END statement? How does it differ than the HALT instruction?

7.7 The following program fragment has an error in it. Identify the error and explain how to fix it.

```
        ADD     R3, R3, #30
        ST      R3, A
        HALT
A       .FILL   #0
```

Will this error be detected when this code is assembled or when this code is run on the LC-2?

7.8 We want the following program fragment to shift R3 to the left by 4 bits, but it has an error in it. Identify the error and explain how to fix it.

```
          AND     R2, R2, #0
          ADD     R2, R2, #4
LOOP      BRz     DONE
          ADD     R2, R2, #-1
          ADD     R3, R3, R3
          BRnzp   LOOP
DONE      HALT
```

7.9 What does the following program do?

```
          .ORIG   x3000
          AND     R5, R5, #0
          AND     R3, R3, #0
          ADD     R3, R3, #8
          LDI     R1, A
          ADD     R2, R1, #0
AG        ADD     R2, R2, R2
          ADD     R3, R3, #-1
          BRnp    AG
          LD      R4, B
          AND     R1, R1, R4
          NOT     R1, R1
          ADD     R1, R1, #1
          ADD     R2, R2, R1
          BRnp    NO
          ADD     R5, R5, #1
NO        HALT
B         .FILL   xFF00
A         .FILL   x4000
          .END
x         x
```

7.10   1. Assemble the following program:

```
          .ORIG   x3000
          STI     R0, LABEL
          OUT
          HALT
LABEL     .STRINGZ ''%''
          .END
```

2. The programmer intended the program to output a '%' to the monitor, and then halt. Unfortunately, the programmer got confused about what all the opcodes

mean. Replace exactly **one** opcode in the above program with correct opcode, which will then make the program work as intended.

3. The original program from part 1 was executed. However, execution exhibited some very strange behavior. The strange behavior was in part due to the programming error, and in part due to the fact that the value in R0 when the program started executing was x3000. Explain what the strange behavior was and why the program behaved that way.

7.11 The following LC-2 program is assembled. When it is executed, how many times will the instruction at the memory address labeled LOOP execute?

```
        .ORIG   x3005
        LEA     R2, DATA
        LDR     R4, R2, #0
LOOP    ADD     R4, R4, #-3
        BRzp    LOOP
        TRAP    x25
DATA    .FILL   x000B
        .END
```

7.12 Assume a sequence of non-negative integers is stored in consecutive memory locations, one integer per memory location, starting at location x4000. Each integer has a value between 0 and 30,000 (decimal). The sequence terminates with the value -1 (ie., xFFFF).

What does the following program do?

```
            .ORIG   x3000
            AND     R4, R4, #0
            AND     R3, R3, #0
            LD      R0, NUMBERS
LOOP        LDR     R1, R0, #0
            NOT     R2, R1
            BRz     DONE
            AND     R2, R1, #1
            BRz     L1
            ADD     R4, R4, #1
            BRnzp   NEXT
L1          ADD     R3, R3, #1
NEXT        ADD     R0, R0, #1
            BRnzp   LOOP
DONE        TRAP    x25
NUMBERS     .FILL   x4000
            .END
```

7.13 The following LC-2 program compares two character strings of the same length. The source strings are in the .STRINGZ form. The first string starts at memory location FIRST, and the second string starts at memory location SECOND. If the strings are the same, the program terminates with the value 0 in R5. If the strings are different, the program terminates with the value 1 in R5. Fill in the blanks labeled (a), (b) and (c), that will complete the program.

```
             .ORIG   x3000
             LD      R1, FIRST
             LD      R2, SECOND
             AND     R0, R0, #0
      LOOP   --------------   (a)
             LDR     R4, R2, #0
             BRz     NEXT
             ADD     R1, R1, #1
             ADD     R2, R2, #1
             --------------   (b)
             --------------   (c)
             ADD     R3, R3, R4
             BRz     LOOP
             AND     R5, R5, #0
             BRnzp   DONE
      NEXT   AND     R5, R5, #0
             ADD     R5, R5, #1
      DONE   TRAP    x25
      FIRST  .FILL   $4000
      SECOND .FILL   $4100
             .END
```

7.14 The following is a LC-2 program that performs a function. Assume a sequence of integers is stored in consecutive memory locations, one integer per memory location, starting at the location x4000. The sequence terminates with the value x0000.

What does the following program do?

```
      .ORIG   $3000
             LD      R0, NUMBERS
             LD      R2, MASK
      LOOP   LDR     R1, R0, $0
             BRz     DONE
             AND     R5, R1, R2
             BRz     L1
             BRnzp   NEXT
      L1     ADD     R1, R1, R1
             STR     R1, R0, 0
```

```
NEXT      ADD    RO, RO, $1
          BRnzp  LOOP
DONE      HALT
NUMBERS  .FILL   $4000
MASK     .FILL   $8000
         .END
```

7.15 What does the pseudo-op `.FILL xFF004` do? Why?

7.16 Suppose you write two separate assembly language modules that you expect to be combined by the Linker. Each module uses the label AGAIN, and neither module contains the pseudo-op `.EXTERNAL AGAIN`. Is there a problem using the label `AGAIN` in both modules. Why or why not?

7.17 The following code fragment requires a value obtained from a module that was written and assembled separately. We know the location of the value in that module is labeled NOT_HERE. So, we include the pseudo-op `.EXTERNAL` to handle the reference.

Is there anything wrong with this code fragment? Explain.

```
.EXTERNAL  NOT_HERE

  . . .

LD         R2, NOT_HERE

  . . .
```

7.18 1. The LC-2 Assembler must be able to "map" an instruction's mnemonic into its binary opcode. For instance, given an "ADD", it must generate the binary pattern 0001. Write an LC-2 assembly language program which prompts the user to type in an LC-2 Assembly instruction and then displays it's binary opcode. If the assembly instruction is invalid, it displays an error message.

   2. The LC-2 Assembler must also convert constants represented in ASCII into their appropriate binary values. For instance, x2A translates into 101010 and #12 translates into 1100. Write an LC-2 assembly program which reads a decimal or hexadecimal constant from the keyboard (i.e., it's preceded by a '#' character signifying it's a decimal, or 'x' signifying it's HEX) and prints out the binary. Assume the constants are all 1 or 2 digits.

Chapter 8

I/O.

Up to now, we have paid little attention to I/O. We did note (in Chapter 4) that input/output is an important component of the Von Neumann model. There must be a way to get information into the computer in order to process it, and there must be a way to get the result of that processing out of the computer so humans can use it. Figure 4.1 lists a number of different input and output devices.

And we did suggest (in Chapter 5) that input and output can be accomplished by executing the TRAP instruction, which asks the operating system to do it for us. Figure 5.8 illustrates this for input (at address x3002) and for output (at address x3010).

In this chapter, we are ready to do I/O by ourselves.

We have chosen to study the keyboard as our input device and the monitor display as our output device. Not only are they the simplest I/O devices and the most familiar to us, but they have characteristics that allow us to study important concepts about I/O without getting bogged down in unnecessary detail.

8.1 I/O Basics.

8.1.1 Device Registers.

Although we often think of an I/O device as a single entity, interaction with a single I/O device usually means interacting with more than one *device register*. The simplest I/O devices usually have at least two device registers: one to hold the data being transfered between the device and the computer, and one to indicate status information about the device. An example of status information is whether the device is available, or is still busy processing the most recent I/O task.

163

8.1.2 Memory-mapped I/O vs. Special Input/Output Instructions.

An instruction that interacts with an input or output device register must identify the particular input or output device register that it is interacting with. Two schemes are used. Some computers use special input and output instructions. Other computers prefer to use the same data movement instructions that are used to move data in and out of memory.

The Digital Equipment Corporation's PDP-8 is an example of a computer that used special input and output instructions. The 12-bit PDP-8 instruction contained a three-bit opcode. If the opcode was 110, an I/O instruction was indicated. The remaining nine bits of the PDP-8 instruction identified which I/O device register and what operation was to be performed.

Most computer designers prefer not to specify an additional set of instructions for dealing with input and output. They use the same data movement instructions that are used for loading and storing data between memory and the general purpose registers. For example, a load instruction, where the source address is that of an input device register, is an input instruction. Similarly, a store instruction where the destination address is that of an output device register is an output instruction.

Since the same data movement instructions are used as are used for memory, every input device register and every output device register must be uniquely identified in the same way that memory locations are uniquely identified. To do this, each device register is assigned an address from the memory address space of the ISA. That is, the I/O device registers are **mapped** to a set of addresses that are allocated to I/O device registers rather than to memory locations. Hence, the name *memory-mapped I/O*.

The original PDP-11 ISA had a 16-bit address space. All addresses wherein bits[15:13] = 111 were allocated to I/O device registers. That is, of the 2^{16} addresses, only 57,344 corresponded to memory locations. The remaining 2^{13} were memory-mapped I/O addresses.

The LC-2 uses memory-mapped I/O. Table A.1 lists the memory-mapped addresses of all LC-2 device registers.

8.1.3 Asynchronous vs. synchronous.

Most I/O is carried out at speeds very much slower than the speed of the processor. A typist, typing on a keyboard, loads an input device register with one ASCII code every time he/she types a character. A computer can read the contents of that device register every time it executes a load instruction, where the operand address is the memory-mapped address of that input device register.

Many of today's microprocessors execute instructions under the control of a clock that operates well in excess of 300 MHz. Even for a microprocessor operating at only 300 MHz, a clock cycle lasts only 3.3 nanoseconds. Suppose a processor executed one instruction at a time (as the LC-2 does), and it took the processor 10 clock cycles to execute each instruction. At that rate, the processor could read the contents of the input device register once every 33 nanoseconds, **if** it could be supplied at that rate. Unfortunately, people do not type at the rate of 300 million words/minute. Question: If the processor reading characters at the rate of one every 33 nanoseconds can keep up with a typist typing at the rate of 300 million words/minute, what is the maximum average number of characters in a word?

We could mitigate this speed disparity by designing hardware that would accept typed characters at some slower fixed rate. For example, we could design a piece of hardware that accepts one character every 30 million cycles. This would require a typing speed of 100 words/minute, which is certainly doable. Unfortunately, it would also require that the typist work in lockstep with the computer's clock. That is not acceptable since the typing speed (even of the same typist) varies from moment to moment.

What's the point? The point is that I/O devices frequently operate at speeds very different from that of a microprocessor, and not in lock step. This latter characteristic we call *asynchronous.* Most interaction between a processor and I/O is asynchronous. To control processing in an asynchronous world requires some protocol or *handshaking* mechanism. So it is with our keyboard and monitor display. In the case of the keyboard, we will need a one-bit status register, called a flag, to indicate if someone has or has not typed a character. In the case of the monitor, we will need a one-bit status register to indicate whether or not the most recent character sent to the monitor has been displayed.

These flags are the simplest form of *synchronization.* A single flag, called the *Ready* bit, is enough to synchronize the output of the typist who can type characters at the rate of 100 words/minute with the input to a processor which can accept these characters at the rate of 300 million characters/second. Each time the typist types a character, the Ready bit is set. Each time the computer reads a character, it clears the Ready bit. By examining the Ready bit before reading a character, the computer can tell whether it has already read the last character typed. If the Ready bit is clear, no characters have been typed since the last time the computer read a character, and so no additional read would take place. When the computer detects that the Ready bit is set, it could only have been caused by a **new** character being typed, so the computer would know to again read a character.

The single Ready bit provides enough handshaking to ensure that the asynchronous transfer of information between the typist and the microprocessor can be carried out accurately.

If the typist could type at a constant speed, and we did have a piece of hardware that would accept typed characters at precise intervals (for example, one character every 30 million cycles), then we would not need the Ready bit. The computer would simply know, after 30 million cycles of doing other stuff, that the typist had typed exactly one more character, and the computer would read that character. In this hypothetical situation, the typist would be typing in lock step with the processor, and no additional synchronization would be needed. We would say the computer and typist were operating *synchronously,* or the input activity was synchronous.

8.1.4   Interrupt-driven vs. Polling.

The processor, which is computing, and the typist, who is typing, are two separate entities. Each is doing its own thing. Still, they need to interact – that is, the data that is typed has to get into the computer. The issue of *interrupt-driven* vs. *polling* is the issue of who controls the interaction. Does the processor do its own thing until being interrupted by an announcement from the keyboard, "Hey, a key has been struck. The ASCII code is in the input device register. You need to read it." This is called **interrupt-driven** I/O, where the keyboard controls the interaction. Or, does the processor control the interaction, specifically by interrogating (usually, again and again) the Ready bit until it (the processor) detects that the Ready bit is set. At that point the processor knows it is time to read the device register. This second type of interaction is called **polling**, since the Ready bit is polled by the processor, asking if any key has been struck.

Section 8.2.2 describes how the polling method works. Section 8.5 further explains interrupt-driven I/O.

8.2   Input from the Keyboard.

8.2.1   Basic Input Registers (the KBDR and the KBSR).

We have already noted that, in order to handle character input from the keyboard, we need two things: a data register that contains the character to be input, and a synchronization mechanism to let the processor know that input has occurred. The synchronization mechanism is contained in the status register associated with the keyboard.

These two registers are called the Keyboard Data Register (KBDR) and the Keyboard Status Register (KBSR). They are assigned addresses from the memory address space. As shown in Table A.1, KBDR is assigned to xF401. KBSR is assigned to xF400.

Even though a character needs only 8 bits and the synchronization mechanism needs only one bit, it is easier to assign 16 bits (like all memory addresses in the LC-2) to each. In the case of KBDR, bits [7:0] are used for the data, and bits [15:8] contain x00. In the case of KBSR, bit [15] contains the synchronization mechanism, i.e., the Ready bit.

Figure 8.1 shows the two device registers needed by the keyboard. If you look back at the overall structure of the LC-2 Data Path (shown in Figure 5.9), you can see how KBSR and KBDR fit within the overall scheme of things.

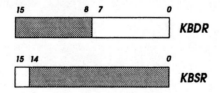

Figure 8.1: Keyboard Device Registers.

8.2.2 The Basic input service routine.

KBSR[15] controls the synchronization of the slow keyboard and the fast processor. When a key on the keyboard is struck, the ASCII code for that key is loaded into KBDR[7:0] and the electronic circuits associated with the keyboard automatically set KBSR[15] to 1. When the LC-2 reads KBDR, the electronic circuits associated with the keyboard automatically clear KBSR[15], allowing another key to be struck. If KBSR[15] = 1, the ASCII code corresponding to the last key struck has not yet been read, and so the keyboard is disabled.

If input-output is controlled by the processor (i.e., via polling), then a program can repeatedly test KBSR[15] until it notes that the bit is set. At that point, the processor can load the ASCII code contained in KBDR into one of the LC-2 registers. Since the processor only loads the ASCII code if KBSR[15] is 1, there is no danger of reading a single typed character multiple times. Furthermore, since the keyboard is disabled until the previous code was read, there is no danger of the processor "missing" characters that were typed. In this way, KBSR[15] provides the mechanism to guarantee that each key typed will be loaded exactly once.

The following input routine loads R0 with the ASCII code that has been entered through the keyboard, and then moves on to the NEXT_TASK in the program.

```
01      START   LDI     R1, A           ; Test for character input
02              BRzp    START
03              LDI     R0, B
04              BR      NEXT_TASK       ; branch to what comes next
05      A       .FILL   xF400           ; Address assigned to KBSR
06      B       .FILL   xF401           ; Address assigned to KBDR
```

As long as KBSR[15] is 0, no key has been struck since the last time the processor read the data register. Lines 01 and 02 comprise a loop that tests bit[15] of KBSR. Note the use of the LDI instruction, which loads R1 with the contents of xF400, the memory-mapped address of KBSR. If the ready bit, bit[15], is clear, BRzp will branch to START, and another iteration of the loop. When someone strikes a key, KBDR will be loaded with the ASCII code of that key and the Ready bit of KBSR will be set. This will cause the branch to fall through, and the instruction at line 03 to be executed. Again, note the use of the LDI instruction, which this time loads R0 with the contents of xF401, the memory-mapped address of KBDR. The input routine is now done, so the program branches unconditionally to its NEXT_TASK.

8.3 Output to the monitor.

8.3.1 Basic Output Registers (the CRTDR and the CRTSR).

Output works in a way very similar to input, with CRTDR and CRTSR replacing the roles of KBDR and KBSR, respectively. The letters CRT are used in deference to the Cathode

Ray Tube, an old electronic device used in monitor displays. In the LC-2, CRTDR is assigned address xF3FF. CRTSR is assigned address xF3FC.

As is the case with input, even though an output character needs only 8 bits and the synchronization mechanism needs only one bit, it is easier to assign 16 bits (like all memory addresses in the LC-2) to each output device register. In the case of CRTDR, bits[7:0] are used for data, and bits[15:8] contain x00. In the case of CRTSR, bit[15] contains the synchronization mechanism, i.e., the Ready bit.

Figure 8.2 shows the two device registers needed by the monitor. Figure 5.9 shows how CRTSR and CRTDR fit within the overall structure of the LC-2 Data Path.

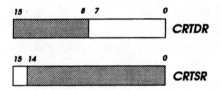

Figure 8.2: Monitor Device Registers.

8.3.2   The Basic output service routine.

CRTSR[15] controls the synchronization of the fast processor and the slow monitor display. When the LC-2 transfers an ASCII code to CRTDR[7:0] for outputting, the electronics of the monitor automatically clear CRTSR[15] as the processing of the contents of CRTDR[7:0] begins.   When the monitor finishes processing the character on the screen, it (the monitor) automatically sets CRTSR[15]. This is a signal to the processor that it (the processor) can transfer another ASCII code to CRTDR for outputting. As long as CRTSR[15] is clear, the monitor is still processing the previous character, so the monitor is disabled as far as additional output from the processor is concerned.

If input-output is controlled by the processor (i.e., via polling), then a program can repeatedly test CRTSR[15] until it notes that the bit is set, indicating that it is okay to write a character to the screen. At that point, the processor can store the ASCII code for the character it wishes to write into CRTDR[7:0], setting up the transfer of that character to the monitor's display.

The following routine causes the ASCII code contained in R0 to be displayed on the monitor:

```
01      START   LDI     R1, A           ; Test if output register ready
02              BRzp    START
03              STI     R0, B
04              BR      NEXT_TASK
05      A       .FILL   xF3FC           ; Address assigned to the CRTSR
06      B       .FILL   xF3FF           ; Address assigned to the CRTDR
```

Like the routine for KBDR and KBSR in Section 8.2.2, lines 01 and 02 repeatedly poll CRTSR[15] to see if the monitor electronics is finished yet with the last character shipped by the processor. Note the use of LDI and the indirect access to xF3FC, the memory-mapped address of CRTSR. As long as CRT[15] is clear, the monitor electronics is still processing this character, and BRzp branches to START for another iteration of the loop. When the monitor electronics finishes with the last character shipped by the processor, it automatically sets CRTSR[15] to 1, which causes the branch to fall through, and the instruction at line 03 to be executed. Note the use of the STI instruction, which stores R0 into xF3FF, the memory-mapped address of CRTDR. The write to CRTDR also clears CRTSR[15], disabling for the moment CRTDR from further output. The monitor electronics takes over and writes the character to the screen. Since the output routine is now done, the program unconditionally branches (line 04) to its NEXT_TASK.

8.3.3   Example: Keyboard Echo.

When typing at the keyboard, it is desirable to know exactly what characters one has typed. We can get this "echo" capability easily (without any sophisticated electronics) by simply combining the above two routines, as shown below. The key typed at the keyboard is displayed on the monitor.

```
        START   LDI     R1, KBSR        ; Test for character input
                BRzp    START
                LDI     R0, KBDR
        ECHO    LDI     R1, CRTSR       ; Test output register ready
                BRzp    ECHO
                STI     R0, CRTDR
                BR      NEXT_TASK
        KBSR    .FILL   xF400           ; Address assigned to the KBSR
        KBDR    .FILL   xF401           ; Address assigned to the KBDR
        CRTSR   .FILL   xF3FC           ; Address assigned to the CRTSR
        CRTDR   .FILL   xF3FF           ; Address assigned to the CRTDR
```

8.4   A more sophisticated input routine.

In the example of Section 8.2.2, the input routine would be a part of a program being executed by the computer. Presumably, the program requires character input from the keyboard. But how does the person sitting at the keyboard know when to type a character! Sitting there, the person may wonder whether or not the program is actually running, or if perhaps the computer is busy off doing something else.

To let the person sitting at the keyboard know that the program is waiting for input from the keyboard, the computer typically prints a message on the monitor. Such a message is often referred to as a *prompt*. The symbol that is displayed by your operating system (for example, % or **C:**) or by your editor (for example, :) are examples of prompts.

The program fragment shown in Figure 8.3 obtains keyboard input via polling as we have shown in Section 8.2.2 already, and also includes a prompt to let the person sitting at the keyboard know when it is time to type a key. Let's examine this program fragment in parts.

You are already familiar with lines 13 through 19 and lines 25 through 28, which correspond to the code in Section 8.3.3 for inputting a character via the keyboard and echoing it on the monitor.

Lines 01 through 03, lines 1D through 1F, and lines 22 through 24 recognize that this input routine needs to use general purpose registers R1,R2, and R3. Unfortunately, they most likely contain values that will still be needed after this routine has finished. In order to not lose those values, the ST instructions in lines 01 through 03 saves them in memory locations SaveR1, SaveR2, and SaveR3, before the input routine starts its business. These three memory locations have been allocated by the .FILL pseudo-ops in lines 22 through 24. After the input routine is finished, and before the program branches unconditionally to its NEXT_TASK (line 20), the LD instructions in lines 1D through 1F. restore them to their rightful locations in R1, R2, and R3.

This leaves lines 05 through 08, 0A through 11, 1A through 1C, 29 and 2A. These lines serve to alert the person sitting at the keyboard that it is time to type a character.

Lines 05 through 08 write the ASCII code x0A to the monitor. This is the ASCII code for a *Newline*. Most ASCII codes correspond to characters that are visible on the screen. A few, like x0A are control characters. They cause an action to occur. Specifically, the ASCII code x0A causes the cursor to move to the far left of the next line on the screen. Thus the name "Newline." Before attempting to write x0A, however, as is always the case, CRTSR[15] is tested (line 6) to see if CRTDR can accept a character. If CRTSR[15] is clear, the monitor is busy, and the loop (lines 06 and 07) is repeated. When CRTSR[15] is 1, the conditional branch (line 7) is not taken, and x0A is written to CRTDR for outputting (line 8).

Lines 0A through 11 cause the actual prompt `Input a character>` to be written to the screen. The prompt is specified by the **.STRINGZ** pseudo-op on line 2A, and is stored in 19 memory locations – eighteen ASCII codes, one per memory location, corresponding to the 18 characters in the prompt, and the terminating sentinel x0000.

Line 0C iteratively tests to see if the end of the string has been reached (by detecting x0000), and if not, once CRTDR is free, line 0F writes the next character in the input prompt into CRTDR. When x0000 is detected, the program knows that the input prompt has been written to the screen, and branches to the code that handles the actual keyboard input (starting at line 13).

After the person at the keyboard has typed a character, and it has been echoed, (lines 13 to 19), the program writes one more newline (lines 1A through 1C) before branching to its NEXT_TASK.

```
01        START   ST      R1,SaveR1       ; Save registers needed by this routine
02                ST      R2,SaveR2
03                ST      R3,SaveR3
04        ;
05                LD      R2,Newline
06        L1      LDI     R3,CRTSR
07                BRzp    L1              ; Loop until the Monitor is ready
08                STI     R2,CRTDR        ; Move cursor to new clean line
09        ;
0A                LEA     R1,Prompt       ; Prompt is starting address of prompt string
0B        Loop    LDR     R0,R1,#0        ; Write the input prompt
0C                BRz     Input           ; End of prompt string
0D        L2      LDI     R3,CRTSR
0E                BRzp    L2              ; Loop until the Monitor is ready
0F                STI     R0,CRTDR        ; Write next character of prompt string
10                ADD     R1,R1,#1        ; Increment Prompt pointer
11                BR      Loop            ; Get the next character in the prompt
12        ;
13        Input   LDI     R3,KBSR         ;
14                BRzp    Input           ; Poll until a character is typed
15                LDI     R0,KBDR         ; Load input character into R0
16        L3      LDI     R3,CRTSR
17                BRzp    L3              ; Loop until the Monitor is ready
18                STI     R0,CRTDR        ; Echo input character to the monitor
19        ;
1A        L4      LDI     R3,CRTSR
1B                BRzp    L4              ; Loop until the Monitor is ready
1C                STI     R2,CRTDR        ; Move cursor to new clean line
1D                LD      R1,SaveR1       ; Restore registers to orinal values
1E                LD      R2,SaveR2
1F                LD      R3,SaveR3
20                BR      NEXT_TASK       ; Do the next task of your program
21        ;
22        SaveR1  .FILL   x0000           ; Allocated space for registers saved
23        SaveR2  .FILL   x0000
24        SaveR3  .FILL   x0000
25        CRTSR   .FILL   xF3FC
26        CRTDR   .FILL   xF3FF
27        KBSR    .FILL   xF400
28        KBDR    .FILL   xF401
29        Newline .FILL   x000A           ; ASCII code for newline
2A        Prompt  .STRINGZ "Input a character>"
```

Figure 8.3: The Input Routine for the LC-2 Keyboard

8.5   Interrupt driven I/O.

In Section 8.1.4, we noted that interaction between the processor and an I/O device can be controlled by the processor (i.e., polling) or it can be controlled by the I/O device (i.e., interrupt-driven). In Sections 8.2, 8.3, and 8.4, we have seen several examples of polling. In each case, the processor tested the Ready bit of the status register, and when it was "1," the processor branched to the instruction that did the input or output operation.

We will not study interrupt-driven I/O in this book in detail. However, we will explain the fundamental enabling mechanism. Two elements: are required:

Element 1: a signal from the I/O device indicating that it is ready.

Element 2: a test by the processor during each instruction cycle to see if such a signal is present.

If both elements are present, and the executing program so desires, the program does not need to spin its wheels while it again and again checks to see if the Ready bit is set. Instead, the processor can ignore the I/O device and do whatever processing it needs to, until the I/O device lets the processor know that it is ready for interaction. In fact, that is precisely the advantage of interrupt-driven I/O: the processor does not waste time testing the Ready bit, but is instead free to do other useful work until being informed by the I/O device that there is I/O activity to deal with.

8.5.1   Element 1: The Interrupt Signal.

First, the signal from the I/O device indicates that it is ready for interaction with the processor. If the I/O device is the keyboard, it is ready if someone has typed a character. If the I/O device is the monitor, it is ready if the associated electronic circuits have successfully completed the display of the last character. In both cases, the I/O device is ready when the corresponding Ready bit is set.

In most I/O devices, the Status Register, in addition to the Ready bit, has an Interrupt Enable (IE) bit, shown as bit[14] in Figure 8.4. The **signal from the I/O device** referred to as "element 1" is the logical AND of the IE bit and the Ready bit. It is also shown in Figure 8.4.

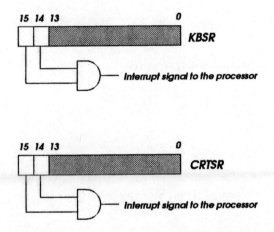

Figure 8.4: Interrupt Enable Bits and their Use.

Note that if bit[14] is clear, it does not matter whether the Ready bit is set, element 1 will not be present, and the I/O device will not be able to interrupt the processor. In that case, the program will have to poll the I/O device to determine if it is ready. Bit[14] can be set or cleared by the processor, depending on whether or not the processor wants polling or interrupt-driven I/O.

If bit[14] is set, then interrupt-driven I/O is enabled. In that case, as soon as someone types a key (or as soon as the monitor has finished processing the last character), bit[15] is set. This in turn asserts the output of the AND gate, causing an interrupt signal to the processor.

8.5.2   Element 2: The Test for Interrupts.

Second, the test to see if the interrupt signal is present. If bit[14] of the relevant Status Register is set, interrupt-driven I/O is enabled. This is implemented by a little additional logic to the control unit of the processor. Recall in Chapter 4 that the instruction cycle sequences through the six phases of FETCH, DECODE, EVALUATE ADDRESS, FETCH OPERAND, EXECUTE and STORE RESULT. Recall further that we said that after the sixth phase, the control unit returns to the first phase, i.e., the FETCH of the next instruction.

The additional logic to test for the interrupt signal is to replace that last sequential step of **always** going from STORE RESULT back to FETCH, as follows. The STORE RESULT phase is instead accompanied by a test for the interrupt signal. If the interrupt signal is asserted, then the control unit will not return to the FETCH phase. Instead, it will initiate the execution of a program fragment to carry out the requirements of the I/O device. How it does that is one more thing we will have to leave for some future semester. If the interrupt signal is not asserted, then it is business as usual, with the control unit returning to the FETCH phase to start processing the next instruction.

8.6 Exercises.

8.1 1. What is a device register?

  2. What is a device data register?

  3. What is a device status register?

8.2 Why is a ready bit not needed if synchronous I/O is used?

8.3 In Section 8.1.1, the statement is made that a typist would have to type at the rate of 3 billion words/minute in order to provide input to a 300 MHz processor at the maximum rate the microprocessor can accept it. This statement makes an assumption about the size of a word. What is that assumption?

8.4 State whether the following interactions are synchronous or asynchronous.

  1. Between a remote control and a television set.

  2. Between the mailman and you, via a mailbox.

  3. Between a mouse and your PC.

8.5 What is the purpose of bit 15 in the KBSR?

8.6 What problem is likely to occur if a program does not check the ready bit of the KBSR before reading the KBDR?

8.7 Which of the following combinations fit the system described in Section 8.2.2?

  1. memory mapped and interrupt driven

  2. memory mapped and polling

  3. special opcode for I/O and interrupt driven

  4. special opcode for I/O and polling

Do any of these combinations not work together? If no, why not?

8.8 Write a program that checks the initial value in memory location x4000 to see if it is a valid ASCII code and if it is a valid ASCII code, prints the character. If the value in x4000 is not a valid ASCII code, the program prints nothing.

8.9 What problem is likely to occur if the keyboard hardware doesn't check the KBSR before writing to the KBDR?

8.10 What problem is likely to occur if the CRT output hardware doesn't check the CRTSR before writing to the screen?

8.11 Some computer engineering students decided to revise the LC-2 for their senior project. In designing the LC-3, they decided to conserve on device registers by combining the KBSR and the CRTSR into one status register: the IOSR (the Input/Output Status register). IOSR[15] is the Keyboard device ready bit and IOSR[14] is the CRT device ready bit. What are the implications for programs wishing to do I/O? Is this a poor design decision?

8.12 Adam H. decided to design a variant of the LC-2 that didn't need a Keyboard Status Register. Instead, he created a readable/writable Keyboard Data and Status Register(KBDSR) which contains the same data as the KBDR. With the KBDSR, a program requiring keyboard input would wait until a non-zero value appeared in the KBDSR. The non-zero value would be the ASCII value of the last key-press. Then the program would write a zero into the KBDSR indicating that it had read the key-press. The following is a modified version of the basic input service routine:

```
            AND    R1, R1, #0     ; Initialize R1 to 0
    IN_LOOP LDI    R0, KBDSR
            BRz    IN_LOOP        ; Wait until KBDSR is non-zero
            STI    R1, KBDSR      ; Clear KBDSR.  R0 has ASCII of key-press
            BR     NEXT_TASK      ; Branch to what comes next
    KBDSR   .FILL xF400           ; Address assigned to KBDSR
```

There are at least two serious flaws with this design. Identify them.

8.13 Is interrupt driven I/O more or less efficient than polling?

Chapter 9

TRAP Routines and Subroutines.

9.1 LC-2 TRAP routines.

9.1.1 Introduction.

Recall Figure 8.3 of the previous chapter. In order to successfully have the program obtain input from the keyboard, it was necessary for the programmer (in chapter 8) to know several things:

> 1: the hardware data registers for both the keyboard and the monitor: the monitor so a prompt could be displayed, and the keyboard, so the program would know where to look for the input character,

> 2: the hardware status registers for both the keyboard and the monitor: the monitor so the program would know when it was okay to display another character in the input prompt, and the keyboard so the program would know when someone had struck a key, and

> 3: the asynchronous nature of keyboard input relative to the executing program.

This is beyond the knowledge of most application programmers. In fact, in the real world, if application programmers (or user programmers, as they are sometimes called) had to understand I/O at this level, there would be much less I/O and far fewer programmers in the business.

In addition, there is another problem with allowing user programs to perform I/O activity for themselves. I/O activity involves the use of device registers that are shared by many programs. This means that if a user programmer were allowed to access the hardware registers, and he/she messed up, it could create havoc for **other** user programs. Thus, it is ill-advised to give user programmers access to these registers. We say the hardware

177

registers are **privileged** and not accessible to programs that do not have the proper degree of *privilege*.

The notion of "privilege" introduces a pretty big can of worms. Unfortunately, we can't do much more than mention it here, and leave it for later courses to give it serious treatment. For now, we simply note that there are resources that are not accessible to the user program, and that access to those resources is controlled by endowing some programs with sufficient privilege and other programs without. Having said that, we move on to our problem at hand, a "better" solution for user programs that require I/O.

The simpler solution as well as the safer solution to the problem of user programs requiring I/O involves the TRAP instruction and the operating system (which does have the proper degree of privilege). We saw its use in Chapter 5. The user program gets the operating system to do the job by invoking the TRAP instruction. That way, the user program does not have to know the gory details mentioned above, and other user programs are protected from the consequences of misguided user programmers.

Figure 9.1 shows a user program that, upon reaching location 1000, needs an I/O task performed. The user program requests the operating system to perform the task in behalf of the user program. The operating system takes control of the machine, handles the request specified by the TRAP instruction, and then returns control back to the user program. We often refer to the request made by the user program as a *service call* or a *system call*.

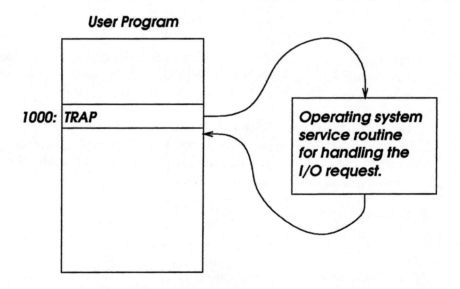

Figure 9.1: Invoking an OS Service Routine by means of the TRAP Instruction.

9.1.2   The TRAP mechanism.

The TRAP mechanism involves several elements.

1: A set of service routines executed on behalf of user programs by the operating system. These are part of the operating system, and start at arbitrary addresses in memory. The LC-2 was designed so that up to 256 service routines can be specified.

2: A table of the starting addresses of these 256 service routines. This table is stored in the first 256 addresses in memory (locations x0000 to x00FF). The table is referred to by various companies by various names. One company calls this table the System Control Block. Another company calls it the Interrupt Vector Table. Figure 9.2 provides a snapshot of the System Control Block of the LC-2, with specific starting addresses highlighted, among them the keyboard input service routine (location x04A0), the character output service routine (location x0430) and the machine halt service routine (location xFD70). Note that, for example, the starting address of the keyboard input service routine (location x04A0) is contained in location x0023.

3: The TRAP instruction. When a user program wishes to have the operating system take control of the computer, execute a specific service routine on behalf of the user program, and then return control back to the user program, the user program uses the TRAP instruction.

4: The RET instruction. The RET instruction provides the mechanism for the operating system to return control back to the user program.

x0000	
x0001	
:	:
x0021	x0430
x0022	x0450
x0023	x04A0
x0024	x04E0
x0025	xFD70
:	:

Figure 9.2: The System Control Block.

9.1.3   The TRAP instruction.

The TRAP instruction causes the service routine to execute by doing two things:

* it changes the PC to the starting address of the relevant service routine on the basis of its trap vector (to be explained), and

* it provides a way back (a linkage) to the program that initiated the TRAP instruction.

The TRAP instruction works as follows. The TRAP instruction is made up of two parts: the TRAP opcode 1111, and the trap vector (bits[7:0]). Bits [11:8] must be zero. The trap vector identifies the service routine the user program wants the operating system to perform. In the example below, the trap vector is x23.

15	14	13	12	11	10	9	8	7	6	5	4	3	2	1	0
1	1	1	1	0	0	0	0	0	0	1	0	0	0	1	1

TRAP   trapvector

During the EXECUTE phase of the instruction cycle, the trap vector is zero-extended to 16 bits to form an address. In the above case, that address is x0023. The contents at that address, in this case x04A0 (see Figure 9.2), are loaded into the PC. Location x04A0 is the starting address of the TRAP routine to input a character from the keyboard. We say the trap vector "points" to the starting address of the TRAP routine. Thus, TRAP x23 causes the operating system to start executing the keyboard input service routine.

In order to return to the instruction following the TRAP instruction in the user program (after the service routine has completed), there must be some mechanism for saving the address of that next instruction in the user program. The TRAP instruction provides the linkage back by storing the PC in R7 before loading the PC with the starting address of the service routine. This occurs during the EXECUTE phase of the TRAP instruction, so the PC has already been updated (in the FETCH phase) to point to the instruction following the TRAP instruction.

9.1.4   The RET instruction.

The RET instruction is a zero-operand instruction. It consists of the opcode 1101, and no operands. Bits [11:0] of the RET instruction must be zero. The RET instruction is shown below.

15	14	13	12	11	10	9	8	7	6	5	4	3	2	1	0
1	1	0	1	0	0	0	0	0	0	0	0	0	0	0	0

RET

During the EXECUTE phase of the RET instruction, the PC is loaded with the contents of R7. If R7 is not changed during the TRAP routine (i.e., during the time since the TRAP instruction executed), control of the computer will return to the program at the instruction following the TRAP instruction that initiated the service routine.

Figure 9.3 shows how the LC-2 uses the TRAP instruction and the RET instruction to implement the example of Fig. 9.1. The flow of control goes from (A) within a user program that needs a character input from the keyboard, to (B) the operating system service routine that performs that task in behalf of the user program, back to the user program (C) that presumably uses the information contained in the input character.

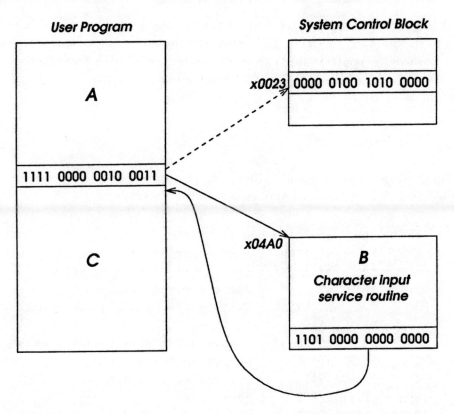

Figure 9.3: Flow of Control from a User Program to an OS Service Routine and Back.

Recall that the computer continually executes its instruction cycle (FETCH, DECODE, etc.) so that the way to change the flow of control is to change the contents of the PC. In that way, the next FETCH will be at a redirected address.

Thus, to request the character input service routine, the TRAP instruction, with trap vector x23, is used. Execution of that instruction causes the contents of memory location x0023 (which in this case contains x04A0) to be loaded into the PC, and the address of the instruction following the TRAP instruction to be loaded into R7. The dashed lines on Figure 9.3 show the use of the trap vector to obtain the starting address of the trap service routine from the System Control Block.

The next instruction cycle starts with the FETCH of the contents of x04A0, which is the first instruction of the operating system service routine that requests (and accepts) keyboard input. That service routine, as we will see momentarily, is patterned after the keyboard input routine we studied in Section 8.4. Recall that upon completion of that input routine (see Figure 8.3), R0 contains the ASCII code of the key that was typed.

The TRAP service routine executes to completion, ending with the RET instruction. Execution of the RET instruction loads the PC with the contents of R7. If R7 was not changed during execution of the service routine, this would be the address of the instruction following the TRAP instruction in the initiating user program. Thus, the user program resumes execution, with R0 containing the ASCII code of the keyboard character that was typed.

If R7 had been changed during execution of the service routine, we would have a problem returning to the initiating program. To be sure nothing destroys the linkage to the initiating program, we save the contents of R7 in some memory location before starting the service routine. We restore that value to R7 after completing the service routine and just before executing the RET instruction.

9.1.5 An example.

The following program is provided to illustrate the use of the TRAP instruction. It can also be used to amuse the average four-year-old.

```
01              .ORIG x3000
02              LD    R2,TERM   ; Load negative of terminating character
03              LD    R3,ASCII  ; Load ASCII difference x0020
04      AGAIN   TRAP  x23       ; Request keyboard input
05              ADD   R1,R2,R0  ; Test for terminating character
06              BRz   EXIT
07              ADD   R0,R0,R3  ; Change upper case to lower case
08              TRAP  x21       ; Output to the monitor
09              BRnzp AGAIN     ; ... and do it again!
0A      TERM    .FILL xFFC9     ; FFC9 = -7
0B      ASCII   .FILL x0020
0C      EXIT    TRAP  x25       ; Halt
```

The idea of the program is as follows. A person is sitting at the keyboard. Each time the person types a capital letter, the program outputs the lower case version of that letter. If the person types a "7," the program terminates.

The program executes as follows: The program first loads constants xFFC9 and x0020 into R2 and R3. The constant xFFC9, which is the negative of the ASCII code for 7, is used to test the character typed at the keyboard. The constant x0020 is the zero-extended difference between the ASCII code for a capital letter and the ASCII code for that letter's lower case representation. For example, the ASCII code for "A" is x41; the ASCII code for "a" is x61. The ASCII codes for "Z" and "z" are x5A and x7A respectively.

Then TRAP x23 is executed, which invokes the keyboard input service routine. When control returns to the applicaton program (at line 05), R0 contains the ASCII code of the character typed. The ADD and BRz instructions test for the terminating character "7." If the character typed is not a "7," the ASCII upper case/lower case difference is added to the character, storing the result in R0, and a TRAP to the monitor output service routine is called. This causes the lower case representation of the same letter to be displayed on the monitor. When control returns to the application program (this time at line 09), an unconditional BR to AGAIN is executed, and another request for keyboard input.

Before leaving this example, we note that correct operation of the program assumes that the person sitting at the keyboard only types capital letters and the value "7." What if the person types a "$"? A "better" program would be one that tests the character typed to be sure it really is a capital letter from among the 26 capital letters in the alphabet, and if it is not, takes corrective action. Question: Augment the above program to add that test for bad data. That is, write a program that will type the lower case representation of any capital letter typed, and will terminate if anything other than a capital letter is typed.

9.1.6 TRAP routines for handling I/O.

Using the constructs described above, the input routine described in Figure 8.3 can be slightly modified to be the input service routine shown in Figure 9.4. There are three changes. (1) We add the appropriate .ORIG pseudo-op, which corresponds to the starting address found at location x0023 in the System Control Block, and the terminating .END pseudo-op. (2) We save and restore R7, which contains the linkage back to the initiating program. And, (3) we terminate the input routine with the RET instruction, rather than the BR NEXT_TASK, as is done in Figure 8.3, since this service routine is invoked by means of the TRAP x23 instruction, rather than as part of the user program.

The output routine of Section 8.3.2 can be modified in a similar way, as shown in Figure 9.5.

The results are input (Figure 9.4) and output (Figure 9.5) service routines that can be invoked simply and safely by the TRAP instruction with the appropriate trap vector. In the case of input, upon completion of TRAP x23, R0 contains the ASCII code of the keyboard character typed. In the case of output, the initiating program must load R0 with the ASCII code of the character it wishes displayed on the monitor before invoking TRAP x21.

9.1.7 TRAP routine for halting the computer.

Recall in Section 4.4, we discussed the RUN latch that is ANDed with the crystal oscillator to produce the clock that controls the operation of the computer. We noted that if that one-bit latch was cleared, the output of the AND gate would be 0, stopping the clock.

Years ago, most ISAs had a HALT instruction for stopping the clock. Given how infrequently that instruction is executed, it seems wasteful to devote an opcode for it. In many

```
        ;   Service Routine for Keyboard Input
        ;
                .ORIG   x04A0
        START   ST      R7,SaveR7       ; Save the linkage back to the program.
                ST      R1,SaveR1       ; Save the values in the registers
                ST      R2,SaveR2       ; that are needed to use so that they
                ST      R3,SaveR3       ; can be restored before RET
        ;
                LD      R2,Newline
        L1      LDI     R3,CRTSR        ; Check CRTDR --  is it free?
                BRzp    L1
                STI     R2,CRTDR        ; Move cursor to new clean line
        ;
                LEA     R1,Prompt       ; Prompt is starting address
                                        ; of prompt string
        Loop    LDR     R0,R1,#0        ; Get next prompt character
                BRz     Input           ; Check for end of prompt string
        L2      LDI     R3,CRTSR
                BRzp    L2
                STI     R0,CRTDR        ; Write next character of
                                        ; prompt string
                ADD     R1,R1,#1        ; Increment Prompt pointer
                BRnzp   Loop
        ;
```

Figure 9.4: Character input service routine.

```
Input   LDI     R3,KBSR         ; Has a character beenn typed?
        BRzp    Input
        LDI     R0,KBDR         ; Load it into R0
L3      LDI     R3,CRTSR
        BRzp    L3
        STI     R0,CRTDR        ; Echo input character
                                ; to the monitor
;
L4      LDI     R3,CRTSR
        BRzp    L4
        STI     R2,CRTDR        ; Move cursor to new clean line

        LD      R1,SaveR1       ; Service routine done, restore
        LD      R2,SaveR2       ; original values in registers.
        LD      R3,SaveR3
        LD      R7,SaveR7       ; Restore linkage back prior to RET
        RET                     ; Return to calling program
;
SaveR7  .FILL   x0000           ; Location set aside for saving R7
SaveR1  .FILL   x0000
SaveR2  .FILL   x0000
SaveR3  .FILL   x0000
CRTSR   .FILL   xF3FC
CRTDR   .FILL   xF3FF
KBSR    .FILL   xF400
KBDR    .FILL   xF401
Newline .FILL   x000A           ; ASCII code for newline
Prompt  .STRINGZ "Input a character>"
        .END
```

Figure 9.4: Character input service routine, continued.

```
                    .ORIG   x0430           ; System call starting address
                    ST      R7, SaveR7      ; Save R7 so we can RET
                                            ; at the bottom
                    ST      R1, SaveR1      ; R1 will be used to poll the CRT
                                            ; hardware
; Write the character
TryWrite            LDI     R1, CRTSR       ; Get status
                    BRzp    TryWrite        ; Bit 15 on says CRT is ready
WriteIt             STI     R0, CRTDR       ; Write character

; return from trap
Return              LD      R1, SaveR1      ; Restore registers
                    LD      R7, SaveR7      ; Restore jump return R7
                    RET                     ; Return from trap

CRTSR               .FILL   xF3FC           ; Address of CRT status register
CRTDR               .FILL   xF3FF           ; Address of CRT data register
SaveR1              .FILL   x0000
SaveR7              .FILL   x0000
                    .END
```

Figure 9.5: Character output service routine

modern computers, the RUN latch is cleared by a TRAP routine. In the LC-2, the RUN latch is bit[15] of memory-mapped location xFFFF. Figure 9.6 shows the TRAP service routine for halting the processor; that is, for stopping the clock.

First, registers R7, R1 and R0 are saved – R7 because it contains the linkage back to the running program, and R1, R0 because they are needed by the service routine. Then (lines 08 through 0D), the banner **Halting the machine** is displayed on the monitor. Finally (lines 11 through 14), the RUN latch (MCR[15]) is cleared by ANDing the MCR with 0111111111111111. That is MCR[14:0] remains unchanged, but MCR[15] is cleared.

Question: What instruction (or TRAP service routine) starts the clock?

Table A.3 contains a complete list of the operating system service routines available via the TRAP instruction on the LC-2.

```
01                      .ORIG   xFD70           ; where this routine resides
02              ST      R7, SaveR7       ; save R7 for subsequent  RET
03              ST      R1, SaveR1       ; R1: a temp for MC register
04              ST      R0, SaveR0       ; R0 is used as working space
05
06      ; print message that machine is halting
07
08              LD      R0, ASCIINewLine
09              TRAP    x21
0A              LEA     R0, Message
0B              TRAP    x22
0C              LD      R0, ASCIINewLine
0D              TRAP    x21
0E
0F      ; clear bit 15 at $FFFF to stop the machine
10
11              LDI     R1, MCR          ; load MC register into R1
12              LD      R0, MASK         ; R0 = $7FFF
13              AND     R0, R1, R0       ; mask to clear the top bit
14              STI     R0, MCR          ; store R0 into MC register
15
16      ; return from HALT routine.  Make sure you understand how this works...
17      ; (how can this routine return if the machine is halted above?)
18      ;
19              LD      R1, SaveR1       ; restore registers
1A              LD      R0, SaveR0
1B              LD      R7, SaveR7       ; restore trap return
1C              RET
1D
1E      ; Some constants
1F
20      ASCIINewLine    .FILL   x000A
21      SaveR0          .FILL   x0000
22      SaveR1          .FILL   x0000
23      SaveR7          .FILL   x0000
24      Message         .FILL   "Halting the machine."
25      MCR             .FILL   xFFFF    ; location of machine control register
26      MASK            .FILL   x7FFF    ; mask to clear the top bit
27                      .END
```

Figure 9.6: Halt service routine for the LC-2.

9.1.8 Saving and Restoring Registers.

One item we have mentioned in passing that we should emphasize more explicitly is the need to save the value in a register if

> (a) its value will be destroyed by some subsequent action, and

> (b) we will need to use the value after that subsequent action.

Consider the following example: Suppose we want to input from the keyboard ten decimal digits, convert their ASCII codes into their binary representations, and store the binary values in ten successive memory locations, starting at the address Binary. We write the following program fragment to do the job:

```
                         ...

01                       LEA    R3,Binary
02                       LD     R6,ASCII   ; ASCII template for line 05
03                       LD     R7,COUNT   ; Initialize COUNT to 10.
04          AGAIN        TRAP   x23        ; Get keyboard input.
05                       ADD    R0,R0,R6   ; Strip ASCII template
06                       STR    R0,R3,#0   ; Store binary digit.
07                       ADD    R3,R3,#1   ; Increment pointer to storage.
08                       ADD    R7,R7,#-1  ; Decrement COUNT.
09                       BRp    AGAIN      ; Still more characters to input.
0A                       BRnzp  NEXT_TASK  ;
0B          ASCII        .FILL  xFFD0      ; negative of x0030.
0C          COUNT        .FILL  #10
0D          Binary       .BLKW  #10
                         ...
```

The first step in the program fragment is initialization. We load R6 with the negative of the ASCII template, in order to easily subtract x0030 from each ASCII code. We load R7 with ten, the initial count. Then we execute the loop ten times, each time getting a character from the keyboard, stripping away the ASCII template, storing the binary result, and testing if we are done.

Only the program does not work! Why?

Answer: The TRAP instruction in line 04 wiped out the value ten that was loaded into R7 in line 03. Therefore, the instructions in lines 09 and 0A did not do what they thought they were doing!

Exercise: What will the program fragment in lines 01 to 0D do?

The problem is that the TRAP instruction, in addition to loading the PC with the starting address of the service routine, **also** stores in R7 the linkage back to the initiating program.

And, because we needed the value we had put in R7 before the TRAP instruction, our program executed incorrectly.

The message is: If a value in a register will be needed after something else is stored in that register, we must *save* it before the something else happens and *restore* it before we can subsequently use it. We save a register value by storing it in memory; we restore it by loading it back into the register. In Figure 9.6, line 02 contains the ST instruction that saves R7, line 1B contains the LD instruction that restores R7, and line 23 sets aside the location in memory for storing R7.

The save/restore problem can be handled either by the initiating program before the TRAP occurs, or by the called program (for example, the service routine) after the TRAP executes. We will see in Section 9.2 that the exact same problem exists for another class of calling/called programs, the subroutine mechanism. But, we will get to that in Section 9.2.

We use the term *caller-save* if the calling program handles the problem. We use the term *callee-save* if the called program handles the problem. The appropriate one to handle the problem is the one that knows which registers will be destroyed by subsequent actions.

The callee knows which registers it needs to do its job. Therefore, before it starts, it saves those registers with a sequence of stores. After it finishes, it restores those registers with a sequence of loads. And it sets aside locations to save those register values. In Figure 9.6, the HALT routine needs R0 and R1. So, it saves their values with ST instructions in lines 03 and 04, restores their values with LD instructions in lines 19 and 1A, and sets aside locations for these values in lines 21 and 22.

The caller knows what damage will be done by instructions under its control. Again, in Figure 9.6, the caller knows that each instance of the TRAP instruction will destroy what is in R7. So, before the HALT instruction even starts, it saves R7, and before it finishes, it restores R7.

9.2 Subroutine calls/returns.

We have just seen how a programmer's productivity can be enhanced if he/she does not have to learn details of the I/O hardware, but can rely instead on the operating system to supply the program fragments needed to perform those tasks. And, we also mentioned in passing that it is kind of nice to have the operating system access these device registers so we don't have to be at the mercy of some other user programmer.

We have seen that a request for the service routine is invoked in the user program by the TRAP instruction, and handled by the operating system. Return to the initiating program is obtained via the RET instruction.

It is often useful to be able to invoke a program fragment multiple times within the same program, without having to retype the program fragment in the source code each time. In addition, it is sometimes the case that one person writes a program that requires such fragments and another person writes the fragments.

Finally, one might require a fragment that has been supplied by the manufacturer as part of the operating system. It is almost always the case that the operating system includes collections of such fragments in order to free the programmer from having to write his/her own. These collections are referred to as *libraries*. An example is the *Math Library*, which consists of fragments to execute such functions as **square root, sine,** and **arctangent**.

Such a program fragment is called a *subroutine* (or alternatively, a *procedure*), or in C terminology, a *function*.

9.2.1 The JSR/RET mechanism.

Figure 9.4 provides a simple illustration of a fragment that must be executed multiple times within the same program. Note the three instructions starting at symbolic address L1. Note also the three instructions starting at address L2, L3, and L4. Each of these four three-instruction sequences do the following:

```
LABEL     LDI     R3,CRTSR
          BRzp    LABEL
          STI     Reg,CRTDR
```

Two of the four program fragments store R0 and the other two store R2, but that is easy to take care of, as we will see. The main point is that, aside from the small nuisance of which register is being stored, the four program fragments do exactly the same thing. The pair of instructions **JSR** and **RET** allows us to execute this one three-instruction sequence multiple times, while requiring us to include it as a subroutine in our program only once.

The JSR instruction acts very much like the TRAP instruction in that it redirects control to a subroutine, while saving a linkage back to the calling program. The PC is loaded with the starting address of the subroutine, while R7 is loaded with the address of the instruction following the JSR instruction in the initiating program. The last instruction in a subroutine is the RET instruction, which loads PC with the contents of R7, thereby returning control to the instruction following the JSR instruction.

An important difference between the JSR instruction and the TRAP instruction, somewhat beyond the scope of this course, is the nature of the routine that the JSR or TRAP instruction is requesting. In the case of the TRAP instruction (as we saw), these routines (called service routines) usually involve hardware resources. Generally, these routines are only available as part of the operating system, which has the required degree of privilege because presumably it knows what it is doing. In the case of the JSR instruction, these routines (called subroutines) are either written by the same programmer who wrote the program containing the JSR instruction, or they are written by a colleague, or they are provided as part of a library. In all cases, they involve resources that can not mess up other people's programs, and so we are not concerned that they are part of a user program.

9.2.2 The JSR and JSRR instructions.

The LC-2 specifies two opcodes for calling subroutines, **JSR** and **JSRR**. The only difference between the two instructions is the addressing mode that is used for evaluating the starting address of the subroutine. JSR evaluates its address in **exactly** the same way that LD and ST do. JSRR evaluates its address in **exactly** the same way that LDR and STR do.

JSR (JMP)

The JSR instruction consists of four parts. Bits[15:12] contain the opcode, 0100. Bits[8:0], as is the case for the LD and ST instructions, contain the pgoffset9, which when concatenated with the page number (PC[15:9]), forms the operand address. In the case of the JSR instruction, this is the starting address of the subroutine. Bit[11], called the L (for **Link**) bit indicates whether the linkage back to the address of the instruction following the JSR instruction will be saved. If bit[11] = 1, that address is saved in R7. If bit[11] = 0, that address is not saved. Bits[10:9] contain zeroes.

If the JSR instruction shown below is stored in location x4200, its execution will cause the PC to be loaded with x43F2, and R7 to be loaded with x4201.

15	14	13	12	11	10	9	8	7	6	5	4	3	2	1	0
0	1	0	0	1	0	0	1	1	1	1	1	0	0	1	0

JSR   L   pgoffset9

In the above instruction, if Bit[11] had contained a 0, R7 would have remained unchanged. The LC-2 Assembly Language distinguishes two instructions, depending on whether the linkage back is saved: JSR and JMP. If Bit[11] = 1, the linkage back is saved in R7 so a subsequent RET instruction can return control to the instruction following the JSR instruction. The Assembly Language notes that feature with the acronym JSR, for **J**ump**S**ub**R**outine. If Bit[11] = 0, the linkage is not saved so the program can not return to the next instruction. The Assembly Language notes that with the acronym **Ju**MP, which stands for unconditional jump.

Question: Is there any other instruction in the LC-2 that carries out **exactly** the function of the JMP instruction?

JSRR (JMPR)

The JSRR instruction is exactly like the JSR instruction, except for the addressing mode. That is, it forms its operand address in the same way the LDR and STR instructions do, rather than the way the LD and ST do. Bits[15:12] contain the opcode 1100, bit[11] contains the L bit, and bits[10:9] contain zeroes.

The starting address of the subroutine is computed by adding ZEXT(bits[5:0]) to the base register (obtained from bits[8:6]).

If R5 contains x3000, and if the **JSRR** instruction shown below is stored in location x420A, its execution will cause the PC to be loaded with x3002, and R7 to be loaded with x420B.

15	14	13	12	11	10	9	8	7	6	5	4	3	2	1	0
1	1	0	0	1	0	0	1	0	1	0	0	0	0	1	0

JSRR	L	BaseR	index6

In the above instruction, if bit[11] had contained a 0, R7 would have remained unchanged. As is the case with JSR and JMP, here too the LC-2 Assembly Language distinguishes two instructions, depending on whether the linkage back is saved: JSRR and JMPR. If Bit[11] = 1, the linkage back is saved in R7 so a subsequent RET instruction can return control to the instruction following the JSRR instruction. If bit[11] = 0, the linkage is not saved so the program has no way to automatically return to the instruction following a JMPR instruction.

Question: What important feature does the JMPR instruction provide that the JMP instruction does not provide?

9.2.3 An example.

Let's look again at the keyboard input service routine of Figure 9.4. In particular, let's look at the three-line sequence that occurs at L1, L2, L3, and L4 :

```
LABEL   LDI     R3,CRTSR
        BRzp    LABEL
        STI     Reg,CRTDR
```

Can the JSR/RET mechanism enable us to replace these four occurrences of the same sequence with a single subroutine. Answer: Yes, **almost.**

Figure 9.7, our "improved" keyboard input service routine, contains

```
        JSR     WriteChar
```

at lines 05, 0B, 11, and 14, and the four-instruction subroutine

```
WriteChar       LDI     R3,CRTSR
                BRzp    WriteChar
                STI     R2,CRTDR
                RET
```

at lines 1D through 20. Note the RET instruction that is needed to terminate the subroutine.

Note the hedging: "almost." In the original sequences starting at L2 and L3, the STI instruction forwards the contents of R0 (not R2) to the CRTDR. We can fix that easily enough, as follows:

In line 09 of Figure 9.7, we use

```
        LDR        R2,R1,#0
```

instead of

```
        LDR        R0,R1,#0.
```

This causes each character in the prompt to be loaded into R2. The subroutine Writechar forwards it from R2 to the CRTDR.

In line 10 of Figure 9.7, we insert the instruction

```
        ADD        R2,R0,#0
```

in order to move the keyboard input (which is in R0) into R2. The subroutine Writechar forwards it from R2 to the CRTDR. Note that R0 still contains the keyboard input. Furthermore, since no subsequent instruction in the service routine loads R0, R0 still contains the keyboard input after control returns to the user program.

Finally, in line 13 of Figure 9.7, we insert the instruction

```
        LD     R2,Newline
```

in order to move the "newline" character into R2. The subroutine Writechar forwards it from R2 to the CRTDR.

Figure 9.7 is the actual LC-2 TRAP service routine provided for keyboard input.

9.2.4   Another subroutine: Writing a character string to the monitor.

Before we leave the example of Fig. 9.7, note the code on lines 09 through 0D. This fragment of the service routine is used to write the sequence of characters **Input a character** to the monitor. A sequence of characters is often referred to as a *string of characters* or a *character string*. This fragment is also present in Fig. 9.6, with the result that **Halting the machine** is written to the monitor. In fact, it is so often the case that a user program needs to write a string of characters to the monitor that this function is given its own trap vector in the LC-2 operating system. Thus, if a user program requires a character string to be written to the monitor, it need only provide (in R0) a pointer to the starting address of the character string, and then invoke TRAP x22. In LC-2 Assembler this TRAP is called **PUTS**.

Thus, PUTS (or TRAP x22) causes control to be passed to the operating system, and the procedure shown in Figure 9.8 is executed. Note that PUTS is the code of Lines 09 through 0D, with a few minor adjustments.

```
01                         .ORIG    x04A0
02      START      ST       R7,SaveR7
03                 JSR      SaveReg
04                 LD       R2,Newline
05                 JSR      WriteChar
06                 LEA      R1,PROMPT
07      ;
08      ;
09      Loop       LDR      R2,R1,#0        ; Get next prompt char
0A                 BRz      Input
0B                 JSR      WriteChar
0C                 ADD      R1,R1,#1
0D                 BR       Loop
0E      ;
0F      Input      JSR      ReadChar
10                 ADD      R2,R0,#0        ; Move char to R2 for writing
11                 JSR      WriteChar       ; Echo to monitor
12      ;
13                 LD       R2, Newline
14                 JSR      WriteChar
15                 JSR      RestoreReg
16                 LD       R7,SaveR7
17                 RET
18      ;
19      SaveR7     .FILL    x0000
1A      Newline    .FILL    x000A
1B      Prompt     .STRINGZ "Input a character>"
1C      ;
1D      WriteChar  LDI      R3,CRTSR
1E                 BRzp     WriteChar
1F                 STI      R2,CRTDR
20                 RET
21      CRTSR      .FILL    xF3FC
22      CRTDR      .FILL    xF3FF
```

Figure 9.7: The LC-2 TRAP service routine for character input.

```
23        ;
34        ReadChar        LDI     R3,KBSR
35                        BRzp    ReadChar
36                        LDI     R0,KBDR
37                        RET
38        KBSR            .FILL   xF400
39        KBDR            .FILL   xF401
3A        ;
3B        SaveReg         ST      R1,SaveR1
3C                        ST      R2,SaveR2
3D                        ST      R3,SaveR3
3E                        ST      R4,SaveR4
3F                        ST      R5,SaveR5
40                        ST      R6,SaveR6
41                        RET
42        ;
43        RestoreReg      LD      R1,SaveR1
44                        LD      R2,SaveR2
45                        LD      R3,SaveR3
46                        LD      R4,SaveR4
47                        LD      R5,SaveR5
48                        LD      R6,SaveR6
49                        RET
4A        SaveR1          .FILL   x0000
4B        SaveR2          .FILL   x0000
4C        SaveR3          .FILL   x0000
4D        SaveR4          .FILL   x0000
4E        SaveR5          .FILL   x0000
4F        SaveR6          .FILL   x0000
50                        .END
```

Figure 9.7: The LC-2 TRAP service routine for character input, continued

```
; puts.asm
; This service routine writes a NULL-terminated string to the console.  It
;          services the PUTS service call (TRAP x22).
; Inputs: R0 is a pointer to the string to print.
; Context Information: R1 and R2 are saved, and R7 is lost in the jump to
;          this routine

          .ORIG    x0450                ; where this ISR resides
                   ST       R7, SaveR7     ; save R7 for later return
                   ST       R1, SaveR1     ; save other registers that
                   ST       R3, SaveR3     ;   are needed by this routine
;
; loop through each character in the array
;

Loop               LDR      R1, R0, #0     ; retrieve the character(s)
                   BRz      Return         ; if this word is 0, done
L2                 LDI      R3,CRTSR
                   BRzp     L2
                   STI      R1, CRTDR      ; write the character
                   ADD      R0, R0, #1     ; increment pointer
                   BR       Loop           ; do it all over again

; return from the request for service call
Return             LD       R3, SaveR3
                   LD       R1, SaveR1
                   LD       R7, SaveR7
                   RET
;
; Register locations
CRTSR              .FILL    xF3FC
CRTDR              .FILL    xF3FF
SaveR1             .FILL    x0000
SaveR3             .FILL    x0000
SaveR7             .FILL    x0000
                   .END
```

Figure 9.8: The LC-2 PUTS Service Routine.

9.2.5 Library Routines.

We noted early in this section that there are many uses for the JSR/RET mechanism, among them the ability of a user program to call library subroutines that are provided as part of the operating system. Libraries are provided as a convenience to the user programmer. They are legitimately advertised as "productivity enhancers" since they allow the user programmer to use them without having to know or learn much of their inner details. For example, a user programmer knows what "square root" is, (we abbreviate **sqrt**) and may need to use sqrt(x) for some value x, but does not have a clue as to how to write a program to do it, and probably would rather not have to learn how.

A simple example illustrates the point. We have lost our key and need to get into our apartment. We can lean a ladder up against the wall so that the ladder touches the bottom of our open window, 24 feet above the ground. There is a 10 foot flower bed on the ground along the edge of the wall, so we need to keep the base of the ladder outside the flower bed. How big a ladder do we need so that we can lean it against the wall and climb through the window. Or, stated less colorfully: If the sides of a right triangle are 24 feet and 10 feet, how big is the hypotenuse (see Figure 9.9).

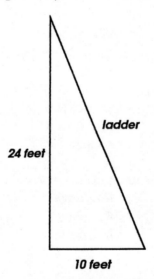

Figure 9.9: Solving for the length of the hypotenuse.

We remember from high school that Pythagoras answered that one for us:

$$c^2 = a^2 + b^2$$

Knowing a and b, we can easily solve for c by taking the square root of the sum of a^2 and b^2. Taking the "sum" is not hard – the LC-2 ADD instruction will do the job. The "square" is also not hard; we can multiply two numbers by a sequence of additions. But how does one get the "square root"?

The structure of our solution is shown in Figure 9.10.

```
                  . . .
                  . . .
          LD      R0,SIDE1
          BRz     1$
          JSR     SQUARE
1$        ADD     R1,R0,#0
          LD      R0,SIDE2
          BRz     2$
          JSR     SQUARE
2$        ADD     R0,R0,R1
          JSR     SQRT
          ST      R0,HYPOT
          BRnzp   NEXT_TASK
SQUARE    ADD     R2,R0,#0
          ADD     R3,R0,#0
AGAIN     ADD     R2,R2,#-1
          BRz     DONE
          ADD     R0,R0,R3
          BRnzp   AGAIN
DONE      RET
SQRT      . . .            ; R0 <-- SQRT(R0)
          . . .            ;
          . . .            ; How do we write this subroutine?
          . . .            ;
          . . .            ;
          RET
SIDE1     .BLKW   1
SIDE2     .BLKW   1
HYPOT     .BLKW   1
          . . .
          . . .
```

Figure 9.10: A Program Fragment to Compute the Hypotenuse of a Right Triangle.

The subroutine SQRT has yet to be written. If it weren't for the Math Library, the programmer would have to pick up a math book (or get someone to do it for him/her), check out the Newton-Raphson Method, and produce the missing subroutine.

However, with the Math Library, the problem pretty much goes away. Since the operating system supplies a number of subroutines (including SQRT), the user programmer can continue to be ignorant of the likes of Newton-Raphson. The user still needs to know the label of the target address of the library routine that performs the square root function, where to put the argument x, and where to expect the result sqrt(x). But these are easy conventions that can be obtained from the documentation associated with the Math Library.

If the library routine starts at addresss SQRT, and the argument is provided to the library routine at R0, and the result is obtained from the library routine at R0, Figure 9.10 reduces to Figure 9.11.

Two things are worth noting.

Thing 1: the programmer no longer has to worry about how to compute the square root function. The library routine does that for him/her.

Thing 2: the pseudo-op .EXTERNAL. We already saw in Section 7.4.2 that this pseudo-op tells the Assembler that the label (SQRT) needed to perform the JSRR instruction will be supplied by some other program fragment, and will be combined with this program fragment when the *executable image* is produced. The executable image is the binary module that actually executes. The executable image is produced at *link* time.

This notion of combining multiple modules at link time to produce an executable image is the normal case. You will see concrete examples of this process when we work with the programming language C in the second half of this course.

Most application software requires library routines from various libraries that it would be very inefficient for the typical programmer to produce all of them – assuming the typical programmer could produce such routines in the first place. We have mentioned routines from the Math Library. There are also a number of preprocessing routines for producing "pretty" graphics images. There are other routines for a number of other tasks where it would make no sense at all to have the programmer write the routines from scratch. It is much easier to require only (1) appropriate documentation so that the interface between the library routine and the program that calls that routine is clear, and (2) the use of the proper pseudo-ops such as .EXTERNAL in the source program. The linker can then produce an executable image at link time from the separately assembled modules. Figure 9.12 illustrates the process.

```
            . . .
            . . .
            .EXTERNAL SQRT
            . . .
            . . .
            LD       R0,SIDE1
            BRz      1$
            JSR      SQUARE
1$          ADD      R1,R0,#0
            LD       R0,SIDE2
            BRz      2$
            JSR      SQUARE
2$          ADD      R0,R0,R1
            LD       R4,BASE
            JSRR     R4,#0
            ST       R0,HYPOT
            BRnzp    NEXT_TASK
SQUARE      ADD      R2,R0,#0
            ADD      R3,R0,#0
AGAIN       ADD      R2,R2,#-1
            BRz      DONE
            ADD      R0,R0,R3
            BRnzp    AGAIN
DONE        RET
BASE        .FILL    SQRT
SIDE1       .BLKW 1
SIDE2       .BLKW    1
HYPOT       .BLKW    1
            . . .
            . . .
```

Figure 9.11: The Program Fragment of Figure 9.10, using a Library Routine.

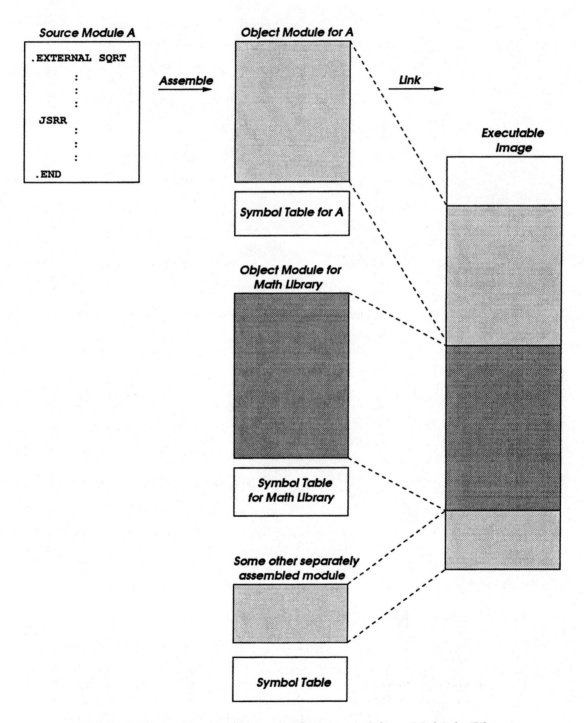

Figure 9.12: An Executable Image Constructed from Multiple Files.

9.3 Exercises.

9.1 Name some advantages to doing I/O through a trap routine instead of writing the routine yourself each time you would like your program to perform I/O?

9.2 Why is the starting address of the trap routine stored at the address specified in the trap instruction instead of the routine itself? For example, why have the TRAP x25 instruction look in address x25 for the begging of the halt routine instead of having x25 be the beginning of the routine?

9.3 1. How many TRAP service routines can be implemented in the LC-2?

 2. Why must a RET instruction be used to return out of a TRAP routine? Why won't a BRnzp (Unconditional BR) instruction work instead?

 3. How many accesses to memory are made during the processing of the TRAP instruction? Assume the TRAP is already in the IR.

9.4 Refer to Figure 9.6, the halt service routine, how can the halt service routine return after bit 15 of the machine control register is cleared?

9.5 1. What instruction (or TRAP routine) starts the clock after the machine is HALTed?

 2. Refer to the HALT service routine in Figure 9.6. Which instruction actually halts the machine?

 3. What is the first instruction executed when the machine is started again?

 4. Where will the RET of the HALT routine return to?

9.6 Given the following LC-2 assembly program:

```
            .ORIG   x3000
    L1      LEA     R1, L1
            AND     R2, R2, x0
            ADD     R2, R2, x2
            LD      R3, P1
    L2      LDR     R0, R1, xC
            OUT
            ADD     R3, R3, -1
            BRZ     GLUE
            ADD     R1, R1, R2
            BRNZP   L2
    GLUE    HALT
    P1      .FILL   x14
            .STRINGZ "awPrloenngtYiofuuAlrLeaRcikgOhftWNiotw"
            .END
```

 1. After this program is assembled and loaded, what binary pattern is stored in memory location x3005?

2. Which instruction (provide a memory address) is executed after instruction x3005 is executed?

3. Which instruction (provide a memory address) is executed prior to instruction x3006?

4. What is the output of this program?

9.7 Consider the following LC-2 assembly language program:

```
          .ORIG   x3000
          LEA     R0,DATA
          AND     R1,R1,#0
          ADD     R1,R1,#9
LOOP1     ADD     R2,R0,#0
          ADD     R3,R1,#0
LOOP2     JSR     SUB1
          ADD     R4,R4,#0
          BRZP    LABEL
          JSR     SUB2
LABEL     ADD     R2,R2,#1
          ADD     R3,R3,#-1
          BRP     LOOP2
          ADD     R1,R1,#-1
          BRP     LOOP1
          HALT
DATA      .BLKW   10 x0000
SUB1      LDR     R5,R2,#0
          NOT     R5,R5
          ADD     R5,R5,#1
          LDR     R6,R2,#1
          ADD     R4,R5,R6
          RET
SUB2      LDR     R4,R2,#0
          LDR     R5,R2,#1
          STR     R4,R2,#1
          STR     R5,R2,#0
          RET
          .END
```

Assuming that the memory locations at DATA get filled in before the program executes, what is the relationship between the final values at DATA and the initial values at DATA?

9.8 Below is part of a program that was fed to the LC-2 assembler. The program is supposed to read a series of input lines from the console into a buffer, search for a particular character and output the number of times the character occurs in the text.

The input text is terminated by an EOT and is guaranteed to be no more than 1000 characters in length. After the text has been input, the program reads the character to count.

The subroutine labeled COUNT that actually does the counting was written by another individual and is located at address x3500. When called, the subroutine expects the address of the buffer to be in R5 and the address of the character to count to be in R6. The buffer should have a NUL to mark the end of the text. It returns the count in R6.

The OUTPUT subroutine that converts the binary count to ASCII digits and displays them was also written by another individual, and is at address x3600. It expects the number to print to be in R6.

Here is the code that reads the input and calls COUNT:

```
        .ORIG   x3000
        LEA     R1, BUFFER
G_TEXT  TRAP    x20                 ; Get input text
        ADD     R2, R0, x-04
        BRZ     G_CHAR
        STR     R0, R1, #0
        ADD     R1, R1, #1
        BR      G_TEXT

G_CHAR  STR     R2, R1, #0          ; Store NUL to terminate buffer
        TRAP    x20                 ; Get character to count
        ST      R0, S_CHAR
        LEA     R5, BUFFER
        LEA     R6, S_CHAR
        LD      R4, CADDR
        JSRR    R4, #0              ; Count character
        LD      R4. OADDR
        JSRR    R4, #0              ; Convert R6 and display
        TRAP    x25
CADDR   .FILL   x3500               ; Address of COUNT
OADDR   .FILL   x3600               ; Address of OUTPUT
BUFFER  .BLKW   1001    x0000
S_CHAR  .FILL   x0000
        .END
```

1. There is a problem with this code. What is it, and how might it be fixed? (The problem is **not** that the code for COUNT and OUTPUT is missing)

2. What happens when you run the fixed code through the LC-2 assembler (you'll have to comment out the JSRR instructions)?

9.9 Recall the machine busy example. Suppose the bit pattern indicating which machines are busy and which are free is stored in memory location x4001. Write functions that do the following:

1. check if no machines are busy and return 1 if none are busy;

2. check if all machines are busy and return 1 if all are busy;

3. check how many machines are busy and return the number of busy machines;

4. check how many machines are free and return the number of free machines;

5. check if a certain machine number, passed as an argument in R5 is busy and return 1 if that machine is busy;

6. return the number of a machine that is not busy.

Chapter 10

And, finally...

In this chapter we will complete the ISA-level introduction to computing structures. We have finished our treatment of the ISA of the LC-2. Before moving up in Chapter 11 to programming in C, there are two concepts that we feel it is important to spend some time with: the *stack* and data conversion between ASCII and 2's complement integers. You will find both concepts useful in much of what you do in computer science and engineering, long after this book is just a pleasant memory. After that, we will close out our ISA-level introduction with the design of a calculator, a comprehensive application that makes use of both.

10.1 The Stack – A very important storage structure.

10.1.1 The Stack – An abstract data type.

Throughout your future usage (or design) of computers, you will encounter the storage mechanism known as a *stack*. Stacks can be implemented in many different ways, and we will get to that momentarily. Like everything else in this book, we will attempt to understand how stacks work by building them out of elements we already understand.

But first, it is also important to know that the "concept" of a stack has nothing to do with how it is implemented. The concept of a stack is the specification of how it is to be **accessed**. That is, the defining ingredient of a stack is that the **last** thing you stored in it is the **first** thing you remove. That is what makes a stack different from everything else in the world. Simply put: Last In, First Out. ...or, LIFO.

In the terminology of computer programming languages, we say the stack is an example of an *abstract data type*. That is, an abstract data type is a storage mechanism that is defined by the operations performed on it, and not at all by the specific manner in which it is implemented. In Chapter 19 we will write programs in C that use linked lists, another example of an abstract data type.

207

10.1.2   Two example implementations.

A coin holder in the armrest of an automobile is an example of a stack. The first quarter you take to pay the highway toll is the last quarter you previously added to the stack of quarters. As you add quarters, you physically push the "earlier" quarters down into the coin holder.

Figure 10.1 shows the behavior of a coin holder. Initially, as shown in Figure 10.1a, the coin holder is empty. The first highway toll is 75 cents, and you give the gate keeper a dollar. He gives you 25 cents change, a 1995 quarter, which you insert into the coin holder. The coin holder appears as shown in Figure 10.1b.

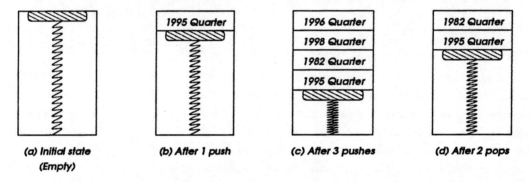

    (a) Initial state   **(b) After 1 push**   **(c) After 3 pushes**   **(d) After 2 pops**
         (Empty)

Figure 10.1: A coin holder in an auto armrest (Example of a stack).

There are special terms for insertion and removal of elements from a stack. We say we *push* an element onto the stack when we insert it. We say we *pop* an element from the stack when we remove it.

The second highway toll is $4.25, and you give the gate keeper 5 dollars. The gatekeeper gives you 75 cents change, which you insert into the coin holder: first a 1982 quarter, then a 1998 quarter, and finally, a 1996 quarter. Now the coin holder is as shown in Figure 10.1c. The third toll is 50 cents, and you remove ("pop") the top two quarters from the coin holder: the 1996 quarter first and then the 1998 quarter. The coin holder is then as shown in Figure 10.1d.

The coin holder is an example of a stack, **precisely** because it obeys the LIFO requirement. Each time you insert a quarter, you do so at the TOP. Each time you remove a quarter, you do so from the TOP. The last coin you inserted is the first coin you remove – THEREFORE, it is a stack.

Another implementation of a stack, sometimes referred to as a hardware stack, is shown in Figure 10.2. Its behavior resembles that of the coin holder we just described. It consists of some number of registers, each of which can store an element. The example of Figure 10.2 contains five registers. As each element is added to the stack or removed from the stack, the elements **already** on the stack **move**.

In Figure 10.2a, the stack is initially shown as empty. Access is always via the first element, which is labeled TOP. If the value 18 is pushed on the stack, we have Figure 10.2b. If the

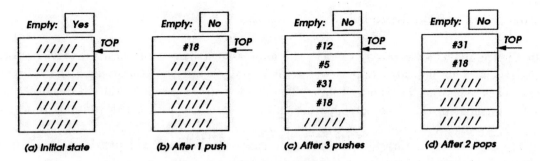

Figure 10.2: A Stack, implemented in hardware – Data entries move.

three values, 31, 5, and 12 are pushed (in that order), the result is Figure 10.2c. Finally, if two elements are popped from the stack, we have Figure 10.2d. The distinguishing feature of the stack of Figure 10.2 is that, like the quarters in the coin holder, as each value is added or removed, all the values already on the stack move.

10.1.3   Implementation in Memory.

By far, the most common implementation of a stack in a computer is as shown in Figure 10.3. The stack consists of a sequence of memory locations, along with a mechanism, called the *stack pointer*, that keeps track of the TOP of the stack, that is, the location containing the most recent element pushed. Each value pushed is stored in one of the memory locations. In this case, the data already stored **does not physically move.**

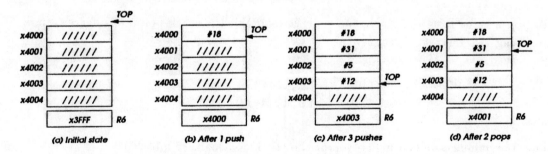

Figure 10.3: A Stack, implemented in memory – Data entries do not move.

In the example shown in Figure 10.3, the stack consists of five locations x4000 through x4004. R6 is the stack pointer.

Figure 10.3a shows an intially empty stack. Figure 10.3b shows the stack after pushing the value 18, Figure 10.3c shows the stack after pushing the values 31, 5, and 12 in that order. Figure 10.3d shows the stack after popping the top two elements on the stack. Note that those top two elements (the values 5 and 12) are still present in memory locations x4002 and x4003. However, as we will see momentarily, those values 5 and 12 can not be accessed from the stack.

Push.

In Figure 10.3a, R6 contains x3FFF, the address just before the first (BASE) location in the stack. This indicates that the stack is initially empty. We first push the value 18 in the stack, resulting in Figure 10.3b. The stack pointer provides the address of the last value pushed, in this case, x4000, where 18 is stored. Note that the contents of locations x4001, x4002, x4003 and x4004 are not shown. As will be seen momentarily, the contents of these locations are irrelevant since they can never be accessed provided that locations x4000 through x4004 are accessed **only** as a stack.

To push a value on the stack, the stack pointer is incremented, and the value stored. The two-instruction sequence

```
PUSH          ADD     R6,R6,#1
              STR     R0,R6,#0
```

pushes the value contained in R0 onto the stack. Thus, for the stack to be as shown in Figure 10.3b, R0 must have contained the value 18 before the two-instruction sequence was executed.

The three values 31, 5, and 12 are pushed on the stack by loading each in turn into R0, and then executing the two-instruction sequence. In Figure 10.3c, R6 (the stack pointer) contains x4003, indicating that 12 was the last element pushed.

Pop.

To pop a value from the stack, the value is read and the stack pointer is decremented. The following two-instruction sequence

```
POP           LDR     R0,R6,#0
              ADD     R6,R6,#-1.
```

pops the value contained in the top of the stack and loads it into R0.

If the stack is as shown in Figure 10.3c and we executed the sequence twice, we would pop two values from the stack. In this case, we would first remove the "12," and then the "5." We would, of course, have to move the 12 from R0 to some other location before calling POP a second time.

Figure 10.3d shows the stack after that sequence of operations. R6 contains x4001, indicating that 31 is now at the top of the stack. Note that the values 12 and 5 are still stored in memory locations x4002 and x4003, respectively. However, since the stack requires that we push by executing the PUSH sequence and pop by executing the POP sequence, we can not access these two values if we obey the rules. The fancy name for "the rules" is the *stack protocol.*

Underflow.

What happens if we now attempt to pop three values from the stack? Since only two values remain on the stack, we would have a problem. Attempting to pop items which have not been previously pushed results in an *underflow* situation. In our example, we can test for underflow by comparing the stack pointer with x3FFF, which would be the contents of R6 if there were nothing left on the stack to pop. If UNDERFLOW is the label of a routine that handles the underflow condition, our resulting POP sequence would be

```
POP     LD      R1,EMPTY        ; EMPTY contains -3FFF
        ADD     R2,R6,R1        ; Compare stack pointer with 3FFF.
        BRz     UNDERFLOW
        LDR     R0,R6,#0
        ADD     R6,R6,#-1
        RET
EMPTY   .FILL   xC001
```

Rather than have the POP routine immmediately jump to the UNDERFLOW routine if the POP was unsuccessful, it is often useful to have the POP routine return to the calling program, with the "underflow" information contained in a register.

A common convention for doing this is to use a register to provide success/failure information. Figure 10.4 is a flow chart showing how the POP routine could be augmented, using R5 to report this success/failure information.

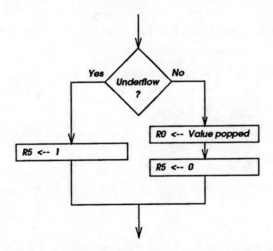

Figure 10.4: POP routine, including test for underflow.

Upon return from the POP routine, the calling program would examine R5 to determine whether the POP completed successfully (R5 = 0), or not (R5 = 1).

Note that since the POP routine reports success or failure in R5, whatever was stored in R5 **before** the POP routine was called is lost. Thus, it is the job of the calling program to save the contents of R5 before the JSR instruction is executed. Recall from Section 9.1.8 that this is an example of a caller-save situation.

The resulting POP routine is shown below. Note that since the instruction immediately preceding the RET instruction sets/clears the condition codes, the calling program can simply test Z to determine whether the POP completed successfully.

```
POP       LD      R1,EMPTY        ; EMPTY contains -3FFF
          ADD     R2,R6,R1
          BRz     Failure
          LDR     R0,R6,#0
          ADD     R6,R6,#-1
          AND     R5,R5,#0
          RET
Failure   AND     R5,R5,#0
          ADD     R5,R5,#1
          RET
EMPTY     .FILL   xC001
```

Overflow.

What happens when we run out of available space, and we try to push a value onto the stack? Since we can not store values where there is no room, we have an *overflow* situation. We can test for overflow by comparing the stack pointer with (in the example of Figure 10.3) x4004. If they are equal, we have no room to push another value on the stack. If OVERFLOW is the label of a routine that handles the overflow condition, our resulting PUSH sequence would be

```
PUSH      LD      R1,MAX          ; MAX contains -4004
          ADD     R2,R6,R1
          BRz     OVERFLOW
          ADD     R6,R6,#1
          STR     R0,R6,#0
          RET
MAX       .FILL   xBFFC
```

In the same way that it is useful to have the POP routine return to the calling program with success/failure information, rather than immediately jumping to the UNDERFLOW routine, it is useful to have the PUSH routine act similarly.

We augment the PUSH routine with instructions to store 0 (success) or 1 (failure) in R5, depending on whether or not the push completed successfully. Upon return from the PUSH routine, the calling program would examine R5 to determine whether the PUSH completed successfully (R5 = 0), or not (R5 = 1).

Note again that since the PUSH routine reports success or failure in R5, we have another example of a caller-save situation. That is, since whatever was stored in R5 before the PUSH routine was called is lost, it is the job of the calling program to save the contents of R5 before the JSR instruction is executed.

Also, note again that since the instruction immediately preceding the RET instruction sets/clears the condition codes, the calling program can simply test Z or P to determine whether the POP completed successfully.

The resulting PUSH routine is shown below.

```
PUSH      LD      R1,MAX        ; MAX contains -4004
          ADD     R2,R6,R1
          BRz     Failure
          ADD     R6,R6,#1
          STR     R0,R6,#0
          AND     R5,R5,#0
          RET
Failure   AND     R5,R5,#0
          ADD     R5,R5,#1
          RET
MAX       .FILL   xBFFC
```

10.1.4 The Complete Picture.

The POP and PUSH routines allow us to use memory locations x4000 through x4004 as a five-entry stack. If we wish to push a value on the stack, we simply load that value into R0, and execute JSR PUSH. To pop a value from the stack into R0, we simply execute JSR POP. If we wish to change the location or the size of the stack, we adjust BASE and MAX accordingly.

Before leaving this topic, we should be careful to clean up one detail. The subroutines PUSH and POP make use of R1, R2, and R5. If we wish to use the values stored in those registers after returning from the PUSH or POP routine, we had best save them before using them. In the case of R1 and R2, it is easiest to save them in the PUSH and POP routines before using them, and then restore them before returning to the calling program. That way, the calling program does not even have to know that these registers are used in the PUSH and POP routines. This is an example of the callee-save situation described in Section 9.1.8. In the case of R5, the situation is different, since the calling program does have to know that success or failure is reported in R5. Thus, it is the job of the calling program to save the contents of R5 before the JSR instruction is executed if the calling program wishes to use the value stored there again. This is an example of the caller-save situation.

The final code for our PUSH and POP operations is shown in Figure 10.5.

```
;
; Subroutines for carrying out the PUSH and POP functions.  This
; program works with a stack consisting of memory locations x4000
; (BASE) through x4004 (MAX).  R6 is the stack pointer.
;
POP             ST      R2,Save2        ; are needed by POP.
                ST      R1,Save1
                LD      R1,BASE         ; BASE contains -x4000.
                ADD     R1,R1,#1        ; R1 contains -x3FFF.
                ADD     R2,R6,R1        ; Compare stack pointer to x3FFF
                BRz     fail_exit       ; Branch if stack is empty.
                LDR     R0,R6,#0        ; The actual "pop."
                ADD     R6,R6,#-1       ; Adjust stack pointer
                BRnzp   success_exit
PUSH            ST      R2,Save2        ; Save registers that
                ST      R1,Save1        ; are needed by PUSH.
                LD      R1,MAX          ; MAX contains -4004
                ADD     R2,R6,R1        ; Compare stack pointer to x4004
                BRz     fail_exit       ; Branch if stack is full.
                ADD     R6,R6,#1        ; Adjust stack pointer
                STR     R0,R6,#0        ; The actual "push."
success_exit    LD      R1,Save1        ; Restore original
                LD      R2,Save2        ; register values.
                AND     R5,R5,#0        ; R5 <--- success.
                RET
fail_exit       LD      R1,Save1        ; Restore original
                LD      R2,Save2        ; register values.
                AND     R5,R5,#0
                ADD     R5,R5,#1        ; R5 <--- failure.
                RET
BASE            .FILL   xC000           ; BASE contains -x4000.
MAX             .FILL   xBFFC
Save1           .FILL   x0000
Save2           .FILL   x0000
```

Figure 10.5: The Stack Protocol.

10.2 Arithmetic using a stack.

10.2.1 The Stack as temporary storage.

There are computers that use a stack instead of general purpose registers to store temporary values during a computation. Recall our add instruction:

```
ADD      R0,R1,R2
```

takes source operands from R1 and R2 and writes the result of the addition into R0. We call the LC-2 a *three-address* machine because all three locations (the two sources and the destination) are explicitly identified. Some computers use a stack for source and destination operands and explicitly identify NONE of them. The instruction would simply be

```
ADD
```

We call such a computer a stack machine, or a *zero-address* machine. The hardware would know that the source operands are the top two elements on the stack, which would be "popped" and then supplied to the ALU, and that the result of the addition would be "pushed" on the stack.

To perform an ADD on a stack machine, the hardware would execute two pops, an add, and a push. The two "pops" would remove the two source operands from the stack, the "add" would compute their sum, and the "push" would place the result back on the stack. Note that the pop, push, and add are not part of the ISA of that computer, and therefore not available to the programmer. They are control signals that the hardware uses to make the actual pop, push, and add occur. The control signals are part of the microarchitecture and beyond what we are concentrating on right now. The programmer simply instructs the computer to ADD, and the microarchitecture does the rest.

Sometimes (as we will see in our final example of this chapter), it is useful to process arithmetic using a stack. Intermediate values are maintained on the stack rather than in general purpose registers, such as the LC-2's R0 through R7. Most general purpose microprocessors, including the LC-2, use general purpose registers. Most hand calculators use a stack.

10.2.2 An example.

For example, suppose you wanted to evaluate (A + B) * (C+ D), where A contains 25, B contains 17, C contains 3, and D contains 2, and store the result in E. If the LC-2 had a multiply instruction (we would probably call it MUL), we could use the following program:

```
LD    R0,A
LD    R1,B
ADD   R0,R0,R1
LD    R2,C
LD    R3,D
ADD   R2,R2,R3
MUL   R0,R0,R2
ST    R0,E
```

With a hand calculator, you could execute the following eight operations

```
(1)    push     25
(2)    push     17
(3)    add
(4)    push     3
(5)    push     2
(6)    add
(7)    multiply
(8)    pop      E
```

with the final result popped being the result of the computation, that is, 210. Figure 10.6 shows a snapshot of the stack after each of the eight operations.

In Section 10.4, we will write a program to cause the LC-2 (with keyboard and monitor) to act like such a hand calculator. We say the LC-2 simulates the hand calculator when it executes that program.

But first, let's examine the subroutines we will need to do the various arithmetic operations.

10.2.3   OpAdd, OpMult, and OpNeg.

The calculator we will simulate in Section 10.4 will have the ability to enter values, add, subtract, multiply, and display results. To add, subtract, and multiply, we will need three subroutines:

   1: OpAdd, which will pop two values from the stack, add them, and push the result on the stack,

   2: OpMult, which will pop two values from the stack, multiply them, and push the result on the stack, and

   3: OpNeg, which will pop the top value, form its 2's complement negative value, and push the result on the stack.

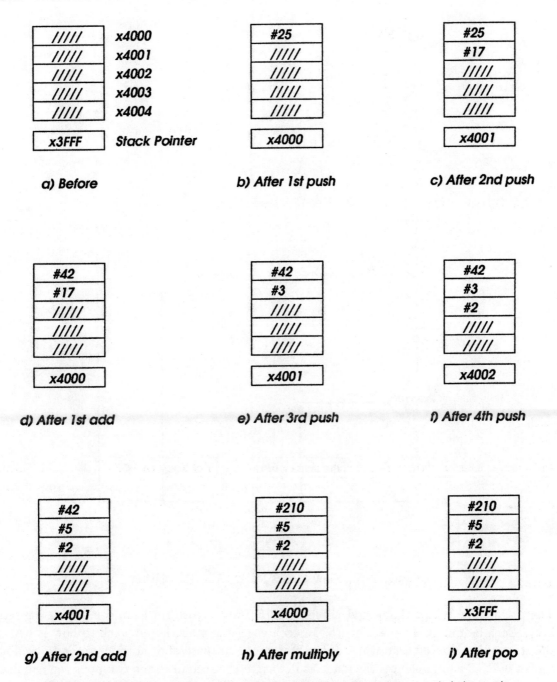

Figure 10.6: Stack Usage During the Computation of (25 + 17) * (3 + 2).

The OpAdd Algorithm.

Figure 10.7 shows the flow chart of the OpAdd algorithm. Basically, the algorithm attempts to pop two values off the stack, and if successful, add them. If the result is within the range of acceptable values (that is, an integer between -999 and +999), then the result is pushed on the stack.

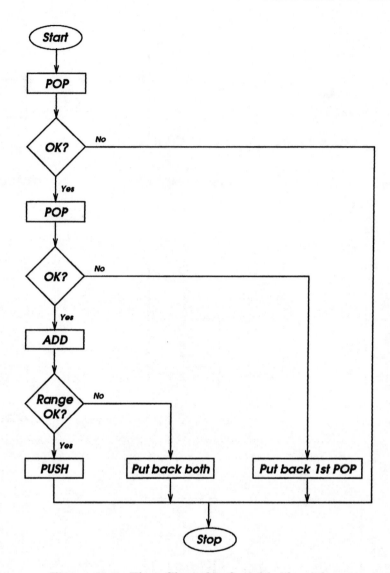

Figure 10.7: Flow Chart for OpAdd Algorithm.

There are three things that could prevent the OpAdd algorithm from completing success-fully. Each is indicated by a 1 in R5. In each case, the stack is put back to how it was at the start of the OpAdd algorithm. If the first pop is unsuccessful, nothing needs to be done since the POP routine leaves the stack as it was. If the second of the two pops reports back unsuccessfully, the stack pointer is incremented, which effectively returns the first value popped to the top of the stack. If the result is outside the range of acceptable values, then the stack pointer is incremented twice, returning both values to the top of the stack.

The OpAdd algorithm is shown in Figure 10.8.

Note that the OpAdd Algorithm calls the RangeCheck Algorithm. This is a simple test to be sure the result of the computation is within what can be successfully stored in a single stack location. For our purposes, suppose we restrict values to be integers in the range -999 to +999. This will come in handy in Section 10.4 when we design our home-brew hand

```
;
;           Routine to pop the top two elements from the stack,
;           add them, and push the sum onto the stack.  R6 is
;           the stack pointer.
;
OpAdd       JSR     POP             ; Get first source operand.
            ADD     R5,R5,#0        ; Test if POP was successful.
            BRp     Exit            ; Branch if not successful.
            ADD     R1,R0,#0        ; Make room for second operand
            JSR     POP             ; Get second source operand.
            ADD     R5,R5,#0        ; Test if POP was successful.
            BRp     Restore1        ; Not successful, put back first.
            ADD     R0,R0,R1        ; THE Add.
            JSR     RangeCheck      ; Check size of result.
            BRp     Restore2        ; Out of range, restore both.
            JSR     PUSH            ; Push sum on the stack.
            RET                     ; On to the next task...
Restore2    ADD     R6,R6,#1        ; Increment stack pointer.
Restore1    ADD     R6,R6,#1        ; Increment stack pointer.
Exit        RET
```

Figure 10.8: The OpAdd Algorithm.

calculator. The flow chart for the RangeCheck algorithm is shown in Figure 10.9. The
LC-2 program that implements this algorithm is shown in Figure 10.10.

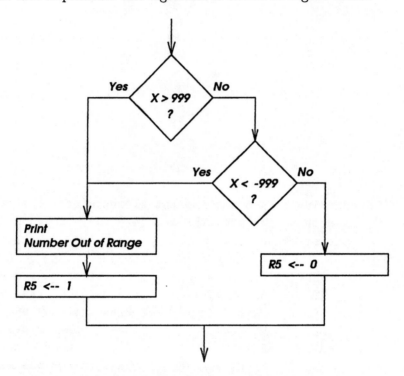

Figure 10.9: The RangeCheck Algorithm – Flow Chart.

The OpMult Algorithm.

Figure 10.11 shows the flow chart of the OpMult algorithm, and Figure 10.12 shows the LC-
2 program that implements that algorithm. Similar to the OpAdd algorithm, the OpMult
algorithm attempts to pop two values off the stack, and if successful, multiplies them. Since
the LC-2 does not have a "multiply" instruction, multiplication is performed as we have
done in prior situations as a sequence of "adds." Lines 17-19 of Figure 10.12 contain the
crux of the actual multiply.

If the result is within the range of acceptable values, then the result is pushed on the stack.

If the second of the two pops reports back unsuccessfully, the stack pointer is incremented,
which effectively returns the first value popped to the top of the stack.

If the result is outside the range of acceptable values, which as before will be indicated by
a 1 in R5, then the stack pointer is incremented twice, returning both values to the top of
the stack.

```
;
;       Routine to check that the magnitude of a value is
;       between -999 and +999.
;
RangeCheck      LD              R5,Neg999
                ADD             R4,R0,R5        ; Recall that R0 contains the
                BRp             BadRange        ; result being checked.
                LD              R5,Pos999
                ADD             R4,R0,R5
                BRn             BadRange
                AND             R5,R5,#0        ; R5 <--- success
                RET
BadRange        ST              R7,Save         ; R7 is needed by TRAP/RET
                LEA             R0,RangeErrorMsg
                TRAP            x22             ; Output character string
                LD              R7,Save
                AND             R5,R5,#0        ;
                ADD             R5,R5,#1        ; R5 <--- failure
                RET
Neg999          .FILL           #-999
Pos999          .FILL           #999
Save            .FILL           x0000
RangeErrorMsg .FILL            x000A
                .STRINGZ        "Error: Number is out of range."
```

Figure 10.10: The RangeCheck Algorithm.

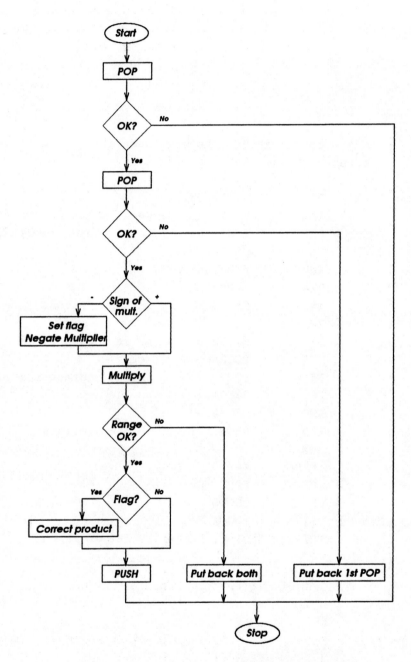

Figure 10.11: Flow Chart for the OpMult Algorithm.

```
01    ;
02    ;      Algorithm to pop two values from the stack, multiply them
03    ;        and if their product is within the acceptable range, push
04    ;        the result on the stack.   R6 is stack pointer.
05    ;
06    OpMult         AND     R3,R3,#0        ; R3 holds sign of multiplier.
07                   JSR     POP             ; Get first source from stack.
08                   ADD     R5,R5,#0        ; Test for successful POP
09                   BRp     Exit            ; Failure
0A                   ADD     R1,R0,#0        ; Make room for next POP
0B                   JSR     POP             ; Get second source operand
0C                   ADD     R5,R5,#0        ; Test for successful POP
0D                   BRp     Restore1        ; Failure; restore first POP
0E                   ADD     R2,R0,#0        ; Moves multiplier, tests sign
0F                   BRzp    PosMultiplier
10                   ADD     R3,R3,#1        ; Sets FLAG: Multiplier is neg
11                   NOT     R2,R2
12                   ADD     R2,R2,#1        ; R2 contains -(multiplier)
13    PosMultiplier  AND     R0,R0,#0        ; Clear product register
14                   ADD     R2,R2,#0
15                   BRz     PushMult        ; Multiplier = 0, Done.
16    ;
17    MultLoop       ADD     R0,R0,R1        ; THE actual "multiply"
18                   ADD     R2,R2,#-1       ; Iteration Control
19                   BRp     MultLoop
1A    ;
1B                   JSR     RangeCheck
1C                   ADD     R5,R5,#0        ; R5 contains success/failure
1D                   BRp     Restore2
1E    ;
1F                   ADD     R3,R3,#0        ; Test for negative multiplier
20                   BRZ     PushMult
21                   NOT     R0,R0           ; Adjust for
22                   ADD     R0,R0,#1        ; sign of result
23    PushMult       JSR     PUSH            ; Push product on the stack.
24                   RET
25    Restore2       ADD     R6,R6,#1        ; Adjust stack pointer.
26    Restore1       ADD     R6,R6,#1        ; Adjust stack pointer.
27    Exit           RET
```

Figure 10.12: The OpMult Algorithm.

The OpNeg Algorithm.

We have provided algorithms to add and multiply the top two elements on the stack. To subtract the top two elements on the stack, we can use our OpAdd algorithm if we first replace the top of the stack with its negative value. That is, if the top of the stack contains A, and the second element on the stack contains B, and we wish to pop A,B and push B-A, we can accomplish this by first negating the top of stack, and then performing OpAdd.

The algorithm for negating the element on the top of the stack, OpNeg, is shown in Figure 10.13.

```
;
;       Algorithm to pop the top of the stack, form its negative,
;       and push the result on the stack.
;
OpNeg           JSR     POP             ; Get the source operand
                ADD     R5,R5,#0        ; test for successful pop
                BRp     Exit            ; Branch if failure
                NOT     R0,R0
                ADD     R0,R0,#1        ; Form the negative of the source.
                JSR     PUSH            ; Push the result on the stack.
Exit            RET
```

Figure 10.13: The OpNeg Algorithm.

10.3 Data type conversion.

It has been a long time since we talked about data types – recall our definition in Section 2.1.2: a data type is a representation of information such that the ISA provides instructions that operate on that representation. We have been exposed to several data types: unsigned integers for address arithmetic, 2's complement integers for integer arithmetic, 16-bit binary strings for logical operations, floating point numbers for scientific computation, and ASCII codes for interaction with input and output devices.

It is important that every instruction be provided with source operands of the data type that the instruction requires. For example, **ADD** requires operands that are 2's complement integers. If the ALU were supplied with floating point operands, the computer would produce garbage results.

It is not uncommon in high level language programs to find an instruction of the form

```
A = R + I
```

where R (floating point) and I (2's complement integer) are represented in different data types.

If the operation is to be performed by a floating point adder, then we have a problem with I. To handle the problem, one must first convert the value I from its original data type (2's complement integer) to the data type required by the operation (floating point).

Even the LC-2 has this data type conversion problem. Consider a multiple-digit integer that has been entered via the keyboard. It is represented as a string of ASCII characters. To perform arithmetic on it, you must first convert the value to a 2's complement integer. Consider a 2's complement representation of a value that you wish to display on the monitor. To do so, you must first convert it to an ASCII string.

In this section, we will examine routines to convert between ASCII strings of decimal digits and 2's complement binary integers.

10.3.1 Example: The bogus program: 2+3=e.

First, let's examine Figure 10.14, a concrete example of how one can get into trouble if one is not careful about keeping track of the data type of each of the values one is working with.

Suppose we wish to enter two digits from the keyboard, add them, and display the results on the monitor. At first blush, we write the following simple program:

```
TRAP    x23        ; Input from the keyboard.
ADD     R1,R0,#0   ; Make room for another input.
TRAP    x23        ; Input another character.
ADD     R0,R1,R0   ; Add the two inputs.
TRAP    x21        ; Display result on the monitor.
TRAP    x25        ; Halt.
```

Figure 10.14: ADDITION without paying attention to Data Types.

What happens?

Suppose the first digit entered via the keyboard is a 2 and the second digit entered via the keyboard is a 3. What will be displayed on the monitor before the program terminates? The value loaded into R0 as a result of entering a 2 is the ASCII code for 2, which is x0032. When the 3 is entered, the ASCII code for 3, which is x0033 will be loaded. Thus, the ADD instruction will add the two binary strings x0032 and x0033, producing x0065. When that value is diplayed on the monitor, it will be treated as an ASCII code. Since x0065 is the ASCII code for a lower case e, that is what will be displayed on the monitor.

The reason why we didn't get 5 (which, at last calculation, was the correct result when adding 2 + 3) was that we didn't (a) convert the two input characters from ASCII to 2's complement integers before performing addition, and (b) convert the result back to ASCII before displaying it on the monitor.

Exercise: Correct Figure 10.14 so that it will add two one-digit positive integers and give a one-digit positive sum. Assume that the two digits being added do in fact produce a single digit sum.

10.3.2   ASCII to Binary.

It is often useful to deal with numbers that require more than one digit to express them. Figure 10.15 shows the ASCII representation of the three digit number 295, stored as an ASCII string in three consecutive LC-2 memory locations, starting at ASCIIBUFF. R1 contains the number of decimal digits in the number.

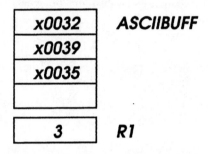

Figure 10.15: The ASCII Representation of 295 Stored in Consecutive Memory Locations.

Note that in Figure 10.15 a whole LC-2 word (16 bits) is allocated for each ASCII character. One can (and in fact, more typically, one does) store each ASCII character in a single byte of memory. In this example, we have decided to give each ASCII character its own word of memory in order to simplify the algorithm.

Figure 10.16 shows the flow chart for converting the ASCII representation of Figure 10.15 into a binary integer. The value represented must be in the range 0 to +999, i.e., it is limited to three decimal digits.

The algorithm systematically takes each digit, converts it from its ASCII code to its binary code by stripping away all but the last four bits, and then uses it to index into a table of ten binary values, each corresponding to the value of one of the ten digits. That value is then added to R0. R0 is used to accumulate the contributions of all the digits. The result is returned in R0.

Figure 10.17 shows the LC-2 program that implements this algorithm.

Exercise: [Very challenging] Suppose the decimal number is arbitrarily long. Rather than store a table of ten values for the "thousands" digit, another table for the ten "ten-thousands" digit, and so on, can we design an algorithm to do the conversion without resorting to any tables whatsoever?

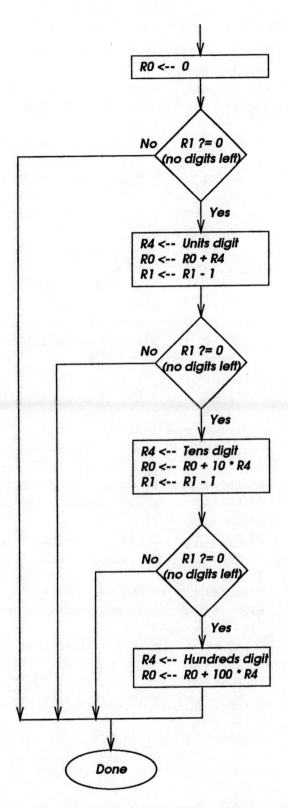

Figure 10.16: Flowchart, Algorithm for ASCII to Binary Conversion.

```
;
; This algorithm takes an ASCII string of three decimal digits and
; converts it into a binary number.  R0 is used to collect the result.
; R1 keeps track of how many digits are left to process.  ASCIIBUF
; contains the most significant digit in the ASCII string.
;
ASCIItoBinary  AND   R0,R0,#0        ; R0 will be used for our result
               ADD   R1,R1,#0        ; Test number of digits.
               BRz   DoneAtoB        ; There are no digits
;
               LD    R3,NegASCIIOffset  ; R3 gets xFFD0, which is -x0030
               LEA   R2,ASCIIBUFF
               ADD   R2,R2,R1
               ADD   R2,R2,#-1       ; R2 now points to "ones" digit
;
               LDR   R4,R2,#0        ; R4 <-- "ones" digit
               ADD   R4,R4,R3        ; Strip off the ASCII template
               ADD   R0,R0,R4        ; Add ones contribution to running sum
;
               ADD   R1,R1,#-1
               BRz   DoneAtoB        ; The original number had one digit
               ADD   R2,R2,#-1       ; R2  now points to "tens" digit
;
               LDR   R4,R2,#0        ; R4 <-- "tens" digit
               ADD   R4,R4,R3        ; Strip off ASCII  template
               LEA   R5,LookUp10     ; LookUp10 is BASE of tens values
               ADD   R5,R5,R4        ; R5 points to the right tens value
               LDR   R4,R5,#0
               ADD   R0,R0,R4        ; Add tens contribution to total
;
               ADD   R1,R1,#-1
               BRZ   DoneAtoB        ; The original number had two digits
               ADD   R2,R2,#-1       ; R2 now points to "hundreds" digit
;
               LDR   R4,R2,#0        ; R4 <-- "hundreds" digit
               ADD   R4,R4,R3        ; Strip off ASCII template
               LEA   R5,LookUp100    ; LookUp100 is BASE of hundreds values
               ADD   R5,R5,R4        ; R5 points to the right hundreds value
               LDR   R4,R5,#0
               ADD   R0,R0,R4        ; Add hundreds contribution to total
;
DoneAtoB       RET
```

Figure 10.17: ASCII to Binary Conversion Routine.

```
NegASCIIOffset .FILL   xFFD0
ASCIIBUFF      .BLKW   4,x0000
LookUp10       .FILL   #0
               .FILL   #10
               .FILL   #20
               .FILL   #30
               .FILL   #40
               .FILL   #50
               .FILL   #60
               .FILL   #70
               .FILL   #80
               .FILL   #90
;
LookUp100      .FILL   #0
               .FILL   #100
               .FILL   #200
               .FILL   #300
               .FILL   #400
               .FILL   #500
               .FILL   #600
               .FILL   #700
               .FILL   #800
               .FILL   #900
```

Figure 10.17: ASCII to Binary Conversion Routine, continued.

10.3.3 Binary to ASCII.

Similarly, it is useful to convert the 2's complement integer into an ASCII string so that it can be displayed on the monitor. Figure 10.18 shows the algorithm for converting a 2's complement integer stored in R0 into an ASCII string stored in four consecutive memory locations, starting at ASCIIBUFF. The value initially in R0 is restricted to be in the range -999 to +999. After the algorithm completes execution, ASCIIBUFF contains the sign of the value initially stored in R0. The following three locations contain the three ASCII codes corresponding to the three decimal digits representing its magnitude.

The algorithm works as follows. First, the sign of the value is determined, and the appropriate ASCII code is stored. The value in R0 is replaced by its absolute value. The algorithm determines the "hundreds digit" by repeatedly subtracting 100 from R0 until the result goes negative. This is next repeated for the "tens digit." The value left is the "ones digit."

```
;
; This algorithm takes the 2's complement representation of a signed
; integer, within the range -999 to +999, and converts it into an ASCII
; string of a sign digit, followed by three decimal digits.  R0 contains
; the initial value being converted.
;
BinarytoASCII   LEA     R1,ASCIIBUFF  ; R1 points to string being generated
                ADD     R0,R0,#0      ; R0 contains the binary value
                BRN     NegSign       ;
                LD      R2,ASCIIplus  ; First store the ASCII plus sign
                STR     R2,R1,#0
                BR      Begin100
NegSign         LD      R2,ASCIIminus ; First store ASCII minus sign
                STR     R2,R1,#0
                NOT     R0,R0         ; Convert the number to its absolute
                ADD     R0,R0,#1      ; value; it is easier to work with.
;
Begin100        LD      R2,ASCIIoffset ; Prepare for "hundreds" digit
;
                LD      R3,Neg100      ; Determine the hundreds digit
Loop100         ADD     R0,R0,R3
                BRN     End100
                ADD     R2,R2,#1
                BR      Loop100
;
```

Figure 10.18: Binary to ASCII Conversion Routine.

```
End100          STR     R2,R1,#1        ; Store ASCII code for hundreds digit
                LD      R3,Pos100
                ADD     R0,R0,R3        ; Correct R0 for one-too-many subtracts
;
                LD      R2,ASCIIoffset ; Prepare for "tens" digit
;
                LD      R3,Neg10        ; Determine the tens digit
Loop10          ADD     R0,R0,R3
                BRN     End10
                ADD     R2,R2,#1
                BR      Loop10
;
End10           STR     R2,R1,#2        ; Store ASCII code for tens digit
                ADD     R0,R0,#10       ; Correct R0 for one-too-many subtracts
;
                LD      R2,ASCIIoffset ; Prepare for "ones" digit
                ADD     R2,R2,R0
                STR     R2,R1,#3
                RET
;
ASCIIplus       .FILL   x002B
ASCIIminus      .FILL   x002D
ASCIIoffset     .FILL   x0030
Neg100          .FILL   xFF9C
Pos100          .FILL   x0064
Neg10           .FILL   xFFF6
```

Figure 10.18: Binary to ASCII Conversion Routine, continued.

Exercise: This algorithm always produces a string of four characters, independent of the sign and magnitude of the integer being converted. Devise an algorithm that eliminates unnecessary characters in common representations, i.e., an algorithm that does not store leading 0s nor a leading + sign.

10.4   Our final example: the Hand Calculator.

We conclude Chapter 10 with the code for a comprehensive example: the simulation of a hand calculator. The intent is to demonstrate the use of many of the concepts discussed thus far, as well as to show an example of well-documented, clearly written code, where the example is much more complicated than what can can fit on one or two pages. The calculator simulation consists of eleven separate routines.

You are encouraged to study this example before moving on to Chapter 11 and the next topic – High Level Language Programming.

The hand calculator works as follows: We use the keyboard to input commands and decimal values. We use the monitor to display results. We use a stack to perform arithmetic operations as described in Section 10.2. Values entered and displayed are restricted to three decimal digits, that is, only values between -999 and +999, inclusive. The available operations are

> 1: X – exit the simulation.
>
> 2: D – Display the value at the top of the stack.
>
> 3: C – Clear all values from the stack.
>
> 4: + – Replace the top two elements on the stack with their sum.
>
> 5: * – Replace the top two elements on the stack with their product.
>
> 6: - – Negate the top element on the stack.
>
> 7: value – Push the value typed on the keyboard on the top of the stack.

Figure 10.19 is a flow chart that gives an overview of our hand calculator simulation. Simulation of the calculator starts with initialization, which includes setting R6, the Stack Pointer, to an empty stack. Then the user sitting at the keyboard is prompted for input.

Input is echoed, and the calculator simulation systematically tests the character to determine the user's command. Depending on the user's command, the calculator simulation carries out the corresponding action, followed by a prompt for another command. The calculator simulation continues in this way until the user presses X, signalling that the user is done using the "hand calculator."

Eleven routines comprise the calculator simulation. Figure 10.20 is the main algorithm. Figure 10.21 takes an ASCII string of digits typed by a user, converts it to a binary number, and pushes the binary number on the top of the stack. Figure 10.17 provides the ASCII to binary conversion routine. Figure 10.22 pops the entry on the top of the stack, converts it to an ASCII string, and displays the ASCII string on the monitor. Figure 10.18 provides the binary to ASCII conversion routine. Figure 10.23 clears the stack. Figures 10.8 (OpAdd), 10.12 (OpMult) and 10.13 (OpNeg) supply the basic arithmetic algorithms using a stack. Figures 10.24 and 10.25 contain versions of the POP and PUSH routines tailored for this application.

Note that a few changes are needed if the various routines are to work with the main program of Figure 10.15. For example, OpAdd, OpMult, and OpNeg must all terminate with

```
BRnzp NewCommand
```

instead of RET. Also, some labels are used in more than one subroutine. If the subroutines are assembled separately, and certain labels are identified as .EXTERNAL (see Section 9.2.5), then the use of the same label in more than one subroutine is not a problem. However, if the entire program is assembled as a single module, then duplicate labels are not allowed. In that case, one must rename some of the labels (e.g., Restore1, Restore2, Exit, and Save) so that all labels are unique.

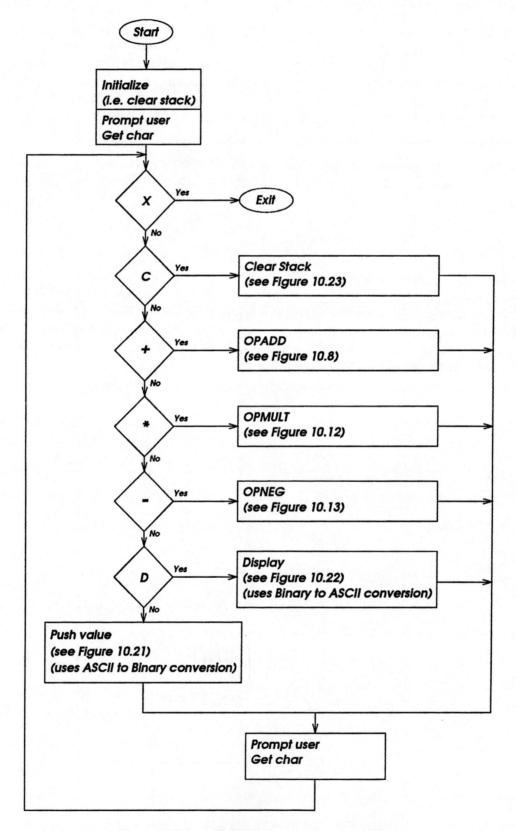

Figure 10.19: The Hand Calculator, Overview.

```
;
;   The Hand Calculator, Main Algorithm
;
                        LEA     R6,StackBase   ; Initialize the Stack.
                        ADD     R6,R6,#-1      ; R6 is stack pointer
                        LEA     R0,PromptMsg
                        PUTS
                        GETC
                        OUT

;
; Check the command
;
Test                    LD      R1,NegX        ; Check for X
                        ADD     R1,R1,R0
                        BRz     Exit

;
                        LD      R1,NegC        ; Check for C
                        ADD     R1,R1,R0
                        BRz     OpClear        ; See Figure 10.23

;
                        LD      R1,NegPlus     ; Check for +
                        ADD     R1,R1,R0
                        BRz     OpAdd          ; See Figure 10.8

;
                        LD      R1,NegMult     ; Check for *
                        ADD     R1,R1,R0
                        BRz     OpMult         ; See Figure 10.12

;
                        LD      R1,NegMinus    ; Check for -
                        ADD     R1,R1,R0
                        BRz     OpNeg          ; See Figure 10.13

;
                        LD      R1,NegD        ; Check for D
                        ADD     R1,R1,R0
                        BRz     OpDisplay      ; See Figure 10.22
```

Figure 10.20: The Hand Calculator's Main Algorithm.

```
;
; Then we must be entering an integer
;
                        BRnzp      PushValue      ; See Figure 10.21
;
NewCommand              LEA        R0,PromptMsg
                        PUTS
                        GETC
                        OUT
                        BRnzp      Test
Exit                    HALT
PromptMsg               .FILL      x000A
                        .STRINGZ "Enter a command:"
NegX                    .FILL      xFFA8
NegC                    .FILL      xFFBD
NegPlus                 .FILL      xFFD5
NegMinus                .FILL      xFFD3
NegMult                 .FILL      xFFD6
NegD                    .FILL      xFFBC
```

Figure 10.20: The Hand Calculator's Main Algorithm, continued.

```
;
; This algorithm takes a sequence of ASCII digits typed by the user,
; converts it into a binary value by calling the ASCIItoBinary
; subroutine and pushes the binary value onto the stack.
;
PushValue          LEA      R1,ASCIIBUFF   ; R1 points to string being generat
                   LD       R2,MaxDigits
;
ValueLoop          ADD      R3,R0,xFFF6    ; Test for carriage return
                   BRz      GoodInput
                   ADD      R2,R2,#0
                   BRz      TooLargeInput
                   ADD      R2,R2,#-1      ; Still room for more digits
                   STR      R0,R1,#0       ; Store last  character read
                   ADD      R1,R1,#1
                   GETC
                   OUT                     ; Echo it
                   BRnzp    ValueLoop
;
GoodInput          LEA      R2,ASCIIBUFF
                   NOT      R2,R2
                   ADD      R2,R2,#1
                   ADD      R1,R1,R2       ; R1 now contains no. of char.
                   JSR      ASCIItoBinary
                   JSR      PUSH
                   BRnzp      NewCommand
;
TooLargeInput      GETC                    ; Spin until carriage return
                   OUT
                   ADD      R3,R0,xFFF6
                   BRnp     TooLargeInput
                   LEA      R0,TooManyDigits
                   PUTS
                   BRnzp    NewCommand
TooManyDigits      .FILL    x000A
                   .STRINGZ "Too many digits"
MaxDigits          .FILL    x0003
```

Figure 10.21: The Hand Calculator's PushValue routine.

```
;
; This algorithm calls BinarytoASCII to convert the 2's complement
; number on the top of the stack into an ASCII character string, and
; then calls PUTS to display that number on the screen.
;
OpDisplay     JSR      POP              ; R0 gets the value to be displayed
              ADD      R5,R5,#0
              BRp      NewCommand       ; POP failed, nothing on the stack.
;
              JSR      BinarytoASCII
              LD       R0,NewlineChar
              OUT
              LEA      R0,ASCIIBUFF
              PUTS
              ADD      R6,R6,#1         ; Put displayed number back on stack
              BRnzp    NewCommand
NewlineChar   .FILL    x000A
```

Figure 10.22: The Hand Calculator's Display routine.

```
;
; This routine clears the stack by reseting the stack pointer (R6).
;
OpClear       LEA      R6,StackBase  ; Initialize the Stack.
              ADD      R6,R6,#-1     ; R6 is stack pointer
              BRnzp    NewCommand
```

Figure 10.23: The OpClear routine.

```
;
;   This algorithm POPs a value from the stack and puts it in
;   R0 before returning to the calling program.  R5 is used to
;   report success (R5=0) or failure (R5=1) of the POP operation.
;
POP             LEA     R0,StackBase
                NOT     R0,R0
                ADD     R0,R0,#2         ; R0 = -(addr.ofStackBase -1)
                ADD     R0,R0,R6         ; R6 = StackPointer
                BRz     Underflow
                LDR     R0,R6,#0         ; The actual POP
                ADD     R6,R6,#-1        ; Adjust StackPointer
                AND     R5,R5,#0         ; R5 <-- success
                RET
Underflow       ST      R7,Save          ; TRAP/RET needs R7
                LEA     R0,UnderflowMsg
                PUTS                     ; Print error message.
                LD      R7,Save          ; Restore R7
                AND     R5,R5,#0
                ADD     R5,R5,#1         ; R5 <-- failure
                RET
Save            .FILL   x0000
StackBase       .BLKW   9, x0000
StackMax        .FILL   x0000
UnderflowMsg    .FILL   x000A
                .STRINGZ "Error: Too Few Values on the Stack."
```

Figure 10.24: The Hand Calculator's POP Routine.

```
;
;  This algorithm PUSHes on the stack the value stored in R0.
;  R5 is used to report success (R5=0) or failure (R5=1) of
;  the PUSH operation.
;
PUSH            ST      R1,Save1        ; R1 is needed by this routine
                LEA     R1,StackMax
                NOT     R1,R1
                ADD     R1,R1,#1        ; R1 = - addr. of StackMax
                ADD     R1,R1,R6        ; R6 = StackPointer
                BRz     Overflow
                ADD     R6,R6,#1        ; Adjust StackPointer for PUSH
                STR     R0,R6,#0        ; The actual PUSH
                BR      Success_exit
Overflow        ST      R7,Save
                LEA     R0,OverflowMsg
                PUTS
                LD      R7,Save
                LD      R1, Save1       ; Restore R1
                AND     R5,R5,#0
                ADD     R5,R5,#1        ; R5 <-- failure
                RET
Success_exit    LD      R1,Save1        ; Restore R1
                AND     R5,R5,#0        ; R5 <-- success
                RET
Save            .FILL   x0000
Save1           .FILL   x0000
OverflowMsg     .STRINGZ "Error: Stack is Full."
```

Figure 10.25: The Hand Calculator's PUSH Routine.

10.5   Exercises.

10.1 What are the defining characteristics of a stack?

10.2 What is an advantage to using the model in Figure 10.3 to implement a stack versus the model in Figure 10.2?

10.3 Write a function that implements another stack function, peek. Peek returns the value of the first element on the stack without removing the element from the stack. Peek should also do underflow error checking. (Why is overflow error checking unnecessary?)

10.4 Rewrite the push and pop routines (in Figure 10.5) to model a stack implemented as in Figure 10.2, i.e., one in which the data entries move with each operation.

10.5 Re-write the push and pop routines such that the stack on which they operate holds elements that take up 2 memory locations.

10.6 Re-write the push and pop routines to handle stack elements of arbitrary sizes.

10.7 How would you check for underflow and overflow conditions if you implemented a stack using the model in Figure 10.2?

10.8 The following operations are performed on a stack.

Push A, Push B, Pop, Push C, Push D, Pop, Push E, Pop, Pop, Push F

1. What does the stack contain after the final Push?
2. At which point does the stack contain the most elements?
   Without removing the elements left on the stack from the previous operations, now we perform:
   Push G, Push H, Push I, Push J, Pop, Push K, Pop, Pop, Pop, Push L, Pop, Pop, Push M
3. What does the stack contain now?
4. Now at which point does the stack contain the most elements?

10.9 Say that the input stream of a stack is a list of all the elements we pushed onto the stack, in the order that we pushed them. The input stream from both parts of the previous problem was:

ABCDEFGHIJKLM

Say the output stream is a list of all the elements which are popped off the stack, in the order that they are popped off.

1. What is the output stream from both parts of the previous problem? Hint: BDC...
2. If the input stream is ZYXWVUTSR, create a sequence of pushes and pops such that the output stream is YXVUWZSRT.

3. If the input stream is ZYXWVUTSR, how many different output streams can be created?

10.10 Describe, in your own words, how the "Multiply" step of the OpMult Algorithm in Figure 10.11 works.

Is there a way to make the "Multiply" step work faster, i.e., to have it compute the product using fewer total instructions?

10.11 Correct Figure 10.14 so that it will add two one-digit positive integers and give a one-digit positive sum. Assume that the two digits being added do in fact produce a single digit sum.

10.12 Correct Figure 10.14, assuming that the input numbers are one-digit positive hex numbers. Assume that the two hex digits being added together do in fact produce a single hex digit sum.

10.13 The code in Figure 10.17 converts a decimal number represented as ASCII digits into binary. Extend this code to also convert a hexadecimal number represented in ASCII into binary. If the number is preceded by an 'x', then the subsequent ASCII digits (three at most) represent a hex number, otherwise it is decimal.

10.14 Refer to the flowchart in Figure 10.16 and the code in Figure 10.17. Suppose the decimal number is arbitrarily long. Rather than store a table of ten values for the "thousands" digit, another table of ten values for the "ten-thousands" digit, and so on, can we design an algorithm to do the conversion without resorting to any tables whatsoever?

10.15 The code in Figure 10.18 always produces a string of four characters, independent of the sign and magnitude of the integer being converted. Modify the code such that it eliminates unnecessary characters in common representations, i.e., an algorithm that does not store leading 0s nor a leading + sign.

Chapter 11

Introduction to Programming in C.

11.1 Our objective.

Congratulations! You have now completed an introduction to the basic underlying structure of computer systems. With this foundation solidly in place, you are now well prepared to move upwards in the levels of transformation, and to deal with a high-level computer programming language called C.

In the second half of this book, we will cover C from a unique perspective. We'll rely on your understanding of the low-level computing hardware to teach you high-level programming in C. At every step, with every new high-level concept, we will be able to make a connection to the lower levels of the computer system. From this perspective, nothing will be mysterious, nothing will be abstract. We approach the computer system from the bottom-up in order to reveal that there indeed is no "magic" going on when you execute the programs you write. It is our belief that with the mystery removed, you will comprehend programming concepts more quickly and deeply and in turn become better programmers.

Let's begin with a quick overview of the first half. In the first ten chapters, we described the LC-2, a simple computer that contains the basic elements of all computers. A basic idea behind the design of the LC-2 is that simple elements are systematically combined to form more sophisticated devices. MOS transistors are connected together to build logic gates. Logic gates are used to build the memory and datapath elements and these elements are combined to create the LC-2. This systematic connection of simpler devices to form more sophisticated devices is an important concept that is pervasive throughout computing. You will continue to see many examples of it in this half of the book.

After describing the hardware of the LC-2, we described how to program it. We started by programming in the 1's and 0's of its native machine language and quickly moved to the more user-friendly LC-2 assembly language. We learned how to systematically decompose a programming problem into pieces that could be easily coded on the LC-2. We examined how low-level TRAP subroutines perform commonly needed tasks on behalf of the programmer, tasks such as I/O. The concepts of systematic decomposition and subroutines are important not only for low-level programming but for high-level languages as well. You will continue to see examples of them many times before we are through.

Our intention for this half of the text is to go through the major components of the C programming language. The parts of the language not described within the second half are covered in the complete C reference manual in Appendix D. Our primary objective is to introduce fundamental high-level programming constructs—variables, control structures, functions, arrays, pointers, simple data structures. Along the way, we will discuss C syntax and, to a lesser degree, programming style, often relying on the many examples of C code to convey these points.

In this chapter, we will dive head-first into C by looking at a simple example program. With this example, we will point out some important details that you will need to know in order to start programming in C. But before we look at this example, let's examine why high-level languages are necessary in the first place and let's look at the techniques by which high-level programs are converted into machine language.

11.2   Bridging the gap.

As computing hardware becomes faster and more powerful, software becomes more complex and sophisticated. New generations of computer systems spawn new generations of software that can do more powerful things than previous generations. As the software gets more sophisticated, the job of developing it becomes more difficult. To prevent overwhelming the programmer, it is critical that the process of programming be kept as simple as possible. Any part of this process that can be done automatically (e.g., by the computer itself) is a welcome enhancement.

As we made the transition from LC-2 machine language in Chapters 5 and 6 to LC-2 assembly language in Chapter 7, you no doubt noticed and appreciated how assembly language greatly simplified programming the LC-2. The 1's and 0's became mnemonics and memory addresses became symbolic labels. The assembler filled some of the *gap* between the Algorithm level and the ISA level in the levels of transformation (see Figure 1.6). It would be desirable for the Language to fill more of that gap. And High-level languages do just that. Let's look at how.

All higher level programming languages (and to some degree even assembly language) allow the programmer to give symbolic names to values. In machine language, if we wanted to keep track of the iteration count of a loop, we need to set aside a memory location or a register in which to store the counter value. Accessing the counter means recalling its memory address and filling it into the appropriate LOAD or STORE instruction. In assembly language, we could assign a label to that memory location giving a more natural handle with which to refer to it. In a higher level language such as C, the programmer simply assigns the value a name (and, as we will see later, provide the *type* and indicate the *scope*) and the programming language takes care of allocating storage for it and performing the appropriate data movement operations whenever the programmer refers to it. Since programs often contain many values, having such a convenient way to handle values is a useful enhancement.

Often, a programmer will want to do an operation that is not naturally supported by the instruction set. In the LC-2, there is no one instruction that performs an integer multiply. Instead, an LC-2 programmer must write a small piece of code to perform multiplication. The operations supported by a high-level language is usually larger than the set supported by the ISA. The language will generate the necessary code to carry out the operation whenever the programmer uses it. The programmer than can concentrate on the actual programming task knowing that these operations will be performed correctly and without worrying about the low-level implementation.

Because of the systematic way in which programming tasks are broken down (as with systematic decomposition in Chapter 6), several control "patterns" appear frequently in the code we write. A construct to test a condition and do something if the condition is true or another if the condition is false, for instance, is a very common programming construct. The assembly language programmer almost always has to recreate this construct from scratch every time it's needed. In high-level languages, these common programming structures have simple expressions fashioned after those we use in English. For example, if we want to do taskA if condition is true, else do taskB if it is false, then in C we can use the following C *control structure*:

```
if (condition)
    taskA;
else
    taskB;
```

Since these common code structures are expressed using simple, English-like statements, the program itself becomes easier to read. One can look at a program in a high-level language and notice loops and decision constructs and quickly discern the intent of the code with less effort than with an assembly language program. As you will no doubt discover if you already haven't, the readability of code is very important in programming. Often as programmers, we are given the task of debugging or building upon someone else's code. If the *syntax* and *semantics* of the language are natural and intuitive to begin with, then understanding code in that language by reading it becomes a simpler task. The syntax of a programming language defines how its various components (declarations, expressions, statements) must be connected together to form proper code. The semantics of this code specify what the program does.

Certain high-level languages even provide safeguards against bugs. By making the programmer adhere to a strict set of rules, the language can make checks as the program is being translated or as the program is being executed. If certain rules or conditions are violated, an error message will direct the programmer to the spot in the code where the bug is likely to exist.

11.3   Translating higher level programs.

Just as LC-2 Assembly Language programs need to be translated (or more specifically, *assembled*) into machine code, high-level programs must be somehow translated into machine code. How this is done depends on the particular high-level language. And it can be done in one of two ways. One translation technique is called *interpretation*. With interpretation, a translation program called an *interpreter* reads in the high-level program and performs the operations indicated by the programmer. The high-level program doesn't directly execute, but rather is "executed" by the interpreter program. The other technique is called *compilation* and the translator, called a *compiler*, completely translates the high-level program into machine language. The translated program can then execute directly on the hardware. Keep in mind that both interpreters and compilers are themselves programs running on the computer system.

11.3.1   Interpretation.

With interpretation, a high-level program is just a set of commands for the interpreter program. The interpreter reads in the commands and carries them out as defined by the language. The high-level program never gets directly executed by the hardware, and in fact is just input data for the interpreter program. Without the interpreter, the program cannot execute; it is required every time the program is executed. Often, with interpreters, the high-level program is interpreted section-by-section, a single line, command, or subroutine at a time. High-level languages that are often interpreted include LISP, BASIC, perl, and Java. Special-purpose languages tend to be interpreted, such as the symbolic math language called Maple. The LC-2 simulator is also a form of interpreter.

11.3.2   Compilation.

With compilation, on the other hand, our high-level program is translated into machine language and can execute directly on the hardware. To do this effectively, the compiler must analyze the source program as a larger unit (usually, the entire source file) before producing the translation. A program need only to be compiled once, and can be executed many times. Many programming languages including C, C++, and FORTRAN, are typically compiled. The LC-2 Assembler is a rudimentary compiler.

11.3.3   Pros and cons.

There are advantages and disadvantages with either translation technique. With interpretation, developing and debugging a program is easier. Interpreters often allow the ability to execute through a program one section (single line, for example) at a time. This allows the programmer to examine intermediate results and make code modifications and additions on-the-fly. However, with interpretation, programs take longer to execute as there is a middle-man, the interpreter, which is actually doing the work. With compilation, the programmer has more control of what happens during execution. The programmer, with the compiler's assistance, can produce code which executes more quickly and uses memory more efficiently. Since compilation can produce more efficient code which doesn't require an interpreter to run, most real-world software, including the software we buy, tends to be produced using compiled languages.

11.4 The C programming language.

The C programming language was developed in 1972 by Dennis Ritchie at Bell Laboratories. The language was developed for use in developing compilers and operating system software and for this reason, the language has a low-level bent to it. The language allows the programmer to manipulate data items at a very low level (similar to assembly language) yet it still provides the expressiveness and convenience of a high-level language. It is for these reasons that C is very widely used today as more than just a language to develop compilers and system software.

In this book, all the examples and specific details will be based on a standard version of C called ANSI C. As with many programming languages, many variants of C have been introduced throughout the years. We will limit our discussion here to what is considered a standard and popular version of C. Most compilers support ANSI C and in order to compile and execute the sample code in the text, having access to an ANSI C compiler will be essential.

11.4.1 The C compiler.

The C compiler is the typical mode of translation from a C source program to an *executable image*. Recall from Section 7.4.1 that an executable image is a machine language representation of a program that is ready to be loaded into memory and executed. A typical compiler consists of several major components, as shown in Figure 11.1.

The C *preprocessor* performs the first phase. You will no doubt soon discover the importance of the preprocessor in C programming. As its name implies, the C preprocessor "preprocesses" the C program before handing it off to the actual compiler. The C preprocessor scans through the source files (the source files contain the actual C program) looking for and acting upon C preprocessor directives. These directives are similar to pseudo-ops in LC-2 Assembly Language. They . instruct the preprocessor to transform the C source file in some controlled manner, for example by substituting the character string PI with 3.14159 or by inserting the contents of file XYZ.h into the current file. All preprocessor directives begin with a pound sign # as the first character. All useful C programs rely on the preprocessor. We will deal with several important preprocessor directives in detail later in this chapter.

After the preprocessor transforms the input source file, the program is ready for compilation. The compiler transforms the program into an *object module*. Recall from Section 7.4.2 that an object module is the machine code for one section of the eventual program. There are

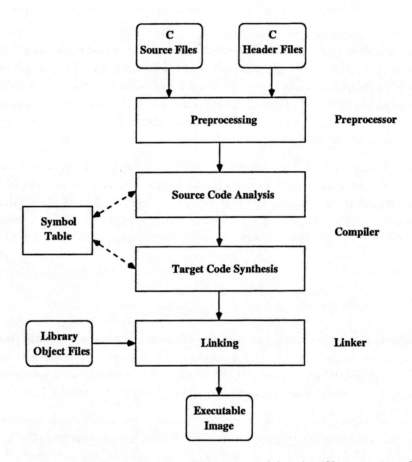

Figure 11.1: The C compilation process. C source and header files are translated into an executable image.

two major phases of compilation: analysis, where the source program is broken down or *parsed* into it constituent parts, and synthesis, where a machine code version of the program is generated. Often, the two portions of a compiler corresponding to these two phases are called the compiler's front end and the compiler's back end. It is the job of the front end to read in, parse, and build an internal representation for, the original program. The back end generates machine code and, if directed, attempts to optimize this code to run more quickly and efficiently on the particular computer its targeted for. Each of these two phases is typically divided into subphases where a specific task, such as parsing, register allocation, or instruction scheduling, is accomplished. Some compilers generate assembly code and use an assembler to complete the translation to machine code.

One of the most important internal representations a compiler uses in translating a program is called the *symbol table*. A symbol table is the compiler's internal representation of all the variables, functions, and other programmer-defined items in the program being compiled. It is similar to the symbol table maintained by the LC-2 assembler (see Section 7.3.3), but slightly different information is kept within each entry. We'll examine the C compiler's symbol table in more detail in the next chapter.

The linker takes over after the compiler has translated the source code into object code. It is the linker's job to link together all necessary object modules and form an executable image of the program. The process is the same as the assembly language process of linking together object modules to form an executable image. The executable image is a version of the program that can be loaded into memory and executed. When you click on the icon for the web browser on your computer, you are instructing the operating system to read the web browser executable image from your hard drive and load it into memory and start executing it.

Often, C programs rely upon library routines. Library routines perform common and useful tasks (such as I/O) and are prepared for general use by the programmers who developed the system software (the operating system and compiler, for example). Library routines are very similar to the LC-2 TRAP routines we examined in Chapter 9. If a program uses a library routine, then the linker will find the object code corresponding to the routine and link it within the final executable image. Usually library objects are stored in a particular place depending on the computer system. In UNIX, some library objects can be found in **/usr/lib**.

11.4.2 Using the C compiler.

Now let's examine how to use the C compiler. To compile a C source file named **prog_file1.c** into an executable image named **program**, we use the following command in UNIX:

```
cc -o program prog_file1.c
```

This command tells the C compiler (called **cc**, for C compiler) to read and process the file **prog_file1.c**. The **-o** (called the "dash-oh" switch or flag, in UNIX terminology) tells the compiler to generate an output file with the name program. In this case, we are invoking all the major phases of compilation: the preprocessor, the compiler, and the linker. After the compilation successfully completes, we can run the program by typing its name (in this case, program) at the command prompt. This, in turn, instructs the operating system to load the executable image into memory and to start executing it—this is the command line equivalent of double-clicking on an icon. Note that the extension on the name of the source file is important: the compiler assumes that since the input file has the extension .c, it is a C source file.

Instead of generating an executable image, sometimes it is useful to only generate a file containing the object module, or object file, particularly if the program being compiled consists of many source files. Typically, each source file will be compiled into an object file and after all the objects are generated, the linker is used to tie the objects together into an executable image. The following command runs the preprocessor and compiler but not the linker to generate an object file.

```
cc -c prog_file1.c
```

The switch, -c, causes the linker to be suppressed. The default output file generated will have the same base name as the input file with the extension .o, i.e., prog_file.o.

Once all the object files have been generated, we can link them together to form an executable image using the following command. Here, the program consists of 4 object files and we are creating an executable image called program.

```
cc -o program prog_file1.o prog_file2.o prog_file3.o prog_file4.o
```

The file name extension .o informs the compiler that the input files are all object files and that preprocessing and compilation need not be performed. The linker is automatically invoked to generate the executable image.

There are many other switches to the compiler which control the various phases of compilation. Some switches instruct the compiler to aggressively optimize the code, some switches instruct the compiler to insert extra information into the executable for debugging purposes. As you build expertise in C and want to explore the various controls on the C compiler, the UNIX command man will provide a detailed listing of all the cc switches. The man command is the UNIX version of a help command. It displays the manual pages associated with a particular topic.

```
man cc
```

We are now ready to start our exploration of the C programming language. Many of the new C concepts we present will be coupled with LC-2 code generated by a hypothetical LC-2 C compiler. In some cases, we will describe what actually happens when this code is executed. Although many of the examples and specific details will be for C, we will point out things which are fundamental to most high-level programming languages. Many of the examples are complete programs which you can compile and execute. When examples are not complete programs, we'll call them *code segments*.

11.5   A simple example.

Let us begin by diving head first into the example C program listed in Figure 11.2. We will use this example to point out some important structural features of C and to jump-start the process of learning C. The example is a simple one: it prompts the user to type in a number and then counts down from that number to 0, displaying each number along the way on the screen. At this point, it is not important to completely understand the purpose of each individual line of code. There are, however, several components that are useful to understand now. Understanding these components will help you in writing your first few C programs and help you better comprehend the examples that will be presented in the subsequent chapters.

At this point, you should be able to type in this code (or download it from the web), compile it, and try it out.

The code contains several important components. There are *comments* to help document the code. There are *preprocessor directives*, each beginning with the # character, which instruct the preprocessor to transform the source file in a particular way. There is *C source code* which begins at the line main() and ends at the closing brace, }. Within this C code, there are several *function calls* to perform I/O. We will describe each of these components in detail in the following subsections.

11.5.1   C source code.

First, we deal with the C source code. As we mentioned, the actual code begins at the line main() and ends at the closing brace at the last line of the program. This code is a *function definition* for a function called main. At this point, it is appropriate to think of functions as the C equivalent to LC-2 subroutines (which we discussed in Chapter 9). Functions are a very important part of C and we will devote all of Chapter 14 to them. For now, we point out that all C programs require a function named main. The function main is where the execution of every C program begins.

Within the function definition for main, the code can be broken down into three sections. The first section *declares* two variables called i and start which will be used within the function main. Variables are a very useful high-level programming device, essentially giving us a way to name values which we want to use within a program. More on variables in the next chapter. The second section displays a message and prompts the user to input a positive number. The output generated by this section looks as follows:

```
/* ============================================================ */
/*                                                              */
/*                   Countdown program                          */
/*                                                              */
/* ============================================================ */

/* Description : This program first prompts the user to type in
      a positive number and then counts down from that number to 0,
      displaying each number along the way. */

/* This is a preprocessor directive to include the standard I/O
      library's header file.  All programs that use the standard
      I/O library, i.e., all programs that perform I/O, require it */
#include <stdio.h>

#define STOP 0

/* All programs also require a function called main.  It is
      where execution of the program begins. */
main()
{
  /* Variable declarations */
  int i = 0;
  int start;

  /* Prompt the user for input */
  printf("Counting program ----\n");
  printf("Enter a positive number: ");
  scanf("%d", &start);

  /* Count down from the input number to 0 */
  for (i = start; i >= STOP; i--)
    printf("%d\n", i);
}
```

Figure 11.2: A program prompts the user for a decimal number and counts down from that number to 0.

```
Countdown Program ----
Enter a positive number:
```

Once the user enters a number, the program execution moves to the third section. Here, the program enters a `for` loop (a type of iteration construct which we will discuss in Chapter 13) which performs the countdown. For example, if the user entered the number 5, then the program's output would look as follows:

```
Countdown Program ----
Enter a positive number: 5
5
4
3
2
1
0
```

11.5.2   Comments, formatting and style.

Next, the comments and formatting. C's commenting style is different from LC-2 assembly language. Comments in C begin with `/*` and end with `*/`. They can span multiple lines. C source files often begin comments that contain the name of the program, the programmer's name, the date modified, etc., and a description of the code in the file. Comments are usually interspersed within the code to explain the intent of sections of the code. Too many comments, particularly ones which provide no additional information than what is obvious from reading the code, can clutter up the program making it hard to read.

Keep in mind that C is a generally free-format language. The amount of spacing between words within a program does not change the meaning of the program. The programmer is free to structure the program in whatever manner they see fit, while obeying the syntactic rules of C. There are some conventional forms of indentation which make the flow of the code more apparent, such as the indentation of the `for` loop at the end of the code in the example. The C code examples throughout this book use a conventional indentation style typical for C.

Notice in this example that many lines are terminated by semicolons, `;`. In C, semicolons are used to terminate variable *declarations* and *statements* and are necessary for the compiler to unambiguously break the program down into its constituent components. More on C syntax in the next chapter.

11.5.3   The C preprocessor.

We've briefly mentioned the C preprocessor in Section 11.4.1. Recall that it transforms the original C program before it is handed off to the compiler. Our simple example contains two commonly used preprocessor directives: `#define` and `#include`. The C examples in this book rely only on these two directives; the appendix D however describes several others.

The `#define` directive is simple, yet powerful directive: it instructs the C preprocessor to replace occurrences of any text that matches X with text Y, a process formally referred to as *macro substitution*. In the example, the `#define` causes the text STOP to be substituted with the text 0. So the following source line

```
for (i=start; i >= STOP; i--)
```

is transformed (internally, only between the preprocessor and compiler) into:

```
for (i=start; i >= 0; i--)
```

Often, the `#define` directive is used to create fixed values within a program, such as:

```
#define NUMBER_OF_STUDENTS 25
#define MAX_LENGTH    80
#define LENGTH_OF_GAME 300
#define COST_OF_WIDGET  19.69
#define PI  3.14159
```

The common programming style is to use uppercase for the text to be replaced. More examples and a more precise description of `#define` can be found in appendix D.

The `#include` directive instructs the preprocessor to literally insert another file into the source file. Essentially, the `#include` directive itself is replaced by the contents of another file. At this point, the usefulness of this command may not be completely apparent, but as we progress deeper into the C language, you'll understand how *C header files* can be used to contain `#defines` and declarations which are useful within several source files.

For instance, all programs which use the C I/O functions must include the I/O library's header file `stdio.h`. This file defines some relevant information about the I/O functions in the library. The preprocessor directive, `#include <stdio.h>` is used to insert the header file before compilation begins.

There are two variations of the `#include` directive:

```
#include <stdio.h>
#include "program.h"
```

The first variation uses angle brackets (< >) around the filename. This tells the preprocessor that the header file can be found in a predefined directory, usually determined by the configuration of the system and which contains many system-related and library-related header files. Often, we will want to include headers files we've created ourselves. The second variation, using double quotes (" ") around the filename, the instructs the preprocessor that the header file can be found in the same directory as the C source file.

More information about the `#include` command can be found in appendix D.

11.5.4 Input and output.

We close this chapter by pointing out some simple C input and output functions. We'll describe these functions at a high level and save the details for Chapter 18 when we've introduced enough background material to understand C I/O at a low level. Since all useful programs perform some form of I/O, learning the I/O capabilities of C is an important first step. In C, I/O is performed by library functions, similar to the IN and OUT trap routines provided by the LC-2 system software.

Several lines of the example program perform output using the C library function `printf`. The function `printf` performs output to the standard output device, which is typically defined to be the screen. It requires a *format string* in which we can provide two things: (1) text to print out and (2) specifications on how to print out values. The text is simply the text we want output to the standard output device when the `printf` is executed. In addition to text, it's often useful to print out values generated by the program. The specifications indicate the format in which these values are to be printed out. Let's examine a few examples:

```
printf("%d is a prime number.", 43);
printf("43 plus 58 in decimal is %d.", 43 + 58);
printf("43 plus 58 in hexadecimal is %x.", 43 + 58);
printf("43 plus 58 as an ASCII character is %c.", 43 + 58);
printf("The value of variable a is %d.", a);
```

The first example contains the format specification `%d` in its format string. It causes the value listed after the format string to be *embedded* in the output as a decimal number. So the output of the first example would be:

```
43 is a prime number.
```

The subsequent examples show variants of the `printf`. In the second example, the format specification will cause the value 101 (43 + 58) to be printed out as a decimal number. In the third example, the format specification `%x` causes 101 to be displayed as a hexadecimal number. Similarly, in the fourth example, the format specification of `%c` displays the value interpreted as an ASCII character (which in this case would be lower case e). Table F.1 contains a list of format specifications which can be used with `printf`—all format specifications begin with the percent sign, `%`. The last example demonstrates a common usage of `printf`. Here, a value generated during the execution of the program, in this case the *variable* a, is output as a decimal number. The value displayed depends on the value of a when this particular line of code is executed. More on variables in the next chapter.

If you were to execute the five `printf` statements above, you would notice that they are all displayed on one single line, i.e., without any line breaks. If we want line breaks to appear, we must put them explicitly within the format string in the places we want them to occur. Newlines, tabs, and other special characters require the use of a special backslash '\' sequence. For example, to print a newline character (and thus cause a line break), we use the special sequence '\n'. We can re-write the `printf` statements above as such:

```
printf("%d is a prime number.\n", 43);
printf("43 plus 58 in decimal is %d.\n", 43 + 58);
printf("43 plus 58 in hexadecimal is %x.\n", 43 + 58);
printf("43 plus 58 as an ASCII character is %c.\n", 43 + 58);
printf("The value of variable a is %d.\n", a);
```

Notice that each format string ends by printing the newline character '\n'. Each subsequent `printf` will begin on a new line. Appendix D.2.4 contains a list of other special characters which are useful when generating output.

In our sample program, `printf` appears three times in the source. The first two versions only display text and no values (thus they have no format specifications). The third version prints out the value of variable i. Generally speaking, we can display as many values as we like within a single `printf`. The number of format specifications (for example, `%d`) must correspond to the number of values being displayed.

Question: what if we replaced the third `printf` in the sample program with the following? (The expression "`start - i`" calculates the value of `start` minus the value of `i`.)

```
printf("%d %d\n", i, start - i);
```

Having dealt with output, we now turn to the corresponding input function `scanf`. The function `scanf` performs input from the standard input device, which is the keyboard by default. It requires a format string (similar to the one required by `printf` and a list of variables into which the values retrieved from the input device will be stored. The function `scanf` reads input from this device (say, the keyboard) and according to the conversion characters in the format string, converts the input and assigns the converted values to the variables listed.

In the sample program, we use `scanf` to read in a single decimal number using the format specification `%d`. Recall from our discussion on LC-2 keyboard input, the value received via the keyboard will be in ASCII. The format specification `%d` informs `scanf` to interpret the incoming sequence of ASCII keystrokes as a decimal number and to convert it into an integer representation. The result will be stored in the variable called `start`. A very important thing to remember is that all variables which are being modified by the `scanf` function (for example, `start`) must be preceded by an `&` character. This may seem mysterious now, but once we've covered pointers in Chapter 17 this notation will make sense. The format specification `%d` is one of several that can be used with `scanf`. Table F.2 lists them all. There are specifications to read in a single character, a floating point value, an integer expressed as a hexadecimal value, etc. Below are several more examples of scanf including one which reads in two decimal numbers.

```
scanf("%c", &new_char);   /* Reads in a character and stores it in new_char */
scanf("%f", &x);          /* Reads in a float and stored it in variable x */
scanf("%d %d", &a, &b);   /* Reads two decimal numbers, stores them in a and b */
```

11.6   Exercises.

11.1 Describe some problems or inconveniences you found when programming in lower level languages. How do higher level languages help reduce the tedium of programming in lower level languages?

11.2 What is the difference between an interpreted language and a compiled language?

11.3 What is the primary advantage to writing in a compiled language? What are some disadvantages to programming in a higher level language.

11.4   1. Describe the input to the C preprocessor.

   2. Describe the input to the C compiler.

   3. Describe the input to the linker.

11.5   1. What happens if we changed the second to last line of the program in Figure 11.2 from:

```
printf("%d\n", i);
```

   to:

```
printf("%c\n", i);
```

   2. What if we replaced it with:

```
printf("%d %d\n", i, start - i);
```

11.6 The following lines of C code appear in a program. What will be the output of each
printf statement.

```
#define LETTER '1'
#define ZERO    0
#define NUMBER 123

printf("%c", 'a');

printf("x%x", 12288);

printf("$%d.%c%d\n", NUMBER, LETTER, ZERO);
```

11.7 The scanf reads in a character from the keyboard and the printf prints it out. What
do the following two statements accomplish?

```
scanf("%c", &new_char);
printf("%d\n", new_char);
```

Chapter 12

Variables and operators.

In this chapter we'll cover two basic concepts of programming: variables and operators. *Variables* hold the values upon which the program acts and *operators* are the programming devices for manipulating them. Variables and operators together allow the programmer to more easily express the computations which constitute the real work to be done by a program.

The code segment below contains two lines of C code:

```
int i = 0;

i = i + 4;
```

The first line `int i = 0;` declares the variable `i`. The second line performs an operation based on `i`. In general, *declarations* inform the compiler of the variables we intend on using whereas the subsequent C *statements* describe the actual work we plan on doing with those variables. The first part of this chapter is devoted to variables. We'll cover the basic types of variables available in C and how they are declared. In the second part, we'll cover operators.

12.1   Variables.

A value is any data item upon which the program performs an operation. Examples of values include the iteration count for an executing loop or an input value entered by the user or a partial sum of a series of numbers which are being added together. Managing these values is a central concept in programming. When programming in LC-2 assembly language, we explicitly stored these values in memory or in a register and wrote code to move them from place to place in order to operate on them.

Since values are such an elementary component of programs, it makes sense that high-level languages should make the process of managing them simpler. High-level languages

261

allow the programmer to refer to the value *abstractly*. First, in all high-level languages, a programmer can select a symbolic name for a value. This is similar to the way we created labels for memory locations in LC-2 assembly language programming. These names can be chosen to reflect a characteristic of the value, allowing the programmer to more easily recall the intent of the value. For example, a value used to keep track of the number of iterations of a loop could be called `iteration_count`. Secondly, high-level languages completely manage the storage of a value so that a programmer can focus on writing the program and need not worry about where in memory to store a value or about juggling the value between memory and the registers. In high-level languages, these symbolically named values are called variables.

In C, variables must be *declared* before they can be used. Declaring a variable informs the compiler about the name of the variable, the type of information the variable will contain, and where in the program the variable will be used. The compiler needs this information in order to completely manage the variable. Optionally, the variable can be *initialized* in the declaration. This gives the variable an initial value.

In the example code at the beginning of this chapter, we declared a variable called `i` using the declaration:

```
int i = 0;
```

This declaration creates a variable which is to contain an integer value (as indicated by the `int`) and is initialized to the value 0. The compiler then reserves an integer's worth of memory for `i` (sometimes, the compiler can optimize the program such that `i` is stored in a register and therefore doesn't require a memory location, but that is a subject for later). Whenever `i` is referred to in the subsequent C code, the compiler will generate the appropriate machine code to access it.

Variables (except for global variables, which we will learn about shortly) can only be declared at the beginning of a *block*. We haven't built up enough knowledge of C syntax to formally define a block, but we roughly define it for the moment as a subsection of a program. All blocks begin with a open brace character { and end with a closing brace }. So any variables that need to be declared within a block are declared immediately after the start of the block, immediately after the open brace.

A variable's declaration conveys three pieces of information to the compiler: the variable's *identifier*, its *type*, and its *scope*. The first two of these the C compiler gets explicitly from the variable's declaration. In the case of the example declaration `int i = 0;`, the identifier is `i` and the variable is of integer type, as indicated by the `int` preceding its name. The third piece of information is the variable's scope. The scope of a variable is the region of the program in which the variable is accessible. It is implicitly specified by the place in the code where the declaration occurs.

Before we take a look at identifiers and type and scope in more detail, we note a fourth attribute called *storage class*. For variables in C, storage class can be either automatic or static. We will not deal with storage class in our coverage of C. Instead, we defer treatment of storage class to the C reference manual in appendix D.3.4.

12.1.1 Three basic data types: int, char, double.

We have already encountered the concept of data type in Chapter 2. Essentially, all data within a computer system exists as a pattern of bits. In order to give meaning to this pattern, we impose a type upon it. For example, the binary pattern 0110 0101 might be the lower case e or it might be the decimal number 101 depending on whether we treat it as an ASCII data type or as an integer data type.

In C, there are three commonly used data types: `int` or signed integer, `char` or character, and `double` or floating point (actually, double-precision floating point).

The `int` type declares a signed integer value. The range in value of an `int` depends on the particular Instruction Set Architecture of the computer and compiler being used. In the LC-2 an `int` is a 16-bit 2's complement integer with which we can represent numbers between +32767 and -32768.

The following line of code declares an integer variable called `count`.

```
int count;
```

Notice that this declaration is different from the declaration of `int i = 0;` from the previous section: the declaration for `count` does not have an initializer. In C, the initializer is an optional component of a variable's declaration.

The `char` type declares a variable whose data value represents a character. Although 8 bits are sufficient to hold an ASCII character, for purposes of making the examples in this textbook less cluttered, all `char` variables will be allocated 16 bits by our LC-2 C compiler.

Below are two example declaration for variables of type `char`. The variable `lock` is initialized to hold the ASCII value of upper case Q whereas `key` is not explicitly initialized. (What value will this uninitialized variable start off with? We will be able to answer this question shortly). Also notice that the upper case Q is surrounded by single quotes ' '. In C, characters which are to be interpreted as ASCII constants are surrounded by single quotes. In other words, the variable `lock` is initialized to the ASCII value of Q.

```
char lock = 'Q';
char key;
```

The C type `double` refers to a double-precision floating point variable. The representation of floating point numbers is different than that of integers. As we learned in Section 2.7.1, floating point numbers are represented very similarly to the scientific notation we learned in high school, except they are represented in base 2 rather than base 10. There is another floating point type in C called `float`, which declares a single-precision floating point number, however `double` is more commonly used because of its increased precision. The size of the `double` type is dependent on the Instruction Set Architecture of the computer and compiler. It almost always is at least the size of an integer. Floating point numbers are often used in situations where the calculation demands precision to many decimal places. Floating point constants are represented containing either a decimal point or an exponent, or both, as demonstrated in the example code below. The exponent signified by the character e or E can be positive or negative and represents the power of 10 the fractional part (the part that preceeds the e or E) is multiplied by. Note that the exponent must be an integer value. For more information on floating point constants, see Appendix D.2.4.

```
double average;
double one_point_one = 1.1;       /* This number is 1.1   */
double one_hundred_ten = 1.1E2;   /* This number is 110.0 */
double one_hundred = 1E2;         /* This number is 100.0 */
double one_tenth = 1E-1;          /* This number is 0.1   */
```

The programmer actually has a small degree of flexibility in selecting the size these basic types. The words `long` and `short` can be attached to `int` or `double` with the intent of extending or shortening the default size. For example, a `long int` can declare a integer which has twice the number of bits as a regular `int` thereby allowing us to represent a larger range of numbers. The exact operation of these size declarations depends on the particular implementation of C being used. Similarly, the specifier `long` can be attached to the `double` type to create a larger floating point type (if supported by the particular system) with greater range and precision. See Appendix D.3.3 for more examples and additional information on `long` and `short`.

Another useful variation of the basic `int` data type is the unsigned integer. We can declare an unsigned integer using the `unsigned` type specifier. With unsigned integers, all bits are used to represent positive numbers. In the LC-2 for instance, which has 16-bit integers, an unsigned integer has a value between 0 and 65535. For additional information and examples, see Appendix D.3.3.

The type of a variable is used by the compiler to allocate the proper amount of space in memory for the variable. A variable's type also indicates how to generate proper code for performing operations on the variable. For instance, performing an addition on two integer variables can be done on the LC-2 with one ADD instruction. If the two variables, were double-precision floating point numbers, then our LC-2 compiler would have to generate a small sequence instructions to perform the addition since no single LC-2 instruction performs a floating-point addition.

For some programming languages, the type of a variable is implicit. In FORTRAN, the name (actually, the first letter of the name) of a variable tells the compiler if the variable is implicitly an integer. In some interpreted languages, the interpreter allows the programmer to fluidly switch a variable from one type to another (often in these languages, the variables don't even need to be declared). Neither of these is the case with the C programming language.

In C, variables can also be specified as *constants* by adding the `const` qualifier before its type. These constants are really variables whose values do not change during the execution of a program. For example, in writing a program which calculates the area of a circle given a radius as input, it might be useful to create a constant called `pi` initialized to the value 3.14159. More information on constants can be found in appendix D.2.4.

12.1.2 Identifiers.

Giving variables meaningful names is important for writing good code. Most high-level languages have flexible rules for the names (or more formally, identifiers) that can be chosen. C allows you to create identifiers composed of upper and lower case letters of the alphabet, digits, and the underscore character _. Only letters and the underscore character, however, can begin an identifier. An identifier can be of any length, but only the first 31 characters are used by C compiler to differentiate variables—only the first 31 characters matter to the compiler. Variables beginning with an underscore (e.g., `_index_`) are conventionally only used in special library code. Even though upper case is allowed, C programmers generally use lower case for identifiers reserving upper case for special items such as preprocessor macros. See 11.5.3.

There are certain *keywords* in C which have special meaning and therefore restricted from being used as identifiers. A list of C keywords can be found in appendix D.2.6. One keyword we've encountered already is `int` and we cannot name a variable `int`. The rationale for preventing keywords from being used as variables is a simple one: to avoid situations of ambiguity where the programmer expresses one thing and the compiler interprets another.

12.1.3 Scope: globals and locals.

The third piece of information the compiler gleans from a variable's declaration is its scope. The scope of a variable defines the region of the program in which the variable is accessible. Some variables can be accessed throughout the program. These are referred to as global variables. Some variables can only be accessed in smaller regions of a program. These variables are local to the region in which they are accessible. In C, the programmer doesn't explicitly state the scope of a variable. Instead the compiler infers the scope from the place in the program a variable is declared.

In C variables are accessible within the block in which they are declared. We will provide a more precise definition for a block after we have introduced more C syntax, but roughly stated a block is a programmer-defined subsection of the program. Blocks are organized within a hierarchy; blocks can contain other blocks. As mentioned earlier, blocks in C code begin with the open brace character { and end with a closing brace }.

To begin with, the entire program is a conceptually a block (but it is an exception to the rule stated above—it is NOT surrounded by an open brace and a closing brace). Any variable declared in this outermost block is accessible anywhere within the program. They are called *global* variables. Using global variables within a program should be done judiciously. They can be extremely helpful in certain programming situations, but can add complications later when debugging or modifying code. For this reason, novice programmers are often instructed to not use global variables.

The entire program is divided up into smaller subprograms (or subroutines, as we saw in LC-2 assembly language) called functions. Each function is also considered a block. We will devote all of Chapter 14 to functions. Variables declared within a functions are *local* to that functions and they can be accessed only within the body of the function. Furthermore, a programmer can create a sub-block of C code anywhere within a function. Variables declared within a sub-block are local to that sub-block. It is possible, and sometimes useful, to declare two different variables with the same name as long as they are defined within different blocks.

Whenever a reference is made to variable within a program, the compiler will use the most local declaration in the block hierarchy to identify the variable. Put another way: if a local variable is declared within a block that same name as a global variable, then the local variable gets accessed within the block and not the global. We will present examples of such scoping rules in the next section.

12.1.4 Some examples.

In this section, we present some examples of variable declarations in C.

The following examples demonstrate declarations of the three basic types discussed in this chapter. Some declarations have no initializers. Some do. Note how floating point and character constants are expressed in C.

```
double w;
double p = 9.44;
double mole = 6.02E23;
double very_small = 9.1094E-31;
int average = 2;
int i = 0;
int jump;
int k;
int l = 4;
char key = 'A';
```

What happens if no initializer is specified? In C, all variables of automatic storage class are not initialized. For us, this means that all local variables have an unknown value when they are first encountered. Their value depends on whatever is in the memory location to which they are assigned. In C, it is the programmer's responsibility to ensure the variables are somehow initialized during the course of execution. In the example above, the variables w, jump, and k have will some unknown value to start with. As a side note, variables of static storage class (global variables, for example) are automatically initialized to 0.

Shown below are some sample variations on the three basic types.

```
long int q;
unsigned int r, s = 900;
float t = 9.24;
float c = 2.998E8;
```

For sake of a more complete coverage of C syntax, we present the following example. In this line of code, four integer variables are declared on a single line. Each different variable is separated by a comma and the complete declaration ends with a semicolon. Though this form of declaration is legal in C, such style is typically discouraged for people new to C. Instead, the preferred style is to declare each variable on a separate line.

```
int i, j, k, l;
```

The following example demonstrates scoping within C. Recall that the braces mark the beginning and end of a block. For this code segment, only the variable declaration are shown; all other code has been omitted.

```
int i = 1;  /* This version of i is global */
            /* because it is outside all other blocks */
{
   /* Block A */
   int i = 2;

   printf("%d\n", i);     /* Outputs a 2 */
}

{
   /* Block B */
   int i = 3;

   printf("%d\n", i);     /* Outputs a 3 */

   {
      /* Block C */
      int i = 4;

      printf("%d\n", i);  /* Outputs a 4 */
   }

   {
      /* Block D */
      printf("%d\n", i);  /* Outputs a 3 */
   }

}

{
   /* Block E */
   printf("%d\n", i);     /* Outputs a 1 */
}
```

There are four different variables each called i declared in this code segment. The first declaration occurs outside of all other blocks, i.e., within the "block" of the whole program, and therefore is a global variable. The other declarations are local within the blocks in which they are declared.

To illustrate the scoping rules, we've output the values of i at various points within the program using printf. The printf in block A will display a 2, the printf in block B will output a 3, and the printf in block C outputs a 4. Each printf refers to the variable declared locally within its block. The printf in block D will display a 3; it refers to the variable i declared within block B. This declaration is the innermost declaration of i in relation to block D. Finally, the `printf` in block E outputs a 1. No local declarations of i apply to it. It refers to the global version of i declared outside all other blocks.

12.1.5   Symbol table.

In chapter 7, we examined how the assembler systematically keeps track of labels within an assembly program by using a *symbol table*. Labels for memory locations at the assembly level are in many ways like variables in higher level programming languages. Like the assembler, the C compiler keeps track of variables through a symbol table in order to translate the original program into machine language. Whenever the compiler reads a variable declaration, it creates a new entry in its symbol table for the variable. The entry contains enough information for the compiler to manage the new variable—each entry contains the name of the variable, its type, an offset into a storage area in memory (which helps the compiler generate the address of the memory location in which to store the variable), and an identifier which indicates the block in which it is defined. In the next few chapters we'll examine more closely how the symbol table information is used by the compiler to generate correct machine code.

The symbol table keeps track of more than just variables, though. Anything that the programmer provides an identifier for is entered into the symbol table. Functions, enumerated types, structures, in addition to variables, are examples of things a programmer might name. As we introduce these concepts, we shall see how the compiler uses information contained in the symbol table to translate a high-level program into machine code. ' Figure 12.1 shows the symbol table entries corresponding to the variables declared in the example program at the end of Chapter 11. The declarations from this program are shown below. There are two variables declared, thus two entries are added to the symbol table for them. Both have a scope local to `main`. The variable i is an integer variable with an offset of 3. The variable `start` is of also type `int` and has an offset of 4. More on offsets in a moment.

```
int i = 0;
int start;
```

The variable i has an initializer. The compiler will generate code to initialize this variable at the beginning of the block in which it is defined. In this case, at the beginning of the function `main`, there will exist code to set i to 0. In general, variables can be initialized to any legal value when they are declared using the optional initializer. As we mentioned before (which we mention again to stress its importance), in C all global variables are initialized to 0, but all local variables must be initialized by the programmer.

12.1.6   Allocating space for variables.

The offset field in the symbol table provides information about where in memory variables are actually stored. For all examples in this textbook, all variables will be assigned a memory location. However, real compilers perform code optimizations which allocate variables in

Symbol Table

Name	Type	Offset	Scope
i	int	3	main

Name	Type	Offset	Scope
start	int	4	main

Figure 12.1: The compiler's symbol table when it compiles the program from chapter 10.

registers (since registers take less time to access than memory, the program will run faster if frequently accessed values are put into registers) or remove unused variables altogether.

There are two regions of memory in which C variables are allocated storage. The global data section is where all global variables are stored. The offset attribute in the symbol table indicates the location where the variable is stored by expressing it as the distance in memory locations from the start of the region. For instance, if a global variable x had an offset of 4 and the global data section started at memory location 0x8000, then x would be stored in location 0x8004. For all our examples in this text, R5 contains the address of the beginning of the global data section. Loading the variable x into R3, for example, can be accomplished with the following LC-2 instruction:

```
LDR  R3, R5, #4
```

The run-time stack is where all local variables are stored. We will describe the mechanics of the run-time stack in Chapter 14. For now, whenever we are executing instructions within a particular function, then R6 will contain the address of the beginning (or top) of the run-time stack. We will describe the mechanism by which R6 gets properly in Chapter 14 when we discuss functions. So referring to the code from the example from the previous chapter, the LC-2 code generated by our LC-2 C compiler to initialize the variable i is listed below. It's important to remember that other compilers, such as the one you use on your PC, will not generate LC-2 code, but rather code in the particular Instruction Set Architecture of your computer.

```
AND  R2, R2, #0   ;   Zero out R2
STR  R2, R6, #3   ;   Store a 0 into i
```

Figure 12.2 shows the organization of memory when a program is running. The program itself occupies a region, so does the run-time stack and the global data section. There are other regions as well which we will describe in upcoming chapters. Notice that R5 is

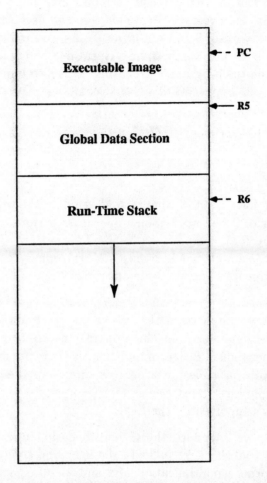

Figure 12.2: A few of the regions of memory defined for program execution.

anchored to point to the global data section. R6 points to the current top of the run-time stack and the PC points to an instruction in the region where the executable image resides.

When our LC-2 C compiler analyzes a block of code, it allocates memory space for each variable declared within the block. The outermost block in a C program is the program itself and variables declared there are global variables. In our LC-2 compiler, they are allocated space in the global data segment on a first declared, first allocated basis. So the first variable declared gets the first spot, offset 0. The second variable declared gets the next available spot, offset 1, and so forth. Local variables are allocated on the run-time stack and are also allocated in the order the compiler sees the declarations. The first declared variable gets offset 3. Why offset 3 and not offset 0? As we shall see in upcoming chapters, there is vital information kept in the first three locations which are used by the computer to manage the stack while the program is executing. It is also important to realize that this scheme is particular to our hypothetical LC-2 C compiler. Other compilers may perform this variable allocation differently.

12.2   Operators.

All high-level languages have a set of operators that allow the programmer to manipulate variables in order to perform real work. Some operators perform arithmetic, some perform logic functions, others perform comparisons between two values. These operators allow the programmer to express a computation in a more natural, convenient, and compact way than by expressing it as a sequence of assembly instructions.

The first thing to realize is that even with a small set of operate instructions, the LC-2 can be programmed to do any computation that we can do by hand. The LC-2 only supports ADD, AND, and NOT instructions, but these operations are complete enough for it to do other, more complex operations. Programmers can, if they are so inclined, have the LC-2 calculate the square root of a value. In a process similar to the construction of the LC-2 datapath from very simple logic gates, one can perform very sophisticated operations using the simple ones natively supported by the LC-2.

To illustrate this point, we introduce the C multiplication operator, *. We've declared three unsigned integer variables, x, y, and z in the following code segment. The last line is a statement which performs a multiplication of x and y and *assigns* the result to z.

```
    unsigned int x = 7;
    unsigned int y = 5;
    unsigned int z;

    z = x * y;
```

Our LC-2 C compiler will generate LC-2 code which first initializes the values of x to 7 and y to 5 and then performs the multiplication by repeatedly adding the value of x to itself a total of y times, similar to the code we saw in the calculator example in Chapter 10. The

LC-2 code generated by our hypothetical compiler looks like the following. Keep in mind that R6 contains the address of the top of the run-time stack where all local variables are allocated storage.

```
              AND  R4, R4, #0    ;  zero out R4
              ADD  R4, R4, #7    ;  R4 <- 7
              STR  R4, R6, #3    ;  x = 7; -- recall x has offset 3

              AND  R4, R4, #0    ;  zero out R4
              ADD  R4, R4, #5    ;  R4 <- 5
              STR  R4, R6, #4    ;  y = 3; -- recall y has offset 4

              AND  R4, R4, #0    ;  zero out R4
              LDR  R2, R6, #3    ;  load the value of x into R2
              LDR  R3, R6, #4    ;  load the value of y into R3
LOOP          BRZ  DONE
              ADD  R4, R4, R2    ;  The multiply loop, the result is in R2
              ADD  R3, R3, #-1
              BR   LOOP

DONE:         STR  R4, R6, #5    ;  z = x * y; -- recall z has offset 5
```

The C version of this code is more like the standard mathematical expression for multiplication than the corresponding LC-2 code.

12.2.1 Expressions and statements.

Before proceeding, let's take a moment to define a little C syntax. At this point, we've covered variables and constants. We can combine variables and constants with operators, such as the multiply operator from the previous example, to form C an *expression*. In the previous example, x * y is an expression.

Expressions can be grouped to form a *statement*. Again from the previous example, z = x * y; is a statement. Statements in C are like complete sentences in English. Just as a sentence captures a complete thought or description or action, a C statement expresses a complete unit of work to be carried by the computer. All simple statements in C end with a semicolon character, ;. The semicolon separates the end of one statement from the beginning of another in much the same way a period separates two sentences in English.

In C it is possible to create pathological statements which do not express any computation, but are nonetheless syntactically. The null statement is just simply a semicolon, as shown in the example below. Also shown is another form of a null statement. Both are legal C statements.

```
    z = x * y;      /* This statement accomplishes some work */
    ;               /* Null statement */
    5;              /* also a null statement */
```

One or more simple statements can be grouped together to form a compound statement, or block, by enclosing the simple statements within braces, { }. Syntactically, compound statements are equivalent to simple statements. We shall see examples of compound statements in the next chapter. By the end of this chapter, you should be familiar not only with variables and operators, but using variables and operators to form expressions and simple C statements.

12.2.2 The assignment operator.

The first C operator we formally introduce is the C assignment operator. Its symbol is simply the equal sign, =. The operator works as follows: the right-hand side of the assignment operator is evaluated and the left-hand side is set to the value of the right hand side. Let's take a look at a segment of C code and its LC-2 translation.

```
    int x = 9;   /* x will have the offset 3 */

    x = x + 4;   /* We now expect the value of x to be 13 */
```

The LC-2 code looks like:

```
                        ;   initialize x
        AND  R2, R2, #0     ;   Clear out R2
        ADD  R2, R2, #9     ;   R2 contains the value 9
        STR  R2, R6, #3     ;   x = 9;

        LDR  R2, R6, #3     ;   Get the value of x
        ADD  R2, R2, #4     ;   calculate x + 4
        STR  R2, R6, #4     ;   x = x + 4;
```

The LC-2 translation includes an instruction to reload the value of x into R2 (the LDR instruction) even though this instruction is unnecessary. The compiler could have removed that instruction and the program would still work (in fact, it would run faster). For the sake of making the examples clearer, in all the LC-2 code presented in this half of the book, we will include the translation corresponding to each individual C statement. Keep in mind that a real compiler will attempt to eliminate unnecessary instructions when generating optimized machine code, but that is a subject for a more advanced course.

Notice that even though the algebraic symbol for equality is the same as the C symbol for assignment, they have different meanings. In mathematics, by using the equal sign = one is making the assertion that the right hand and left hand expressions are equivalent. In C, using the = operator causes the compiler to generate code which will make the left-hand side change its value to equal the value of the right-hand side. In other words, the left-hand side is assigned the value of the right.

In C, all expressions evaluate to a value of particular type. From the previous example, the expression x + 4 evaluates to the integer value of 13. This integer value of 13 is assigned to the integer variable x. What would happen if we constructed an expression of mixed type, for example x + 4.3? The general rule is that the mixed expressions will be *promoted* from character to integer and from integer to floating-point. Also, shorter types are converted to longer types. Thus the expression x + 4.3 takes on a floating point type. What if we attempted to assign an expression of one type to a variable of another, for example x = x + 4.3? The type of a variable remains immutable in C, so the expression is converted to the type of the variable. More on the specific of both these situations in Section 12.2.10 of this chapter.

The fact that all C expressions evaluate to a value is an important concept to keep in mind; some programmers tend to rely on this fact heavily. The assignment operator generates the value begin assigned. For example, the expression x = 3 itself has the integer value 3. The following is a valid C statement:

```
y = x = 3;  /* Here, y will get the value 3 because x = 3  */
            /* evaluates to the value 3                     */
```

12.2.3 Arithmetic operators.

The arithmetic operators are easy to understand. Many of the operations and corresponding symbols are ones we are accustomed to, having used them since learning arithmetic in grade school. For instance, + performs addition, - subtraction, * performs multiplication (which is different from the symbol we are accustomed to for multiplication in order ambiguity with the letter x). The symbol / performs division. These operators are interpreted slightly differently depending on the type of the expression they are used in. For instance, the C compiler will generate a different stream of LC-2 instructions if the two operands being added together are doubles (recall, these are double-precision floating point numbers) than if the operands are integers. Adding two integers in the LC-2 can be done with an ADD instruction, whereas adding two floating point values requires a sequence of instructions.

What happens when we divide two integer values? When performing an integer divide, the C convention is to drop the fractional part and keep the integral part as the result. The expression 11 / 4 evaluates to 2. The modulus operator %, can be used to calculate the integer remainder. For example, 11 % 4 evaluates to 3. The modulus operator can only be used with integral (char and int) data types.

Below we show several C statements formed using the arithmetic operators.

```
distance = rate * time;

net_income = income - taxes_paid;

fuel_economy = miles_traveled / fuel_consumed;

area = 3.14159 * radius * radius;

y = a*x*x + b*x + c;

z = x / y;    /* If x and y are integers, then the result is the
                 integral portion of the result: e.g., 7 / 2 = 3 */

z = x % y;    /* The result is x mod y, for example 7 % 2 = 1 */
```

Table 12.1 lists all the arithmetic operations.

Operator symbol	Operation	Example usage
*	multiplication	x * y
/	division	x / y
%	modulus	x % y
+	addition	x + y
-	subtraction	x - y

Table 12.1: Arithmetic operators in C. Multiplication, division, and modulus have higher precedence than addition and subtraction. Arithmetic operators of equal precedence associate from left-to-right.

12.2.4 Precedence and associativity.

Before proceeding on to the next set of operators, we diverge momentarily to answer an important question. What value is stored in x as a result of the following statement?

```
x = 2 + 3 * 4;
```

Just as when doing arithmetic, there is an order in which expressions are evaluated. For instance, when evaluating a formula in algebra, multiplication and division have higher precedence than addition and subtraction. For operations of equal precedence, evaluation is carried out from left to right, i.e., they associate left-to-right. In programming language terms, operators are arranged in terms of *precedence* and *associativity*. For the arithmetic operators, the C precedence rules are the same as we are taught in arithmetic. In the statement above, x is assigned the value 14 because the multiplication operator has higher precedence than addition.

Here's an example of associativity. What will be the value of x after this statement executes?

```
x = 2 + 3 - 4 + 5;
```

The operators + and - are of equal precedence, but they associate left-to-right. The value of 6 is assigned to x.

The complete set of precedence and associativity rules for all operators is provided in Table 12.6 at the end of this chapter and also in Appendix D.5.10. Attempting to memorize this table is counter-productive to learning C. Instead it is important to realize that precedence rules exist and to roughly comprehend the logic behind them and to refer to the table when necessary. There is a safeguard, however: parentheses.

Parentheses override the evaluation rules by explicitly specifying which operations are to be performed ahead of others. Evaluation always begins at the innermost parentheses. Parentheses help make code more readable (since most of the people reading your code will not have memorized the precedence rules either). We can surround a subexpression with parentheses if we want that subexpression evaluated first. So in the example below, say the variables a, b, c, and d are all equal to 4. The statement:

```
x = a * b + c * d / 2;
```

could equivalently be written as:

```
x = (a * b) + ((c * d) / 4);
```

For both statements, x is set to the value 20. Here the compiler will always evaluate the innermost subexpression first and move outwards before falling back on the precedence rules. What would the value of this expression be written as below, a, b, c, d still equal to 4? The answer 32 should not surprise you.

```
x = a * (b + c) * d / 4;
```

12.2.5   Bitwise operators.

Now we continue our treatment of the C operators, covering the bitwise operators in this section. The C operator corresponding to the LC-2 instruction AND is &. The & operator performs an AND, *bitwise* (bit-by-bit) across the two input operands. The C operator | performs a bitwise OR. The operator ˜ performs a bitwise NOT and takes only one operand, i.e., it is a unary operator. The operator ^ performs a bitwise XOR. Examples of expression using these operators are given below. Recall, in C hexadecimal constants are preceded by a 0x.

```
0x1234 & 0x5678   /* equals 0x1230 */
0x1234 | 0x5678   /* equals 0x567C */
0x1234 ^ 0x5678   /* equals 0x444C */
~0x1234           /* equals 0xEDCB */
1234 & 5678       /* equals 1026  */
```

There are two shift operators: << and >> which accomplish a left shift and right shift respectively. They are both binary operators, meaning they require two operands. The second operand, which must be an integer or character type, indicates the number of bit positions to shift the value of the first operand. Neither of these operators modifies the value of the operands. Examples of expressions using the shift operators is given below.

```
0x1234 << 3       /* equals 0x91A0 */
0x1234 >> 2       /* equals 0x048D */
1234 << 3         /* equals 9856  */
1234 >> 2         /* equals 308   */
```

The operand to be shifted can be of any type. The programmer, if he or she wanted, could shift a `char` variable or a `double` variable. This is an example of the flexibility of C which has helped make it so popular. A programmer can manipulate the bits of an arbitrary variable in whatever fashion he or she feels necessary. However, it also allows one to shoot themselves in the foot and spend countless hours tracking down and fixing bugs.

Below we show several C statements formed using the bitwise operators.

```
int f = 7;
int g = 8;
int h = 0;

h = f & g;      /* h will equal 0  */

h = f | g;      /* h will equal 15 */

h = ~f | ~g;    /* h will equal -1 */
```

```
h = f << 1;      /* h will equal 14.  f will not be modified */

h = g << f;      /* h will equal 1024. g or f will not be modified */
```

Table 12.2 shows all the bitwise operators.

Operator symbol	Operation	Example usage
~	bitwise NOT	~x
<<	left shift	x << y
>>	right shift	x >> y
&	bitwise AND	x & y
^	bitwise XOR	x ^ y
|	bitwise OR	x | y

Table 12.2: Bitwise operators in C. The operators are grouped in order of precedence, the NOT operator having highest precedence, and the left and right shift operators having equal precedence, followed by AND, then XOR, then OR. They all associate from left-to-right. See table 12.6 for a complete listing of operator precedence.

12.2.6 Logical operators.

Logical operators are so closely related to bitwise operators that beginning programmers often confuse the two. The three logical operators in C are &&, ||, and !. The && operator performs a logical AND of its two operands: it evaluates to an integer value of 1 if both its operands are logically true. C adopts the notion that a non-zero (i.e., something other than zero) value is logically true. Anything with a value of zero is logically false. It is an important concept to remember and we shall see it surface many times as we go through the various components of the C language. So, the && operator evaluates to a 1 (logically true) if **both** operands are non-zero (logically true). For example, 3 && 4 evaluates to a 1. The expression x && y evaluates to a 1 only if x AND y are both not zero. It evaluates to 0 otherwise.

The || operator is the logical OR. The expression x || y evaluates to a 1 if either x OR y are not zero. The negation operator ! changes the logical state of its operand. So !x is 1 only if x equals 0. It evaluates to 0 otherwise.

Here are some examples of the logical operators, with several previous examples of bitwise operators included to highlight the difference.

```
int f = 7;
int g = 8;
```

```
    int h = 0;

    h = f & g;      /* h will equal 0  */

    h = f && g;     /* h will equal 1  */

    h = f | g;      /* h will equal 15 */

    h = f || g;     /* h will equal 1  */

    h = ~f | ~g;    /* h will equal -1 */

    h = !f && !g    /* h will equal 0  */
```

Table 12.3 lists all the logical operators.

Operator symbol	Operation	Example usage
!	logical NOT	!x
&&	logical AND	x && y
||	logical OR	x || y

Table 12.3: Logical operators in C. The NOT operator has highest precedence, then AND, then OR. See table 12.6 for a complete listing of operator precedence.

12.2.7 Relational operators.

C has several operators to test the relationship between two values. These operators are often used to change the control flow of a program based on values calculated within that program. An example is the equality operator, ==, which tests if two values are equal. It evaluates to a 1 if its two operands are equal and to a 0 otherwise. In the following C code, the variable z will equal 1 if x and y are equal and 0 if they are not. In other words, the == operator has higher precedence than the = operator.

```
    z = x == y;     /* Looks confusing, huh? */
```

In the example above, the right-hand side of the assignment operator = is the expression x == y, which evaluates to a 1 or a 0. Once evaluated, the right-hand side is assigned to the left-hand side.

Similarly, the not equal != operator evaluates to a 1 if the operands are not equal. Other relational operators test for greater than, less than, etc., as described below.

```
int f = 7;
int g = 8;
int h = 0;

h = f == g;      /* Equal To operator.  h will equal 0 */

h = f > g;       /* Greater Than operator. h will equal 0  */

h = f != g;      /* Not Equal To operator. h will equal 1  */

h = f <= g;      /* Less Than Or Equal To operator. h will equal 1 */

h = f == (g - 1);   /* What will h equal here? */

h = f == g - 1;     /* What about here? */
```

The next example is a preview of coming attractions. The C relational operators are very useful for performing tests on variables in order to change the flow of the program. In the next chapter we will describe the C **if** statement in more detail. However, the concept of an if-then construct is not a new one—we've been dealing with if-then decision constructs ever since learning how to program the LC-2 in Chapterchapt:lc2.

```
if (h==5)
    x = 0;
else
    x = 1;
```

Here, only if h is equal to 5 will x be set to 0. Otherwise it will be set to 1.

Table 12.4 lists all the relational operators and provides a simple example of each.

Operator symbol	Operation	Example usage
>	greater than	x > y
>=	greater than or equal	x >= y
<	less than	x < y
<=	less than or equal	x <= y
==	equal	x == y
!=	not equal	x != y

Table 12.4: Relational operators in C. The first four operators have higher precedence than the last two. Both sets associate from left-to-right.

12.2.8   Advanced topic: C's special operators.

The C programming language has a collection of unusual operators which have become a trademark of C programming. Most of these operators are combinations of operators we've seen already. The combinations are such that they make expressing commonly used computations even simpler. However, to someone who isn't accustomed to the shorthand notation of these operators, reading and trying to understand C code which contains these operators can be difficult.

The ++ operator *increments* a variable to the next higher value. The -- operator *decrements* it. For example, the expression x++ increments the value of integer variable x by 1. These operators can be used within more complicated expressions, for example:

```
y  = 2 * x++;
```

Here, assuming both x and y are integers, the original value of x is multiplied by 2 and then assigned to the variable y. After the original value of x has been used, it is incremented. Here, the code *roughly* corresponds to the following:

```
y  = 2 * x;
x  = x + 1;
```

The ++ and -- operators can be used on either side of a variable. The expression ++x operates in a slightly different order than x++. If the expression x++ is part of a larger expression, then the value of x is used before it is incremented; with ++x, the value of x is incremented before it is used. If the operator ++ appears before the variable, then it is used in *prefix* form. If is appears after the variable, it is in *postfix* form.

```
y  = 2 * ++x;
```

The code above *roughly* corresponds to the following:

```
x  = x + 1;
y  = 2 * x;
```

This subtle distinction is not too important to understand for now. For most of the examples we present in this book, the prefix and postfix forms of these operators can be used interchangeably. You can find a precise description of this difference in the appendix D.5.6.

C also allows certain arithmetic and bitwise operators to be combined with the assignment operator. For instance, if we wanted to add 29 to variable x, we could use the shorthand operator += as follows:

```
x   += 29;
```

This code is equivalent to:

```
x  = x + 29;
```

Table 12.5 lists some of the special operators provided by C.

Operator symbol	Operation	Example usage
++	increment (postfix)	x++
--	decrement (postfix)	x--
++	increment (prefix)	++x
--	decrement (prefix)	--x
+=	add and assign	x += y
-=	subtract and assign	x -= y
*=	multiply and assign	x *= y
/=	divide and assign	x /= y
%=	modulus and assign	x %= y
&=	and and assign	x &= y
|=	or and assign	x |= y
^=	xor and assign	x ^= y
<<=	left shift and assign	x <<= y
>>=	right shift and assign	x >>= y

Table 12.5: Special operators in C. Among these operators, the postfix operators have highest precedence, followed by prefix. The assignment operators have lowest precedence. **Note:** Each group associates from right-to-left

More examples:

```
int f = 7;
int g = 8;
int h = 0;

h += g;        /* h will equal 8           */

h %= f;        /* Equivalent to h = h % f;  */
               /* Initially, h = 8, f = 7.  */
               /* Afterwards, h will equal 1 */

h <<= 3;       /* Equivalent to h = h << 3; */
               /* Initially, h equals 1.    */
               /* Afterwards, h will equal 8 */
```

Conditional expressions.

There is a unique operator in C whose symbols are the question mark and colon, ? and :, and which takes three operands. The best way to describe this operator is to jump into an example:

```
x = a ? b : c;
```

Here variable **x** will get either the value of **b or** the value of **c** based on the value of **a**. If **a** is non-zero (logically true), then **x** will be assigned the value of **b**. Otherwise, **x** will be assigned the value of **c**. Figure 12.3 is a complete program which uses the conditional expression.

```
#include <stdio.h>

main()
{
    int max;
    int a, b;

    printf("Input an integer :");
    scanf("%d", &a);
    printf("Input another integer :");
    scanf("%d", &b);

    max = (a > b) ? a : b;
    printf("The larger number is %d\n", max);
}
```

Figure 12.3: A C program which uses a conditional expression.

The example program prompts the user for two integers, stores them in the variables **a** and **b** and then assigns the variable **max** to either the value of **a** or the value of **b** depending on which is larger. The value of **max** is output using **printf**.

12.2.9 Tying it together.

We can combine these operators to form complex expressions. Almost always, the operand to an operator can be an expression. The exception is the left-hand side of any assignment operator must be a variable. After all, it makes no sense to assign a value to an expression. Also, the operands to the increment and decrement operators, **++** and **--** must be variables.

Table 12.6 lists all the C operators (including some which we have not yet covered) and their order of evaluation. Using the information presented in the table, we can evaluate complex expressions such as the one below (which uses a peculiar blend of operators).

```
y = x & z + 3 || 9 - w-- % 6;
```

According to the rules of evaluation, the above statement is equivalent to the following:

```
y = (x & (z + 3)) || (9 - ((w--) % 6));
```

Another more useful expression is given below. In this example, if the value of variable **x** is between 5 and 10, the expression evaluates to 1. Otherwise it is 0.

```
5 <= x && x <= 10
```

We will see many examples of this type of expression when we discuss control structures in the next chapter.

Precedence group	Associativity	Operators
1	l-to-r	*function call* () [ ] . ->
2	r-to-l	*postfix* ++ *postfix* --
3	r-to-l	*prefix* ++ *prefix* --
4	r-to-l	*dereference* * *address* &
		unary + *unary* -
		˜ ! sizeof
5	r-to-l	*cast* (type)
6	l-to-r	*multiply* * / %
7	l-to-r	+ -
8	l-to-r	<< >>
10	l-to-r	< > <= >=
11	l-to-r	== !=
12	l-to-r	&
13	l-to-r	^
14	l-to-r	|
15	l-to-r	&&
16	l-to-r	||
17	l-to-r	?:
18	r-to-l	= += -= *= etc...

Table 12.6: Operator Precedence, highest to lowest.

12.2.10   Mixed-type expressions.

What if we did the following:

```
int x = 10;
double y = 3.14159;
double z;

z = x * y;
```

This is a legal sequence of C code. Here the compiler will *promote* or convert the integer value of x into a double value before multipling. Note that the value stored at x remains the same. The value of z is 31.4159. Keep in mind that promotion is performed within C and the general rule is that when operands of different type are used, the shorter type is converted to the longer type and integer and character types are converted to floating point.

12.3   A comprehensive example.

Figure 12.4 is a complete C program which performs some simple operations on integer variables and displays the results of these operations. There is one globally declared variable, b, and 3 variables, a, c, d, which are local to the function main. First, values are assigned to a and b (note, this initialization could have been expressed when we declared the variables). Second, the variables c and d are updated based on two calculations performed using a and b. Finally, using the C library function printf, the values of c and d are printed out. Notice, because we are using printf, we must include the Standard I/O library header file, stdio.h.

The LC-2 C compiler when analyzing this code, will assign the global variable b the first available spot in the global data section, at offset 0. When analyzing the function main, it will assign a, c, and d slots 3, 4, and 5 on the top of the run-time stack. Recall that offsets 0, 1, 2 off the top of the stack contain information to which helps maintain the stack. A snapshot of the compiler's symbol table corresponding to this program is shown in figure 12.6.

The resulting assembly code generated by the LC-2 C compiler is listed in figure 12.5.

```
/* Include the standard I/O header file */
#include <stdio.h>

int b;         /* Variable b is a global variable since it is declared outside
                  the function main */

main()
{
  int a;       /* Variables a,c,d are all local to main */
  int c;
  int d;

  /* Initialize */
  a = 2;
  b = 3;

  /* Perform calculations */
  c = a++ & ~b;
  d = (a + b) - (a - b);

  /* Print out results */
  printf("The results are : c = %d, d = %d\n", c, d);
}
```

Figure 12.4: A C program which performs simple operations.

```
AND   R0, R0, #0
ADD   R0, R0, #2    ;  The compiler assigns variable a an offset of 3
STR   R0, R6, #3    ;  a = 2;

AND   R0, R0, #0
ADD   R0, R0, #3    ;  The compiler assigns b to offset 0 in the global area
STR   R0, R5, #0    ;  b = 3;

LDR   R0, R5, #0    ;  get value of b
NOT   R0            ;  ~b
LDR   R1, R6, #3    ;  get value of a
AND   R2, R0, R1    ;  calculate a & ~b
ADD   R1, R1, #1    ;  increment a
STR   R1, R6, #3    ;  a++
STR   R2, R6, #4    ;  c = a++ & ~b;
                    ;  The variable c is assigned an offset of 4

LDR   R0, R6, #3    ;  get value of a
LDR   R1, R5, #0    ;  get value of b
ADD   R0, R0, R1    ;  calculate a + b

LDR   R2, R6, #3    ;  get value of a
LDR   R3, R5, #0    ;  get value of b
NOT   R3
ADD   R3, R3, #1    ;  calculate -b
ADD   R2, R2, R3    ;  calculate a - b
NOT   R2
ADD   R2, R2, #1    ;  calculate -(a - b)
ADD   R0, R0, R2    ;  calculate (a + b) + -(a - b)
STR   R0, R6, #5    ;  d = (a + b) - (a - b);
                    ;  The variable d is assigned an offset of 5
:
:
<code for calling the function printf>
:
:
```

Figure 12.5: The LC-2 code for the previous C program.

Symbol Table

Name	Type	Offset	Scope
b	int	0	global

Name	Type	Offset	Scope
a	int	3	main

Name	Type	Offset	Scope
c	int	4	main

Name	Type	Offset	Scope
d	int	5	main

Figure 12.6: The LC-2 C compiler's symbol table when compiling this program.

12.4   Exercises.

12.1 Assuming that space for the variable `ff` is allocated at offset 3, generate the compiler's symbol table for the following code.

```
{
    float ff;
    char cc;
    int ii;
    char dd;

    /* ... */

}
```

12.2 The following variable declaration appears in a program.

```
int r;
```

  1. If `r` is a local variable, to what value will it be initialized?
  2. If `r` if a global variable, to what value will it be initialized?

12.3 Evaluate the following floating point constants. Write their values in standard notation.

  1. 111 E -11
  2. -0.00021 E 4
  3. 101.101 E 0

12.4 For the code below, state the values that are printed out by each `printf` statement. Assume that the statements are executed in the order A, B, C, D.

```
int t;  /* This variable is globally declared */

{
   int t = 2;

   printf("%d\n", t);      /*  A  */

   {
      printf("%d\n", t);  /*  B  */

      t = 3;
   }

   printf("%d\n", t);      /*  C  */
}

{
   printf("%d\n", t);      /*  D  */
}
```

12.5 Write the LC-2 code that would result if the following variable declarations were compiled using the LC-2 C compiler.

```
{
   char c = 'a';
   int  x = 3;
   int  y;
   int  z = 10;
}
```

12.6 Given that a and b are both integers, where a and b have been assigned the values 6 and 9 respectively, what is the value of each of the following expressions? Also, if the value of a or b changes, give their new value.

1. ++a + b--
2. a | b
3. a || b
4. a & b
5. a && b

6. !(a + b)

7. a % b

8. b / a

9. a = b

10. a = b = 5

11. a = (++b < 3) ? a : b

12. a <<= b

12.7 Explain the difference between the following C statements:

1. j = i++;

2. j = ++i;

3. j = i + 1;

4. i += 1;

5. j = i += 1;

6. Which statements modify the value of i? Which ones modify the value of j? If i
   = 1 and j = 0 initially, what will the values of i and j be after each statement
   is run separately?

12.8 Say variables a and b are both declared locally as long int.

1. Translate the following expression: a + b into LC-2 code, assuming a long int
   occupies 2 bytes. Assume a is allocated offset 3, and b is at offset 4.

2. Translate the same expression assuming a long int occupies 4 bytes and a is
   allocated offset 3, and b is at offset 5.

12.9 If initially, a = 1, b = 1, c = 3, and result = 999, what are the values of the variables after the following C statement is executed?

result = ((b+1) | --c) + a;

12.10 Recall the machine busy example from previous chapters. Say the integer variable
   machineBusy tracks the busyness of all 16 machines. Recall that a 0 in a particular bit
   position indicates the machine is busy and a 1 in that position indicates that machine
   is idle.

1. Write a C statement to make machine 5 busy.

2. Write a C statement to make machine 10 idle.

3. Write a C statement to make machine n busy. I.e., the machine which has become
   busy is in integer variable n.

4. Write a C expression to check if machine 3 is idle. If it is idle, the expression
   returns a 1. If it is busy, the expression returns a 0.

5. Write a C expression which evaluates to the number of idle machines. For example, if the binary pattern in `machineBusy` were 1011 0010 1110 1001, then the expression will evaluate to 9.

12.11 What purpose does the semicolon serve in C?

12.12 Say we are designing a new computer programming language that includes the operators @, #, $ and U.

How would the following expression get evaluated

`w @ x # y $ U z`

under the following constraints.

1. If the precedence of @ is higher than # is higher than $ is higher than U. Use parentheses to indicate the order.
2. If the precedence of # is higher than U is higher than @ is higher than $.
3. If their precedence is all the same, but they associate left-to-right.
4. If their precedence is all the same, but they associate right-to-left.

12.13 Modify the example program in Chapter 11 (Figure 11.2) such that it prompts the user to type a character and then prints every character from that character down to the character ! in the order they appear in the ASCII table.

12.14 Write a C program to calculate the sales tax on a sales transaction. Prompt the user to enter the amount of the purchase and the tax rate. Output the amount of sales tax and the total amount (include tax) on the whole purchase.

12.15 Suppose your program contains the two integer variables, x and y which have values 3 and 4 respectively. Write C statements that will exchange the values in x and y such that after the statements are executed, x = 4 and y = 3.

1. First, write this routine using a temporary variable for storage.
2. Now re-write this routine without using a temporary variable for storage.

Chapter 13

Control structures.

In Chapter 6, we introduced the three constructs of systematic decomposition: the sequential construct, the conditional construct, and the iteration construct. Using step-wise refinement, we broke down a large task into one which we could more easily program on a computer. Once the task was refined down to a low enough level, it was relatively simple to write the program in LC-2 instructions. We want to apply the same systematic decomposition when programming in C. In order to do so, we need the ability to create all three types of constructs within our C programs. Using the expressions and statements covered in the previous chapter, we can create sequential constructs. In this chapter, we cover C's version of conditional and iteration constructs.

We begin this chapter by describing C's conditional constructs: the if and if-else statements and the slightly more sophisticated switch statement. After conditional constructs, we'll move on to C's iteration constructs: the for, while, and do-while statements. With many of these constructs, we will present the corresponding LC-2 code generated by our hypothetical LC-2 C compiler. This chapter closes with several example C programs which use the concepts presented in Chapters 11, 12, and 13.

13.1 Conditional constructs.

The conditional construct allows a programmer to select an action based on some condition within the program. This is a very common programming construct and is supported by every useful programming language. C provides two types of basic conditional constructs: if and if-else. There is also a special purpose conditional construct called switch.

13.1.1 The if statement.

Simply put, the if statement performs an action if a condition is true. The action is a C statement and it is executed only if the condition, which is a C expression, evaluates to a non-zero (logically true) value. Let's take a look at an example.

```
if (x <= 10)
   y = x * x + 5;
```

Here, the statement, y = x * x + 5; is only executed if the condition x <= 10 is non-zero. Recall from our discussion of the <= operator that it evaluates to 1 if the relationship is true, 0 otherwise.

Syntactically, the condition we are testing must be surrounded by parentheses. The parentheses allow the compiler to unambiguously separate the condition from the rest of the if statement. The statement that follows can be any legal statement. Recall from the previous chapter: in C, a legal statement is any legal expression ending with a semicolon.

The statement following the condition can also be a *compound statement*, or *block*, which is a sequence of statements beginning with an open brace and ending with a closing brace. Compound statements are used in order to group one or more simple statements into a single entity. This entity is itself equivalent to a simple statement. Using compound statements with an if statement we can base the execution of several statement on a single condition. For example, in the following code, both y and z will be modified if x is less than or equal to 10.

```
if (x <= 10) {
   y = x * x + 5;
   z = (2 * y) / 3;
}
```

The spacing of variables and operators and indentation of lines is flexible in C. The indentation used in the example above is one form of conventional indentation for an if statement. It allows someone reading the code to quickly identify the portion which executes if the condition is true. It however does not affect the behavior of the program. For example, the following code behaves differently from the previous version even though the indentation is the same:

```
if (x <= 10)
   y = x * x + 5;
   z = (2 * y) / 3;
```

In which way do the two versions behave differently?

Here are more examples of if statements.

```
if (1 <= x && x <= 10)   /* What values of x make this true? */
    y = y + 1;

if (y & x)               /* When is this true? */
    z = z / 10;

if (y && x)              /* When is this true? */
    z = z / 10;

/* This condition is always true.  The variable y
   will always be set to 5.  Why? */
if (x = 2)
    y = 5;
```

The final example above points out a very common mistake made when programming in C (even C experts sometimes make this mistake). The condition is constructed with the assignment operator = which causes the value of x to change to 2. The condition is always true: recall from our discussion on the assignment operator that it evaluates to the value being assigned. Since the condition is always non-zero, y will always get assigned the value 5 and x will always be assigned 2. The above code is very different from:

```
if (x == 2)
    y = 5;
```

Here, a test for equality is performed. If x equals 2, then the variable y is set to 5. The variable x is not modified. Let's look at the LC-2 code which is generated, assuming that x and y are integers and their offsets on the run-time stack are 3 and 4 respectively.

```
        LDR  R0, R6, #3   ;   load x into R0
        ADD  R0, R0, #-2  ;   subtract 2 from x
        BRNZ NOT_TRUE     ;   If the condition is not true,
                          ;   then skip the assignment statement

        AND  R1, R1, #0   ;   R1 <- 0
        ADD  R1, R1, #5   ;   R1 <- 5
        STR  R1, R6, #4   ;   y = 5;

NOT_TRUE :                ;   the rest of the program
        :
```

Notice that it is most straightforward for the LC-2 C compiler to generate code that tests for the opposite of the original condition (x not equal to 2) and to branch based on its outcome.

The `if` statement is itself a statement. Therefore it is legal to *nest* them as demonstrated in the following C code. Since the statement following the first `if` is a simple statement (i.e., composed of only one statement) no braces are required.

```
if (x == 3)
   if (y != 6) {
      z = z + 1;
      w = w + 2;
   }
```

The inner `if` statement only executes if **x** is equal to 3. There is an easier way to express the code above. Can you do it with only one `if` statement?

13.1.2   The `if-else` statement.

If we wanted to perform one set of actions if a condition were true and another set if the same condition were false, we could use the following sequence of `if` statements:

```
if (x == 2)
   y = 4;

if (x != 2)
   y = 9;
```

Here, **y** will be set to 4 if **x** equals 2, otherwise **y** will be assigned the value 9. Since this is a tedious way to express a very common programming construct, C provides a more convenient method: the `if-else` statement.

The following code is functionally equivalent to the previous code segment.

```
if (x == 2)
    y = 4;
else
    y = 9;
```

As with the `if` statement, each component of an `if-else` can be a compound statement, as in the following example.

```
if (x) {
    y++;
    z--;
}
else {
    y--;
    z++;
}
```

If the variable **x** is non-zero, then the **if** condition is true, **y** is incremented and **z** decremented. Otherwise, **y** is decremented and **z** incremented. The LC-2 code generated by the LC-2 C compiler is listed in Figure 13.1. We are assuming that **x**, **y**, and **z** are integer variables declared as locals. Their offsets are 3 for **x**, 4 for **y**, and 5 for **z**.

```
        LDR  R0, R6, #3   ;   load the value of x
        BRZ  ELSE         ;   if x is equal to 0, perform the else part

        ; x is not equal to 0
        LDR  R1, R6, #4   ;   load y into R1
        ADD  R1, R1, #1
        STR  R1, R6, #4   ;   y++;

        LDR  R1, R6, #5   ;   load z into R1
        ADD  R1, R1, #-1
        STR  R1, R6, #5   ;   z--;

        BR DONE

        ; The condition is false
ELSE:   LDR  R1, R6, #4   ;   load y into R1
        ADD  R1, R1, #-1
        STR  R1, R6, #4   ;   y--;

        LDR  R1, R6, #5   ;   load z into R1
        ADD  R1, R1, #1
        STR  R1, R6, #5   ;   z++;

DONE:   :
        :
```

Figure 13.1: The LC-2 code generated for an **if-else** statement.

We can connect conditional constructs together to form a longer sequence of conditional tests. The following example shows a complex decision structure created using the `if` and `if-else` statements. No other control structures are used.

```
if (x == 2)
   z = z + 1;                        /* statement A */
else
   if (y == 2) {
      z = z + 2;                     /* statement B */
      w = w - 1;
   }
   else if (x == 3 && y != 6) {
      z = z + 1;                     /* statement C */
      w = w + 2;
   }
```

Which values of x and y cause each of the statements A, B, C to be executed? Can more than one of A, B, C ever execute?

Finally, we point out a C syntax rule for associating `if`s with `else`s: an `else` is associated with the most recent, unassociated `if`. The following example points out why this is important.

```
if (x != 10)
   if (y > 3)
      z = z / 2;
   else
      z = z * 2;
```

Without this rule, it would not be clear whether the `else` associates with the outer `if` or the inner `if`. For this situation, the rule states that the `else` is coupled with the inner `if`, so this code is equivalent to the following:

```
if (x != 10) {
   if (y > 3)
      z = z / 2;
   else
      z = z * 2;
}
```

Just as parentheses can be used to redirect and clarify the evaluation of expressions, braces can be used to associate statements. If we wanted to associate the `else` with the outer `if`, we could write the code as such:

```
if (x != 10) {
   if (y > 3)
      z = z / 2;
}
else
  z = z * 2;
```

13.1.3 The switch statement.

Another control structure that often appears in our programs is a series of tests of the same variable. For example,

```
char c;

:
:
if (c == 'a') {
   /* statement A */
   :
   :
}
else if (c == 'b') {
   /* statement B */
   :
   :
}
else if (c == 'x') {
   /* statement C */
   :
   :
}
else if (c == 'y') {
   /* statement D */
   :
   :
}
```

In this code, one (or none) of the statements labeled A, B, C, or D will be executed depending on the value of the character variable c. If c is equal to the character a, then statement A is performed, if it is equal to the character b, then statement B is performed, and so forth. If c doesn't equal a or b or x or y, then none of the statements are executed.

If there are many cases to check, then many tests will be required in order to find the "matching" case. In order to give the compiler an opportunity to better optimize this code by bypassing some of this testing, the C programming language includes the `switch` statement.

The following code segment behaves the same as the code in the previous example.

```
char c;

switch (c) {
case 'a':
  /* statement A */
  :
  break;

case 'b':
  /* statement B */
  :
  break;

case 'x':
  /* statement C */
  :
  break;

case 'y':
  /* statement D */
  :
  break;
}
```

Essentially, a `switch` statement consists of an expression to test a series of `cases`, each labeled with a constant. Each `case` indicates the computation to perform if the expression matches the constant label.

Let's go through it piece by piece. The `switch` keyword precedes the expression on which to base the decision. This expression must be of integral type, which means it must be either an `int` or a `char`. If the value of the expression matches one of the `case` constants, the code following the `case` keyword will be executed. Each `case` consists of a sequence of zero or more statements similar to a compound statement however no delimiting braces are required. Conceptually, each `case` is an entry point into the compound statement of the `switch`. The place within this compound statement to start executing is determined by which `case` matches the value of the `switch` expression.

Each `case` label within a `switch` statement must be different. If two were the same, then an ambiguous situation would be presented about which to execute if the expression matched the labels. Furthermore, each `case` label must be a constant expression. It cannot be based on a value which changes as the program is executing. The following is not a legal `case` label (assuming `i` is a variable):

```
case i:
```

In the `switch` example above, each `case` ends with a `break` statement. The `break` exits the `switch` construct and changes the flow of control directly to the statement after the closing brace of the `switch`. The `break` statements are optional. If they are not used, then control will go from the current `case` to the next. For example, if the `break` after statement C were omitted, then a match on `case 'x'` would cause statement C AND statement D to be executed. However, in practice, each `case` will end with a `break`.

We can also include a `default` case. This case is selected if the `switch` expression matches none of the `case` constants. If no `default` case is given and the expression matches none of the constants, then nothing within the `switch` is executed.

For a detailed description of the `switch` statement, see appendix D.7.3.

13.1.4　An example program.

The program in Figure 13.2 performs a function similar to the calculator example from Chapter 10. The user is prompted for three items: an integer operand, an operation to perform, and another integer operand. The program then performs the operation on the two input values and displays the results on the screen. The program makes use of a `switch` to decide which operation the user has selected.

```c
#include <stdio.h>

main()
{
  /* Variable declarations */
  int operand_1;
  int operand_2;
  int result;
  char operation;

  /* Get the input values */
  printf("\n\n=== Calculator program ===\n\n");
  printf("Enter first operand: ");
  scanf("%d", &operand_1);
  printf("Enter operation to be performed (+, -, *, /): ");
  scanf("\n%c", &operation);
  printf("Enter second operand: ");
  scanf("%d", &operand_2);

  /* Perform the calculation */
  switch(operation) {
  case '+':
   result = operand_1 + operand_2;
   break;

  case '-':
   result = operand_1 - operand_2;
   break;

  case '*':
   result = operand_1 * operand_2;
   break;

  case '/':
   result = operand_1 / operand_2;
   break;

  default:
   printf("Invalid operation!\n");
   result = 0;
  }

  /* Print out the result */
  printf("The answer is %d\n", result);
}
```

Figure 13.2: Calculator program in C.

13.2   Iteration constructs.

Iteration constructs repeat a sequence of code in a controlled manner. In C, there are three looping constructs: the `while` statement, the `for` statement, and the `do-while` statement.

13.2.1   The `while` statement.

We begin by describing C's simplest iterations statement: the `while`. Simply put, `while` statement allows a C statement to execute repeatedly until a condition becomes false. Before each iteration of the statement, the condition is checked. If the condition evaluates to a logical true (non-zero) value, then the statement is executed.

In the example below, the loop keeps iterating while the value of `x` is less than 10.

```
x = 0;
while (x < 10) {
    printf("x = %d\n", x);
    x = x + 1;
}
```

It produces the following output:

```
0 1 2 3 4 5 6 7 8 9
```

The `while` statement breaks down into two components:

```
while (test)
    loop_body;
```

The `test` component is an expression used to determine whether or not to continue executing the loop. It is tested before each repetition of the loop. The statement `loop_body` expresses the work to be done within the loop and it can be a compound statement. In other words, the loop executes the `loop_body` *while* the `test` is true.

Figure 13.3 shows the control flow using the notation of systematic decomposition. There are two branches required: one conditional branch to exit the loop and one unconditional branch to loop back to the test to determine whether or not to execute another iteration.

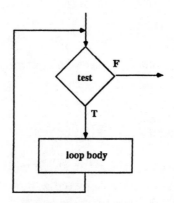

Control flow for a **while** statement

Figure 13.3: The C **while** statement pictorially represented.

The LC-2 code generated by the compiler for the **while** example at the beginning of this section which counts from 0 to 9 is listed in Figure 13.4. The variable **x** is a local integer variable stored at offset 3 on the run-time stack.

The **while** statement is useful for coding loops where the iteration process involves testing for a *sentinel* condition. When the sentinel is encountered, the loop terminated. For example, when we wrote the character counting program in Chapters 5 and 7, we created a loop which terminated when the sentinel EOT character (a character with ASCII code 4) was detected.

The following complete program uses the **while** statement to test for a sentinel condition. Can you determine what this program does without running it on a computer?

```c
#include <stdio.h>

main()
{
    char echo = 'A';    /* Initialize char variable echo */

    while (echo != '\n') {
      scanf("%c", &echo);
      printf("%c", echo);
    }
}
```

```
              AND   R0, R0, #0    ;    clear out R0
              STR   R0, R6, #3    ;    x = 0;

              ; while (x < 10)
              ; test
              ;
LOOP:         LDR   R0, R6, #3    ;    perform the test
              ADD   R0, R0, #-10
              BRPZ DONE           ;    x is not less than 10

              ; loop body
              ;
              LDR   R0, R6, #3    ;    get x
              :
              :
              <code for calling the function printf>
              :
              :
              ADD   R0, R0, #1    ;    x + 1
              STR   R0, R6, #3    ;    x = x + 1;
              BR    LOOP          ;    another iteration?

DONE:         :
              :
              :
```

Figure 13.4: The LC-2 code generated for a **while** statement.

We end our treatment of the `while` statement by pointing out a common mistake when using `while` loops. The program below will never terminate because the loop body (which consists of a simple statement) does not change the looping condition. It always remains true. Though often a bug, sometimes such *infinite loops* are intentionally used in certain situations.

```
x = 0;
while (x < 10)
    printf("x = %d\n", x);
```

13.2.2 The `for` statement.

The syntax for the C `for` statement may look a little intimidating at first but after analyzing the pieces of its syntax and examining the resulting LC-2 code, the notation begins to make sense.

In its most straightforward form, the `for` statement allows us to repeat a statement a specific number of times. For example:

```
for (i = 0; i < 10; i++)
    printf("%d ", i);
```

will produce the following output:

```
0 1 2 3 4 5 6 7 8 9
```

The `for` statement is composed of four components, broken down as follows:

```
for (init; test; reinit)
    loop_body;
```

The three components within the parenthesis, `init`, `test`, and `reinit`, control the behavior of the loop and must be separated by semicolons. The final component, `loop_body`, specifies the actual computation to be performed within the loop. As always, if the work to be performed within the loop cannot be stated with a single simple statement, then a compound statement can be used by enclosing several simple statements with braces.

Let's take a look at each component of the `for` loop in detail. The `init` component is an expression which is evaluated before the **first** iteration. It typically is used to initialize variables in preparation for executing the loop.

The `test` component is an expression which gets evaluated before **every** iteration to determine another iteration should be executed. If the `test` expression evaluates to zero, then the **for** terminates and the control flow is passed to the next statement. If the expression is non-zero, then another iteration of the **loop_body** is performed.

The **reinit** component is an expression which is evaluated at the end of **every** iteration. It is used to prepare (or reinitialize) for the next iteration.

The **loop_body** is a statement which defines the work to be performed each iteration. It can be a compound statement.

Figure 13.5 shows the flow of control for a **for** statement using the notation we developed for systematic decomposition. There are four blocks, one for each of the four components of the **for** statement. There is a conditional branch which determines whether to exit the loop based on the outcome of the **test** expression or to proceed with another iteration. The unconditional branch loops back to the **test** at the end of each iteration, after the **reinit** expression is evaluated.

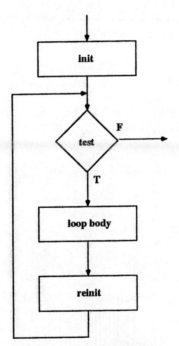

Control flow for a **for** **statement**

Figure 13.5: The C **for** statement.

Even though the syntax of a **for** statement allows it to be very flexible, most of the **for** loops you will encounter (or will write) are of a standard form. They are almost always used to execute a body of code for a certain number of iterations. In the example above at the beginning of this section, 10 iterations of the loop were executed.

Below are some examples of code with **for** loops. The indentation used for these loops is stylistic and does not affect the behavior of the loops when they execute. The convention is to indent loop bodies so that they can be quickly identified by someone scanning through the code.

```
/* --- What is the output of loop? --- */
for (i = 0; i <= 10; i++)
   printf("%d ", i);


/* --- What does this one output?  --- */
letter = 'a';

for (c = 0; c < 26; c++)
   printf("%c ", letter+c);



/* --- What does this loop do?      --- */
number_of_ones = 0;

for (bit_num = 0; bit_num < 16; bit_num++) {
   if (input_value & (1<<bit_num))
      number_of_ones++;
}
```

Here is another example of a **for** where the loop body is composed of another **for** loop. This construct is referred to as a *nested loop*.

```
/* What will sum equal at the end of the outer for loop? */
sum = 0;

for (i = 1; i <= 10; i++) {
   for (j = 0; j < i; j++) {
      sum += j;
   }
}
```

Let's take a look at the LC-2 translation of a simple **for** loop. Assume i is a local integer variable whose offset is 3 off the top of the run-time stack. The loop body is a simple one: the local variable x (offset 4) is incremented by the current value of i.

```
int x = 0;

for (i = 0; i < 10; i++)
   x += i;
```

The LC-2 code generated by the compiler is shown below in figure 13.6.

```
                AND   R0, R0, #0     ;   clear out R0
                STR   R0, R6, #4     ;   x = 0;

                ; init
                ;
                AND   R0, R0, #0     ;   clear out R0
                STR   R0, R6, #3     ;   init (i = 0)

                ; test
                ;
LOOP:           LDR   R0, R6, #3     ;   perform the test
                ADD   R0, R0, #-10
                BRPZ  DONE           ;   i is not less than 10

                ; loop body
                ;
                LDR   R0, R6, #4     ;   get x
                LDR   R1, R6, #3     ;   get i
                ADD   R0, R0, R1     ;   x + i
                STR   R0, R6, #4     ;   x += i;

                ; reinit
                ;
                LDR   R0, R6, #3
                ADD   R0, R0, #1
                STR   R0, R6, #3     ;   i++
                BR    LOOP

DONE:           :
                :
                :
```

Figure 13.6: The LC-2 code generated for a **for** statement.

Here is a common mistake made when using **for** loops within C code.

```
x = 0;
for (i = 0; i < 10; i++);
    x = x + 1;

printf("x = %d\n", x);
printf("i = %d\n", i);
```

What gets output by the first `printf`? The answer is `x = 1`. Why? The second `printf` outputs `i = 10`. Why?

A `for` loop can be constructed using a `while` loop (actually, vice versa as well). In programming, they can be used interchangeably, to a degree. When to use which looping construct may seem confusing at first. Using one instead of the other in a particular situation depends on several factors, such as programming style and taste, but there are certain tasks which lend themselves to a particular type of loop. As we've seen, `while` loops are particularly useful for sentinel loops, whereas `for` loops are useful for counter-controlled loops.

13.2.3   The `do-while` statement.

With a `while` loop, the condition is always evaluated **before** an iteration is performed. Therefore, it is possible for the `while` loop to execute zero iterations (i.e., when the condition is false from the start). There is a slight variant in C of the `while` statement called `do-while` which always performs at least one iteration. In a `do-while` loop, the condition is evaluated **after** an iteration is performed. The operation of the `do-while` is demonstrated in the following example.

```
x = 0;
do {
    printf("x = %d\n", x);
    x = x + 1;
} while (x < 10);
```

Here, the conditional test, `x < 10`, is evaluated at the end of each iteration. Thus, the loop body will execute at least once. The next iteration is performed only if the test evaluates to a non-zero value. The code above produces the same output as the code in Figure 13.2.1.

Syntactically, a `do-while` is composed of two components.

```
do
  loop_body;
while (test);
```

The `loop_body` component is a statement (simple or compound) which describes the computation performed by the loop. The `test` is an expression which determines whether another iteration is to be performed.

Figure 13.7 shows the control flow using the systematic decomposition notation. Notice the slight change from the flow of a `while` loop. The loop body and the test are interchanged. A conditional branch loops back to the top of the loop body, initiating another iteration. Notice that one iteration is always executed.

At this point, the differences between the three types of C loop constructs may seem subtle and inconsequential, but once you become comfortable using them and build up experience

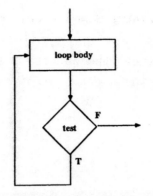

Control flow for a do-while statement

Figure 13.7: The C do-while statement.

using these constructs, you will be able to appreciate their differences. To a large degree, these constructs can be used interchangeably. Three flavors of iteration were provided as a convenience to the programmer. As you build experience with C programming, you will begin to see situations where one construct will fit the task at hand more naturally than the others.

13.2.4 Advanced topic: The break and continue statements.

For sake of completeness, in this section, we will describe two constructs that are sometimes used in conjunction with the C iteration constructs. The break statement causes the compiler to generate code which will prematurely exit a loop and the continue statement causes the compiler to generate code which will end the current iteration and start the next. These statements occur within the loop body and apply to the iteration construct immediately enclosing them. Essentially, the break and continue statements cause the compiler to generate an unconditional branch instruction somewhere in the loop body. See D.7.7 in Appendix D for additional information. Below are two example code segments which use break and continue. The output generated by each is also given.

```
/* This code segment produces the output: 0 1 2 3 4 */
for (i = 0; i < 10; i++) {
    if (i == 5)
        break;
    printf("%d ", i);
}
```

The following example is similar, except it uses a `continue` statement.

```
/* This code segment produces the output: 0 1 2 3 4 6 7 8 9 */
for (i = 0; i < 10; i++) {
   if (i == 5)
      continue;
   printf("%d ", i);
}
```

13.3   C syntax.

Up until this point, we have mentioned bits and pieces of C syntax in passing. Here, we'll summarize what we've learned and put C syntax into a logical framework. C syntax is fairly straightforward and regular (i.e., there are not many special cases), however it is filled with opportunities for shooting oneself in the foot. Keep in mind that the point of the syntax of any high-level language is to remove ambiguity. The programming language is a connection between our human languages, which are riddled with ambiguity and imprecision, and the precise mechanical language of the machine.

We have seen two broad categories of constructs in the C programming language: declarations and statements. We use declarations to inform the compiler of variables we intend on using within the program. Statements, on the other hand, describe the work we wish to perform.

13.3.1   Declarations.

The variable declarations we have discussed have a very simple form, shown below. The brackets [ ] are used to indicate that the initializer is optional.

```
type identifier [= initializer];
```

The type designates the data type for the variable and can be one of the standard types supported by C (`int`, `char`, `double`, for example) or a type defined by the programmer. See Appendix D.3.5 on programmer-defined types. Identifiers can be almost any sequences of upper and lower case letters, digits, and the underscore character. They cannot begin with a digit. The initializer is optional, and is specified with an = followed by a expression which is typically a constant. As a matter of convenience, variables of the same type can be declared together in a single declaration, separated by a commas. Here, three integer variables are declared, and y is initialized to 3. As we stated before, for stylistic reasons, this form of declaration is discouraged.

```
int x, y = 3, z;
```

13.3.2 Statements.

Statements are composed of expressions. An expression is a sequence of variable identifiers, constants, and operators used in a legal fashion. An expression ending in a semicolon signifies a simple statement. A statement can also be combined with other statements and declarations to form a compound statement or *block*. A compound statement is syntactically equivalent to a single statement and any place a statement is required, a compound statement can be used. The control constructs (if, if-else, switch, for, while, do-while) create statements which execute conditionally, partially, or iterate.

A block can also contains variable declarations. They must appear before any statements. Any variables declared within a block are local to that block—they are accessible only within the block. For example:

```
int i, k;

for (i = 0; i < 10; i++) {
  for (k = 0; k < 20; k++) {
      int i = 10;
      :
      :
  }
}
```

The variable i declared within the loop body of the inner for statement is different than the i declared at the outermost level. The inner i is only accessible within the loop body in which it is defined. The outer i is accessible everywhere except in the inner loop body. Each i will be allocated to a different memory location, thus they are essentially different variables sharing the same name.

13.4 Examples.

13.4.1 Example 1 : finding prime numbers between 1 and 100.

The program in Figure 13.8 prints out all the numbers less than or equal to 100 that are prime. There are two for loops within the program, one of which is nested within the other. The outer loop sequences through all the integers between 2 and 100 and the second loop determines if the number generated by the outer loop has any divisors. The second loop only needs to check for divisors between 2 and 10 since all numbers in the range 2 to 100 have at least one divisor that is less than or equal to 10. If a divisor between 2 and 10 is found, then a flag variable, called prime in the code, is set to FALSE. It is set to TRUE before the divisor loop begins. If it remains TRUE, then the particular number generated by the outer loop has no divisors and is therefore prime.

Here, we are utilizing the C preprocessor's macro substitution facility. We've defined, using `#define`, two symbolic names, `FALSE` which maps to the value 0 and `TRUE` which maps to 1. The preprocessor will simply replace each occurrence of the word `TRUE` in the source file with 1 and each occurrence of `FALSE` with 0. Note that these preprocessor macros are case sensitive so that `TRUE` and `true` will not match.

```
#include <stdio.h>
#define FALSE 0
#define TRUE  1

main()
{
  int current_number, divisor, prime;

  /* Start with 2 and go until 100  */
  for (current_number = 2; current_number <= 100; current_number++) {

    prime = TRUE;    /* Assume the number is prime */
    /* Test if the candidate number is a prime */
    for (divisor = 2; divisor <= 10; divisor++) {
      if (((current_number % divisor) == 0) && current_number != divisor)
        prime = FALSE;
    }

    if (prime)
      printf("The number %d is prime\n", current_number);
  }
}
```

Figure 13.8: A program that finds all primes between 2 and 100.

13.4.2 Example 2 : detecting a sequence of text.

The example program in Figure 13.9 reads in input from the keyboard until the newline character is typed. Within that entire stream of input, the program determines the number of occurrences of the character sequence 'the'.

The following program makes use of a C standard I/O function called `getchar`. The function `getchar` is very much like the LC-2 TRAP routine IN. It gets input from the keyboard and *returns* the ASCII value of the key that was typed. In C, a function can also return a value (a concept we will explore in the next chapter). The function call `getchar()` returns the ASCII value of the key. In the program, this value is assigned to the variable `c`. The program contains the expression:

```
((c = getchar()) != '\n')
```

to control the **while** loop. To explain what this expression accomplishes, we'll dissect it into its constituents parts. Because of the parentheses, the first subexpression that is evaluated is `(c = getchar())` . As mentioned, the value returned by the `getchar` function is assigned to the variable c. Since the assignment operator = is used, this subexpression then evaluates to the value assigned to c, so `(c = getchar())` equals whatever keystroke was detected by `getchar`. The subexpression is an operand to the relational operator `!=`, the "not equal to" operator. The other operand is the ASCII constant `'\n'` or newline. The entire expression evaluates to 1 if the ASCII value assigned to c is not the ASCII value of the newline character. Otherwise it is zero.

With each character read in from the keyboard, the program evaluates whether the character is part of the sequence "the". The variable named `match` records the *state* of the current sequence. For example, if the previous input character was a "t", then match is set to 1. If the previous two characters were "th", then match equals 2. Otherwise, match is set to 0.

```
#include <stdio.h>
#define FALSE 0
#define TRUE  1

main()
{
  char c;
  int count = 0, match = 0;

  /* When the user types a newline, the program will end */
  while ((c = getchar()) != '\n') {
    switch (match) {
      /* Starting point */
      case 0:
        if (c == 't')
          match++;
        else
          match = 0;
        break;

      /* Got a 't' already. If this character is an 'h', then proceed to 'e'.
         If it is a 't', the start from match = 1, otherwise start over */
      case 1:
        if (c == 'h')
          match++;
        else if (c == 't')
          match = 1;
        else
          match = 0;
        break;

      /* Got 'th' already, so if we get an 'e', increment and start over,
         Else, if we get a 't' start from match = 1, else start over. */
      case 2:
        if (c == 'e') {
          count++;
          match = 0;
        }
        else if (c == 't')
          match = 1;
        else
          match = 0;
        break;
    }
  }
  printf("The number of times 'the' was detected: %d\n", count);
}
```

Figure 13.9: A program that counts the occurrences of 'the' in the input stream.

13.4.3 Example 2 : approximating the value of pi.

The program in Figure 13.10 calculates the value of pi using its power series expansion. The formula is :

$$\pi = 4 - \frac{4}{3} + \frac{4}{5} - \frac{4}{7} + \cdots + (-1)^n \frac{4}{2n+1} + \cdots$$

The program first reads in a number from the keyboard to determine the number of terms of the power series to evaluate. Then it performs the calculation using a for loop. The final step is to print out the approximation.

```c
#include <stdio.h>

main()
{
  int NumberOfTerms, i;
  double pi;
  double plus_minus = 1.0;

  printf("Number of terms : ");
  scanf("%d", &NumberOfTerms);

  pi = 4;

  for (i = 1; i <= NumberOfTerms; i++) {
    plus_minus = plus_minus * (-1.0);
    pi = pi + (plus_minus * (4.0 / (2.0 * i + 1)));
  }

  printf("The approximate value of pi is %f\n", pi);
}
```

Figure 13.10: A program to calculate π.

13.5   Exercises.

13.1 Create the LC-2 compiler's symbol table for the calculator program listed in Figure 13.2.

13.2   1. Write what the following code looks like after it is processed by the preprocessor.

```
#define VERO -2

if (VERO)
    printf("True!");
else
    printf("False!");
```

   2. What is the output produced when the compiled version of this code is run?

   3. If we modified the code to the following, does the code behave differently?

```
#define VERO -2

if (VERO)
    printf("True!");
else if (!VERO)
    printf("False!");
```

13.3 An **if-else** statement can be used in place of the C conditional operator (See Section 12.2.8). Rewrite the following statement using an **if-else** rather than the conditional operator.

```
x = a ? b : c;
```

13.4 Describe the behavior of the following statements for the case when **x** equals 0 and when **x** equals 1.

   1.
```
        if (x = 0)
            printf("x equals 0\n");
        else
            printf("x does not equal 0\n");
```

   2.
```
        if (x == 0)
            printf("x equals 0\n");
        else
            printf("x does not equal 0\n");
```

3.
```
        if (x == 0)
            printf("A\n");
        else if (x != 1)
            printf("B\n");
        else if (x < 1)
            printf("C\n");
        else if (x)
            printf("D\n");
```

4.
```
        int x;
        int y;

        switch (x) {

        case 0:
            y = 3;

        case 1:
            y = 4;
            break;

        default:
            y = 5;
            break;
        }
```

5. What happens if x if not equal to 0 or 1 for part (c)?

13.5 What will the LC-2 code for the switch statement in part (c) of the previous problem look like?

13.6 Can the following if-else statement be converted into a switch? If yes, convert it. If no, why not?

```
        if (x == 0)
            y = 3;
        else if (x == 1)
            y = 4;
        else if (x == 2)
            y = 5;
        else if (x == y)
            y = 6;
        else
            y = 7;
```

13.7 How many times are we guaranteed that the loop body of each of the following constructs is executed?

Construct 1:

```
while(condition)
    loopBody
```

Construct 2:

```
do
    loopBody
while(condition);
```

Construct 3:

```
for(initialization; condition; increment)
    loopBody
```

13.8 Compile the following three code segments into non-optimized LC-2 assembly code. Also what is the output of each code segment?

Segment 1:

```
a = 2;
while(a > 0) {
    a--;
}
printf("%d", a);
```

Segment 2:

```
a = 2;
do {
    a--;
} while(a > 0)
printf("%d", a);
```

Segment 3:

```
b = 0;
for (a = 3; a < 10; a += 2)
    b = b + 1;
printf("%d %d", a, b);
```

13.9 The following is a part of C program which is not completed. Below the C program, its LC-2 translation is presented. Based on the LC-2 code, complete the C program.

```
/* The C program */
main() {
    int a, b;

    /* The LC-2 translation */
    .ORIG    x3000
    LEA      R6, STACK
    AND      R0, R0, #0
    ADD      R0, R0, #10
    STR      R0, R6, #4
    AND      R0, R0, #0
    ADD      R0, R0, #5
    STR      R0, R6, #3
    LDR      R0, R6, #4
    LDR      R1, R6, #3
    NOT      R1, R1
    ADD      R1, R1, #1
    ADD      R0, R1, R0
    STR      R0, R6, #3
    LDR      R0, R6, #3
    ADD      R0, R0, R0
    STR      R0, R6, #4
    LDR      R0, R6, #3
    BRP      Print
    HALT
Print    LD      R0, Value
    OUT
    HALT
Value    .FILL x31
```

13.10 Assume x is an integer that has been assigned the value 4.

1. What output is generated by the following code segment?

```
if (7 > x > 2)          /* be careful here */
    printf("True.");
else
    printf("False.");
```

2. Does the following code cause an infinite loop?

```
while(x > 0)
    x++;
```

3. Does the following code cause an infinite loop?

```
while(x > 0);
    x++;
```

4. What is the value of **x** after the following code has executed?

```
for ( ; x < 4; x--) {
    if (x < 2)
        break;
    else if (x == 2)
        continue;
    x = -1;
}
```

13.11 Change this program so that it uses a **do-while** loop instead of a **for** loop.

```
main() {
    int i;
    int sum;

    for(i=0; i<=100; ++i) {
        if (i % 4 == 0)
            sum = sum + 2;
        else if (i % 4 == 1)
            sum = sum - 6;
        else if (i % 4 == 2)
            sum = sum * 3;
        else if (i % 4 == 3)
            sum = sum / 2;
    }
    printf("%d\n", sum);
}
```

13.12 Write a C program which accepts as input a single integer **k**, then writes a pattern consisting of a single 1 on the first line, two occurrences of 2 on the second line, and so on, until it writes **k** occurrences of **k** on the last line.

For example, if the input is 5, the output should be the following:

```
1
2   2
3   3   3
4   4   4   4
5   5   5   5   5
```

13.13 1. Convert the following while loop into a for loop.

```
while (condition)
    loopBody;
```

2. Convert the following for loop into a while loop.

```
for (init; condition; reinit)
    loopBody;
```

13.14 What is the output of the following code:

```
int r = 0;
int s = 0;
int w = 12;
int sum = 0;

for (r = 1; r <= w; r++)
    for (s = r; s <= w; s++)
        sum = sum + s;

printf("sum =%d\n", sum);
```

Chapter 14

Functions.

14.1 Introduction.

Functions are the soul of C programming. Functions, also called subroutines or procedures in other programming languages, are a programming concept that allows the programmer to create a program from smaller, simpler components. We've seen this concept of building complex things from simple components several times at various levels of a computer system. Functions provide *abstraction*; they allow low-level details to be buried deeper within a program, giving the program a clear high-level structure.

Functions also allow code to be reused. Often within a program, the same subtask will be repeated from different places at different times. Instead of rewriting the code to perform the subtask at each spot it's required, the programmer can create a function to perform the subtask and *call* it when it is needed. Functions that perform subtasks common enough to be required by many programs can be put into a collection called a *library* of functions. Most C programmers heavily utilize C's standard library functions, examples of which include the I/O functions `printf`, `scanf` and `getchar`.

We've seen examples of functions when we programmed in LC-2 assembly language. The IN and OUT routines were examples of system functions—functions written by the system designers which perform common, useful tasks which require low-level knowledge of the hardware.

C is a language oriented around functions. When we examine a C source file, we are looking at a collection of functions. This collection of functions makes up a program. Every statement belongs to one (and only one) function. All C programs start executing at a function called `main`. The function `main` may contain calls to other functions, which in turn may call other functions. After the last statement in `main` completes, the program terminates.

In this chapter we will examine C functions in detail. We will describe why they are useful as programming constructs and present some of the terminology associated with functions.

327

We will also describe, again using the LC-2 as a model, the low-level mechanics of functions in C.

14.2 High-level programming structure.

Below is an example of the function **main** of a chess program. The program is organized such that the functions SetUpBoard, DetermineSides, WhitesTurn, BlacksTurn, and NoOutcomeYet perform the major subtasks.

```
main()
{
   /* Set up the chess board */
   SetUpBoard();

   /* Determine who is black, who is white */
   DetermineSides();

   /* Play the game! */
   do {
      WhitesTurn();
      BlacksTurn();
   } while(NoOutcomeYet());
}
```

While the internal workings of the algorithm are not apparent, this structured programming style reveals the flow and organization of the program. The details of the algorithm are hidden within the functions, whose names describe the jobs they do.

Often, we can treat a function as a small program which performs a well defined subtask. The first function, **SetUpBoard**, sets up the chess board. This function will initialize the internal representation for the chess board and place the pieces in the correct initial spots. The task is well-defined. Once the code is written, it can be tested independently of the other functions. Functions are good places to divide a large programming task among several programmers. For example, one programmer can work on the **SetUpBoard** function while another works on the **DetermineSides** function. By treating functions as individual sub-programs, the whole programming process easier to manage, simplifying coding and reducing the amount of time needed to get a complex program debugged and running.

14.3 Functions in C.

We begin with a simple example program. Figure 14.1 lists a program which simply prints a message via a function called **print_banner**. This is a C function call in its simplest form. Program execution begins at the function **main** which calls the function **print_banner**. The function `print_banner` calls the function `printf` which, as we know, is a C library function. Once the message is printed, the flow of control returns to `main` and the program terminates.

```c
#include <stdio.h>

void print_banner();

main()
{
    print_banner();
}

void print_banner()
{
    printf("A simple example of a C function.\n");
}
```

Figure 14.1: A C program which uses a function to print a banner message.

Now we move to a slightly more sophisticated example. Figure 14.2 lists an example C program which contains two functions, `main` and `factorial`:

In this program, the function `main` reads a decimal number from the keyboard. This number is stored in the variable `number`. Using the value of `number`, a function call is made to the function `factorial`. Within the function `factorial`, the value passed by the function `main` is assigned to the parameter n. The actual factorial of n is calculated by multiplying all positive integers less than n together (algebraically, factorial(n) =n! = 1*2*3*...*n). The result is stored in the variable `result`. The value of `result` is then returned (using the `return` statement) to the function that called `factorial`. When control passes back to `main`, the return value from `factorial` is assigned to the variable `answer` which is then displayed using a call to `printf`. Notice that the function `factorial` is different from the function `print_banner` from the previous example in figure 14.1. The function `factorial` requires an *argument* and it returns a value.

Notice that the four statements of `main` and the two statements of `factorial` are numbered within the comments. The flow of control goes from statement 1 to 2 to 3 to 5 to 6 then back to 4. There is a subtlety, however, which is worth pointing out: statement 3 does not completely execute until the call to `factorial` (statements 5 and 6) is complete. The return value must be generated before the assignment to `answer` can be performed.

There are three essential components associated with functions in C: a function *declaration* (also known as the *prototype*), a function *definition*, which contains the source code for the function, and the function *call*, which invokes the function.

```
#include <stdio.h>

/* This is the declaration (or prototype) for the function factorial.
   All functions which are called within the source must be prototyped    */
int factorial(int n);                                              /* -- A -- */

/* The function main --- all C programs must contain a function
   called main.  Else where will execution start?                         */
main()
{
    int number;
    int answer;

    printf("Input a number: ");     /* 1. Function call to a library function
                                          -- where is its prototype?        */

    scanf("%d", &number);           /* 2. Function call to a library function */

    answer = factorial(number);     /* 3. Function call to factorial   -- B -- */

                                    /* 4. Output results                      */
    printf("The factorial of %d is %d\n", number, answer);
}

/* The function definition for factorial.                          -- C -- */
int factorial(int n)
{
    /* Declarations */
    int i;
    int result = 1;

    /* Statements */
    for (i = 1; i <= n; i++)        /* 5. for loop calculates factorial */
        result = result * i;

    return result;                  /* 6. Return to caller            -- D -- */
}
```

Figure 14.2: A C program to calculate factorial.

14.3.1   The declaration.

In the example above, the source code line marked -- **A** -- (near the right margin, within the comments) is the function declaration for **factorial**. A function's declaration informs the compiler about the function, similar to how a variable's declaration informs the compiler about a variable. Sometimes called a function prototype, a function declaration describes the number and type of the input *parameters* required by the function and describes the type of the value the function returns. Often the names of the parameters are also included, but are not required. Parameters are data items the function expects to receive as input and are listed in parentheses following the function's name. The return value is the function's output. In the example above, the function `factorial` takes one integer parameter (called n within the function) and returns an integer value. Functions are not required to return a value. For example the function `print_banner` from the previous example did not return a value. If a function doesn't return a value, then its return type must be declared as `void`. Similarly, some functions may not require any input. Again, the function `print_banner` required no parameters. It's parameter list was empty. The function declaration ends with a semicolon.

14.3.2 The call.

The line marked `-- B --` is the actual function call to `factorial`. In this statement, the function `factorial` is called upon to perform its task. The values which are to be transmitted to the function, called *arguments*, are enclosed within parenthesis immediately following the name of the function being called. Arguments can be any legal expression which matches the type expected by the function being called. In this example, we want the function `factorial` to compute the factorial of the integer value in the variable called `number`. The value returned by `factorial` is then assigned to the integer variable `answer`.

14.3.3 The definition.

The code beginning at the line marked `-- C --` indicates the beginning of the definition for the function `factorial`. Notice that this first line matches the function declaration. Within the parentheses after the name of the function is the function's *formal parameter list*. This is an ordered list of values the function is expecting to receive whenever it is called. The actual arguments in all calls to this function should also match the type and ordering of the formal parameter list.

The actual function's body appears in the braces following the parameter list. A function's body consists of declarations and statements which define the computation the function performs. Any variable declared within these braces is local to the function. Notice that a function's body is precisely a compound statement.

14.3.4 The return value.

The line marked `-- D --` is where control passes back from `factorial` to whichever function called it, which in this case, is the function `main`. Since `factorial` is returning a value, then an expression must follow the `return` keyword and the type of this expression must match the return type declared for the function. In the case of factorial, the statement `return result` transmits the calculated factorial stored in `result` back to the caller. In general, functions which return a value must include at least one `return` statement in their body. Functions which do not return a value (functions declared as type `void`) do not require a `return` statement; the `return` is optional. For these functions, control passes back to the calling function after the last statement has been executed.

In the program source listed in Figure 14.2, the function `main` appeared before the function `factorial`. If all called functions are properly prototyped, then the ordering of functions within a source file has no bearing on program behavior. The convention we will follow is that the function `main` will be defined first and all other functions will follow.

Let's summarize: a function declaration (or prototype) informs the compiler of a function, indicating the number and types of parameters the function expects and indicating what type of value the function returns. A function definition is the actual source code for the function. The formal parameter list of the definition indicates the names of the function's parameters and in which order they will be passed by the caller. And finally, a function is invoked via a function call. Input values, or arguments, for the function to act upon are listed within the parenthesis of the function call. Literally, the value of each argument listed in the function call will be assigned to each parameter in the parameter list, the first argument assigned to the first parameter, the second argument to the second parameter, and so forth.

14.4   Another example.

Figure 14.3 lists an example program whose source consists of three functions: `main`, `print_banner` (this version is slightly different than the previous one), and `max_of_four`. The program computes the maximum of four input values.

The function `print_banner` simply prints out some information about the program and prompts the user to provide the input. This function takes no input parameters and generates no return value.

The function `max_of_four` performs the actual determination of the maximum. It takes four integers as input and returns the value of the largest.

Notice in the call to `max_of_four`, that the arguments are a, b, c, d. The values of these arguments will be assigned to the parameters of `max_of_four` when it starts executing. The parameter w will be assigned the value of a, x will get the value of b, and so forth.

At this point, in may not be completely clear to you when a subtask should be made into a function. There sometimes is no clear answer. With experience, you will become a better judge.

```
/* This program takes four numbers as input and prints out
   the maximum of the four */

#include <stdio.h>

/* Function declarations */
void print_banner();
int max_of_four(int w, int x, int y, int z);


main()
{
  int a, b, c, d;  /* Variables for input */
  int max;         /* Holds maximum of input */

  print_banner();

  scanf("%d %d %d %d", &a, &b, &c, &d);

  max = max_of_four(a, b, c, d);

  printf("The maximum value of the inputs is : %d\n", max);
}

/* Simply prints out the input banner */
void print_banner()
{
  printf("\nThis program will find the maximum of four input values.\n");
  printf("Please enter four integers: ");
}

/* This function returns the maximum input parameter */
int max_of_four(int w, int x, int y, int z)
{
  int local_max;

  if ((w >= x) && (w >= y) && (w >= z))
    local_max = w;
  else if ((x >= y) && (x >= z))
    local_max = x;
  else if (y >= z)
    local_max = y;
  else
    local_max = z;

  return local_max;
}
```

Figure 14.2: A C program that calculates the maximum of four values.

14.5   The run-time stack.

Before we jump into a detailed exploration of functions, we need to understand a mechanism central to the execution of C functions: the run-time stack. As we shall see, the run-time stack is necessary to enable functions to call themselves, which is central to a programming technique called *recursion*. Since it's an important programming concept, we will devote all of Chapter 16 to it.

14.5.1   The activation record.

When analyzing the code of function, the LC-2 compiler firsts creates entries in its symbol table (see 12.1.5) for all local variables declared within the function. Within each symbol table entry, the compiler keeps track of where in memory the variable has been allocated storage. Recall that variables are assigned offsets beginning at a region of memory whose base address is in R6. Each function's local variables are allocated storage in this manner. But in order for this to work properly, as different functions are called, we need a systematic means of changing R6 as control passes from one function to another. Each C function is translated into LC-2 instructions assuming that R6 contains the base address of a region of memory allocated for its local variables.

In order to make this happen, the compiler creates a memory template of all the local variables within a function while processing the source code for that function. This template is called the *activation record*. The activation record is essentially a systematic means of organizing the memory in which a function's local variables are stored. As we shall see, certain bookkeeping information is also stored in the activation record—this bookkeeping information is used to maintain the stack and control flow during execution.

An activation record has a very simple structure, which we describe using the following code. Figure 14.4 shows the activation record for this function called **noname**. Notice that function **noname** has three local variables and two parameters.

```
int noname(int a, int b)
{
    int w, x, y;

    /* Function body */
    :
    :
    return y;
}
```

The first three entries of all LC-2 activation records for all functions are reserved for book-keeping information. The first entry is reserved for the return value, regardless of whether a function returns a value or not. The function **noname** returns an integer value. The **return** statement at the end of the function body causes the value of integer variable y to be written into the space reserved for the return value in the activation record. This happens just before control is passed back to the calling function.

The second entry in the activation record is the return address. This is the address of the instruction to execute after the function noname has completed execution. In LC-2 terms, it is the same as the link address of a JSR instruction. As we shall see, function calls and returns in C are implemented using LC-2 JSR and RET instructions.

The final bookkeeping entry is called the *dynamic link*. It is the memory address of the activation record of the function which called this function. More on the dynamic link later.

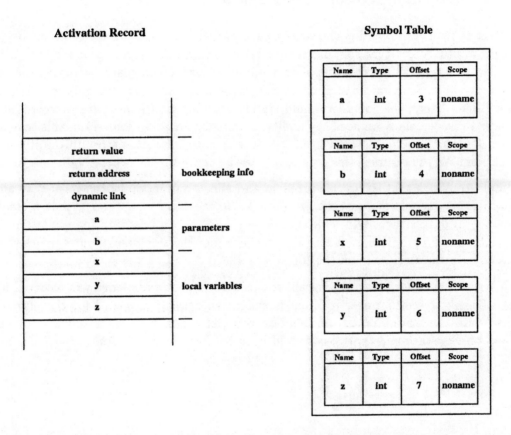

Figure 14.4: The activation record and symbol table entries for the function noname.

Each of the formal parameters are given entries in the activation record immediately following the three bookkeeping entries. In this case there are two parameters each requiring one memory location. Following the entries for the parameters, the entries for local variables are allocated. In this case there are three local variables, thus three entries are created. The compiler is able to determine the structure of any function's activation record as it analyzes the function's definition.

When the function `noname` executes, the *stack pointer* R6, which points to the top of the run-time stack, will point to the beginning of this activation record. In other words, when function `noname` is called, its activation record is *pushed* on top of the run-time stack.

The layout of a function's activation record allows the compiler to determine the memory address of each of the parameters and local variables when generating the machine code for the function. The offsets from the top of the activation record indicate where in memory, starting from the stack pointer, each variable and parameter is stored. For example, in order to load the value of local variable x into register R3, the compiler simply generates an LDR R3, R6, #5.

14.5.2 Activation records during execution.

We want to give each function the same execution environment: R6 contains the beginning of a region of memory that contains its activation record. A simple approach is to have the compiler assign each function a spot in memory where it can place its activation record. So, for example, function `main` gets location x1000, function `noname` gets location x1020, and so forth. Here, the compiler would simply ensure that the activation records did not overlap. However, since we need the ability of functions to call themselves, this scheme will not work—when a function calls itself it will overwrite the values stored from its previous invocation. We will examine this extensively in the next chapter, when we discuss recursion.

A simple approach that solves this problem and allows a function to call itself is to allocate the activation records at run time on a stack. Recall from Chapter 10, that a stack is a fundamental data structure in which *Push* and *Pop* are the two data manipulation operations. The Push operation adds an item to the top of the stack and Pop removes the item last added to the stack, i.e., off the top of the stack.

With a run-time stack, when a program is executed, a region of memory is reserved for the stack. During execution, as a function is called, an activation record for that function is pushed onto the stack. When the function completes, the function's activation record is popped off the stack and control is passed back to the calling function.

Let's look at an example and look at this process in more detail:

```
main()
{
  int a;
  int b;

  :
  :
  b = noname(a, 10);
  :
  :
}

int noname(int a, int b)
{
  int w, x, y;

  /* Function body */
  :
  :
  return y;
}
```

Figure 14.5 shows the run-time stack at several points during the execution of the program containing these functions. The run-time stack begins at some fixed point in memory and grows towards higher numbered memory addresses. In this figure, since higher numbered addresses are at the bottom of the diagram, the stack grows downwards. The point where the stack begins is determined by the designers of the operating system and varies from one computer system to another. In the LC-2, the stack begins at 0x4000.

Execution begins with a call by the LC-2 operating system to the function main. At this point, the activation record of main (which is similar in format to other activation records) is pushed on to the run-time stack and R6 contains the address of the beginning of main's activation record. This is shown in Figure 14.5(A). The LC-2 code associated with the call to noname will manipulate the stack in such a way that once noname begins execution, the activation record for noname will be on top of the stack and R6 will contain the address for it. Figure 14.5(B) shows the activation record for noname at the top of the stack. When noname completes, its activation record will be popped off the stack and main's record will once again be at the top, as shown in Figure 14.5(C). The mechanism to make all this happen is all done by LC-2 code generated by the compiler. In translating a function call, the compiler generates LC-2 code to push a record onto the stack. When translating a function return, the compiler generates LC-2 code to pop a record off the stack. Let's look at how this is done.

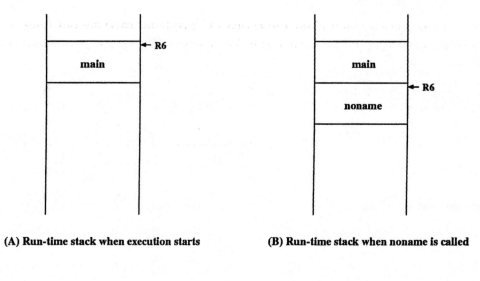

(A) Run-time stack when execution starts   (B) Run-time stack when noname is called

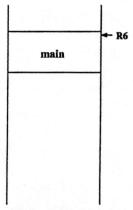

(C) Run-time stack when noname completes

Figure 14.5: Several snapshots of the run-time stack while the previous program executes.

14.6 Implementing functions in C.

In this section we describe the mechanics of function calls in C.

There are four segments of code that carry out the process of pushing and popping activation records: First, code in the *calling* function (the function in which the call occurs) performs the push of an activation record onto the stack. Second, the code at the beginning of the *called* function (the function to which the call was made) saves some bookkeeping information so that control can be successfully passed back to the calling function when the called function completes. Third, the code in the called function pops its activation record off the stack and returns control back to the calling function. Finally, once control is back in the calling function, code is executed to retrieve called function's return value.

In the next few sections we present the actual LC-2 code for carrying out these operations. We do so by closely examining the statement b = noname(a, 10); from the code in the previous example.

14.6.1 The call.

In the statement b = noname(a, 10);, the function noname is called with two arguments. The value returned by the function is assigned to the local integer variable b.

In translating this function call, the compiler generates LC-2 code which:

1. Transmits the value of the two arguments to the function noname by writing the values in the parameter fields of a **new** activation record.

2. Stores the value of R6 into the dynamic link field of this new activation record.

3. Modifies R6 to contain the address of this new activation record. This effectively pushes a new activation record on the stack.

4. Transfers control to noname via the JSR instruction.

The LC-2 code to perform this function call looks as follows:

```
    LDR  R0, R6, #3   ; load a
    STR  R0, R6, #8   ; store the first argument to noname

    AND  R0, R0, #0   ; R0 <- 0
    ADD  R0, R0, #10  ; R0 <- 10
    STR  R0, R6, #9   ; store the second argument to noname

    STR  R6, R6, #7   ; store R6 into the dynamic link slot of the new record
                      ; we have now effectively pushed a new record on the stack

    ADD  R6, R6, #5   ; move R6 to point to beginning of the new record
    JSR  noname
```

The first seven LC-2 instruction accomplish the task of transmitting the argument values. When generating the code to accomplish this, the compiler only needs to be aware of the size of the activation record of the calling function. The calling function in this case is the function **main** and it has an activation record size of 5 (three bookkeeping entries plus two local variables). The compiler knows that the new activation record will begin **immediately** after the activation record for **main**. It doesn't need to know anything about the function being called, except for the number, order, and type of its parameters. It knows this from the function declaration.

The sixth instruction (STR R6, R6, #7) stores the current value of R6 into the dynamic link field of the new activation record. The dynamic link is used, as we shall see, to correctly pop a record off the stack. It stores the value of the old top-of-stack. The seventh instruction increments R6 just beyond the current activation record and points it to the activation record for noname. Finally, a JSR instruction initiates execution of the called function. Recall that the LC-2 JSR instruction places the return address in R7.

Figure 14.6 shows the layout in memory of these two activation records after the code above has executed. Some values have not been generated, such as the return value for main. These values are marked with a --.

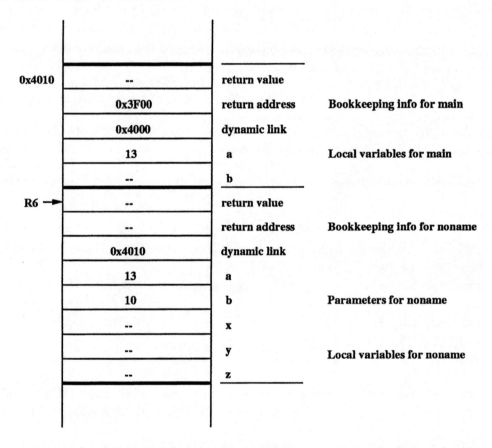

Figure 14.6: The run-time stack after the activation record for noname is pushed on the stack.

14.6.2   Starting the called function.

The instruction executed after the JSR is the first instruction in the called function noname. Before the compiler can generate the code corresponding to the statements within a function, it must take care of some bookkeeping due to the function call. All functions in C (including main) are called from somewhere, thus all functions must start off by saving the value of

R7 (it contains the return address of where they need to return control) into the return address entry in the activation record. The LC-2 code to do this is quite simple:

```
noname:
        STR R7, R6, #1    ; recall that R6 points to the beginning of
                          ; the current record.
```

When the JSR in the calling function executes, the address of the instruction following the JSR in the code is put into R7. The first task of the called function is to store the value in a safe place in memory—loosing the return address would mean that there would be no way to return control to the calling function. For this reason, each activation record contains a spot where we can safely store the return address.

14.6.3 Ending the called function.

Several things need to be performed to return control back to the calling function. Firstly, a function which returns a value needs a mechanism for the return value to be properly transmitted back to the calling function. This transmission happens via the activation record. Secondly, all functions must pop the current activation record. To enumerate:

1. If there is a return value, it is written into the return value entry of the activation record.

2. The return address is loaded into R7.

3. The value of the dynamic link entry is loaded into R6. The activation is effectively popped from the stack.

4. The RET instruction returns control back to the calling function.

The LC-2 instruction corresponding to this for noname are:

```
        LDR  RO, R6, #7   ; load the value of y
        STR  RO, R6, #0   ; store it into the return value entry

        LDR  R7, R6, #1   ; load the return address
        LDR  R6, R6, #2   ; load the dynamic link

        RET
```

The first two instructions write the return value, which in this case is the local variable y, into the first entry of the activation record. The second instruction copies the value of the return address into R7. It was written into the activation record when the called function started execution. The third instruction copies back the dynamic link (the old top of stack) into R6. This effectively pops the activation record off the stack. Even though the activation record is popped off the stack, the values still remain in memory (a fact which should not be surprising, having dealt with the physical operation of memory in Chapter 3). Once control is passed back to the calling function, it will read the return value from the activation record that was just popped.

14.6.4 Returning to the calling function.

After the called function executes the RET instruction, control is passed back to the calling function. In some cases, there will be no return value (if the function called declared of type void) and in some cases, the calling function will ignore the return value. Again, from our previous example the return value is assigned to local variable b. The code after the JSR looks as follows:

```
    :
    :
JSR   noname

LDR   R0, R6, #5   ; load the return value
                   ; (just beyond the record for main, which has 5 entries)
STR   R0, R6, #4   ; b = noname(a, 10);
    :
    :
```

The LDR instruction loads the return value of the called function from the activation record that was just popped off the stack. The act of popping a record only moves the stack pointer R6; the values in memory from the popped record persist until they are overwritten (i.e., after a new record is pushed on the stack) or the computer is halted and powered-down.

14.6.5 Tying it all together.

The code for the call site in main and the beginning and end of noname is listed in Figure 14.7. Here, the LC-2 code segments presented in the previous sections are all combined, showing the overall structure of the code.

```
main:
        :
        :
      LDR  RO, R6, #3   ; load a
      STR  RO, R6, #8   ; store the first argument to noname

      AND  RO, RO, #0   ; RO <- 0
      ADD  RO, RO, #10  ; RO <- 10
      STR  RO, R6, #9   ; store the third argument to noname

      STR  R6, R6, #6   ; store R6 into the dynamic link slot of the new record
                        ; we have now effectively pushed a new record on the stack

      ADD  R6, R6, #6   ; move R6 to point to beginning of new record
      JSR  noname

      LDR  RO, R6, #4   ; load the return value
                        ; (just beyond the current record)
      STR  RO, R6, #4   ; b = noname(a, 10);
        :
        :


noname:
      STR R7, R6, #1    ; recall that R6 points to the beginning of
                        ; the current record.


        :
        :         ; the body of noname
        :
      LDR  RO, R6, #8   ; load the value of y
      STR  RO, R6, #0   ; store it into the return value entry

      LDR  R7, R6, #1   ; load the return address
      LDR  R6, R6, #2   ; load the dynamic link

      RET
```

Figure 14.7: The LC-2 code corresponding to a C function call and return.

14.7   A detailed example, with complete translation.

At this point, we have discussed the syntax of C functions, the translation of C code containing functions, and the run-time behavior of programs with function calls. Let us walk through another example of code containing function to solidify the concepts.

Figure 14.8 shows an example C program which takes input from the keyboard, converts each input character into uppercase, and prints out the result. When the input character is the newline character, the program terminates. The conversion process from lower case to upper case is done by the function **to_upper**.

```c
#include <stdio.h>

/* Function Prototype */
char to_upper(char inchar);

/* Function definition */
main()
{
  char key;
  char upcase;

  printf("Input a line of text : ");

  while((input = getchar()) != '\n') {
    /* Function call */
    upcase = to_upper(input);
    putchar(upcase);
  }
}

/* Function definition */
/* If the parameter is lower case then return
   its uppercase ASCII value */
char to_upper(char inchar)
{
  if (inchar >= 'a' && inchar <= 'z')
    return(inchar - ('a' - 'A'));
  else
    return(inchar);
}
```

Figure 14.8: A program with a function to convert lower case letters to uppercase.

The corresponding LC-2 code for this example follows. Because the LC-2 ISA is not byte-addressable, a character variable occupies a full word of memory to make this example easier to understand.

```
main:
        STR   R7, R6, #1    ;   even main needs to store away the return address
        :
        :                   ;   code for call to printf and the test for the while loop
        :
        LDR   R0, R6, #3    ;   load value of key
        STR   R0, R6, #8    ;   store key as first parameter
        STR   R6, R6, #7    ;   store the current top of stack as the dynamic link
        ADD   R6, R6, #5    ;   move the top of stack to the new activation record
        JSR   to_upper      ;   the call
        LDR   R0, R6, #5    ;   load the return value and stick it into upcase
        STR   R0, R6, #4    ;   upcase = to_upper(key);
        :
        :                   ;   code for call putchar
to_upper:
        STR   R7, R6, #1    ;   store away the return address
        LDR   R0, R6, #3    ;   load the parameter inchar
        LD    R1, ASCII_a   ;   load the ascii value of 'a'
        NOT   R1
        ADD   R1, R1, #1    ;   R1 contains -'a'
        ADD   R1, R0, R1    ;   inchar - 'a'
        BRN   FALSE         ;   inchar is less than 'a'
        LD    R1, ASCII_z   ;   load the ascii value of 'z'
        NOT   R1
        ADD   R1, R1, #1    ;   R1 contains -'z'
        ADD   R1, R0, R1    ;   inchar - 'z'
        BRN   FALSE         ;   inchar is greater than 'z'
        ;  The condition is true (inchar >= 'a' && inchar <= 'z')
        LD    R1, neg_ASCII_a_minus_A   ; load the ascii value of -('a'-'A')
        LDR   R0, R6, #3    ;   load inchar
        ADD   R0, R1, R0    ;   calculate (inchar - ('a' - 'A'))
        STR   R0, R6, #0    ;   store it into the return value entry
        LDR   R7, R6, #1    ;   load the return address
        LDR   R6, R6, #2    ;   load the dynamic link
        RET                 ;   return (inchar - ('a' - 'A'));
ASCII_a:                .FILL #97
ASCII_z:                .FILL #122
neg_ASCII_a_minus_A:    .FILL #-32
FALSE:
        LDR   R0, R6, #3    ;   load inchar
        STR   R0, R6, #0    ;   store it into the return value entry
        LDR   R7, R6, #1    ;   load the return address
        LDR   R6, R6, #2    ;   load the dynamic link
        RET                 ;   return (inchar + 'a');
```

Figure 14.9: LC-2 version of the C uppercase program.

14.8 Exercises.

14.1 What is the significance of the function **main**? Why must all programs contain this function?

14.2   1. What is the purpose of the dynamic link?

2. What is the purpose of the return address?

3. What is the purpose of the return value?

14.3   1. What is a function declaration? What is its purpose?

2. What is a function prototype?

3. What is the function definition?

4. What are arguments?

5. What are parameters?

14.4 For each of the items below, identify whether the calling function or the called function performs the action.

1. Writing the arguments into the activation record.

2. Writing the return value

3. Writing the dynamic link

4. Modifying the value in R6 to contain the address of the called function's activation record.

14.5 Just before Paul was to turn in his C program, his computer crashed and the file was destroyed except for the following lines.

```
main()
{
    int i, j;
```

Fortunately, the LC-2 translation of his program was saved. Help Paul by reconstructing his C program.

```
        MAIN    AND     R0, R0, #0
                ADD     R0, R0, #10
                STR     R0, R6, #3

                AND     R0, R0, #0
                STR     R0, R6, #4

        LOOP1   LDR     R0, R6, #4
                ADD     R0, R0, #1
```

```
                    STR     R0, R6, #4

                    LDR     R0, R6, #3
                    ADD     R0, R0, #-1
                    STR     R0, R6, #3


                    LDR     R0, R6, #3
                    BRNZ    LOOP1

            EXIT1   HALT
```

14.6 What is the output of the following program?

```
#include <stdio.h>

int multiply(int d, int b);

int d = 3;

main() {
  int a, b, c;
  int e = 4;

  a = 1;
  b = 2;

  c = multiply(a, b);
  printf("%d %d %d %d %d\n", a, b, c, d++, ++e);
}

int multiply(int d, int b) {
  int a;

  a = 2;
  b = 3;

  return (a * b);
}
```

14.7 Below is the code for a C function name **goofy**. The diagram beside the code is its activation record.

  1. Write one of the following in each entry of the activation record to indicate what is stored there.

(a) local variable

(b) argument

(c) address of an instruction

(d) address of data

(e) other

```
int goofy(int x)
{
        int a;

        a = x + 1;

        return (a);
}
```

2. Some of the entries in the activation record above are written by the function which calls **goofy**; some are written by **goofy** itself. Place an "X" beside the entries written by **goofy**.

14.8 What is the output of the program below? Explain.

```
void myFunc(int z) {
  printf("%d ", z);
  z++
}

main() {
  int z = 2;

  myFunc(z);
  myFunc(z);
}
```

14.9 The following code was generated by the LC-2 compiler while compiling a C **return** statement:

```
        AND   RO, RO, #0
        STR   RO, R6, #0
        LDR   R7, R6, #1
        LDR   R6, R6, #2
        RET
```

1. What will the return value of this function always be?

2. Could the third and fourth instructions be swapped without changing the behavior of the program? Why or why not?

14.10 Are the arguments to a function placed on the stack before or after the JSR to that function? Why?

14.11 A C program containing a function food has been compiled into LC-2 assembly language. The translation of the function looks like this.

```
food    STR     R7, R6, #1
        STR     R6, R6, #12
        ADD     R6, R6, #10
        JSR     pizza
        LDR     R7, R6, #1
        LDR     R6, R6, #2
        RET
```

1. How many entries does the activation record for food have?

2. If the function pizza takes no arguments, then how many local variables must it have?

14.12 Below is a function written in C and its translation into LC-2 assembly code. Unfortunately, the compiler that made the translation had a bug and made two mistakes (some compilers really make mistakes). Identify and correct the mistakes and explain why they are mistakes.

```
int smaller(int x, int y) {
    if (x < = y)
        return x;
    else
        return y;
}
```

```
        smaller STR     R7, R6, #1

                LDR     R0, R6, #3
                LDR     R1, R6, #4
                NOT     R2, R1
                ADD     R2, R2, #1
                ADD     R2, R0, R2
                BRZ     LABEL1

                LDR     R0, R6, #3
                STR     R0, R6, #0
                BR      LABEL2
        LABEL1  LDR     R0, R6, #4
                STR     R0, R6, #0

        LABEL2  LDR     R6, R6, #2
                LDR     R7, R6, #1
                RET
```

14.13 Give the translation of the following C function into LC-2 assembly language. Draw the activation record for the function.

```
#define SIDES 6

int sum_dice (int num) {
    int i, sum;

    sum = 0;
    for (i = 0 ; i < num ; i++)
        sum = roll_dice(SIDES) + sum;
    return sum;
}
```

14.14 The following C program is compiled into LC-2 machine language and loaded into address x3000 before execution. Not counting the JSRs to library routines for I/O, the object code contains 3 JSRs (one to function f, one to g, and one to h). Suppose the addresses of the three JSR instructions are x3102, x3301, and x3304. And suppose the user provides 4 5 6 as input values. Draw a picture of the run-time stack, providing the contents of locations if possible, when the program is about to return from function f. Assume the stack starts at location x4000.

```c
#include <stdio.h>

main() {
    int a,b,c;

    printf("Type three numbers: ");
    scanf("%d%d%d", &a, &b, &c);
    printf("%d", f(a,b,c));
}

int f(int x, int y, int z) {
    int x1;

    x1 = g(x);
    return h(y,z) * x1;
}

int g(int arg) {
    return arg*arg;
}

int h(int arg1, int arg2) {
    return arg1/arg2;
}
```

14.15 Modify the code in Figure 14.3 to also print out the minimum of the four values. Use a function similar to max_of_four to calculate the minimum.

14.16 Modify the example in Figure 14.8 to **also** convert each character to lower case. The new program should print out both the lower and upper case versions of each input character.

Chapter 15

Debugging.

15.1   Introduction.

Programmers often spend more time debugging their programs than they spend writing them. The C programming language is particularly notorious for bugs because of the large amount of flexibility given to the programmer. Because of this, developing effective debugging skills is critical for someone seeking to master the art of programming.

As we mentioned before, debugging is applied common sense. Using information about a program and its execution, a programmer can deduce (using common sense) where things are possibly going wrong. Debugging a program is a bit like solving a puzzle. The available clues logically lead to the solution. Often there is a critical piece of information, which once when found, immediately reveals the bug.

In this chapter, we will describe some techniques you can use to find the bugs within a program. We will describe some very simple debugging techniques to detect bugs, such as tracing variables and adding error-checking code. These techniques however are not practical for all debugging jobs; larger programs require more sophisticated debugging techniques. For larger tasks, a source-level debugger is invaluable. A source-level debugger is a tool which allows the programmer to interactively monitor a program during its execution. Different computer systems, Windows NT or UNIX, for example, support different specific debuggers. However, almost all debuggers support a set of core operations which is required in order to debug effectively. We will describe these core operations and how to use them within the context of the UNIX source-level debugger dbx.

15.2   Types of errors.

With programming in general, be it at a high-level or low-level, there are several types of errors we introduce into our programs. *Syntactic errors* are the easiest to deal with since we are writing code which confuses the translation mechanism. The translator notifies us of such errors when we attempt to translate the program, often pointing out exactly where the error occurred. *Semantic errors* are problems, sometimes easily caught, but which can often be very difficult to find. They occur when we program something that is syntactically correct but not exactly what we intended. Once they are found, they are often easy to fix. Both syntactic and semantic errors are typographic errors: we typed something we didn't mean to type. *Algorithmic errors*, on the other hand, are errors where where our approach to solving a problem is wrong. They are often hard to detect and once detected can be very hard to fix. This classification of errors is based on broad strokes and intended to clarify how errors get into our programs. There are many errors which are not clearly of a single type.

15.2.1   Syntactic errors.

In C, syntactic errors (often casually called syntax errors) are always caught by the compiler. We are asking the compiler to translate code which is not legal. For instance, the code listed in Figure 15.1 contains a syntax error which the compiler will flag when the code is compiled.

```
#include <stdio.h>

main()
{
    int i
    int j;

    for (i = 0; i <= 10; i++) {
        j = i * 7;
        printf("%d x 7 = %d\n", i, j);
    }
}
```

Figure 15.1: This program contains a syntactic error.

The declaration for the variable i is missing a semicolon. Often missing semicolons and missing variable declarations account for a significant number of syntax errors you will encounter. It's hard to write a complete program without missing a semicolon somewhere. The good news is that these types of errors are easy to detect (because the compiler detects them for us) and easy to fix. The more sophisticated compilers will attempt to keep analyzing a program past any syntax errors it encounters. This enables multiple syntax errors to be detected with a single compilation. However, the compiler sometimes cannot gracefully recover from a syntax error causing it to detect errors where none existed or which were caused by an earlier error. Fixing the first one will remove many subsequent ones.

15.2.2 Semantic errors.

Semantic errors are similar to syntactic errors in that they occur for the same reason: because our minds and our fingers are not completely coordinated when typing in a program. Semantic errors, however, don't involve incorrect syntax therefore the program gets translated and we are able to execute it. It isn't until we analyze the output that we discover that the program isn't doing what we expected. Figure 15.2 lists an example of the same program as above, with a simple semantic error (the original syntax error is fixed). The program prints out a multiplication table for the number 7.

```
#include <stdio.h>

main()
{
  int i;
  int j;

  for (i = 0; i <= 10; i++)
    j = i * 7;
    printf("%d x 7 = %d\n", i, j);
}
```

Figure 15.2: A program with a semantic error.

Here, a single execution of the program will reveal the problem. Only one entry of the multiplication table is printed. You should be able to deduce, given your knowledge of C programming, why this program behaves incorrectly. Why is "11 x 7 = 70" printed out? This program demonstrates something called a *control flow* error. Here, the program's control flow, i.e., the order in which statements are executed, is different than what the programmer intended.

Figure 15.3 lists another, more subtle, semantic error. The program should display one of two messages depending on whether the input value can is between 0 and 100. Why does this particular program always give the same output message?

A common semantic error involving local variables is listed in Figure 15.4. This example uses the factorial program we encountered in Section 14.3.

The program above calculates the factorial of a number input from the keyboard. The program keeps repeating, prompting for input and calculating its factorial, until the user enters a number less than or equal to 0, in which case it stops. Try executing this program on several numbers. Why doesn't it work properly? Hint: draw out the run-time stack for an execution of this program.

Semantic errors are particularly troubling because they often go undetected by both the compiler AND the user until a particular set of inputs triggers the error. Some are caught

```
#include <stdio.h>

main()
{
    int number;
    int temp;

    printf("Enter a integer: ");
    scanf("%d", &number);

    if (0 < number < 100)
      printf("The number is postive and less than a hundred\n");
    else
      printf("The number is NOT postive or it's NOT less than a hundred\n");
}
```

Figure 15.3: A program with a subtle semantic error.

during execution because an illegal action is performed by the program. Almost all computer systems (even PCs) have safeguards which prevent a program from doing certain things, one of which is reading or writing certain parts of memory. For instance, it is undesirable for a user's program to modify the memory which stores the operating system. When such an illegal action is performed by a program, the operating system terminates its execution and prints out a *run-time error* message. Often, these types of illegal actions are inadvertently put into programs due to poor programming. Here's an example. Let's modify the scanf statement from the previous example to the following:

```
    scanf("%d", in);
```

The ampersand & character, as we shall see in Chapter 17, is a special operator in the C language. Omitting it here causes a run-time error message to be displayed when the program is executed. On most UNIX environments, the message displayed is **Bus Error**. (The name of this error has historical significance. The error has little to do with the actual buses within the computer system). Here, the program has requested that an unmodifiable memory location be written. We shall look at this particular example in more detail in Chapter 18.

15.2.3   Algorithmic errors.

The final type of major programming error is the algorithmic error. Here, due to improper design, the program does not correctly perform the intended task. These types of errors can be serious, as they may not appear until many trials of the program have been run. Once

```
#include <stdio.h>

int factorial(int n);

int main()
{
  int in, fact;

  do {
    printf("Input a number :");
    scanf("%d", &in);

    if (in > 0) {
      fact = factorial(in);
      printf("The factorial of %d is %d\n", in, fact);
    }
  } while (in > 0);
}


/* n must be a positive integer */
int factorial(int n)
{
  int res, i;

  for (i=1; i<=n; i++)
    res = res * i;

  return(res);
}
```

Figure 15.4: A program with bug involving local variables.

detected and isolated, they can be very hard to repair. The good news is that these types of errors can be eliminated by proper planning before sitting in front of a computer to type in the program. A good example of this sort of bug is the Year 2000 computer bug, or Y2K bug. Many computer programs minimize the amount of memory required to store dates. They use enough bits to store only the last two digits of the year, and no more. Thus the year 2000 is indistinguishable from the year 1900 (or 1800 or 2100 for that matter). This presents a problem whenever a crossover occurs. Say, for example, you checked out a book from the University library in late 1999 that was due back sometime in early 2000. If the library's computer system has the Y2K bug, then you may end up getting an overdue notice in the mail with some hefty fines listed on it.

15.3   Debugging techniques.

Because bugs are a significant issue in developing computer software, very sophisticated systems for detecting them and repairing the code. Complex software may behave correctly with a certain set of input, but fail on another. Often, it's hard to find the right set of input to make it fail. Once that input is found, then isolating the cause of the bug is yet another hard task.

Clearly, good techniques for finding errors and eliminating them are necessary. For the process of detecting bugs, most programmers (even large software vendors) resort to brute-force testing with different inputs in hopes of finding one which causes the software to break. When a failure is detected, many different techniques exist to isolate its source.

15.3.1   Ad-hoc techniques.

The simplest thing to do once you realize that there is a problem with your program is to visually inspect the source code. Sometimes the nature of the failure tips you off to the region of the code where the bug is likely to exist. This technique is fine if the region of source code is a small and familiar region.

Another simple technique is to add statements within the code to print out information during execution. You might dump out, or trace, the values of critical variables or any information which you think will be useful in finding the bug. You can also add output statements to monitor a program's control flow, thereby check for control flow errors. If the program is easy to compile and the bug appears quickly during execution, this technique is not unreasonable to use.

Several techniques of defensive programming allow you to identify error conditions before they propagate too far from their source. *Assertions* and error checks are statements added to the source code which flag a condition that the programmer knows should not exist. For example, below we've added the following error check to the factorial function:

```
/* n must be a positive integer */
int factorial(int n)
{
  int res = 0, i;

  /* Check for legal parameter values */
  if (n < 1) {
    printf("Bad input.  The input to factorial must be positive.\n");
    return -1;
  }

  for (i=1; i<=n; i++)
    res = res * i;

  return(res);
}
```

Here, if the input parameter to the factorial function is not positive, then a message is displayed and a -1 returned. When and where to add assertion statements requires deep familiarity with the program. Wantonly placed assertions are not helpful and themselves trigger an error when nothing is wrong. (An aside: What would happen if the check wasn't in place and `factorial` called with a zero or a negative number?)

Another defensive technique is to test your program module-by-module. Once a function is written, be sure the function is behaving as you expect by testing it separate from the rest of the program. This is not always possibly, but highly recommended when it is. A benefit of writing shorter and simpler functions is that it not only better modularizes the programming, but simplifies the debugging.

15.3.2 The source-level debugger.

Sometimes the ad-hoc techniques cannot deliver enough information to quickly uncover the source of a bug. In these cases, programmers often turn to a *source-level debugger* to find problem spots. The debugger is a tool that allows an executing program to be paused and monitored such that variables and control flow can be checked at any point during execution. It is very similar to the LC-2 debugger, except it deals with code generated from high-level source code.

In order to use the source-level debugger on a program, the program must be compiled in a special way. The compiler must *annotate* the executable image with enough additional information so the debugger can map a machine language instruction its corresponding statement in the source program. Also, information about variable names and their allocated locations (i.e., the symbol table) must be included so that a programmer can examine the value of any variable within the program. In UNIX, to compile a program with debug information, use the -g flag. Here is an example:

```
cc -o buggy_program -g buggy_program.c
```

Now to invoke the UNIX debugger dbx on this program, we use the following command.

```
dbx buggy_program
```

Once the debugger is invoked, you will be at the debugger prompt.

Note, some systems may not have the dbx debugger as standard software. Many systems, such as Windows for example, have interactive debuggers with *Graphical User Interfaces* (GUIs for short; pronounced gooey). PC debuggers such as Code Warrior and Visual C support the basic debugger functionality described in this chapter, and they have other useful features to assist in the debugging process.

We will now describe a few commonly used debugger commands.

The list command.

When debugging a program, it is helpful to have a listing of the program's source code within sight. Having the source code in sight is a big help when selecting breakpoints or examining variables or when following the execution of the program within the debugger.

The list command displays lines from the source file on the screen. Typing list with no arguments displays a default number (usually 10) of lines surrounding the current source line (usually the next line to be executed). The list command takes a variety of arguments which control the number of lines to be displayed, the line from which to begin the listing, from which function, and from which source file.

Debuggers with a graphical user interface have no need for a list command. These debuggers will open a window containing the program source when the debugger is started; the source code is always visible on the screen.

The stop command.

Similar to the LC-2 breakpoint command, the stop command allows the programmer to specify points during the execution of a program when the program should stop running and control should be passed back to the debugger. Once the debugger has control, the programmer can then probe the state of the program and examine variables and even modify their values.

A useful form of the stop command is stop at <line_num> where the program is paused when the indicated source line number is reached. Another useful form of stop is stop in <function_name>. Here, the program is paused once a call is made to a function with the specified name.

Debuggers with GUIs make the process of picking breakpoints trivial. In these debuggers, breakpoints can be set by clicking on a line in the source code window. When the program is run, execution will stop at that line.

The run command.

Initially, when the debugger is invoked, the program being debugged is not immediately executed. This gives the programmer an opportunity to set up breakpoints, initialize values, and set up various monitors. Once everything is set up, then the programmer can start execution of the program by using the run command. This causes execution to begin. If no breakpoints are set up, then execution proceeds until the program terminates.

The step command.

The LC-2 debugger has a command that executes a single LC-2 instruction of the program. Similarly, the dbx source-level debugger allows execution to proceed one source line at a time. The step command executes the current source line and then pauses the program again. Single-stepping through a program is very useful, particularly when stepping through the region of a program where the bug is suspected to exist. Single-steeping is a good way to check for control flow errors.

The print command.

We can examine the values of variables using the command print <variable_name> which displays the current value of the variable specified. Often, programmers use the breakpoint command stop to pause execution near where the bug is suspected to exist, then use the print command to examine variables at that point in execution.

Debuggers with GUIs often allow variables and their values to be displayed on the screen in a separate window. As the program executes, and breakpoints are encountered, this window is automatically updated with current values.

Miscellaneous commands.

The dbx command help provides a brief description of all the commands supported by the dbx debugger. The command help <command> give a description of a particular command and its syntax. The command status displays all the active breakpoints (and other info) that have been set up. The command clear removes a breakpoint. The command where displays where in the program source the execution has paused.

15.4   Exercises.

15.1 The following programs each have a single error which prevents them from operating as specified. With as few changes as possible, correct the programs. All of the programs should output a single number which is the sum of the integers from 1 to 10, inclusive.

1. Version 1,

```
#include <stdio.h>

main() {
    int i = 1;
    int sum = 0;

    while (i < 11) {
        sum = sum + i;
        ++i;
        printf("%d\n", sum);
    }
}
```

2. Version 2,

```
#include <stdio.h>

main() {
    int i;
    int sum = 0;

    for (i = 0; i >= 10; ++i)
        sum = sum + i;

    printf("%d\n", sum);
}
```

3. Version 3,

```
#include <stdio.h>

main() {
    int i = 0;
    int sum = 0;

    while (i <= 11)
        sum = sum + i++;

    printf("%d\n", sum);
}
```

4. Version 4,

```
#include <stdio.h>

main() {
    int i = 0;
    int sum = 0;

    for (i = 0; i <= 10;)
        sum = sum + ++i;

    printf("%d\n", sum);
}
```

15.2 What is the output produced by the following C code segment?

```
main() {
    int i, j;

    j = 0;
    i = j + 4;

    while (i != j) {
        printf("%d ", i);
        j = j + 1;
    }
}
```

15.3 The following program fragments have syntax errors and therefore will not compile. Assume that all variables have been properly declared. Fix the errors so that the fragments won't cause compiler errors.

1. Fragment 1.

```
i = 0;
j = 0;
do {
   j = j + 1;
   while (i < 5);
}
```

2. Fragment 2.

```
if (cont == 0)
   a = 2;
   b = 3;
   c = 4;
else
   a = -2;
   b = -3;
   c = -4;
```

3. Fragment 3.

```
#define LIMIT 5;

if (LIMIT)
   printf("True");
else
   printf("False");
```

15.4 The following program compiles successfully but causes an error when run. Explain the error and suggest a solution.

```c
#include <stdio.h>

main() {
    int num, sum;

    num = 0;
    sum = 0;
    printf("Enter a number = ");
    scanf("%d", num);

    if (num != 0)
        sum = sum + num;
    else
        sum = sum -1;

    printf("The sum is = %d\n", sum);
}
```

15.5 Paul wrote the following program. He expected the output of his program to be:

```
The value in b is 0
```

However, when he ran the program, the output turned out to be:

```
The value in b is 3
```

What's wrong with his program?

```c
#include <stdio.h>

main() {
    int a[3];
    int b;

    b = 0;
    for (i = 1 ; i <=3 ; i++)
        a[i] = i;

    printf("The value in b is %d\n", b);
}
```

15.6 The following C code was written to find the minimum of a set of positive integers that a user enters from the keyboard. The user signifies the end of the set by entering the value -1. However, the code contains a serious algorithmic error. Identify and suggest ways to fix the error. Use a source-level debugger, if needed, to find the error.

```c
#include <stdio.h>

main()
{
   /* Initialize variables */
   int smallestNumber = 0;
   int nextInput;

   /* Get the first input number */
   scanf("%d", &nextInput);

   /* Keep reading inputs until user enters -1 */
   while (nextInput != -1) {
      if (nextInput < smallestNumber)
      smallestNumber = nextInput;
      scanf("%d", &nextInput);
   }

   printf("The smallest number is %d\n", smallestNumber);
}
```

15.7 Use a source-level debugger to monitor the execution of the following code.

```c
#include <stdio.h>

int is_divisible\_by(int divisor, int quotient);

main() {
    int i;          /* Iteration variable */
    int j;          /* Iteration variable */
    int f;          /* Tracks return values of is_divisible_by */


    for (i = 2; i < 1000; i++) {
        f = 0;
        for (j = 1; j < i; j++) {
            if (is_divisible_by(i, j))
                f++;
        }
    }
}

int is_divisible_by(int divisor, int quotient)
{
    if (divisor % quotient == 0) {
        printf("%d is evenly divisible by %d\n", divisor, quotient);
        return 1;
    }
    else {
        return 0;
    }
}
```

1. Set a break point at the beginning of function is_divisible_by and examine the parameter values for the first 10 calls. What are they?

2. What is the value of f after the inner for loop completes when the value of i equals 660.

3. Can this program be written more efficiently? Hint: monitor the value of the arguments when the return value of is_divisible_by is 1.

Chapter 16

Recursion.

16.1 Introduction.

When applied correctly, recursion can simplify certain programming tasks considerably. The idea behind recursion is simple: a function performs its task by applying itself to a smaller component of that task. Said another way, the function calls itself in the course of carrying out its task. We shall see many examples of this as we progress through this chapter. Recursion is similar to iteration and often the two can be used interchangeably. There are programming situations, however, where using recursion leads to a much simpler program.

16.2 What is recursion?

A function which calls itself is said to be a recursive function, as in the function running_sum in the example below.

```
int running_sum(int n)
{
  if (n == 0)
    return 0;
  else
    return (n + running_sum(n-1));
}
```

This function calculates the running sum of all the integers between its input parameter and 0. For example, running_sum(4) calculates $4 + 3 + 2 + 1 + 0$. The function body of running_sum contains a function call to itself. Notice that the running sum of 4 is really 4 plus the running sum of 3. Likewise, the running sum of 3 is 3 plus the running sum of 2. This *recursive* definition is the basis for a recursive algorithm. Let's look at another example of recursion, this time a higher level one.

369

Suppose we wanted to sort a set of midterm exams into alphabetical order, one approach would be to take the set, divide it into two sets, sort each smaller set individually, and then merge the two sorted sets back into one. In fact, we might continue dividing the smaller sets into two smaller subsets until we end up with subsets small enough to manageably arrange by hand. If a subset is too large then arranging the papers into order by hand is difficult. This process of dividing and sorting illustrates the essence of recursion: we are sorting a large stack by systematically sorting smaller stacks.

Suppose we want to find a particular student's exam once the exams are in alphabetical order. We might pick a point about halfway through the set and examine the name on the exam at that halfway point. If the student's exam is not there, then we search the appropriate half (depending on the student's name and the name on the exam at the halfway point) using the same technique. For example, say we are looking for the exam of Babe Ruth, and at the halfway point, we find Mickey Mantle's exam. Since we're not looking for Mickey's exam, we repeat the process on the bottom half (i.e., the half containing Mantle through Yastrzemski). Fairly quickly, we will close in on and locate Babe Ruth's exam if it exists in the set. This technique of searching through a sorted set of exams is also recursive because we apply the same searching algorithm to continually smaller and smaller subsets of papers.

You might have already encountered recursion in mathematics. Sometimes, we express a function as a function of smaller values. These are called *recurrence equations*. The following equation is a recurrence equation.

$$f(n) = f(n-1) + f(n-2)$$

With recurrence equations, we must also supply an initial case. So in addition to the formula above, we need to state:

$$f(0) = 1$$
$$f(1) = 1$$

Now, we can evaluate:

$$
\begin{aligned}
f(4) &= f(3) + f(2) \\
&= (f(2) + f(1)) + (f(1) + f(0)) \\
&= ((f(1) + f(0)) + 1) + (1 + 1) \\
&= 1 + 1 + 1 + 1 + 1 \\
&= 5
\end{aligned}
$$

In this chapter we'll present several examples of recursion to help you better grasp the concept. We'll also delve into the inner workings of a recursive function to demonstrate how the run-time stack makes it all happen.

16.3 A high-level example: binary search.

In the previous section, we described in words a recursive technique for finding an exam in a set of alphabetically sorted exams. The technique we described is a commonly used recursive technique for finding an item within a group of sorted items—it's called *binary search*. Here we'll express the binary search algorithm using *pseudo-code*. Pseudo-code is shorthand notation of C code. It isn't quite C code as it doesn't have the details of C code, yet it captures the flow and intent of the algorithm

In order to properly express the algorithm, we'll need to describe a stack of exams as two numbers. Assume the exams are sequentially numbered after they are sorted. To describe a stack of exams, the first number indicates the the exam number at the top of the stack and the second number the exam at the bottom.

```
FindExam(student_name, start, end)
{
  half_way_point = (end + start)/2

  if (end < start)
    /* Error case: exam doesn't exist in the set */
    ExamNotFound();

  if (student_name == NameOfExam(half_way_point))
    /* We found the exam! */
    ExamFound(half_way_point);

  else if (student_name < NameOfExam(half_way_point))
    /* Search the top half */
    FindExam(student_name, start, half_way_point-1);

  else
    /* Search the bottom half */
    FindExam(student_name, half_way_point+1, end);
}
```

The function FindExam is called with three arguments: the name we are searching for, the exam number at the top of the set, and the exam number at the bottom. Each time the function is called, we first calculate the half-way point through the set. If the exam we are searching for is at the half-way point, we are done. If it's not, we search the top half or the bottom half depending on the whether the student's name is greater than or less than the name on the exam at the half-way point. For this we use a recursive call to `FindExam`. Notice that the recursive function has two terminal cases—one where the exam is found and one where the exam is determined not to exist in the set.

16.4   Another high-level example: Towers of Hanoi.

Now let's examine a problem where a recursive solution is the simplest solution. There is a classic puzzle known as the Towers of Hanoi. The puzzle involves a platform with three posts. On one of the posts sit a number of wooden disks, each smaller than the one below it. The objective is to move all the disks from their current post to another post. There are two rules for moving disks: only one disk can be moved at a time and a larger disk can never be placed upon a smaller disk. Figure 16.1 shows the initial configuration of the puzzle.

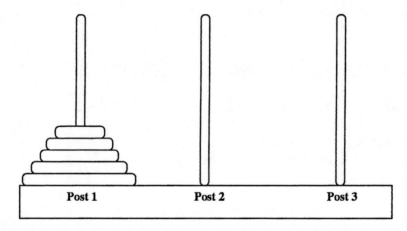

Figure 16.1: The Towers of Hanoi puzzle.

As the legend associated with the puzzle goes, when the world was created, the priests at the Temple of Brahma were given the task of moving 64 disks from one post to another. When they completed their task, the world would end.

Now how would we go about writing a computer program to solve this puzzle? If we view the problem from the end first, we can make the following observation: the last sequence of moves MUST involve moving the largest disk from post 1 to the target post, say post 3, and then moving the other disks back on top of it. Conceptually, we need to move all n-1 disks off the largest disk and onto the intermediate post, then we move the largest disk from its post onto the target post. Then we move all n-1 disks from the intermediate post onto the target post. And we are done! Moving n-1 disks per move is not legal, but we've stated the problem in such a manner that we can solve it if we can solve two smaller versions of it. Once the largest disk is on the target post, we don't need to deal with it any further. Now the n-1'th disk becomes the largest disk and the sub-objective becomes to move it to the target pole. We can therefore apply the same technique. We now have a recursive definition of the problem.

Below is a recursive C function of the algorithm described above.

```
/* Move disk 'disk_number' from the starting_post to the
   target_post using the intermediate_post for temporary storage.
   Disk number 1 is the smallest disk.                              */
MoveDisk(disk_number, starting_post, target_post, intermediate_post)
{
    if (disk_number > 1) {

        /* Move all n-1 disks off the current largest disk and
           put them on the intermediate post */
        MoveDisk(disk_number-1, starting_post, intermediate_post, target_post);

        /* Move the largest disk.  */
        printf("Move disk number %d from post %d to post %d.\n",
                disk_number, starting_post, target_post);

        /* Move all n-1 disks onto the target post */
        MoveDisk(disk_number-1, intermediate_post, target_post, starting_post);
    }
    else
        printf("Move disk number 1 from post %d to post %d.\n",
                disk_number, starting_post, target_post);
}
```

Like with recurrence equations in mathematics, all recursive functions require a terminal case which ends the recursion. Here, we've stated that moving disk 1 (smallest disk) requires no other disks be moved since it is always on top and can be moved directly from the starting post to the target post.

Let's see what happens when we play a game with three disks. We start off by saying that we want to move disk 3 (the largest disk) from post 1 to post 3, using post 2 as the intermediate storage post. By stating this, we are saying that we want to solve a 3-disk Towers of Hanoi puzzle. See Figure 16.2.

```
MoveDisk(3, 1, 3, 2)
```

This call invokes another call to MoveDisk to move disks 1 and 2 off of disk 3 and onto post 2 using post 3 as intermediate storage.

```
MoveDisk(2, 1, 2, 3)
```

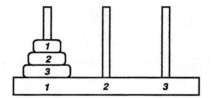

Figure 16.2: The Towers of Hanoi puzzle.

To move disk 2 from post 1 to post 2, we must first move disk 1 off disk 2 and onto post 3 (the intermediate storage). So this triggers another call to `MoveDisk`.

`MoveDisk(1, 1, 3, 2)`

Since disk 1 can always be moved, the (second) `printf` statement is executed and we actually see a disk moved. See Figure 16.3.

Move disk number 1 from post 1 to post 3.

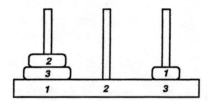

Figure 16.3: The Towers of Hanoi puzzle.

This invocation of the function returns back to its caller. The caller function was the call `MoveDisk(2, 1, 2, 3)`. Recall that we were waiting for all disks on top of disk 2 to be moved to post 3. That having been completed, we can now move disk 2 from post 1 to post 2. The `printf` is the next statement to execute, signaling another disk to be moved. See Figure 16.4.

Move disk number 2 from post 1 to post 2.

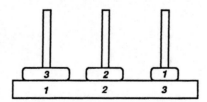

Figure 16.4: The Towers of Hanoi puzzle.

Next, a call is made to move all disks which were on disk 2, back onto disk 2.

```
MoveDisk(1, 2, 3, 1)
```

Again, since disk 1 has no disks on top of it, we see the move printed. See Figure 16.5.

```
Move disk number 1 from post 3 to post 2.
```

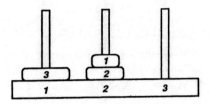

Figure 16.5: The Towers of Hanoi puzzle.

Now, control passes back to the call `MoveDisk(2, 1, 2, 3)` which, having completed its task of moving disk 2 (and all disks on top of it) from post 1 to post 2, returns to its caller. Its caller is `MoveDisk(3, 1, 3, 2)`. Now, all disks have been moved off of disk 3 and onto post 2. Disk 3 can be moved from post 1 onto post 3. The `printf` is the next statement executed. See Figure 16.6.

```
Move disk number 3 from post 1 to post 3.
```

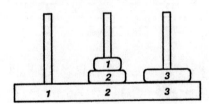

Figure 16.6: The Towers of Hanoi puzzle.

The next sub-task remaining is to move disk 2 (and all disks on top of it) from post 2 onto post 3. We can use post 1 for intermediate storage.

```
MoveDisk(2, 2, 3, 1)
```

In order to do so, we must first move disk 1 from post 2 onto post 1.

```
MoveDisk(1, 2, 1, 3)
```

The move requires no submoves. See Figure 16.7.

`Move disk number 1 from post 2 to post 1.`

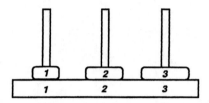

Figure 16.7: The Towers of Hanoi puzzle.

Return passes back to the caller MoveDisk(2, 2, 3, 1) and disk 2 is moved onto post 3. See Figure 16.8.

`Move disk number 2 from post 2 to post 3.`

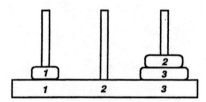

Figure 16.8: The Towers of Hanoi puzzle.

The only thing remaining is to move all disks which were on disk 2 back on top.

`MoveDisk(1, 1, 3, 2)`

The move is done immediately (See Figure 16.9)

`Move disk number 1 from post 1 to post 2.`

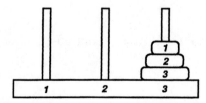

Figure 16.9: The Towers of Hanoi puzzle.

and the puzzle is completed!

16.5 A detailed example in C.

The following recurrence equations generates a well known sequence of numbers.

$$
\begin{aligned}
f(n) &= f(n-1) + f(n-2) \\
f(0) &= 1 \\
f(1) &= 1
\end{aligned}
$$

This function generates a mathematically significant sequence of numbers known as the Fibonacci Numbers. If we wanted to write a C function to generate the nth Fibonacci number, we could simply take the relationship and directly code it into a recursive function, as shown in Figure 16.10. The function `fibonacci` performs the calculation.

```
#include <stdio.h>

int fibonacci(int n);

main()
{
  int t;

  /* Make a simple call to the recursive routine */
  t = fibonacci(3);
  printf("The third Fibonacci number is %d\n", t);
}

int fibonacci(int n)
{
  /* A recursive routine to calculate the nth
     Fibonacci number */
  if (n == 0 || n == 1)
    return 1;
  else
    return(fibonacci(n-1) + fibonacci(n-2));
}
```

Figure 16.10: `fibonacci` is recursive C function to calculate the nth Fibonacci number.

We are stating that calculating the nth Fibonacci number can be done by calculating the n-1th number and the n-2th number and adding them together. The *terminal* condition must be supplied in order for this relationship to have a definite termination point. Notice, in all the previous example, a terminal condition caused the recursion to eventually terminate.

Whenever the function `fibonacci` is called, whether from itself or another function, a new copy of its activation record is pushed on the run-time stack. Each invocation of the function gets a new, private copy of all variables declared within the function. Each copy is completely different than any other copy. They are essentially different variables that share a common name and are defined within the same function. The essence of making recursion work is the run-time stack. If the variables of this function were statically allocated in memory, then each recursive call to `fibonacci` would overwrite the values of the previous call.

Let's see what happens when we call the function `fibonacci` with the parameter 3, `fibonacci(3)`. We start off with the activation record for `fibonacci(3)` on top of the run-time stack. Figure 16.11 shows the progression of the stack as the original function call is evaluated.

Since the parameter n which equals 3 does not meet the terminal condition (i.e., it does not equal 1 or 0), the function will calculate `fibonacci(3-1)` first, as the expression `fibonacci(n-1) + fibonacci(n-2)` is evaluated left to right. A call is made to `fibonacci(2)` and an activation record for `fibonacci(2)` is pushed onto the run-time stack (Figure 16.11, step 2).

For `fibonacci(2)`, the parameter n equals 2 and doesn't meet the terminal condition, therefore a call is made to `fibonacci(1)`. (See Figure 16.11, step 3). This call is made in the course of evaluating `fibonacci(2-1) + fibonacci(2-2)`.

The call `fibonacci(1)` results in no more recursive calls because the parameter n meets the terminal condition. The value 1 is returned back to `fibonacci(2)`, which now can complete the evaluation of `fibonacci(1) + fibonacci(0)` by calling `fibonacci(0)` (See Figure 16.11, step 4). This call (`fibonacci(0)`) immediately returns a 1.

Now, the call `fibonacci(2)` can complete and return its subcalculation (its result is 2) back to its caller, `fibonacci(3)`. Having completed the left hand component of the expression `fibonacci(2) + fibonacci(1)`, `fibonacci(3)` calls `fibonacci(1)` (Figure 16.11, step 5), which immediately returns the value 1. Now `fibonacci(3)` is complete—its result is 3 (Figure 16.11, step 6).

The trace of all function calls made is listed below:

```
fibonacci(3)
fibonacci(2)
fibonacci(1)
fibonacci(0)
fibonacci(1)
```

We could state the recursion of `fibonacci(3)` algebraically, as follows:

```
fibonacci(3) = fibonacci(2) + fibonacci(1)
```

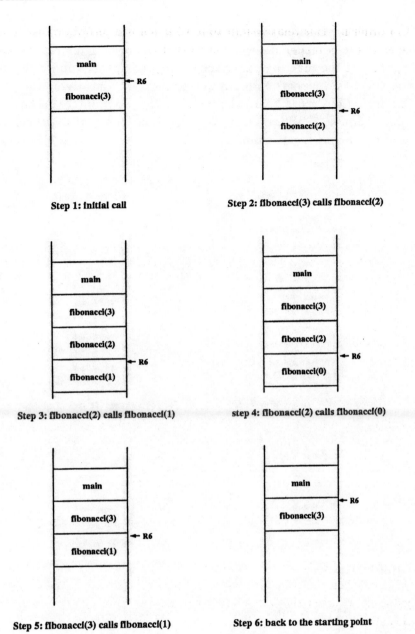

Figure 16.11: Snapshots of the run-time stack for the function call `fibonacci(3)`.

```
= (fibonacci(1) + fibonacci(0)) + fibonacci(1)
= 1 + 1 + 1 = 3
```

Try tracing the execution of `fibonacci(4)`. You'll notice that the trace of `fibonacci(3)` is a component of the trace of `fibonacci(4)`. No surprise since `fibonacci(4)` = `fibonacci(3)` + `fibonacci(2)`.

The LC-2 C compiler generates the following code for this program, listed in Figure 16.12. Now, notice that the compiler determined that it required a temporary variable in order to properly translate the function `fibonacci`. Most compilers will do this when compiling an expression which is composed of many subexpressions. Such temporary values are given storage in the activation record below the space for the programmer declared local variables. This temporary variable is allocated in the activation record of fibonacci at offset 4. The total length of the record is 5 locations.

```
fibonacci:
        STR   R7, R6, #1    ;   store away the return address
        LDR   R0, R6, #3    ;   load the parameter n

        BRZ   FIB_END       ;   n==0
        ADD   R0, R0, #-1   ;
        BRZ   FIB_END       ;   n==1

        LDR   R0, R6, #3    ;   load the parameter n
        ADD   R0, R0, #-1   ;   calculate n-1
        STR   R0, R6, #8    ;   store input as first parameter
        STR   R6, R6, #7    ;   store the current top of stack as the dynamic link
        ADD   R6, R6, #5    ;   move the top of stack to the new activation record
        JSR   fibonacci     ;   the call back to itself: fibonacci(n-1)

        LDR   R0, R6, #5    ;   read the return value
        STR   R0, R6, #4    ;   store it into the compiler generated temporary value

        LDR   R0, R6, #3    ;   load the parameter n
        ADD   R0, R0, #-2   ;   calculate n-2
        STR   R0, R6, #8    ;   store input as first parameter
        STR   R6, R6, #7    ;   store the current top of stack as the dynamic link
        ADD   R6, R6, #5    ;   move the top of stack to the new activation record
        JSR   fibonacci     ;   the call back to itself: fibonacci(n-2)

        LDR   R0, R6, #5    ;   read the return value
        LDR   R1, R6, #4    ;   read the temporary value: fibonacci(n-1)
        ADD   R0, R0, R1    ;   fibonacci(n-1) + fibonacci(n-2)

        STR   R0, R6, #0    ;   write the return value
        LDR   R6, R6, #2    ;   load the dynamic link
        RET

FIB_END:
        AND   R0, R0, #0    ;   clear R0
        ADD   R0, R0, #1    ;   R0 = 1

        STR   R0, R6, #0    ;   write the return value
        LDR   R6, R6, #2    ;   load the dynamic link
        RET
```

Figure 16.12: fibonacci in LC-2.

16.6   Another detailed example in C.

Figure 16.13 lists a recursive C function which takes a positive integer value and converts each digit of the value into ASCII and displays the resulting characters on the screen.

```c
#include <stdio.h>

void int_to_ascii(int i);

main()
{
  /* Make a simple call to the
     recursive routine */
  int_to_ascii(12345);
}


void int_to_ascii(int i)
{
  int pre, curr;

   if (i < 10)
     /* The terminal case - only one digit to convert */
     putchar(i+'0');
   else {

     /* First convert the number, with the least
        significant digit dropped */
     pre = i/10;
     int_to_ascii(pre);

     /* Convert the least significant digit */
     curr = i%10;
     putchar(curr + '0');
   }
}
```

Figure 16.13: `int_to_ascii` is a recursive function which converts integers to ASCII.

The basic idea behind this recursive algorithm is to take the input number, remove the least significant digit by shifting the parameter to the right one digit by dividing by 10, and make a recursive call with this new value. If the input value is a single digit, it is converted to ASCII and displayed to the screen. The output is performed by the C standard output function `putchar` which works like the LC-2 OUT TRAP routine. It displays the ASCII character passed to it on the screen. Once control is passed back after a recursive call, the digit that was removed is converted to ASCII and displayed. To clarify, we present a trace of calls to `int_to_ascii` for the original call of `int_to_ascii(12345)`:

Figure 16.14 contains two pictures of the run-time stack during the execution of this function call.

```
int_to_ascii(12345)
int_to_ascii(1234)
int_to_ascii(123)
int_to_ascii(12)
int_to_ascii(1)
putchar('1')              See Figure (A).
putchar('2')
putchar('3')              See Figure (B).
putchar('4')
putchar('5')
```

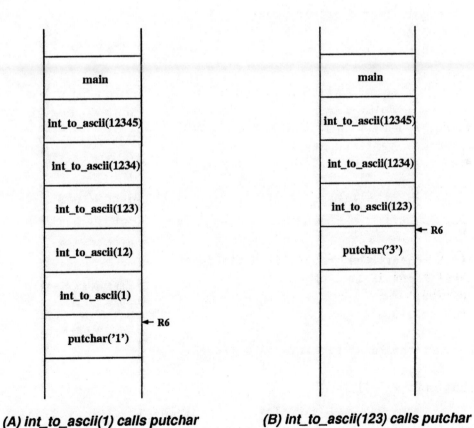

(A) int_to_ascii(1) calls putchar   **(B) int_to_ascii(123) calls putchar**

Figure 16.14: Two snapshots of the run-time stack during the function call `int_to_ascii(12345)`.

What would happen if we reversed the `putchar` call and the recursive call in the code as follows? Now, the least significant digit will be displayed (via `putchar`) before the recursive call to display the other digits. The number will be displayed in reverse order.

```
void int_to_ascii(int i)
{
  int pre, curr;

    if (i < 10)
      /* The terminal case - only one digit to convert */
      putchar(i + '0');
    else {

      /* Now, first convert the least significant digit */
      curr = i%10;
      putchar(curr + '0');

      /* Then convert the number, with the least
         significant digit dropped */
      pre = i/10;
      int_to_ascii(pre);
    }
}
```

What would happen if we omitted the terminal case check? Will anything be displayed? Will the function ever terminate?

```
void int_to_ascii(int i)
{
  int pre, curr;

  /* First convert the number, with the least
     significant digit dropped */
  pre = i/10;
  int_to_ascii(pre);

  /* Convert the least significant digit */
  curr = i%10;
  putchar(curr + '0');
}
```

16.7 Exercises.

16.1 Given the following C program:

```
#include <stdio.h>

int power(int a, int b);

int main(void) {
    int x, y, z;

    scanf("%d%d", &x, &y);

    if (x > 0 && y > 0)
    z = power(x,y);
    else
    z = 0;

    printf("The result is %d\n.", z);
}

int power(int a, int b) {
    if (a < b)
        return 0;
    return 1 + power(a/b, b);
}
```

1. State the complete output if the input is:
   (a) 4 9
   (b) 27 5
   (c) -1 3
2. State in general what the program computes in terms of x and y.

3. Below is a snapshot of the stack after a call to the function **power**. Two activation records are shown, both resulting from calls to **power**, with some of the entries filled in. Assume the snapshot was taken just before execution of one of the **return** statements in **power**. Fill in the entries marked 'X'. Use arrows to show addresses.

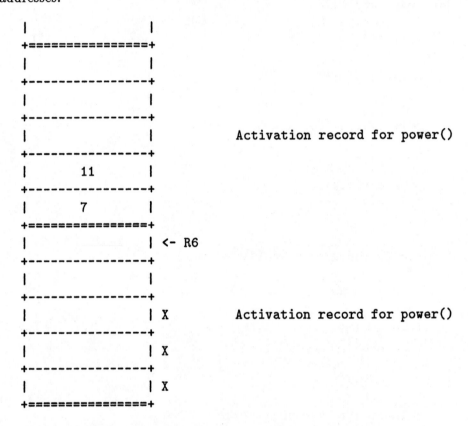

16.2 For this question, refer to the examples which appear in the chapter.

1. How many calls to **running_sum** (See Section 16.1 in the chapter) are made for the call **running_sum(10)**?

2. How about for the call **running_sum(n)**? Give your answer in terms of n.

3. How many calls to **fibonacci** (See Figure 16.10) for the initial call **fibonacci(10)**?

4. How many calls to **MoveDisk** are made in the Towers of Hanoi problem if the initial call is **MoveDisk(4, 1, 3, 2)**. This call plays out a 4 disk game.

5. How many calls are made for an *n* disk game?

16.3 Compile the following C function into an LC-2 assembly code fragment. You may assume that the address of the stack is in R6 and the return address is in R7 when your code begins.

```
int count(int arg) {

    if (arg < 1)
        return 0;

    /*
     * Hint: x % y is the remainder of x divided by y. In this case, the
     * condition will be true if and only if arg is odd. How can you test
     * whether arg is odd or even in LC-2 without doing any division?
     */

    else if (arg % 2)
        return(1 + count(arg - 2));
    else
        return(1 + count(arg - 1));
}
```

16.4 The following C program is compiled and executed on the LC-2. When the program is executed, the runtime stack starts at memory location xC000 and grows towards xFFFF (the stack can occupy up to 32 pages of memory).

```
sevenUp(int x) {
    if (x == 1)
        return 7;
    else
        return (7 + sevenUp(x - 1));
}

main() {
    int a;

    printf("Input a number \n");
    scanf("%d", &a);

    a = sevenUp(a);

    printf("%d is 7 times the number\n", a);
}
```

1. What is the largest input value for which this program will run correctly? Explain your answer.

2. If the runtime stack starts at x4000, what is the largest input value for which this program will run correctly? (In this case, the stack can occupy up to 96 pages of memory.) Explain your answer.

16.5 Write a program without recursive functions equivalent to the following C program.

```
main() {
   printf("%d", m());
}

void m() {
   int num, x;

   printf("Type a number: ");
   scanf("%d", &num);
   if (num <= 0)
      return 0;
   else {
      x = m();
      if (num > x)
         return num;
      else
         return x;
   }
}
```

16.6 Given the following C function,

```
int sigma( int k ) {
   int l;

   l = k -1;

   if (k==0)
      return 0;
   else
      return (k + sigma(l));
}
```

1. Convert the following recursive function into a non-recursive function. Assume sigma will always be called with a non-negative argument.

2. Exactly 1KB of contiguous memory is available exclusively for the run-time stack of the recursive function, and addresses and integers are 16 bits wide. How many recursive function calls can be made before the program runs out of memory? Assume no storage is needed for temporary values.

16.7 Is the return address for a recursive function always the same at each function call? Why or why not?

16.8 What is the returned value of the call `ea(110, 24)` where ea is the following C function?

```c
int ea(int x, int y) {
    int a;

    if (y == 0)
        return x;
    else {
        a = x % y;
        return (ea(y, a));
    }
}
```

16.9 Consider the following recursive function:

```c
int func (int arg) {

    if (arg % 2 != 0)
        return func(arg - 1);
    if (arg <= 0)
        return 1;

    return func(arg/2) + 1;
}
```

1. Is there a value of `arg` that causes an infinite recursion? If so, what is it?

2. Suppose that the function `func` above is part of a program whose main function is given below. How many functions calls are made to `func` when the program is executed?

```c
main() {
    printf("The value is %d\n", func(10));
}
```

3. What value is output by the program?

16.10 What is the output of the following C program?

```c
#include <stdio.h>

void foo(int in);
int even(int n);

int main() {
    foo(10);
}

void foo(int in) {
    if (in == 0)
        return;
    if (even(in))
        printf("%i\n", in);
    foo(in - 1);
    if (!even(in))
        printf("%i\n", in);
    return;
}

int even(int n) {
    return (n % 2) == 0 ? 1 : 0;  /* even, return 1; odd, return 0 */
}
```

Chapter 17

Pointers and Arrays.

17.1 Introduction.

In this chapter we introduce two simple but powerful programming constructs: pointers and arrays. Pointers and arrays are not completely new topics however. We've dealt with the basic concepts behind them when writing assembly code for the LC-2. Now, we examine them in the context of C.

A pointer is simply the address of a variable in memory. With pointers, we can *indirectly* access variables. The ability to indirectly access memory enables some useful capabilities. With pointers, we can create functions which modify the arguments passed by the caller. With pointers, we can create sophisticated ways of organizing data into structures that grow and shrink (like the run-time stack!) during a program's execution. We'll see examples of both uses for pointers over the next few chapters.

Arrays are simply lists of data arranged sequentially in memory. For example, the an itemized list of all the phone calls you've made over the past month might be arranged in memory as an array in the phone company's computer system. To access a particular item in an array, we need to specify which element we want. As we'll see, a[4] will access the 5th element in the array named a. Arrays enable many things, allowing us to conveniently process groups of data such as vectors, matrices, lists, and characters strings.

17.2 Pointers.

In the following C program, the function swap is designed to switch the value of its two arguments. The function swap is called from main with the arguments a which equals 3 and b which equals 4. Once, swap returns control to main we want a and b to have their values swapped. However, compile and execute the code and you will notice that the arguments passed to swap remain unchanged.

```
#include <stdio.h>

void swap(int a, int b);

main()
{
  int a = 3;
  int b = 4;

  printf("Before swap is called: a = %d and b = %d\n", a, b);
  swap(a, b);
  printf("After swap is called: a = %d and b = %d\n", a, b);
}

void swap(int a, int b)
{
  int x;

  x = a;
  a = b;
  b = x;
}
```

Figure 17.1: The function swap attempts to swap the values of its two parameters.

Let's examining the run-time stack during the execution of swap to try to figure out why. Figure 17.2 shows that the function swap modifies the local copies of the parameters a and b. However, when swap completes and control returns to main, the modified values are lost when the activation record for swap is popped off the stack.

The problem here is that C always passes the arguments from the calling function to the called function *by value*. The values of the arguments are placed in the activation record for the function which is called. In order for swap to modify the actual arguments the calling function passes to it, it must have access to the calling function's activation record. The function swap needs the *addresses* of a and b in main in order to change their values. As we shall see next few sections, pointers and their associated operators enable this to happen.

17.2.1   Declaring pointer variables.

Pointer variables contain memory addresses of variables. The pointer is said to *point* to the variable whose address it contains. Associated with a pointer variable is the *type* of value it points to. So for instance, an integer pointer variable points to an integer value. To declare a pointer variable in C, we use the following syntax:

run-time stack

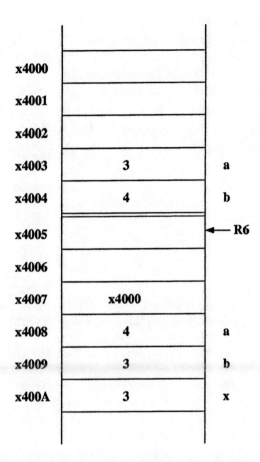

Figure 17.2: A snapshot of the run-time stack when the function `swap` is about to return control.

```
int *ptr;
```

Here we have declared a variable named `ptr` that points to an integer. The asterisk `*` indicates that the identifier that follows is a pointer variable. C programmers will often say that `ptr` is of type "int star". Pointer variables are initialized in C similar to all other variables. If this pointer variable is locally declared, it will not be automatically initialized. Similarly we can declare:

```
char *cp;
double *dp;
unsigned *ip;
```

The variable `cp` points to a character and `dp` points to a double-precision floating point number and `ip` to a unsigned integer. This syntax may seem a bit odd at first, but once we have gone through the pointer operators, the rationale behind the syntax will be clear.

17.2.2   Operators for pointers.

Now that we can declare pointer variables, let's take a look at how they can be used. C has two operators for pointer-related manipulations, the address operator & and indirection operator *. The address operator, whose symbol is an ampersand &, generates the memory address of its operand. Its operand must be something which is stored in memory (more precisely stated, a memory object). A variable, for instance, is a proper operand for the & operator; the number 3, for example, is not. In the following code sequence, the pointer variable ptr will point to the integer variable i. The expression on the right-hand side of the second assignment statement generates the memory address of i.

```
int i;
int *ptr;

i = 4;
ptr = &i;
```

Let's examine the LC-2 code for this sequence. Both declared variables are locals and allocated on the stack. The variable i is allocated offset 3 and ptr offset 4.

```
AND   R0, R0, #0   ;   clear R0
ADD   R0, R0, #4   ;   R0 = 4
STR   R0, R6, #3   ;   i = 4;

AND   R0, R0, #0   ;   clear R0
ADD   R0, R6, #3   ;   generate the memory address of i
STR   R0, R6, #4   ;   ptr = &i;
```

Figure 17.3 shows the top of the run-time stack after the statement ptr = &i; has executed. The current top-of-stack is at memory location x4011. Notice that i contains the integer value 4 and ptr contains the memory address of i.

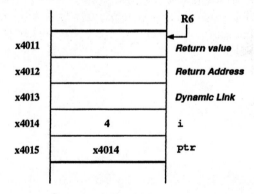

Figure 17.3: A piece of the run-time stack after the statement ptr = &i has executed.

The second pointer operator is called the indirection, or dereferencing, operator and its symbol is the asterisk * (Pronounced "star" in this context). It allows us to indirectly manipulate the value that a pointer is pointing to. In literal terms, the indirection operator * means the "value pointed to by" the variable (or expression) that follows. The expression *x refers to the value pointed to by x. In the previous example, *ptr refers to the value stored in i. Here, *ptr and i can be used interchangeably. Adding to the previous C code example:

```
int i;
int *ptr;

i = 4;
ptr = &i;
*ptr = *ptr + 1;
```

Essentially, *ptr = *ptr + 1; is another way of saying i = i + 1;. Just as with other types of variables we've seen, the *ptr means different things depending on which side of the assignment operator it appears. On the right hand side of the assignment operator, it refers to the value which appears at that location (in this case the value 4). On the left hand side, it indicates the location that gets modified (in this case, the address of i). Notice that this interpretation is the same as with, say, an integer variable. Let's examine the LC-2 code for the final statement.

```
LDR  R0, R6, #4   ;   R0 contains the value of ptr
LDR  R1, R0, #0   ;   load *ptr into R1
ADD  R1, R1, #1   ;   add 1 to *ptr
STR  R1, R0, #0   ;   *ptr = *ptr + 1;
```

Notice that this code is different from what would get generated if the final C statement had been i = i + 1;. With the pointer dereference, the compiler generates two LDR instructions for the indirection operator on the right hand side, one to load the memory address contained in ptr and another to get the value stored at that address. With the dereference on the left hand side, the compiler has generated a STR R1, R0, #0. Had the statement been i = *ptr + 1;, the compiler would have generated a STR R1, R6, #3.

One of the hallmarks of C is the flexibility the programmer is given when dealing with pointer variables. Pointers values are treated as integer values and can be used in general C expressions. Adding to the previous C code example:

```
int i;
int *ptr;

i = 4;
ptr = &i;
*ptr = *ptr + 1;
ptr = ptr + 1;
```

The new statement (ptr = ptr + 1 modifies the memory address stored in ptr. Now ptr is incremented to point to the next memory location. The amount that ptr is incremented depends on the type of object it points to. If the variable occupies two locations of memory (say, for example a double-precision floating point number) then ptr is actually incremented by 2 by the LC-2 compiler. Here, since ptr points to an integer, the ptr will point to the next memory location after the last statement completes. Once incremented, ptr will point to itself—see the activation record in Figure 17.3. Even though ptr is no longer pointing to an integer, the compiler will not complain and will generate code treating the value at *ptr is an integer assuming the programmer knows what they are doing.

What would happen if the following line were added to the end of the previous code example?

```
*ptr = *ptr + 1;
```

17.2.3   Some examples using pointer variables.

Having described the operations of the two C pointer operators, we can now repair the swap function that didn't quite accomplish the the swap of its arguments. We'll use the two new operators to assist.

Figure 17.4 lists the same program with a revised version of swap called new_swap.

The first modification we've made is that the parameters of new_swap are no longer integers but are now pointers to integers (int *). The two parameters are now the memory addresses of the two items which we want swapped. Within the function new_swap, we've added the indirection operator * to signify that the values pointed to by these parameters are to be modified. These values themselves are in the activation record for main. Finally, when we call new_swap from main, we need to supply the proper memory addresses for the two values to be swapped. The & operator does the trick. Figure 17.5 shows the run-time stack when the function new_swap is called and when the function new_swap completes.

We've now seen examples of the two most commonly used methods of passing arguments to a function. By design, C passes most type of arguments *by value*. In a function call, C evaluates each argument and copies its **value** into the called function's activation record. However, we've just seen an example (new_swap) where a *call by reference* is emulated using the address and indirection operators. When an argument is passed by reference, it's **address** is passed to the called function. The called function then uses the indirection operator to get access (and modify) the original value in the caller's activation record.

```c
#include <stdio.h>

void new_swap(int *a, int *b);

main()
{
    int a = 3;
    int b = 4;

    printf("Before new_swap is called: a = %d and b = %d\n", a, b);
    new_swap(&a, &b);
    printf("After new_swap is called: a = %d and b = %d\n", a, b);
}

void new_swap(int *a, int *b)
{
    int x;

    x = *a;
    *a = *b;
    *b = x;
}
```

Figure 17.4: The function **new_swap** swaps the values of its two parameters.

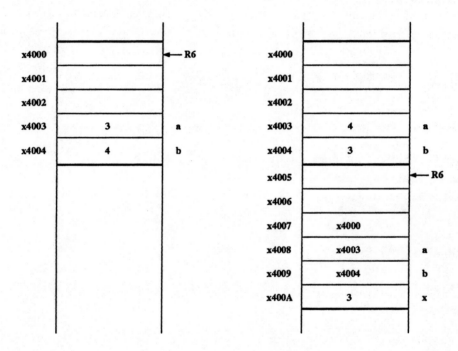

Figure 17.5: Snapshots of the run-time stack when the function new_swap is called and when it completes.

It's now time to revisit some notation that we introduced in Chapter 11. Now that we know how to pass by reference in C, recall how we call the C standard I/O library function `scanf`:

```
scanf("%c", &input);
```

The function `scanf` actually needs to update the variable `input` with the character read from the keyboard. To enable this, `scanf` needs the address of `input`. Therefore we pass its address by preceding it with the address operator &.

The program in Figure 17.6 contains a function `idiv` which takes four arguments, two of which are passed by value, two of which are passed by reference. The function `idiv` divides the first parameter `dividend` by the second parameter `divisor`. The integer portion of the quotient is written into the third parameter `quotient` (which is treated as an address for an integer value), and the integer remainder is written into the fourth parameter `remainder` (which is also treated as an address to an integer). Note that the program also returns a value. The function returns a 1 if the `divisor` is zero, indicating that an error has occurred. It returns zero otherwise.

```c
#include <stdio.h>

main()
{
  int dividend, divisor;
  int quotient, remainder;

  printf("Input dividend\n");
  scanf("%d", &dividend);
  printf("Input divisor\n");
  scanf("%d", &divisor);

  quotient = idiv(dividend, divisor, &remainder);

  printf("Answer: %d remainder %d\n", quotient, remainder);
}

int idiv(int a, int b, int *rem)
{
  *rem = a % b;
  return a / b;
}
```

Figure 17.6: The function `idiv` returns the integer portion of the quotient. The parameter `rem` contains the remainder.

Functions can also return pointer values. The function must be declared as returning a pointer type. The code from Figure 17.4 contains a modified version of the function new_swap: it is modified not only swap the values of the two parameters, but to return the address of the parameter with the larger value.

```
#include <stdio.h>

int *mod_swap(int *a, int *b);

main()
{
    int a = 3;
    int b = 4;
    int *max;

    printf("Before mod_swap is called: a = %d and b = %d\n", a, b);
    max = mod_swap(&a, &b);
    printf("After mod_swap is called: a = %d and b = %d\n", a, b);
    printf("The larger value is %d\n", *max);
}

int *mod_swap(int *a, int *b)
{
  int x;

  x = *a;
  *a = *b;
  *b = x;

  if (*a >= *b)
   return a;
  else
   return b;
}
```

Figure 17.7: The function mod_swap returns a pointer.

17.2.4   The syntax demystified.

Before we complete our introduction to pointers, let's attempt to make sense of the pointer declaration and operator syntax. We've seen that to declare a pointer variable, we use the following declaration:

```
typ *ptr;
```

Where `typ` can be any of the predefined (or programmer defined) types such as `int`, `char`, `double`, etc., and `ptr` is simply any legal variable identifier. Here we are declaring a variable, which when the `*` (dereference) operator is applied to it, generates a variable of type `typ`. That is, `*ptr` is of type `typ`. Similarly when we declare a function to return a pointer type, as `int *mod_swap` in the previous example, we are specifying the type of the value pointed to by the returned memory address.

The operator `*` can be applied to any expression (unlike `&`, which must only be applied to memory object such as variables). We can create something which looks strange, but which can be meaningful in certain contexts. The example below involves evaluating a pointer to a pointer.

```
q = **j;
```

While statements like this one are uncommon, they do occur and you should be aware of and comfortable with their syntax.

Also, as with all other operators, the address and indirection operator are evaluated according to their precedence. The precedence and associativity of these operators is listed in Table 12.6. Notice they both have high precedence with relation to other operators. Let's examine a piece of code that accomplishes a very useful task but has a particularly cryptic notation.

```
char *stringA;
char *stringB;

:
:
while (*stringA++ == *stringB++);
:
:
```

Both pointer variables `stringA` and `stringB` point to character strings. Recall from our LC-2 days that strings are characters stored in sequential memory locations. Strings can represent a word or a phrase, for example. The postfix increment operators `++` are the first to be evaluated, then the dereference operators, and finally the equality test. The values of `stringA` and `stringB` *prior* to the increment are the operands to the dereference operator. Prove to yourself that the `while` loop will find the first character at which the strings differ. We'll revisit this example again at the end of the chapter, after having covered arrays.

17.3   Arrays.

Arrays are similar to pointers in the sense that they give the programmer the ability to specify a variable location indirectly. With pointers, we could specify a variable by referencing it via another variable called a pointer variable. With arrays, we can specify a particular value within a contiguous sequence of values by specifying an offset from the beginning of the sequence. We've seen examples of arrays already when programming the LC-2 (although we never referred to them as arrays). Most programming languages directly support arrays. In this section, we will describe how arrays work in C.

Arrays are most useful when the data the program operates upon is naturally expressed as a contiguous sequence of values. For instance, if we wanted to write a program to take a sequence of 100 numbers entered from the keyboard and *sort* them into ascending order, then an array would be the natural choice for storing these numbers in memory. The program would be almost impossible to write using the simple variables we've been using so far.

17.3.1   Declaring arrays and accessing elements.

First, let's examine how to declare an array. Like all other variables, arrays must have a type associated with them. The type indicates the properties of the values stored in the array. Below is an example of a declaration for an array of 10 integers.

```
int grid[10];
```

The keyword `int` indicates that we are declaring something of type integer. The name of the array is `grid`. We can choose any legal identifier for the name of an array—the rules are the same as those for any variable. The brackets indicate we are declaring an array and the 10 indicates that the array is to contain ten integers, all of which will be sequentially located in memory. Figure 17.8 shows a pictorial representation of memory allocated to `grid`. If the array `grid` were a local variable, then its memory space would be allocated in its function's activation record.

Having declared the array `grid`, let's examine how to access different values in this array. Notice in Figure 17.8 that the array's first element is actually number 0 which means the last element is numbered 9. To access a particular element, we use an *index* within brackets. For example:

```
x = grid[3] + 1;

grid[6] = 5;
```

The first statement reads the value stored in the fourth (remember, we start numbering with 0) element of `grid`, adds 1 to it and stores the result into variable `x`. The second

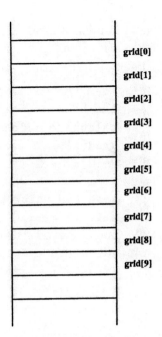

Figure 17.8: The array **grid** allocated in memory.

statement sets the seventh element of grid equal to 5. Let's look at the LC-2 code for this example. Let's say that **x** is a local variable allocated slot 3 in the activation record and **grid** is a local variable occupying slots 4 through 13.

```
ADD   R0, R6, #4    ;    the base of the array (address of grid[0]) is in R0
ADD   R1, R0, #3    ;    calculate address of grid[3]
LDR   R2, R1, #0    ;    grid[3]
ADD   R2, R2, #1    ;    grid[3] + 1
STR   R2, R6, #3    ;    x = grid[3] + 1;

AND   R2, R2, #0    ;
ADD   R2, R2, #5    ;    R2 = 5
ADD   R0, R6, #4    ;    the base of the array (address of grid[0]) is in R0
ADD   R1, R0, #6    ;    calculate address of grid[6]
STR   R2, R1, #0    ;    grid[6] = 5;
```

Notice that the first and eighth instructions calculate the base address of the array and put it into R0. This address corresponds to the location of the first element (element 0) or expressed another way, &grid[0]. We can access any element in the array by adding the index of the desired element to the base address.

The power of arrays comes from the fact that an array's index can be any legal C expression of integer type. The example below demonstrates:

```
grid[x+1] = grid[x] + 2;
```

Let's look at the LC-2 code for the statement above. Assume x is at offset 3 in the current activation record and grid starts at entry 4 and ends on entry 13.

```
LDR  R0, R6, #3    ;    load the value of x
ADD  R1, R6, #4    ;    the base of the array (address of grid[0]) is in R1
ADD  R1, R0, R1    ;    calculate address of grid[x]
LDR  R2, R1, #0    ;    grid[x]
ADD  R2, R2, #2    ;    grid[x] + 2

LDR  R0, R6, #3    ;    load the value of x
ADD  R0, R0, #1    ;    x+1
ADD  R1, R6, #4    ;    the base of the array (address of grid[0]) is in R1
ADD  R1, R0, R1    ;    calculate address of grid[x+1]
STR  R2, R1, #0    ;    grid[x+1] = grid[x] + 2;
```

17.3.2 Examples using arrays.

First, we'll start off with a very simple C program that uses integer arrays. This program adds two *vectors* by adding the corresponding elements from each vector together to form the sum. Said another way: sum[i] = a[i] + b[i], or element 3 of the sum is produced by taken element 3 of the first vector and adding it to element 3 of the second. So if we add a 10 element vector with another 10 element vector, the result will be another 10 element vector. The natural representation for a vector in a C program is an integer array. Figure 17.9 contains the C code to read in two 10 element vectors, add them together, and print out their sum.

A side note: notice the use of the preprocessor macro VECTOR_SIZE to represent a constant value of the size of the input set. This is a common use for preprocessor macros, which are usually found at the beginning of the source file (or within C header files). Now, if we want to increase the size of the vectors, we simply change the definition of the macro (one change) and recompile the program. If we didn't use the macro, the code would need to be changed in multiple spots. The changes could be potentially difficult to track down and missing one update would likely result in a program that didn't work correctly. Using preprocessor macros for such constant values is good, prudent programming practice.

```
#include <stdio.h>

#define VECTOR_SIZE 10

main()
{
  int i;
  int j;
  int VectorA[VECTOR_SIZE];
  int VectorB[VECTOR_SIZE];
  int VectorSum[VECTOR_SIZE];

  /* Input Vector A */
  printf("Enter %d numbers for Vector A.\n", VECTOR_SIZE);
  for (i = 0; i < VECTOR_SIZE; i++) {
    printf("Input VectorA[%d] : ", i);
    scanf("%d", &VectorA[i]);
  }
  printf("\n");

  /* Input Vector B */
  printf("Enter %d numbers for Vector B.\n", VECTOR_SIZE);
  for (i = 0; i < VECTOR_SIZE; i++) {
    printf("VectorB[%d] : ", i);
    scanf("%d", &VectorB[i]);
  }
  printf("\n");

  /* Calculate VectorSum */
  for (i = 0; i < VECTOR_SIZE; i++) {
    VectorSum[i] = VectorA[i] + VectorB[i];
  }

  /* Input Vector B */
  printf("The sum of VectorA and VectorB is \n");
  for (i = 0; i < VECTOR_SIZE; i++) {
    printf("VectorSum[%d] = %d \n", i, VectorSum[i]);
  }
}
```

Figure 17.9: A C program which calculates the sum of two 10 element vectors.

Now on to a slight more complex example. Figure 17.10 lists a C program which reads in 11 different integers from the keyboard and finds the median value of the sequence. The median of a set is its midpoint. The number of elements smaller than the median is equal to the number of elements larger than it.

```c
#include <stdio.h>

#define MAX_NUMS 11

main()
{
  int i;
  int j;
  int larger;
  int numbers[MAX_NUMS];

  /* Get input */
  printf("Enter %d different numbers.\n", MAX_NUMS);
  for (i = 0; i < MAX_NUMS; i++) {
    printf("Input number %d : ", i);
    scanf("%d", &numbers[i]);
  }

  /* Calculate median */
  for (i = 0; i < MAX_NUMS; i++) {
    larger = 0;
    for (j = 0; j < MAX_NUMS; j++) {
        if (numbers[j] > numbers[i])
           larger++;
    }
    if (larger == (MAX_NUMS/2)) {
        printf("The median value is %d\n", numbers[i]);
        break;
    }
  }
}
```

Figure 17.10: A C program which calculates the median of a series of numbers.

The first **for** loop reads in eleven different items from the keyboard and stores them into elements of the array **numbers**. The second **for** loop contains a *nested loop*. Nested loops are common when dealing with arrays. The nested loop in this program actually perform the median calculation. The outer loop iterates through each element of the array and the inner loop takes the element indicated by the outer loop and counts how many elements in the entire array are larger than it. Once an element is found that is smaller than half (remember integer division drops the fractional part) the other elements, the output message is displayed indicating that the median has been found. The **break** statement is an early exit from the outer **for** loop.

17.3.3   Arrays as parameters.

Passing arrays between functions is a useful thing. Say we wanted to create a set of functions which calculated the mean and median on an array of integers. We would need either (1) to pass the entire array from the one function to another or (2) the pass a reference to the array. If an array contains a large number of elements, passing the entire array by pushing each element on the stack could be very costly in execution time and memory space. Instead, C naturally passes arrays by passing the base address of the array to the called function. Figure 17.11 is a segment of C code which contains a function **average** whose single parameter is an array of integers.

When calling the function **average** from **main**, we pass to it the value associated with the array identifier **numbers**. Notice that we are not using the brackets [] of standard array notation here. In C, an array's name refers to the address of the base element of the array. The name **numbers** is therefore equivalent to **&numbers[0]**. The type **numbers** is similar to **int ***. It is an address of memory location containing an integer.

In using **numbers** as the argument to the function **average**, we are causing the address of the array **numbers** to be put onto the stack. Within the function **average**, the parameter **input_values** is assigned the address of the array. Within **average** we can access the elements of the original array using standard array notation. Figure 17.12 shows the run-time stack after **average** has been called.

Since arrays are passed by reference in C, any modifications to the array values made by the called function will be visible to the caller once control returns to it. How would we go about passing only a single element of an array by value? By reference?

17.3.4   Strings in C.

Arrays in C can be used to create *strings*. Strings are sequences of characters and are useful for representing text. Strings are nothing more than character arrays, with each subsequent element containing the next character of the string. For example:

```
char word[10];
```

declares an array capable of storing a string of 10 characters. Longer strings require a larger array. What if we wanted to store a word smaller than 10 characters within this array? In C, the convention is to use the character whose ASCII value is 0 as a sentinel to identify the end of the string. Such string are also called null-terminated strings. '\0' is the special

```
#define MAX_NUMS 11;

int average(int input_values[MAX_NUMS]);

main()
{
  int numbers[MAX_NUMS];
  int mean;

  :
  :
  mean = average(numbers);
  :
  :
}

int average(int input_values[MAX_NUMS])
{
  int i;
  int sum = 0;

  for (i = 0; i < MAX_NUMS; i++) {
    sum = sum + input_values[i]
  }

  return sum/MAX_NUMS;
}
```

Figure 17.11: An example of an array as a parameters to a function.

character corresponding to the end of a string. It is also referred to as the NULL character. Most implementations of C also have a specially defined macro called NULL for it.

Continuing the example above:

```
char word[10];

word[0] = 'H';
word[1] = 'e';
word[2] = 'l';
word[3] = 'l';
word[4] = 'o';
word[5] = '\0';
```

run-time stack

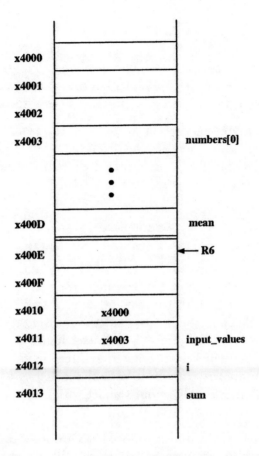

Figure 17.12: The run-time stack immediately after **average** has been called.

```
printf("%s", word);
```

Here, we are assigning the elements of the array individually. The array will contain the string "Hello". Because we need a spot for the NULL character, we can store strings with 9 characters or fewer in the array **word**. We've also used a new **printf** format specification **%s**, which prints out a string of characters, starting with the character pointed to by the corresponding parameter and ending when the NULL character '\0' is encountered.

ANSI C compilers will also allow strings to be initialized within their declarations. For instance the above example can be rewritten to the following. Make note of two things: First, character strings are distinguished from single characters with double quotes " ".
Single quotes are used for single characters, e.g., 'A'. Second, notice that the compiler automatically adds the termination character to the end of the string.

```
char word[10] = "Hello";

printf("%s", word);
```

Let's examine a slightly more complex example involving strings. In this example, listed in Figure 17.13, we read an input string from the keyboard using scanf, then call a function to reverse the string. The reversed string is printed to the screen.

Notice that we are using the format specification %s in the scanf statement. Here, a string of characters ending with *whitespace* is read from the keyboard. In C, any space, tab, newline, carriage return, vertical tab, or formfeed character is considered whitespace. So for the statement scanf("%s", input), if the user typed :

```
Not like the brazen giant of Greek fame,
With conquering limbs astride from land to land;
```

The only the word "Not" will be stored in the string input. The rest of the text line will **not** be discarded, but is retained for subsequent scanfs to read. We'll examine this I/O behavior very closely in Chapter 18. Notice that the maximum word size if 20 characters. What happens if the first word is longer? The scanf function has no information on the size of the array input and will keep storing characters until whitespace is encountered. Question: what then happens to any local variables which are allocated after the array input in the function main? Hint: draw out the activation record before and after the call to scanf.

The function **reverse** performs two tasks in order to properly reverse the string. The first loops calculates the length of the string. The length of this string is needed in order to properly reverse it. The second loop performs the reversal by swapping the first character with the last, the second character with the second to last, the third character with the third to last, etc.

The condition on the **while** loop may seem a little mysterious. There are two parts connected using the AND logical operator &&. If either part evaluates to zero, then the loop terminates. The first part of the condition, string[length], detects the end of the string, which is marked by the NULL character, or ASCII zero (\0). If the character string[length] is NULL, then the first part of the logical AND will be false. The second part of the logical AND, length < MAX_STRING, causes the loop to terminate when there are no more array elements left to check.

The second loop calls the function **swap** on pairs of characters within the string. First, **swap** is called on the first and last character, then on the second and second to last character, and so forth. The function **swap** (as we saw earlier in the chapter) exchanges the value of the two input parameters.

```
#include <stdio.h>

#define MAX_STRING 20

void swap(char *a, char *b);
void reverse(char string[MAX_STRING]);

main()
{
  char input[MAX_STRING];

  printf("Input a word (less than 20 characters) :");
  scanf("%s", input);

  reverse(input);

  printf("The word reversed is %s.\n", input);
}

void swap(char *a, char *b)
{
  char x;

  x = *a;
  *a = *b;
  *b = x;
}

void reverse(char string[MAX_STRING])
{
  int i;
  int length = 0;

  while (string[length] && length < MAX_STRING)
    length++;

  for (i = 0; i < length/2; i++)
    swap(&string[i], &string[length-(i+1)]);
}
```

Figure 17.13: A program which gets a string from the keyboard and prints it with its characters reversed.

The C standard library provides many prewritten functions for strings. For example, functions to copy strings, concatenate strings, compare strings, or to calculate string lengths can be found in the C standard library and the declarations for these functions can be included via the `<string.h>` header file.

More information on these string functions can be found in the Appendix D.8.2.

17.3.5   The relationship between arrays and pointers.

We've mentioned in passing the similarity between an array's name and a pointer variable to an element of the same type. For instance:

```
char word[10];
char *cptr;

cptr = word;
```

is a legal, and sometimes useful, sequence of code. We've assigned the pointer variable `cptr` to point to the base address of the array `word`. Because they are both pointers to characters, `cptr` and `word` can be used interchangeably. One difference, though is that `cptr` is a variable and we can change its value whereas the array identifier `word` is not a variable and we cannot assign it a new value. The identifier is actually a **constant** expression of type **const char *** and always points to a spot chosen by the compiler. The statement `word = cptr` create a syntax error

Table 17.1 shows the equivalence of several expressions involving pointer notation and array notation. Each row in the table is a group of expressions with the same meaning.

cptr	word	&word[0]
(cptr+n)	word+n	&word[n]
*cptr	*word	word[0]
*(cptr+n)	*(word+n)	word[n]

Table 17.1: The relationship between pointers and arrays.

17.3.6   More examples.

The next example program is one we've used in other parts of the text book. We've now seen enough of the C programming language to fully comprehend the C version of the character counting program initially described in Chapter 5. It is listed in Figure 17.14.

In this program we've used an external function called `GetFile`, for which we have not provided the source code. This function is part of another source file, which can be compiled

```
#include <stdio.h>

#define MAX_SIZE 1000

void GetFile(char text[MAX_SIZE]);

main()
{
    int index = 0;
    int count = 0;
    char find;
    char text[MAX_SIZE];

    GetFile(text);

    printf("Please input a character to search for :");
    scanf("%c", &find);

    /* Scan the file */
    while (text[index]) {
        if (text[index] == find)
            count++;
        index++;
    }

    /* Print out the results */
    printf("The number of occurrences of %c is %d\n", find, count);
}
```

Figure 17.14: The character counting program in C

separately, and linked in when the executable image is created. For the purpose of this example, the function GetFile is not necessary. GetFile performs the task of initializing the array text to contain the series of characters which constitute the sequence of text to analyze.

The main loop of the program is trivial. We simply check each character of the array until we encounter the end-of-file sentinel character, which, like for strings, is also equal to the NULL character '\0'. Every array element that matches the character for which we are searching increments the counter variable count. After the end-of-file character is detected, the value of count is displayed.

The next example in Figure 17.15 is a simple sorting program. This program starts off by reading 10 integers from the keyboard and storing them into an array. This array is passed to the function `bubble_sort` which arranges them into ascending order using a sorting technique called bubble sort.

Bubble sort, described at a high level, sorts the array by first finding the largest value within the array and swapping it into the last spot in the array, then finding the next largest value and swapping it into the second to last spot in the array, then the third largest value and swapping it into the third to last spot and so on until all the values have been properly placed. The process is called bubble sort because of the way that values "bubble" their way to their eventual spot in the sorted array.

Let's take a closer look by examining what happens during a single pass of the bubble sort. Say we want to sort the following five numbers:

    53 2 69 32 16

First, the first and second numbers are compared. Since the first number is greater than the second, the numbers are swapped.

    2 53 69 32 16

Next, the second (which used to be the first number in the original order) and third number are compared. Since the second number is **not** greater than the third, nothing changes.

    2 53 69 32 16

Next the third and fourth numbers are compared. Since the third is greater than the fourth, they are swapped.

    2 53 32 69 16

Finally, the fourth and fifth numbers are compared. Since the fourth is greater, it is put into the last spot of the array.

    2 53 32 16 69

This pass through the array has determined that 69 is the largest value, therefore will occupy the last spot in the sorted order. The next pass can ignore this last element of the array since it contains the proper value.

Figure 17.15 contains C code which implements the bubble sort algorithm. In the function `bubble_sort`, the outer `for` loop causes `ii` to vary from 0 to 8. The inner `for` loop then varies from `ii+1` to 9 for each iteration of the outer loop. The first time through, the inner loop varies from 1 to 9, the second time through 2 to 9, then 3 to 9, etc. Basically, first iteration of the outer loop causes the lowest value of the sequence to be placed in the first spot in the array, the second iteration, the second lowest, etc.

```c
#include <stdio.h>

#define MAX_NUMS 10

void bubble_sort(int numbers[MAX_NUMS]);

main()
{
  int i;
  int sum = 0;
  int numbers[MAX_NUMS];

  /* Get input */
  printf("Enter %d numbers.\n", MAX_NUMS);
  for (i = 0; i < MAX_NUMS; i++) {
    printf("Input number %d : ", i);
    scanf("%d", &numbers[i]);
  }

  bubble_sort(numbers);

  /* Print sorted list */
  printf("\nThe input set, in ascending order:\n");
  for (i = 0; i < MAX_NUMS; i++)
    printf("%d\n", numbers[i]);
}

void swap(int *a, int *b)
{
  int x;

  x = *a;
  *a = *b;
  *b = x;
}

void bubble_sort(int numbers[MAX_NUMS])
{
  int ii, jj;

  for (ii = 0; ii < MAX_NUMS-1; ii++) {
    for (jj = ii; jj < MAX_NUMS; jj++) {
      if (numbers[ii] > numbers[jj])
        swap(&numbers[ii], &numbers[jj]);
    }
  }
}
```

Figure 17.15: Bubble sort program

17.3.7 Common pitfalls with arrays in C.

Exceeding the size (or bounds) of an array is one of the most common errors made with arrays in C programming. Unlike some programming languages, C provides no support for ensuring that an array index is actually part of an array. The compiler will blindly generate code for the expression a[i] even if it knows that the index i will access a memory location beyond the end of the array. This is part of C's "surrender control to the programmer" philosophy. Even though this philosophy has contributed greatly to the success of the language, it adds to the effort required to get a C program working. Figure 17.16 lists an example of how an innocent semantic mistake can lead to a serious debugging effort:

```
#include <stdio.h>

main()
{
  int array[10];
  int i;

  for(i=0; i <= 10; i++)
    array[i] = 0;
}
```

Figure 17.16: A C program involving arrays containing a fatal flaw.

Analyze this program by drawing out the activation record for **main** with **array** at offset 3 and i at offset 13. What happens? One note: if you compiled this program using a real compiler, the behavior you see will be different because different compilers arrange variables differently in the activation record. There is no explicit C standard on activation record formats.

C does not support array declarations with using variable expressions. The following code in C is illegal. The size of the array **temp** must be known to the compiler when it analyzes the source code.

```
void SomeArrayFunction(int array, int num_elements)
{
  int temp[num_elements];  /* This will generate a syntax error */

  :
  :
  :
}
```

To deal with limitation, most C programmers make assumptions about the size of the data set the program will operate on and then allocate arrays with extra space. Error checking code is sometimes added to detect the situation of when the allocated space does not suffice. Another option is to use dynamic memory allocation to allocate the array at run-time. More on this later.

17.4   Exercises.

17.1 Write a C function that takes as a parameter a character string of unknown length, containing a single word. Your function should translate this string from English into Pig Latin. This translation is performed by removing the first letter of the string, appending onto the end, and concatenating the letters "ay". You may assume that the array contains enough space for you to add the extra characters.

For example, if your function is passed the string "Hello", after your function returns, the string should have the value "elloHay". The first character of the string should be "e".

17.2 Write a C program which accepts a list of number from the user until a number is repeated (i.e., is the same as the number preceding it). The program then prints out the number of numbers entered (excluding the last) and their sum. When the program is run, the prompts and responses will look like the following.

```
Number: 5
Number: -6
Number: 0
Number: 45
Number: 45
4 numbers were entered and their sum is 44
```

17.3 Modify `new_swap` (See Figure 17.4) to swap character variables instead of integers.

17.4 Write the LC-2 code that gets generated for the statement q = **j, where q and j are both local variables dealing with integers.

17.5 What is the output when the following code is compiled and run?

```
int x;

main() {
    int* px = &x;
    int x = 7;

    *px = 4;
    printf(''x = %d\n'', x);
}
```

17.6 Recall the statement from Section 17.2.4:

```
while (*stringA++ == *stringB++);
```

Using this statement create a string function which returns a 0 if both strings are the same, a 1 if **stringA** appears before **stringB** in sorted order, or a 2 if **stringB** appears before stringA.

17.7 For this question, examine the following program:

```
#include <stdio.h>

main()
{
    int apple;
    int *ptr;
    int **ind;

    ind = &ptr;
    *ind = &apple;
    **ind = 123;

    ind++;
    *ptr++;
    apple++;

    printf("%x %x %d\n", ind, ptr, apple);
}
```

Assuming the activation record for **main** begins at location x4000 on the run-time stack, what gets printed out by the program?

17.8 Show the translation of the following C function into LC-2 assembly language.

```
main() {
    int a[5], i;

    i = 4;
    while (i >= 0) {
        a[i] = i;
        i--;
    }
}
```

17.9 Given the following piece of code:

```
main () {
    int *ptr1, *ptr2;
    int x = 2;

    ptr1 = &x;
    ptr2 = &x;

    if (ptr1 == ptr2)
        printf("Yes\n");
    else
        printf("No\n");
}
```

1. What will be printed when this code runs?

2. Add only two characters (and remove none) to make this print the opposite of what it prints as-is.

17.10 The following code contains a call to the function **triple**. What is the minimum size of the activation record of **triple**?

```
main() {
    int array[3];

    array[0] = 1;
    array[1] = 2;
    array[2] = 3;

    triple(array);
}
```

17.11   1. For the C program written below, what is the size of the activation record for the function `main` and `find_len`?

        2. Show the contents of the stack just before the function `find_len` returns if the input string is `apple`.

```
int find_len(char *);

main() {
   char str[10];

   printf("Enter a string : ");
   scanf("%s", str);

   printf("%s has %d characters\n", str, find_len(str));
}

int find_len(char * s) {
   int len=0;

   while (*s) {
      len++;
      s++;
   }

   return len;
}
```

        3. What would the activation record look like if the above program were run and the user typed a string of length greater than 10 characters? What would happen to the program?

Chapter 18

I/O in C.

18.1 Introduction.

Whether it be to the screen or to a file, output is generated by all useful programs. Most programs also require input. In order to effectively master a programming language, you need to understand how it carries out input and output. Input and output is not directly supported by C, instead it is handled by a set of standard library functions. The behavior of these functions is precisely defined by the ANSI C standard.

In this chapter we will discuss six functions in the C standard I/O library. The functions `putchar` and `printf` write output to the monitor and the functions `getchar` and `scanf` get input the keyboard. The more general function `fprintf` and `fscanf` perform file I/O. We've used most of these functions in the many examples throughout the second half of this book. In this chapter we will examine the details of how these functions work.

18.2 A Brief note about the C standard library.

We've encountered it in passing several times already. The C standard library is a major part of the C programming language. It provides support for I/O, character string manipulations, math functions, system functions, file access functions, and other useful things that are not specific to any single program, but required by many. Information on the library can be found in the Appendix D.8. The library's functions are typically written by designers of the compiler, operating system, and hardware platform because writing them requires intimate knowledge of the underlying hardware and system software.

To use a function defined within the C standard libraries, the proper header file `.h file` must be included. The functions within the library are grouped by the tasks they perform and each of these groups has a header file associated with it. The standard I/O functions use the header file `stdio.h`. This header files contain several things such as the function declarations for the I/O functions and preprocessor macros relating to I/O. A library header file does **not** contain the source code for library functions.

If the header files do not contain source code, then how does the machine code for, say, `printf` get added to our programs? Each library function called within a program is linked in when the executable image is formed. The object files containing the library functions are stored somewhere on the system and are accessed by the linker, which links together our program and all the library functions required by it into an executable image. A preview for a future course: often nowadays, programs can be linked using dynamically linked (DLLs) or *shared* libraries. With these types of libraries, the machine code for a library routine doesn't appear within the executable image but is "linked" in while the program is executing.

18.3   I/O, one character at a time.

Let's start by examining general characteristics of I/O using some of the simplest I/O capabilities that C provides. The functions `getchar` and `putchar` perform input and output *one character at a time*. They provide no conversion functionality; input is read in as ASCII and written out as ASCII, in a manner similar to the `IN` and `OUT` TRAP routines of the LC-2.

Conceptually, C performs all input and output on ASCII text *streams*. In fact, many other popular languages provide a similar abstraction for I/O. The sequence of ASCII characters typed by the user at the keyboard is an example of an input stream. The sequence of ASCII characters printed by a single running program to the computer's monitor is an example of an output stream. By default, the functions `getchar` and `putchar` operate on these two streams. In C the standard input stream from the keyboard is referred to as `stdin` and the standard output stream is referred to as `stdout`.

18.3.1   `putchar`

The function `putchar` is the high-level language equivalent of the LC-2 `OUT` TRAP routine. The function `putchar` displays on the `stdout` output stream the ASCII value of the parameter passed to it. It performs no type conversions–the value passed to it is assumed to be ASCII and is written to the output stream. All the calls to `putchar` in the code segment below cause the same character (h) to be displayed. A `putchar` function call is treated like any other function call. Here the function being called resides within the standard library. Its function declaration is in the `stdio.h` header file. Its code will be linked into the executable during the compiler's link phase.

```
char c = 'h';

 :
 :
putchar(c);
putchar('h');
putchar(104);
```

18.3.2 getchar

The function `getchar` is the high-level language equivalent of the LC-2 IN TRAP function. It returns the ASCII value of the next input character appearing in the `stdin` input stream. By default, the `stdin` input stream is simply the stream of characters typed at the keyboard. In the following code segment, `getchar` returns the ASCII value of next character typed at the keyboard. This return value is assigned to the variable `c`.

```
char c;

c = getchar();
```

18.3.3 Buffered I/O.

Run the following C code and you will notice something peculiar.

```
#include <stdio.h>

main()
{
  char a;
  char b;

  printf("Input character 1:\n");
  a = getchar();

  printf("Input character 2:\n");
  b = getchar();

  printf("Character 1 is %c\n", a);
  printf("Character 2 is %c\n", b);
}
```

The program prompts the user for the first input character and waits for that input to be typed in. Type in a character (say 'z', for example) and nothing happens. The second prompt does not appear, as if the call to `getchar` has missed the keystroke. In fact the program seems to make no progress at all until the newline character (the "Enter" key) is typed in. Such behavior seems unexpected considering that `getchar` is only supposed to read a single character from the keyboard input stream.

This unexpected behavior is due buffering of the keyboard input stream. On most computer systems, I/O streams are buffered. Every key typed on the keyboard is captured by the computer's low-level software and kept in a *buffer* until they are read via an I/O function call, say `getchar`. Conceptually, each I/O stream has it's own buffer, and a buffer is a temporary storage area somewhere in memory.

As for the input buffer, keystrokes are only added after an input line is terminated by the Enter key. On most computer systems, whenever a user types the Enter key, the sequence of characters typed since the last time the Enter key was pressed is added to the input stream. So from the previous code example, it is not until the Enter key is pressed that the program actually see the characters the user typed in (Notice that the Enter key also appears in the input stream as the newline character). There is a good reason for this behavior: pressing the Enter key allows the user to *confirm* the input. Say you mistyped some input and wanted to correct it before the program detects it. You can edit your input using the backspace and delete keys, and then confirm your input by pressing the Enter key.

The output stream is similarly buffered. Examine the behavior of the following program:

```
#include <stdio.h>

#define DELAY 100000000

main()
{
  int sum = 0;
  int i;

  putchar('a');

  /* Generate a small delay */
  for (i = 0; i < DELAY; i++) {
    sum = sum + i;
  }

  putchar('b');
  putchar('\n');
}
```

On most computer systems, you will notice that the delay loop (which may have to be adjusted for your system by modifying the value of DELAY to cause a delay of a several seconds) causes a pause before any output appears on the monitor even though the first putchar appears before the delay loop. The output stream isn't flushed to the output device until a newline character appears in the stream (or the program controlling the output stream completes). The putchar('\n') causes output to be flushed.

Despite the slightly complex implementation of buffered I/O streams, the underlying mechanism used to actually read the keyboard and write to the monitor is very similar to the simpler IN and OUT TRAP routines described in Chapter 8.

18.4 Slightly more sophisticated I/O.

The functions `putchar` and `getchar` suffice for simple I/O jobs, but we require more powerful constructs for typical I/O jobs. The functions `printf` and `scanf` perform more sophisticated *formatted* I/O.

18.4.1 printf

The function `printf` writes formatted text to the output stream. Using `printf` we can print out ASCII text embedded with values generated by the running program. The `printf` function takes care of all the necessary type conversions. We seen many examples of this function throughout the second half of the book. This example prints out the sum of three input values:

```
int x,y,z;

printf("Enter three integer values : ");
scanf("%d %d %d", &x, &y, &z);
printf("The three values are: %d %d %d\n", x, y, z);
printf("The sum of the parameters is %d\n", x+y+z);
```

Generally speaking, `printf` writes it's first parameter to the output stream. The first parameter is the *format string*. It is a character string (i.e., of type `char *`) containing text to be output. Embedded within the format string are zero or more *conversion specifications*.

The conversion specifications indicate how to print out any of the arguments which follow the format string in the function call. Conversion specifications all begin with a `%` character. As their name implies, they indicate how the values which follow should be treated when converted to ASCII. In many of the examples we've encountered so far (including the one above), integers have been printed out as decimal numbers using the `%d` specification. We could also use the `%x` specification to print integers as hexadecimal numbers, or `%b` to print them as binary numbers (represented as ASCII text). Other conversions for other types of values can also be accomplished: `%c` causes a value to be interpreted as straight ASCII (how is this type conversion accomplished?), the `%s` specification is used for strings and causes characters stored consecutively in memory to be output. The null character `\0` signals the end of the string. The specification `%f` displays a floating point number. What if we wanted to print out the `%` character itself? We use the sequence `%%`. See appendix F for a full listing of conversion specifiers and information on controlling the field widths and precisions of the values which are displayed.

As mentioned in Chapter 11, special characters such as a newline can also be embedded in the format string. The `\n` prints a newline and a `\t` character prints a tab; both are examples of these special characters. All special characters begin with a `\` and they can appear anywhere within a format string. In order to print out a backslash character, we use a \\. See Table D.1 in the appendix for a list of special characters.

Here are some examples of various format specifications:

```
int  a = 102;
int  b = 65;
char c = 'z';
char banner[10] = "Hola!"
float pi = 3.14159;

printf("The variable 'a' as a decimal number : %d\n", a);
printf("The variable 'a' as a hex number : %x\n", a);
printf("The variable 'a' as a binary number : %b\n", a);
printf("'a' plus 'b' as an ASCII character : %c\n", a + b);
printf("A character %c.\t A string %s\n A float %f\n", c, banner, pi);
```

The function printf begins by examining the format string a single character at a time. If the current character is not a % or \, then the character is directly written to the output stream. (Remember, the stream may be buffered so the output may not appear on the monitor until a newline is written). If the character is a \, then the next character indicates the particular special character to print out. For instance, the escape sequence \n indicates a newline character. If the current character is a %, indicating a conversion specification, then the next character indicates how the next pending parameter should be interpreted. For instance, if the conversion specification is a %d and the next pending parameter is the bit pattern 000000001101000, then the number 104 is written to the output stream. If the conversion character is a %c, then the character 'h' is written. A different value is printed if %f is the conversion specification. The conversion specifier indicates to printf how the next parameter should be interpreted. It is important to realize that, within the printf routine, there is no relationship between a conversion specification and the type of a parameter. The programmer is free to choose how things are to be interpreted as they are displayed to the screen. Question: what happens with the following function call:

```
printf("The value of nothing is %d\n");
```

There is no argument corresponding to the %d specification. The printf routine assumes the correct number of values were written onto the stack when it is called and blindly reads a value off the stack for the %d spec, assuming it was intentionally placed there. Here, a garbage value will be displayed to the screen.

18.4.2   scanf

The function scanf is used to read formatted ASCII data from the input stream. A call to scanf is similar to a call to printf. Both calls require a format string as the first argument followed by a variable number of other arguments. Both functions are controlled by characters within the format string. The function `scanf` differs in that all arguments following the format string MUST be pointers. The reason for this will be clear to you by the end of this section.

The format string for `scanf` contains ASCII text and conversion specifications, just like the format string for `printf`. The conversion characters are similar to those used for `printf`. A table of these specifications can be found in Appendix F. Essentially, the format string represents the format of the input stream. For example, the format string `"%d"` indicates to `scanf` that the next sequence of non-white space characters (white space is defined as spaces, tabs, newlines, carriage returns, vertical tabs, and formfeeds) will be a sequence of digits in ASCII representing an integer in decimal notation. After this decimal number is read from the input stream, it is converted into an integer and stored into the corresponding argument. Since `scanf` is modifying the values of the variables passed to it, arguments are passed *by reference* using the `&` operator. In addition to conversion specifications, the format string also can contain plain text which `scanf` will attempt to match with the input stream.

We will use the following code to demonstrate.

```
char name[100];
int birth_month, birth_day, birth_year;
double gpa;

printf("Enter data : lastname birthdate(mm/dd/yr) grade_point_average\n");
scanf("%s %d/%d/%d %lf", name, &birth_month, &birth_day, &birth_year, &gpa);

printf("\n");
printf("Name : %s\n", name);
printf("Birthday : %d/%d/%d\n", birth_month, birth_day, birth_year);
printf("GPA : %f\n", gpa);
```

In the `scanf` statement above, the first specification is a `%s` which scans in a string from the input stream. In this context, all characters starting from the first non-white space character and ending with the next white space character (conceptually, the next *word* in the input stream) will be stored in memory starting at the address of `name` and a `\0` character will be automatically added to signify the end of the string. Since the argument `name` is an array, it is automatically passed by reference, i.e., the address of the first element of the array is passed to `scanf`.

The next specification is for a decimal number, `%d`. Now, `scanf` will expect to find a sequence of digits (at least one digit) as the next set of non-white space characters in the standard input stream. Characters from standard input are analyzed, white-space characters are discarded, and the decimal number (i.e., a sequence of digits terminated by a non-digit) is read in. The number is converted from a sequence of ASCII characters into a binary integer and stored in the memory location indicated by the argument `&birth_month`.

The next input field is the ASCII character, '/'. Now, scanf expects to find this character, possibly surrounded by white space, in the input stream. Since this input field is not a conversion specification, it is not assigned to any variable. Once it is read in from the input stream, it is simply discarded, and scanf moves on to the next field of the format string. Similarly, the next three input fields %d/%d read in two decimal numbers separated by a /. These values are converted into integers and stored into birth_day and birth_year.

The last field in the format string specifies that the input stream will contain a *long* floating point number, which is the specification used to read in a value of type double. For this specifier, scanf will expect to see a sequence of decimal numbers, and possibly a decimal point, possibly an 'E' or 'e' signifying exponential notation (see Appendix D.2.4), in the input stream. This field is terminated once a non-digit (excluding the first 'E', or the decimal point or a plus or minus sign for the fraction or exponent) or white space is detected. The scanf routine will take this sequence of ASCII characters and convert them into a properly expressed double-precision floating point number and store it into gpa.

Once it is done processing the format string, scanf returns to the caller. It also returns an integer value. The number of data items which were successfully read from the input stream is passed back to the caller. In this case, if everything went correctly, scanf would return the value 5. In the code above, we chose to ignore the return value.

So for example, the following line of input will yield the following output.

```
Enter data : lastname birthdate(mm/dd/yr) grade_point_average
Mudd 02/16/69 3.02


Name : Mudd
Birthday : 2/16/69
GPA : 3.02
```

Since scanf ignores white space for this format string, the following input stream yields the same results. Remember, newline characters are considered white space.

```
Enter data : lastname birthdate(mm/dd/yr) grade_point_average
Mudd      02
/
16 / 69     3.02

Name : Mudd
Birthday : 2/16/69
GPA : 3.02
```

What if the format of the input stream does not match the format string? For instance, what would happen with the following stream?

```
Enter data : lastname birthdate(mm/dd/yr) grade_point_average
```

Mudd 02 16 69 3.02

Here, the input stream does not contain the / characters encoded in the format string. In this case, `scanf` will return the value 2, since the variables `name` and `birth_month` would be correctly assigned before the mismatch is detected. The remaining variables go unmodified. Since the input stream is buffered, unused input is not discarded and subsequent reads of the input stream begin where this call left off.

If the next two reads of the input stream were:

```
a = getchar();
b = getchar();
```

What will `a` and `b` contain? The answer ' ' (the space character) and 1 should not be puzzling.

What would happen if arguments are not passed to `scanf` as pointers? For example, what happens with the following call?

```
int n = 0;

scanf("%d", n);
```

18.4.3 Variable argument lists.

By now, you might have noticed something different about the functions `printf` and `scanf`. Both can have a *variable* number of arguments passed to them. They therefore requires a special function call mechanism. The number of arguments passed to `printf` and `scanf` depend on the number of items being printed or scanned.

There is a one-to-one correspondence between each conversion specification in the format string and each argument that appears after the format string in these function calls. Recall the following `printf` statement from one of our previous examples:

```
printf("A character %c.\t A string %s\n A float %f\n", c, banner, pi);
```

The format string contains three format specifications therefore three arguments follow it in the function call. The `%c` spec in the string is associated with the first argument which follows (the variable c). The `%s` is associated with `banner`, and `%f` with `pi`. There are three values to be printed, therefore this call contains four arguments altogether. If we want to print five values, the function call will contain six arguments.

The compiler treats a call to `printf` or `scanf` as any other call. Each argument is placed on the stack before the actual function call is performed. The format string (as are all constant strings which appear in C code) is actually a character array and, like all arrays, is passed as the address of the first element. The format string itself is stored in memory by the compiler in a special region of reserved for constants (constants within a program are also called *literal* values). The address of the format string is passed as the first argument and all other arguments follow it. Most compilers will **NOT** check the format string to make sure there are the same number of specifiers and arguments to print (after all, from the compiler's viewpoint, a call to `printf` is just another function call—nothing special needs to be done).

Since the functions `printf` and `scanf`, use variable length argument lists, they require special treatment in order for the activation record and run-time stack to work properly. A modified version of the calling mechanism described in Chapter 14 is used for functions with variable argument lists.

18.5   I/O from Files.

We can now write C programs to read data from the keyboard and write data to the monitor. But what if we wanted to process a large set of data, say the daily stock price for IBM for the last twenty years. To ask the user to type this via keyboard every time the program is run would render it very "user-unfriendly". To handle this, we require the ability to read and write ASCII data *files* from within our C programs. As we will see, I/O in C is conceptually based on file I/O.

The functions `printf` and `scanf` are really special cases of more general-purpose C I/O functions. These two functions operate specifically on the special *file pointers* `stdin` and `stdout`. For our purposes, we will say that a file pointer maps a particular stream (input or output or *input AND output*) to a particular file or device. In C, `stdin` and `stdout` are mapped by default to the keyboard and the monitor.

The general-purpose version of `printf` is called `fprintf` and the general purpose version of `scanf` is called `fscanf`. The functions `fprintf` and `fscanf` work exactly like their counterparts, except they allow us to specify an input or output stream. For example, we can inform `fprintf` to write its output to a specific file.

Let's see how this can be accomplished.

Before we can perform file I/O, we need to declare a file pointer for each physical file we want to manipulate. Typically, physical files are files stored on the file system of the particular computer system. In C, we can declare a file pointer called `fp` as such:

```
FILE *fp;
```

Here we are declaring a pointer to something of type `FILE`. The type `FILE` is defined within the header file `stdio.h`. Its details are not important for the discussion here, so we'll leave them for a later course.

Once the file pointer is declared, we need to map it to a physical file. The C library call `fopen` performs this mapping. Each `fopen` call requires two arguments: the name of the file to open and description of what type of operations we want to perform on the file. Below is a sample.

```
FILE *fp;

fp = fopen("ibm_stock_prices", "r");
```

The first argument to `fopen` is the name of the file to open, `ibm_stock_prices`. The second argument is the operation we want to perform on this file. Several useful *modes* are `"r"` for reading, `"w"` for writing (all previous contents of the file will be lost), `"a"` for appending (previous contents are not lost; new data is added to the end of the file), `"r+"` for reading and writing. Note that both arguments must be character strings, therefore they are surrounded by double quotes in this example. In this case we are opening the file called `"ibm_stock_prices"` for reading.

If the `fopen` call is successful, the function returns a file pointer to the physical file. If the open for some reason fails, then the function will return a `NULL` value. It is **always** good practice to check if the `fopen` call was successful.

```
FILE *fp;

fp = fopen("ibm_stock_prices", "r");

if (!fp)
    printf("fopen unsuccessful!\n");
```

Now with the file pointer properly mapped to a physical file, we can use `fscanf` and `fprintf` to read and write it just as we used `printf` and `scanf` to read the standard devices. The functions `fscanf` and `fprintf` both require a file pointer as their first argument to indicate which stream the operations are to be performed on. The example below demonstrates.

```
#define LIMIT 10000

FILE *fp;
FILE *output_file;
double prices[LIMIT];
int i = 0;
char answer[10];

fp = fopen("ibm_stock_prices", "r");
output_file = fopen("buy_hold_or_sell", "w");

if (!fp || !output_file)
   printf("fopen unsuccessful!\n");
else {
  /*  Read the input data */
  while (fscanf(fp, "%lf", prices[i]) && i < LIMIT)
     i++;

  printf("%d prices read from the data file", i);

  /* Process the data... */
  :
  :

  /* Write the output */
  fprintf(output_file, "%s", answer);
}
```

Here, we are reading from an ASCII text file called ibm_stock_prices and writing to a file called buy_hold_or_sell. The input file contains floating point data item separated by white space. Even though the file may contain more, at most 10000 items will be read in using fscanf. The fscanf function returns a 0 when a floating point number could not be read from the input file, indicating the end of file has been reached (or the file was improperly formatted). This causes the input loop to terminate. After the program processes the input data, the output file is written with the value of the string answer.

The functions printf is equivalent to calling fprintf using stdout as the file pointer. Likewise, scanf is equivalent to calling fscanf using stdin.

18.6 Exercises.

18.1 Write an I/O function call to handle the following tasks. All can be handled by a single call.

1. Print out an integer followed by a string followed by a floating point number.

2. Print out a phone number in (XXX)-XXX-XXXX format. Internally, the phone number is stored as three integers.

3. Print out a student ID number in XXX-XX-XXXX format. Internally, the ID number is stored as three character strings.

4. Read a student ID number in XXX-XX-XXXX format. The number is to be stored internally as three integers.

5. Read in a line of input containing:
   `Last name, First name, Middle initial age sex`
   The name fields are separated by commas. The middle initial and sex should be stored as characters. Age is an integer.

18.2 What does the value returned by `scanf` represent?

18.3 Why is buffering of the keyboard input stream useful?

18.4 What is displayed by the following function call:

```
printf("The value of x is %d\n");
```

18.5 Why does the following code print out a strange value (such as 1073741824)?

```
float x = 192.27163;
printf("The value of x is %d\n", x);
```

18.6 What is the value of `input` for the following function call:

```
scanf("%d", \&input);
```

if the input stream contains :

```
This is not the input you are looking for.
```

18.7 Consider the following program:

```
#include <stdio.h>

main()
{
  int x = 0;
  int y = 0;
  char label[10];

  scanf("%d %d", &x, &y);
  scanf("%s", label);

  printf("%d %d %s\n", x, y, label);
}
```

1. What gets printed out if the input stream is **46 29 BlueMoon**?

2. What gets printed out if the input stream is **46 BlueMoon**?

3. What gets printed out if the input stream is **111 999 888**?

18.8 Write a program to read in a C source file and write it back to a file called "condensed_program" with all *whitespace* removed.

18.9 Write a program to read in a text file and provide an count of:

1. The number of strings in the file, where a string begins with a non whitespace character and ends with a whitespace character.

2. The number of words in the file, where a word begins with an alphabetic character (i.e., a-z or A-Z) and ends with a non-alphabetic character.

3. The number of unique words in the file. Words are as defined in the previous part. The set of unique words has no duplicates.

Chapter 19

Data Structures.

19.1 Introduction.

The data manipulated by the programs we write almost always has some natural higher level organization to it. It's often beneficial to use this natural structure when designing the programs that use the data. If the data is organized properly within the program, the flow of the program will be more intuitive and the program will becomes easier to write, debug, and maintain. For example, if we were writing a program to manage a company's employee database, *bundling* a particular employee's data—such as name, address, job title, social security number, etc.—as one unit would be a natural way to organize the data. This bundling could be be carried further: groups of employees could be organized by departments or divisions.

Data structures are the organization of data in memory. Picking the right structure for the data a program works on is an important step in the development of all programs. At a low level, we want to tightly group related data together (i.e., grouping employee data into one "unit"). At a higher level, want to put the grouped data in a convenient arrangement so that the operations performed by program can be done more efficiently.

In this chapter we will introduce the C support for *structures*. Structures are a way to group related data items together. We will describe the syntax for creating structures in C and look at the LC-2 code generated by the LC-2 C compiler. Next, as a brief foray, we will look at dynamic allocation. Dynamic allocation is not directly related to the concept of data structures, but is a necessary concept for understanding the third item of this chapter: the linked list. The linked list is a fundamental data structure that appears in some form in many programs and is a common technique for high level organization of data items. We will look at functions for adding, deleting, and searching for data items within linked lists.

19.2   Structures.

19.2.1   The basics of structures in C.

Most high-level programming languages have a way to group together related pieces of data. In C, the mechanism for accomplishing this grouping is called a *struct* which is short for structure (called a *record* in other languages). Structures allow related data items to be grouped together and treated as a single data item. Structures are called aggregate data types because the programmer defines them as a collection of simple data items such as `int`, `char`, and `double`. The are similar to arrays in that we can group data items together. The are different from arrays in that we can group data with *different* types together. Structure variables are declared in the same way variables of simple data type are declared. Before any structure variables are declared though, the organization and naming of the data items within the structure must be defined.

Let's say we wanted to write a weather statistics program that contains information about the weather for the past 100 days. Say, for each day, we want to store the high and low temperatures, amount of precipitation, and average wind speed and direction. Each day has a certain set of data associated with it, which we can represent using the following variables:

```
int high_temp;
int low_temp;
double precip;
double wind_speed;
int wind_direction;
```

We'll need this set of variables for each day we want to track in our program. A convenient way to do so is to organize it into a structure:

```
struct day_type {
  int high_temp;
  int low_temp;
  double precip;
  double wind_speed;
  int wind_direction;
};
```

In the declaration above, we have declared a new type containing five *members* elements. We haven't yet declared any storage; we've simply indicated to the compiler what we want this new type to look like. We've given the structure the *tag* `day_type` which is necessary for referring to the structure in other parts of the code. To declare a variable of this new type, we can do the following:

```
struct day_type day;
```

We can access the individual members of this structure variable using the following syntax:

```
struct day_type day;

day.high_temp = 32;
day.low_temp = 22;
```

The variable declaration **day** gets allocated on the stack (if it is a local variable) and occupies a contiguous region of memory big enough to hold each member element.

The allocation of the structure is straightforward. A structure is allocated the same way a variable of a basic data type is allocated: locals are allocated on the run-time stack and globals are allocated in the global data section. Figure 19.1 shows a portion of the activation record for a function which contains the following declarations:

```
int x;
struct day_type day;
int y;
```

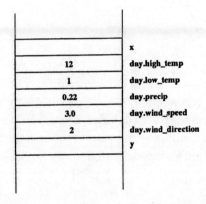

Figure 19.1: An activation record for a function with a local variable of structure type.

Generically, the syntax for a structure declaration is as follows:

```
struct tag {...members...} identifiers;
```

The **tag** provides a handle for referring to the structure again, as in the case of later declaring variables of the structure's format. It is optional and if we don't use it then we need to restate the members of the structure if we intended to use the structure again. The list of member defines the organization of a structure and is syntactically a list of declarations. Finally, we can optionally include identifiers in a structure's declaration to actually declare variables of that structure's type. For instance, if the following declares a variable called **day** of of type **struct day_type**.

```
struct day_type {
  int high_temp;
  int low_temp;
  double precip;
  double wind_speed;
  int wind_direction;
} day;
```

Now that we have seen the technique for declaring and allocating variables of structure type, we now focus on accessing the member fields and performing operations on them. For example, in the following code, the members of a structure variable of type day_type are accessed.

```
int x;
struct day_type day;
int y;

day.high_temp = 12;
day.low_temp = 1;
day.precip = 0.22
day.wind_speed =  3.0;
day.wind_direction = 2;
```

Here, the variable day is of type struct day_type, meaning it has the 5 member fields as we defined previously. The member field labeled high_temp is accessed using the variable's name followed by a period '.' followed by the member field label. The compiler, knowing the layout of the structure, generates code which accesses the structure's member field using another offset. Figure 19.1 shows the layout of the a portion of the activation record for this function. The compiler keeps track, in its symbol table, of the location of each variable and if the variable is an aggregate data type, the position of each field within the variable. Notice that the address of the structure is the address of the first member of that structure.

Below is the code generated by the LC-2 C compiler for the first two assignments in the code segment above.

```
        AND  R1, R1, #0   ;   zero out R1
        ADD  R1, R1, #12  ;   R1 = 12

        ADD  R0, R6, #4   ;   R0 contains address of day
        ADD  R0, R0, #0   ;   R0 contains address of day.high_temp
        STR  R1, R0, #0   ;   day.high_temp = 12;

        AND  R1, R1, #0   ;   zero out R1
        ADD  R1, R1, #1   ;   R1 = 1

        ADD  R0, R6, #4   ;   R0 contains address of day
        ADD  R0, R0, #1   ;   R0 contains address of day.low_temp
        STR  R1, R0, #0   ;   day.low_temp = 1;
        :
        :
```

19.2.2 Arrays and pointers with structures.

For the purpose of our weather program, we want to track the weather for the last 100 days. For this, the following declaration makes sense.

```
struct day_type days[100];
```

The declaration above is similar to the declaration int d[100], except instead of declaring 100 integer values, we've declared a contiguous region of memory containing 100 structures each of which is composed of the 5 members indicated in the structure's declaration. The reference days[12], for example, would refer to the 13th element in the region of 100 in memory. Each element contains enough storage for the 5 member elements of this structure.

Each element of this array is a structure of day_type and can be accessed using standard array notation. Accessing the weather statistics for day 0 can be done using the identifier days[0]. Accessing a member field is done by accessing an element of the array and then specifying a field: days[0].high_temp. The following code segment provides an example. It averages the high temperatures for all 100 days:

```
int i;
int sum = 0;
int average_high_temp;

for (i = 0; i < 100; i++)
   sum = sum + days[i].high_temp;
```

```
    average_high_temp = sum/100;
```

We can also create pointers to structures. The following declaration creates a pointer variable that contains the address of a variable of type day_type.

```
    struct day_type *day_ptr;
```

We can assign this variable as we would any pointer variable.

```
    day_ptr = &day[34];
```

Now, we will introduce a piece of new C syntax: dereferencing a pointer variable which points to a structure. If we want to access any of the member fields pointed to by this pointer variable, we could do the following:

```
    (*day_ptr).high_temp
```

Here, we are dereferencing the variable day_ptr. It points to something of type struct day_type and we can access one of its member field by using the member operator. Since, as we shall see, this is a very common operation and since this expression is not very easy to grasp (or type), a special operator has been defined for it. The above expression is equivalent to:

```
    day_ptr->high_temp
```

The program listed in Figure 19.2 shows a complete example using structures and arrays and pointers. This program uses the weather data structure defined earlier. The program takes input from the keyboard for 10 days worth of weather data (the number of days is defined via the macro NUM_DAYS), calculates and displays the average high temperature and also displays the weather data for the day with the highest temperature. The two functions input_day and output_day perform the task of I/O for a day's worth weather data. Notice that pointers to a day_type structure are used as arguments to these functions.

```
#include <stdio.h>

#define NUM_DAYS 10

/* Structure definition */
struct day_type {
  int high_temp;
  int low_temp;
  double precip;
  double wind_speed;
  int wind_direction;
};


/* Function declarations */
void input_day(struct day_type *day);
void output_day(struct day_type *day);

main()
{
  struct day_type days[NUM_DAYS];
  struct day_type *max_day;
  int max_temp = 0, sum = 0;
  int ii;

  printf("Input data for the previous 10 days\n");
  for (ii = 0; ii < NUM_DAYS; ii++) {
    printf("\nInput information for day %d\n", ii);
    input_day(&days[ii]);
  }

  for (ii = 0; ii < NUM_DAYS; ii++) {
    sum = sum + days[ii].high_temp;

    if (days[ii].high_temp >= max_temp) {
      max_temp = days[ii].high_temp;
      max_day = &days[ii];
    }
  }

  printf("\nThe average temperature was : %d\n", sum / NUM_DAYS);
  printf("The max temperature occurred on this day:\n");
  output_day(max_day);
}
```

Figure 19.2: An example weather data program.

```
void input_day(struct day_type *day)
{
  printf("High temp in deg F  : ");
  scanf("%d", &day->high_temp);
  printf("Low temp in deg F   : ");
  scanf("%d", &day->low_temp);
  printf("Precipitation in inches : ");
  scanf("%lf", &day->precip);
  printf("Ave wind speed in mph : ");
  scanf("%lf", &day->wind_speed);
  printf("Wind direction (1=N,2=E,3=S,4=W) : ");
  scanf("%d", &day->wind_direction);
}

void output_day(struct day_type *day)
{
  printf("High temp      : %d deg F\n", day->high_temp);
  printf("Low temp       : %d deg F\n", day->low_temp);
  printf("Precipitation  : %lf inches\n", day->precip);
  printf("Ave wind speed : %lf mph\n", day->wind_speed);
  printf("Wind direction : %d (1=N,2=E,3=S,4=W)\n", day->wind_direction);
}
```

Figure 19.3: An example weather data program, continued.

19.3   A foray into dynamic allocation.

Variables in C programs are allocated in one of three spots: the run-time stack, the global data section, and the *heap*. Variables declared local to functions are allocated during execution on the run-time stack. Global variables are allocated in the global data section and are accessible by all parts of a program. Dynamically allocated data items—items which are created during run-time—are allocated on the heap.

In the previous example, we declared an array which contained 10 days of weather data. But, what if we wanted to create a flexible program which could handle as many days of weather data as the user was willing to enter? One possible solution would be to declare the array assuming a large upper limit to the number of days worth of data the user might possibly enter. This could result in a lot of potentially wasted space. Another solution is to determine at run-time the number of days which the program will need to manage and to declare the space for the data dynamically. If the user indicates that there will be data for 100 days, then a region of memory is declared with room for 100 day_type structures.

Dynamic allocation in C is handled by standard library functions. Let's take a look at an example which uses the function malloc:

```
int number_of_days;
struct day_type *days;

printf("How many days worth of weather data are in the input set?");
scanf("%d", &number_of_days);

/* A call to a dynamic allocation routine */
days = malloc(10 * number_of_days);
```

Here we use a library call to the routine malloc, which is short for *memory allocate*. The function will allocate a contiguous region of memory of the size in bytes indicated by the single parameter. If the call is successful, it returns a pointer to the allocated region.

Here we allocated 10 * number_of_days bytes of space, where number_of_days is the number indicated by the user as size of the input set and 10 is the size of each day_type structure variable. Why the 10? Recall, that the structure is composed of 5 members—3 integers and 2 doubles—which in the LC-2, all occupy 2 bytes each. As a necessary convenience to programmers, the C language supports a compile-time operator called sizeof. This operator returns the size, in bytes, of the memory object passed to it as an argument. For example, sizeof(struct day_type) will return the number of bytes occupied by a variable of type struct day_type or 10. The programmer does not need to calculate the sizes of various data objects; the compiler can be instructed to perform it automatically.

The function malloc and other similar functions in the standard library which manage memory allocation manage the heap region of memory. Each call updates information associated with the heap. If for some reason, the allocation cannot be accomplished, for example if all the memory of the heap has already been allocated and is in use, then malloc will return a NULL value. The symbol NULL is a preprocessor macro symbol usually defined to the value 0. It is always good, defensive programming practice to check that the return value from malloc indicates the memory allocation was successful.

Another note: the function malloc returns a generic pointer to a generic data item (typically, a char *). We need to *type cast* the pointer returned by malloc to the type of the variable we are assigning it to. In the example above, we assigned the pointer to days, which is of type struct day_type *, so therefore we need to cast the pointer to type day_type. To do so otherwise makes the code less portable across different computer systems and most compilers will generate a warning message. Type casting causes the compiler to treat a value of one type as if it were another type. To type cast a value from one type to a new_type, we use the following syntax. The variable var should be of new_type.

```
var = (new_type) expression;
```

Given type casting and the sizeof operation and the error checking of the return value from malloc, the correct way to write the code from the previous example is given below:

```
int number_of_days;
struct day_type *days;

printf("How many days worth of weather data are in the input set?");
scanf("%d", &number_of_days);

/* A more correctly written call to a dynamic allocation routine */
days = (struct day_type *) malloc(sizeof(struct day_type) * number_of_days);
if (days == NULL) {
    printf("Error in allocating the days array\n");
    exit(1);
}
days[0].high_temp = ...
```

Since the region is contiguous in memory, we can switch between pointer notation and‘ array notation. This is an example of the flexibility which has helped make C a very popular programming language.

The function malloc is only one of several memory allocation functions in the standard library. The function calloc allocates memory and initializes it. The function realloc attempts to grow or shrink previously allocated regions of memory. The deallocation counterpart to these functions is called free, which takes as its parameter a pointer to an allocated region and *deallocates* it. After a region has been free'd, it is once again eligible for allocation. It is good programming practice to deallocate memory objects after we are done with them otherwise the space on the heap available for allocation may quickly start to vanish.

At this point, we have seen limited use for dynamic memory allocation but it is nonetheless a very useful tool in our programming arsenal. All the pieces are now in place for examples involving the linked list data structure which relies heavily on dynamic allocation.

19.4 A fundamental data structure: the linked list.

19.4.1 What is a linked list?

Having the business listings in a phone book organized alphabetically by category makes looking up phone numbers quick and simple. If the listing were haphazardly placed, then finding a phone number would take too long, probably making the phone book useless. The data within the phone book is organized in a manner suited for the task we commonly use it for—looking up phone numbers. Similarly, a programmer can make a program run more quickly by choosing the right arrangement of data within memory. Choosing the correct data structure is an important part of the planning phase of writing a program. The wrong data structure could make your program overly complicated or unnecessarily slow.

In this section, we present a fundamental data structure called the *linked list*. To understand linked lists, we will need to tie together many of the concepts we have examined in the second half of this text.

A linked list is a collection of nodes, where a node is one data "unit" containing an instance of data, such as a day's worth of weather data. Each node also contains a pointer element which points to the next node in the list. As you might have guessed, we create these nodes using C structures. A critical element of a node structure is a member element which points to another node structure.

The linked list has a beginning and an end. Its beginning, or head node, is accessed using a pointer called the head pointer. The final node in the list, or tail, points to the NULL value. Figure 19.4 shows two representations of a linked list data structure: an abstract depiction where nodes are represented as blocks and pointers are represented by arrows and a more physical representation which shows what the data structure might look like in memory.

Conceptually, a linked list and an array are similar data structures. They both hold a sequence of data items, names of students enrolled at a university, for example. They, however, have some strong fundamental differences. An array can be accessed in random order. We can accesses element number 4, followed by element 911, followed by 45, for example. A simple linked list must be traversed starting at its head. If we wanted to access node 29, then we must start at node 0 (the head node) and then go to node 1, then to node 2, etc. Stated another way, a linked list can only be accessed sequentially.

However the linked list has some strong advantages. The linked list is dynamic in nature; additional nodes can be added to it or removed from it. Arrays are static in size. If more students enrolled at the university, then with a linked list, we can dynamically add nodes to make room for more data. A second advantage is that it is much simpler to insert and delete nodes from the middle of a linked list than from the middle of an array.

A linked list in abstract form

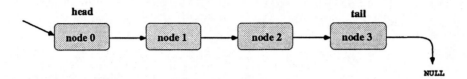

A linked list in memory

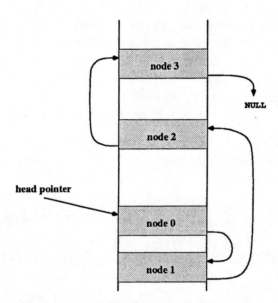

Figure 19.4: Two representations for a linked list.

19.4.2 An example using linked lists.

Say we want to write a program to manage the inventory at a used car lot. At the lot, cars keep coming and going and the database needs to be continually updated—a new entry is created when a car is added to the lot and an entry deleted when a car is sold. Furthermore, the entries are stored in order by vehicle identification number so that queries from the used car salespeople can be handled quickly. (In reality, a vehicle ID is a sequence of characters and number and couldn't be stored as a single `int`. We've simplified reality for sake of this example.) The information we need to keep per car is as follows:

```
int  vehicle_id;
char make[20];
char model[20];
int  year;
```

```
    int mileage;
    double cost;
```

The frequent operations we want to perform—adding, deleting, and searching for entries can be performed simply and quickly using a linked list data structure. Each node in the linked list will contain all the information associated with a car in the lot, as shown above. We can now define the node structure:

```
struct car_node {
  int   vehicle_id;
  char make[20];
  char model[20];
  int   year;
  int mileage;
  double cost;

  struct car_node *next;      /* Points to a car_node */
};
```

Notice that this structure contains a pointer element which points to something of type car_node, meaning it points to something of the same type as it. We will use this member item to point to the next node in the linked list. If the next field is equal to NULL, then the node is the last in the list.

We've defined the elementary data type of the program. Now, we want to focus on a higher level organization of the program which we'll do by writing the function main. The code is listed in Figure 19.5.

Essentially, we've created a menu driven interface for the used car database. The main data structure is accessed using the variable carbase which is of type struct car_node. Although this node can contain information for a car, we will use it as a dummy head node. Using this dummy head node makes the algorithms for inserting and deleting slightly simpler as we do not have to deal with the degenerate case of an empty list. Initially, carbase.next is set equal to NULL indicating no data items are stored in the data base. Make note that we pass a pointer to the node carbase whenever we call the functions to insert, delete, and search the list.

You should note that this higher level representation of the program makes very little reference to the underlying data structure. From main, we can not tell that a linked list will be used to hold the data items. The data structure is abstracted away at this level in the program. The essence of the program is apparent without being cluttered by the details of the implementation.

Now, we will examine each of the functions, staring with AddEntry. Functionally, AddEntry gets information from the user about a newly acquired car and inserts a node containing this information into the proper spot in the linked list. The code is listed in Figure 19.6.

The value passed to this function is actually a pointer to the dummy head node. The first part of the function allocates a `struct car_node` sized chunk of memory in the heap using `malloc`. If the allocation fails, then an error message is displayed and the program exits using the `exit` library call. The second part of the function reads in input from the standard keyboard and assigns it the proper fields within the new node. The third part performs the insertion.

The insertion requires the use of two temporary pointers, `curr` and `prev`. The pointer `curr` scans along the list (in the `while` loop) looking for either the end of the list or a node which has a larger vehicle ID than the one being added. When one of these conditions is encountered, then the new node is added between the node pointed to by `curr` and the one pointed to by `prev`. The `prev` pointer tracks `curr`, but remains one node behind. Figure 19.7 shows a pictorial representation of an insertion. Once the proper spot to insert is found, then the `prev` node's `next` pointer is updated to point to the new node and the new node's `next` pointer is updated to point to the `curr` node. Also shown in the figure is the degenerate case of adding a node to an empty list. Here, `prev` points to the empty head node and its `next` pointer is updated.

The routine to delete a node from the linked list is very similar to `AddEntry`. Functionally, we want to first query the user about which vehicle ID to delete and then use the ID number to find correct node. Once the node is found, the list is manipulated to remove the node. The code is listed in Figure 19.8.

Finding the node to delete involves a similar scan of the linked list as the scan to find the place to insert a node. The `while` loop advances `curr` and `prev` with `curr` one node ahead of `prev`, until either the end of the list is encountered or the node matching the vehicle id is found. Notice that once a node is deleted, its memory is added back to the heap using the `free` function call. Figure 19.9 shows a pictorial representation of the deletion of a node.

The `Search` operation is very similar to the `AddEntry` and `DelEntry` functions, except that the node is not removed from the list. The code is listed in Figure 19.10.

Why is the linked list such an important data structure? For one thing, it is a dynamic structure and we can grow it or shrink it during execution. Arrays need to be statically allocated. This dynamic quality makes it appealing to use in certain situations where the static nature of arrays would be wasteful. More importantly, the model of connecting data elements via pointers is fundamental and applied very frequently in computer programming. Understanding the linked lists will help you understand more elaborate structures such as hash tables and trees.

```
main()
{
  int op;
  struct car_node carbase;

  /* Initialize the data structure. */
  /* carbase is an empty head node. */
  carbase.next = NULL;

  printf("--- Used car database --- \n");

  do {
    printf("Enter an operation:\n");
    printf("1 - Car added to the lot. Add a new entry for it.\n");
    printf("2 - Car sold.  Remove its entry.\n");
    printf("3 - Query.  Look up a car's information.\n");
    printf("4 - Quit.\n");
    scanf("%d", &op);

    switch(op) {
      case 1:
        AddEntry(&carbase);
        break;

      case 2:
        DeleteEntry(&carbase);
        break;

      case 3:
        Search(&carbase);
        break;

      case 4:
        printf("Good bye.\n");
        break;

      default:
        printf("Invalid number.  Try again.\n");
        break;
    }
  }
  while (op != 4);
}
```

Figure 19.5: The function main for our used car database program.

```
void AddEntry(struct car_node *head_pointer)
{
  struct car_node *new_node;
  struct car_node *curr;
  struct car_node *prev;

  /* dynamically allocate memory for this new entry.  Memory will be on the heap */
  new_node = (struct car_node *) malloc(sizeof(struct car_node));

  if (new_node == NULL) {
    printf("Error: could not allocate a new node\n");
    exit(1);
  }

  /* Get input data from the keyboard */
  printf("Enter information about the new car:");
  printf("<vid> <make> <model> <year> <mileage> <cost>\n");
  scanf("%d %s %s %d %d %lf", &new_node->vehicle_id,
                              &new_node->make,
                              &new_node->model,
                              &new_node->year,
                              &new_node->mileage,
                              &new_node->cost);

  /* Point to start of list */
  prev = head_pointer;
  curr = head_pointer->next;

  /* Traverse list looking for the correct place to insert */
  while (curr != NULL && curr->vehicle_id < new_node->vehicle_id) {
    prev = curr;
    curr = curr->next;
  }

  /* Found the place to insert.  Insert between prev and curr */
  prev->next = new_node;
  new_node->next = curr;
}
```

Figure 19.6: A function to add an entry to the database.

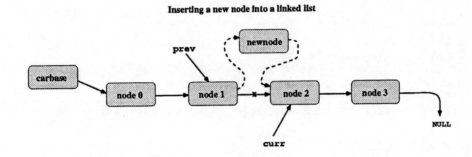

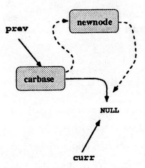

Figure 19.7: Inserting a node into a linked list. The dashed lines indicate newly formed links.

```
void DeleteEntry(struct car_node *head_pointer)
{
  int vehicle_id;
  struct car_node *curr;
  struct car_node *prev;

  printf("Enter the vehicle ID number of the car :\n");
  scanf("%d", &vehicle_id);

  /* Point to start of list */
  prev = head_pointer;
  curr = head_pointer->next;

  /* Traverse list looking for a match */
  while (curr != NULL && curr->vehicle_id != vehicle_id) {
    prev = curr;
    curr = curr->next;
  }

  /* Either we are end of the list, with no match or
     we found the car we're looking for */
  if (curr == NULL)
    printf("The vehicle id %d was not found in the database.\n", vehicle_id);
  else {
    /* curr points to the node we want to delete */
    prev->next = curr->next;
    free(curr);
    printf("Vehicle with id %d deleted.\n", vehicle_id);
  }
}
```

Figure 19.8: A function to delete an entry from the database.

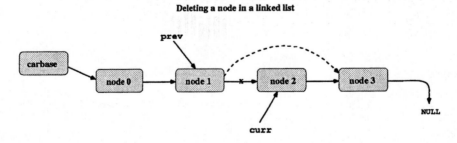

Figure 19.9: Deleting a node from a linked list. The dashed line indicates a newly formed link.

```
void Search(struct car_node *head_pointer)
{
  int vehicle_id;
  struct car_node *curr;
  struct car_node *prev;

  printf("Enter the vehicle ID number of the car :\n");
  scanf("%d", &vehicle_id);

  /* Point to start of list */
  prev = head_pointer;
  curr = head_pointer->next;

  /* Traverse list looking for a match */
  while (curr != NULL && curr->vehicle_id != vehicle_id) {
    prev = curr;
    curr = curr->next;
  }

  /* Either we are end of the list, with no match or
     we found the car we're looking for */
  if (curr == NULL)
      printf("The vehicle id %d was not found in the database.\n", vehicle_id);
  else {
    /* curr points to the node we are looking for */
    printf("vehicle ID : %d\n", curr->vehicle_id);
    printf("make       : %s\n", curr->make);
    printf("model      : %s\n", curr->model);
    printf("year       : %d\n", curr->year);
    printf("mileage    : %d\n", curr->mileage);
    printf("cost       : %f\n", curr->cost);
  }
}
```

Figure 19.10: A function to query the database.

19.5   Exercises.

19.1 Is there a bug in the following program? Explain.

```
struct node {
  int count;
  struct node *next;
};

main()
{
  int data = 0;
  struct node *getdata;

  getdata->count = data + 1;
  printf("%d", getdata->count);
}
```

19.2 The following are a few lines of a C program.

```
struct node {
  int count;
  struct node *next;
};

main()
{
  int data = 0;
  struct node *getdata;

       :
       :

  getdata = getdata->next;

       :
       :
}
```

Write, in LC-2 assembly language, the instructions which are generated by the compiler for the line getdata = getdata->next;.

19.3 The program shown below is compiled on a machine where each basic data type (pointer, character, integer, floating point) occupies one location of memory.

```
struct element {
  char   name[25];
  int    atomic_number;
  float atomic_mass;
};

is_it_noble(struct element t[], int i)
{
  if ((t[i].atomic_number==2)  ||
      (t[i].atomic_number==10) ||
      (t[i].atomic_number==18) ||
      (t[i].atomic_number==36) ||
      (t[i].atomic_number==54) ||
      (t[i].atomic_number==86))
    return 1;
  else
    return 0;
}

main()
{
  int x, y;
  struct element periodic_table[110];


    :
    :
  x = is_it_noble(periodic_table, y);
    :
    :
}
```

1. How many locations will the activation record of the function is_it_noble contain?

2. Assuming that periodic_table, x, and y are the only local variables, how many locations in the activation record for main will be devoted to local variables?

19.4 The following C program is compiled into the LC-2 machine language and executed. The runtime stack begins at x4000. The user types the input

abac

followed by a return.

```
#include <stdio.h>
#define MAX 4
```

```
struct char_rec {
  char ch;
  struct char_rec *back;
};

main()
{
  struct char_rec *ptr, pat[MAX+2];
  int i = 1, j = 1;

  printf("Pattern: ");
  pat[1].back = pat;
  ptr = pat;

  while ((pat[i].ch = getchar()) != '\n') {

    while ((ptr != pat) && (ptr->ch != pat[i].ch))
      ptr = ptr->back;
    ptr[++i].back = ++ptr;

    if (i > MAX) break;
  }

  while (j <= i)
    printf("%d ", pat[j++].back - pat);

  /* Note the pointer arithmetic here: subtraction
     of pointers to structures gives the number of
     structures between addresses, not the number
     of memory locations */
}
```

1. Show the contents of the activation record for main when the program terminates.

2. What is the output of this program for the input abac?

Appendix A

The LC-2 ISA.

A.1 Overview.

The Instruction Set Architecture (ISA) of the LC-2 is defined as follows:

Memory Address Space: 16 bits, corresponding to 2^{16} locations, each consisting of one word (16 bits). Addresses are numbered from 0 (i.e, x0000) to 65,535 (i.e., xFFFF). Addresses are used to identify memory locations and memory-mapped I/O device registers. For convenience, these locations are partitioned into 2^7 pages of 2^9 words each.

General Purpose Registers: Eight 16-bit registers, numbered from 000 to 111.

Program Counter: A 16-bit register.

Bit numbering: Bits of all quantities are numbered, from right to left, starting with bit 0.

Instructions: Instructions are 16 bits wide. Bits[15:12] specify the opcode (operation to be performed), bits[11:0] provide further information that is needed to execute the instruction. Section A.3 provides further information on each of the 16 instructions.

Condition Codes: The load instructions (LD, LDI, LDR, LEA) and the operate instructrions (ADD, AND, and NOT) set the three condition codes, depending on whether the result is negative (N=1, Z=0, P=0), zero (N=0, Z=1, P=0), or positive (N=0, Z=0, P=1).

459

Memory mapped I/O: Input and Output are handled by standard load/store instructions using memory addresses to designate each I/O device register. Table A.1 lists each of the relevant device registers, along with the memory address it has been assigned in the LC-2.

Location	I/O Register Name	I/O Register Function
xF3FC	CRT Status Register	Also known as CRTSR. The ready bit (bit[15]) indicates if the video device is ready to receive another character to print on the screen.
xF3FF	CRT Data Register	Also known as CRTDR. A character written in the low byte of this register will be displayed on the screen.
xF400	Keyboard Status Register	Also known as KBSR. The ready bit (bit[15]) indicates if the keyboard has received a new character.
xF401	Keyboard Data Register	Also known as KBDR. Bits[7:0] contain the last character typed on the keyboard.
xF402	Machine Control Register	Also known as MCR. Bit[15] is the clock enable bit. When cleared, instruction processing stops.

Table A.1: Device Register Assignments.

A.2 Notation.

The following notation will be helpful in understanding the descriptions of the LC-2 instructions (section A.3).

Notation	Meaning
xNumber	The number in hexadecimal notation.
#Number	The number in decimal notation.
A[l:r]	The *field* delimited by bit[l] on the left and bit[r] on the right, from the datum A. For example, if PC contains 0011001100111111, then PC[15:9] is 0011001. PC[2:2] is 1. If l and r are the same bit number, the notation is usually abbreviated PC[2].
A @ B	Concatenation of A and B. For example, if A is 0011 001 and B is 1 1100 1100, A @ B = 0011 0011 1100 1100.
BaseR	Base Register; one of R0..R7, used in conjuncition with a 6-bit offset to compute Base+offset addresses.
page	The set of 2^9 consecutive memory locations whose addresses share the same high 7 address bits.
DR	Destination Register; one of R0..R7 which specifies where the result of an instruction should be written.
imm5	A 5-bit immediate value; bits[5:0] of an instruction, when used as a literal (immediate) value. Taken as a 5 bit, 2's complement integer, it is sign-extended to 16 bits, before it is used. Range: −16..15.
index6	6-bit immediate value; bits[5:0] of an instruction, when used in a Base+offset instruction. Taken as a 6 bit unsigned integer, it is zero-extended to 16 bits, before it is used. Range: 0..63.

Table A.2: Notational Conventions.

Notation	Meaning
LABEL	An assembler construct that identifies a location symbolically (i.e., by means of a name, rather than its 16-bit address).
L	Link bit; differentiates JSR from JMP and JSRR from JMPR instructions. If L =1 (JSR, JSRR), the value of the PC will be saved in R7. If L = 0, the PC is **not** saved in R7.
mem[address]	Denotes the contents of memory at the given address.
PC	Program Counter; 16-bit, processor-internal register which contains the memory address of the **next** instruction to be fetched. For example, during execution of the instruction at address A, the PC contains address A+1.
pgoffset9	9 bits that differentiate the 2^9 locations on a page. PC[15:9] is concatenated with pgoffset9 to form a 16-bit memory address. Range 0..511.
setcc(X)	Indicates that condition codes N, Z and P are set based on the value of X. If X is negative, N=1, Z=0, P=0. If X is zero, N=0, Z=1, P=0. If X is positive, N=0, Z=0, P=1.
SEXT(A)	Sign-extend A. The most significant bit of A is replicated as many times as necessary to extend A to 16 bits. For example, if A = 110000, then SEXT(A) = 1111 1111 1111 0000.
SR, SR1, SR2	Source Register; one of R0..R7 which specifies from where an instruction operand is obtained.
trapvect8	8-bit trap number used in the TRAP instruction. Range 0-255.
ZEXT(A)	Zero-extend A. Zeroes are appended to the left-most bit of A to extend it to 16 bits. For example, if A = 110000, then ZEXT(A) = 0000 0000 0011 0000.

Table A.2: Notational Conventions.

A.3 The Instruction Set.

The 16 LC-2 instructions are summarized in Figure A.1. On the following 16 pages, the instructions will be described in greater detail. For each instruction, we will show the assembly language representation, the actual format of the 16-bit instruction, the operation of the instruction, an English language description of the operation, and one or more examples of the instruction.

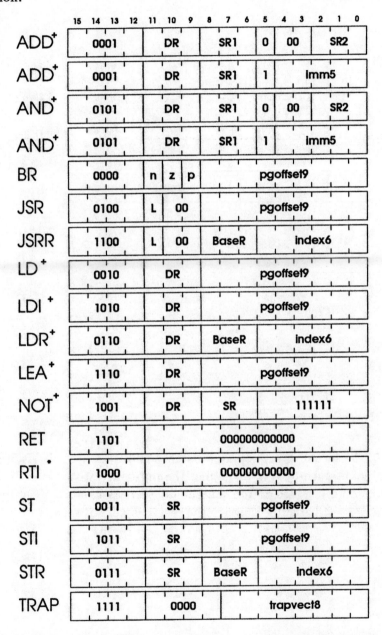

Figure A.1: Formats of the 16 LC-2 Instructions. (+ indicates instructions that modify condition codes; * indicates that meaning and use of RTI is beyond the scope of this book.)

ADD   Addition

Assembler Formats

ADD DR, SR1, SR2
ADD DR, SR1, imm5

Encodings

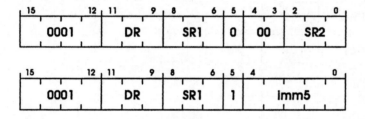

Operation

if (bit[5] == 0)
  DR = SR1 + SR2;
else
  DR = SR1 + SEXT(imm5);
setcc(DR);

Description

If bit[5] is 0, the second source operand is obtained from SR2. If bit[5] is 1, the second source operand is obtained by sign-extending the imm5 field to 16 bits. In both cases, the second source operand is added to the contents of SR1, and the result stored in DR. The condition codes are set, based on whether the result is negative, zero, or positive.

Examples

ADD   R2, R3, R4   ; R2 ← R3 + R4
ADD   R2, R3, #7   ; R2 ← R3 + 7

AND   Bitwise logical AND

Assembler Formats

    AND DR, SR1, SR2
    AND DR, SR1, imm5

Encodings

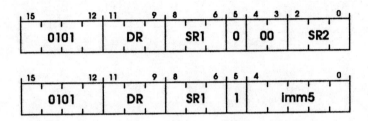

Operation

    if (bit[5] == 0)
      DR = SR1 AND SR2;
    else
      DR = SR1 AND SEXT(imm5);
    setcc(DR);

Description

If bit[5] is 0, the second source operand is obtained from SR2. If bit[5] is 1, the second source operand is obtained by sign-extending the imm5 field to 16 bits. In either case, the second source operand and the contents of SR1 are bitwise ANDed, and the result stored in DR. The condition codes are set, based on whether the binary value produced, taken as a 2's complement integer, is negative, zero, or positive.

Examples

    AND   R2, R3, R4   ; R2 ← R3 AND R4
    AND   R2, R3, #7   ; R2 ← R3 AND 7

BR   Conditional Branch

Assembler Formats

BR   LABEL
BRn   LABEL
BRz   LABEL
BRp   LABEL
BRnz LABEL
BRnp LABEL
BRzp LABEL
BRnzp LABEL

Encoding

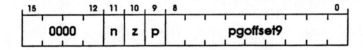

Operation

if ((n AND N) OR (z AND Z) OR (p AND P))
  PC = PC[15:9] @ pgoffset9;

Description

Test the condition codes specified by the state of bits [11:9]. If bit[11] is set, test N; if bit[11] is clear, do not test N. If bit[10] is set, test Z, etc. If any of the condition codes tested is set, branch to the location specified by pgoffset9 on the same page as the branch instruction.

Example

BRzp LOOP   ; Branch to LOOP if the last result was zero or positive.

JSR

JMP

Jump to Subroutine

Jump

Assembler Formats

```
JSR LABEL        (L = 1)
JMP LABEL        (L = 0)
```

Encodings

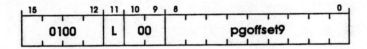

15 12	11	10 9	8 0
0100	L	00	pgoffset9

Operation

```
if (L == 1)
  R7 = PC;
PC = PC[15:9] @ pgoffset9;
```

Description

Unconditionally jump to the location specified by pgoffset9 on the same page as the JSR/JMP instruction. If the link bit L is set, the PC is saved in R7, enabling a subsequent return to the instruction physically following the JSR instruction.

Examples

```
JSR   FOO   ;  Jump to FOO, put return PC into R7.
JMP   FOO   ;  Jump to FOO.
```

JSRR
JMPR

Jump to Subroutine, Base+Offset

Jump, Base+Offset

Assembler Formats

JSRR BaseR, index6   (L = 1)
JMPR BaseR, index6   (L = 0)

Encodings

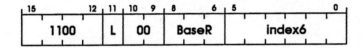

15 12	11	10 9	8 6	5 0
1100	L	00	BaseR	index6

Operation

```
if (L == 1)
    R7 = PC;
PC = BaseR + ZEXT(index6);
```

Description

Unconditionally jump to the location specified by adding ZEXT(index6) to the contents of the base register. If the link bit L is set, the PC is saved in R7, enabling a subsequent return to the instruction physically following the JSRR instruction.

Examples

JSRR   R2, #10   ;   Jump to R2 + #10, put return PC into R7.
JMPR   R2, #10   ;   Jump to R2 + #10.

LD

Load Direct

Assembler Format

LD DR, LABEL

Encoding

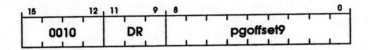

Operation

DR = mem[PC[15:9] @ pgoffset9];
setcc(DR);

Description

Load the register specified by DR from the location specified by pgoffset9 on the same page as the LD instruction. The condition codes are set, based on whether the value loaded is negative, zero, or positive.

Example

LD   R4, COUNT   ;   R4 ← mem[COUNT].

LDI   Load Indirect

Assembler Format

LDI DR, LABEL

Encoding

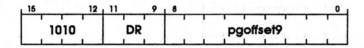

Operation

DR = mem[mem[PC[15:9] @ pgoffset9]];
setcc(DR);

Description

Load the register specified by DR as follows: Construct an address by concatenating the top 7 bits of the program counter with the pgoffset9 field of the LDI instruction. The contents of memory at that address is the address of the data to be loaded into DR. The condition codes are set, based on whether the value loaded is negative, zero, or positive.

Example

LDI   R4, POINTER   ;   R4 ← mem[mem[POINTER]].

LDR   Load Base + Index

Assembler Format

LDR DR, BaseR, index6

Encoding

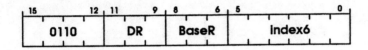

15 12	11 9	8 6	5 0
0110	DR	BaseR	Index6

Operation

DR = mem[BaseR + ZEXT(index6)];
setcc(DR);

Description

Load the register specified by DR from the location specified by a base register and index, as follows: The index is zero-extended to 16 bits and added to the contents of BaseR to form a memory address. The contents of memory at this address are loaded into DR. The condition codes are set, based on whether the value loaded is negative, zero, or positive.

Example

LDR   R4, R2, #10   ;   R4 ← contents of mem[R2 + #10].

LEA   Load Effective Address

Assembler Format

LEA DR, LABEL

Encoding

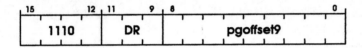

Operation

DR = PC[15:9] @ pgoffset9;
setcc(DR);

Description

Load the register specified by DR with the address formed by concatenating the top 7 bits of the program counter with the pgoffset9 field of the instruction. The condition codes are set, based on whether the value loaded is negative, zero, or positive.

Example

LEA   R4, FOO   ;   R4 ← address of FOO.

NOT   Bitwise complement

Assembler Format

NOT DR, SR

Encoding

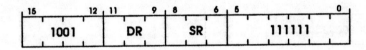

Operation

DR = NOT(SR);
setcc(DR);

Description

Perform the bitwise complement operation on the contents of SR and place the result
in DR. The condition codes are set.

Example

NOT   R4, R2   ;   R4 ← NOT(R2).

RET   Return from subroutine

Assembler Format

RET

Encoding

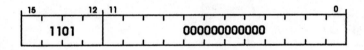

Operation

PC = R7;

Description

Load the PC with the value in R7. This causes a return from a previous JSR or JSRR instruction.

Example

RET   ; PC ← R7.

RTI   Return from Interrupt

Assembler Format

RTI

Encoding

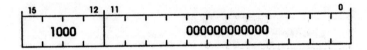

Operation

PC = mem[R6];
R6 = R6 - 1;

Description

Pop the top of the stack, and load the value into PC.

Example

RTI   ;   PC ← top of stack.

Notes

On an external interrupt, the initiating sequence pushes the current PC onto the stack before loading the PC with the starting address of the service routine. The last instruction in the service routine is RTI, which returns control to the interrupted program by popping the stack and loading the value popped into the PC.

This instruction is included in this Appendix only for completeness. Its purpose and use is beyond the scope of the textbook.

ST   **Store direct**

Assembler Format

ST SR, LABEL

Encoding

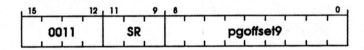

Operation

mem[PC[15:9] @ pgoffset9] = SR;

Description

Store the contents of the register specified by SR into the memory location specified
by pgoffset9 on the same page as the ST instruction.

Example

ST   R4, COUNT   ;   mem[COUNT] ← R4.

STI

Store Indirect

Assembler Format

STI SR, LABEL

Encoding

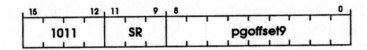

Operation

mem[mem[PC[15:9] @ pgoffset9]] = SR;

Description

Store the contents of the register specified by SR into the memory location whose address is obtained as follows: Construct an address by concatenating the top 7 bits of the program counter with the pgoffset9 field of the STI instruction. The contents of memory at that address is the address of the location to which the data in SR is to be stored.

Example

STI R4, POINTER   ;   mem[mem[POINTER]] ← R4.

STR   Store Base+Offset

Assembler Format

STR SR, BaseR, index6

Encoding

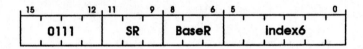

Operation

mem[BaseR + ZEXT(index6)] = SR;

Description

Store the contents of the register specified by SR into the memory location whose
address is specified as follows: the 6-bit offset is zero-extended to 16 bits and added to the
contents of BaseR to form a memory address. This is the address of the location into
which the contents of SR is to be stored.

Example

STR   R4, R2, #10   ;   mem[R2 + #10] ← R4.

TRAP   Operating system call

Assembler Format

TRAP trapvector8

Encoding

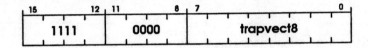

Operation

R7 = PC;
PC = mem[ZEXT(trapvect8)];

Description

Load PC with the contents of the memory location obtained by zero-extending trapvector8 to 16 bits. This is the starting address of the system call specified by trapvector8. Load R7 with the PC, which enables a return to the instruction physically following the TRAP instruction in original program after the service routine has completed.   Each of the first $2^8 = 256$ memory locations contains the starting address for the system call specified by its corresponding trapvector. This region of memory is called the trap vector table. See Table A.3.

Example

TRAP   x23   ;   Direct the operating system to execute the **IN** system call.

TRAP Number	Assembler Name	Description
x20	GETC	Read a single character from the keyboard. The character is not echoed onto the console. Its ASCII code is copied into R0. The high 8 bits of R0 are cleared.
x21	OUT	Write a character in R0[7:0] to the console.
x22	PUTS	Write a string pointed to by R0 to the console.
x23	IN	Print a prompt on the screen and read a single character from the keyboard. The character is echoed onto the console, and its ASCII code is copied into R0. The high 8 bits of R0 are cleared.
x25	HALT	Halt execution and print a message on the console.

Table A.3: TRAP Vector Table.

Appendix B

From LC-2 to x86

Appendix C

The Microarchitecture of the LC-2.

Appendix D

The C Programming Language

D.1 Overview.

This appendix is a C reference manual oriented towards novice C programmers. It covers a significant portion of the language, with an emphasis on the material covered in this book. Each item covered within these nine sections contains a brief summary of the particular feature, stated in an illustrative manner, and an example, if appropriate. The intent of this appendix is to provide a quick reference to various features of the language which may be useful during programming.

D.2 C conventions.

D.2.1 Source files.

The C programming convention is to separate a long programs into files of two types: source files (with the extension .c) and header files (with the extension, .h). Source files, sometimes called .c or dot-c files, contain the C statements for a group of related functions. Each .c file is compiled into an object file and these objects are linked together into an executable image by the linker.

D.2.2 Header files.

Header files typically never contain C statements but rather contain function, variable, and structure declarations and preprocessor macros. The programming convention is to couple a header file to the source file in which the declared items are *defined*. For example, if the source file stdio.c contains the definitions for the functions printf, scanf, getchar, and putchar, then the header file stdio.h contains the declarations for these functions. If one of these functions is called from another .c file, then the stdio.h header file should be included to get the proper function definitions.

D.2.3   Comments.

In C, comments begin with the two character delimiter /* and end with */. Comments within comments, or comments within strings or character constants will not be recognized as comments. They can span multiple lines.

D.2.4   Constants.

Several types of constant values can appear within a program. The type (see D.3.2) of such a value is inferred by the syntax used to express it.

Integer.

Integer constants can be expressed either in decimal, octal, or hexadecimal notation. If the constant is prefixed by a 0, it will be interpreted as an octal number. If the constant begins with a 0x, it will be interpreted as hexadecimal (thus it can contain the letters a through f and A through F). An unprefixed constant indicates that it is in decimal notation. All forms can be preceded by a minus sign - to indicate a negative value.

An integer constant can also be suffixed with the letter l or L to indicate that it is a long. An integer constant suffixed with the letter u or U indicated an unsigned value. Refer to D.3.3 for long and unsigned types.

The first three examples below express the same number, 87. The two last versions express it as an unsigned value and as a long value.

```
87
0x57
0127
-24     /* -24 in decimal */
-024    /* -20 in decimal */
-0x24   /* -36 in decimal */
87U
87L
```

Floating point.

Floating point constants consists of three parts: an integer part, a decimal point, and a fractional part. The fractional or integer part are optional, but one of the two must be present. The number preceded by a minus sign indicates a negative value. Several examples are given below.

```
1.613123
.613123
```

```
1.          /* expresses the number 1.0 */
-.613123
```

Floating point constants can also be expressed in exponential notation, when the form above is followed by an e or E. The e or E signals the beginning of the integer (optionally, signed) exponent, which is the power of 10 by which the part preceeding the exponent is multiplied. The exponent is obviously optional (see the examples above), and if used, then the decimal point is optional. Examples are given below.

```
6.023e23        /* 6.023 * 10^23      */
454.323e-22     /* 454.323 * 10^(-22) */
5e13            /* 5.0 * 10^13        */
```

By default, a floating point type is a `double` or double-precision floating point number, but this can be modified with an optional suffix. The suffix f or F indicates a `float` or single-precision floating point number. The suffix l or L indicates a `long double` (See D.3.3).

Character.

A character constant can be expressed by surrounding a particular character by single quotes, e.g., `'c'`. This converts the character into the internal character code used by the computer, which for most computers, including the LC-2, is ASCII.

The Table D.1 lists special characters. Since they typically cannot be expressed with a single keystroke, the C programming language provides a means to state them via a sequence of characters. The last two forms, octal and hexadecimal, specify ways of stating an arbitrary character by using its code value, stated either octal or hex. For example, the character 'S', which has the ASCII value of 83 (decimal) can be stated as '\0123' or '\x53'.

String constants.

A string constant within a C program must be enclosed within double quote characters, ". String constants have the type `char *` and space for them is allocated in a special section of the address space reserved for constant values. The termination character '\0' is automatically added by the compiler. The following are common examples of a string constants:

```
char greeting[10] = "bon jour!";
printf("This is a string constant");
```

character	sequence
newline	\n
horizontal tab	\t
vertical tab	\v
backspace	\b
carriage return	\r
formfeed	\f
audible alert	\a
backslash \	\\
question mark ?	\?
single quote '	\'
double quote "	\"
octal number	\0nnn
hexadecimal number	\xnnn

Table D.1: Special characters in C.

D.2.5   Formatting.

C is a freely formatted language. The programmer is free to add spaces, tabs, carriage returns, newlines between and within statements and declarations. This feature allows the programmer to adopt a style for coding in C, which can be helpful for making the code more readable.

See 11.5.2 for more information.

D.2.6   Keywords.

The following list is a set of reserved words which have special meaning within the C language.

```
auto        double      int         struct
break       else        long        switch
case        enum        register    typedef
char        extern      return      union
const       float       short       unsigned
continue    for         signed      void
default     goto        sizeof      volatile
do          if          static      while
```

D.3 Identifiers, types and declarations.

D.3.1 Identifiers

A programmer can supply names for various items within a program: variables, functions, members of structures, are a few common examples. In C, identifiers consist of letters, numbers, and the underscore character _. Uppercase letters are different from lower case, so the identifier A is different from a. There are two restrictions, however: the first character of an identifier cannot be a digit and only the first 31 characters of an identifier's name are used by the compiler to distinguish one identifier from another. Also, identifiers must be different from any of the C keywords (See D.2.6).

Several examples of legal identifiers are given below. Each is a distinct identifier.

```
red
Blue
__green__
primary_colors
PrimaryColors
```

See 12.1 for more information.

D.3.2 Basic data types.

In C, all identifiers and expressions (see D.6.1) have a type associated with them. The type indicates how the data referenced by the identifier or the value generated by the expression is to be interpreted. For instance, if the variable kappa is of type int, then it contains a bit pattern which will be interpreted as a signed integer.

There are several predefined basic types within the C language: int, float, double, char. They exist automatically within all implementations of C, though their sizes and range of values depends upon the computer system being used.

int

Integer types deal with signed whole numbers. Typical computers have 32 bit signed integers, expressed in 2's complement form. Such integers would have the range +2147483647 and -2147483648.

float

Objects declared of type float deal with single precision floating numbers.

double

Objects declared of type `double` deal with double precision floating numbers.

char

Objects of character type contain a single character, expressed in the character code used by the computer system. Typical computer systems use the ASCII character code. The size of a `char` is large enough to store a character from character set. C also imposes that the size of a `short int` must be at least the size of a `char`

Collectively, the `int` and `char` types are referred to as integral types whereas `float` and `double` are floating types.

See 12.1.1 for more information on these basic types.

D.3.3   Type qualifiers.

The basic types can be slightly modified with the use of a type qualifier.

signed, unsigned

The integral types `int` and `char` can be modified with the use of the `signed` and `unsigned` qualifiers. By default, integers are signed; the default on characters depends on the particular computer system.

For example, if a particular computer uses 32-bit 2's complement signed integers, then a `signed int` can have any value in the range +2147483647 and -2147483648. On the same machine, an `unsigned int` can have a value any value in the range +4294967295 and 0.

```
signed int c;       /* the signed modifier is redundant */
unsigned int d;

signed char j;      /* forces the char code to be interpreted
                        as a signed value */

unsigned char k;    /* the char will be interpreted as an
                        unsigned number */
```

long, short

The qualifiers `long` and `short` allow the programmer to manipulate the physical size of an integer. Important to note is that there is no strict definition of how much larger one type of integer is than another. The C language only states that the size of a `short int` is less than or equal to the size of an `int` which is less than or equal to the size of a `long int`. Stated more completely and precisely:

```
sizeof(char) <= sizeof(short int) <= sizeof(int) <= sizeof(long int)
```

Several new machines (particularly, machines which support 64-bit data types) make a distinction on the `long` qualifier. To check out the ranges of a particular computer, examine the standard header file `<limits.h>`. On most UNIX systems, it will be in the `/usr/include` directory.

Here are several examples:

```
short int q;
long int p;
unsigned long int r;
```

The qualifier can also be used with the floating type `double` to possibly create a floating point number with higher precision or larger range (if such a type is available on the particular computer) than a `double`. As stated by the ANSI C specification: the size of a `float` is less than or equal to the size of a `double` which is less than or equal to the size of a `long double`.

```
double x;
long double y;
```

`const`

A value which doesn't change through the course of execution can be qualified with the `const` qualifier. For example,

```
const double pi = 3.14159;
```

The base address of an array is a `const` value. For example, if an array is declared with the declaration `int vector[100]`, then the identifier `vector` is of type `const int *`.

D.3.4 Storage class.

Variables can also have a storage class qualifier which directs the compiler on where (if at all) to allocate storage for a particular item. By default (i.e., if no storage class qualifier is specified), variables declared within functions are allocated in on the stack (see 14.5.1); they are given *automatic* storage class by default. Variables declared globally are allocated in the global data section.

Variables declared within a function can be qualified with the `static` qualifier to indicate that they are to be allocated with other static variables, allowing their value to persist across invocations of the function in which they are declared. For example:

```
int count(int x)
{
  static int y;

  y++;
  printf("The function count has been called %d times", y);
}
```

The value of y will not lost when the activation record of `count` is popped off the stack because its storage is allocated in the global data section. Every call of the function `count` updates the value of y.

The initial value of data items in the *static* class are guaranteed to be zero. This is not true for data items in the automatic class; they must be initialized by the programmer.

There is a special qualifier called `register` that can be applied to data items in the automatic class. This qualifier provides a hint to the compiler that the value is frequently accessed within the code, suggesting that allocation within a register may enhance performance. The compiler, however, is not bound to allocate it in a register.

Functions, as well as variables, can be qualified with the qualifier `extern`. This qualifier indicates that the function's or variable's storage is defined in another object module which will be linked together with the current module when the executable is constructed. By default, all global variables are qualified as `externs`.

D.3.5   Derived types.

Using the basic types as elements, different types of derived types can also be constructed within C. These derived types include pointers, arrays, and structures.

arrays.

A variable declared as an array indicates that the variable exists as a contiguous sequence of values, which are individually accessible using an integer index. The elements of an array is numbered starting at 0. The size of the array, i.e., the number of elements it contains, must be stated when the array is declared.

```
char string[100];    /* Declares an array of 100 characters */
int  data[20];       /* Declares an array of 20 integers */
```

To access a particular element within an array, an index is formed using an integer expression (see D.6.1) within square brackets, [ ].

```
data[0]      /* Accesses the first element of the array data */
data[i+3]    /* The variable i must be an integer */
string[x+y]  /* The variable x and y must be an integers */
```

The compiler does not check (nor does it generate code to check) if the value of the index falls within the bounds of the array, but blindly generates the machine code to make the access. The responsibility of ensuring proper access to the array is upon the programmer.

See 17.3 for more information on arrays.

pointers.

Pointers are data items which are addresses of other data items. Pointer types are declared by prefixing an identifier with an asterisk *. The type of a pointer indicates the type of the data item being pointed to by the pointer. For example,

```
int *v;   /* v points to an integer */
```

See 17.2 for more information on pointers.

D.3.6 structures.

Structures are groups of data items treated as a single entity. The programmer can specify and name the data items which compose a structure using the following syntax for a structure declaration:

```
struct tag_id {
  type1 member1;
  type2 member2;
   :
   :
  typeN memberN;
};
```

This structure has member elements named *member1* of type *type1*, *member2* of *type2*, up to *memberN* of *typeN*. The structure is given an optional tag *tag_id*. Variables of this structure type can be declared using this tag.

```
struct tag_id x;
```

This declaration allocates storage the structure variable **x**. This variable will have all the members defined when the structure was declared.

Example:

```
struct point {
   int x;
   int y;
};

struct point function[100];    /* declares an array of structure type variables */
```

See 19.2 for more information on structures.

D.4   Declarations.

In C, variables must be declared before they can be used. Functions declarations are optional. Declarations inform the compiler of characteristics (e.g., its type, storage class, etc.) of the data item so that correct machine code can be generated whenever the data item is used.

D.4.1   Variable declarations.

The format for a variable declaration is as follows:

```
[storage_class] [type_qualifier] {type} {identifier} [ = initializer];
```

The curly braces { } indicate items which are required and the square brackets [ ] indicate optional items.

The initializer for variables of automatic storage, (see D.3.4) can be any expression which uses previously defined values. For variables of the static class or external variables, the initializer must be a constant expression.

Also, multiple identifiers (and initializers) can be placed on the same line, creating multiple variables of the same type, having the same storage class and type qualities.

Examples:

```
static long unsigned int k = 10UL;
register char l = 'Q';
int list[100];
struct node_type n;
```

Declarations can be placed at the beginning of any *block* (see D.6.2), before any statements. Such declarations are visible only within the block in which they appear. Declarations can also appear at the outermost-level of the program, outside of all functions. Such declarations are globally visible, that is visible from all parts of the program.

See 12.1 for more information on variable declarations.

D.4.2 Function declarations.

A function's declaration informs the compiler about the type of value returned by the function and the type, number, and order of arguments the function expects to receive from it's caller.

The format for a function declaration is as follows:

```
{type} {function_id}([type1] [, type2], ...[, typeN]);
```

The curly braces { } indicate items which are required and the square brackets [ ] indicate items which are used if appropriate.

The *type* indicates the type of the value returned by the function and can be of any basic type (see D.3.2) or derived type (see D.3.5). If a function does not return a value, then its type must be declared as **void**.

The *function_id* can be any legal identifier that hasn't already been defined.

Enclosed within parentheses following the *function_id* are the types of each of the arguments expected by the function, indicated by *type1*, *type2*, *typeN*, each separated by a comma. Optionally, an identifier can be supplied for each argument, indicating what the particular argument will be called within the function's definition.

For example, this is a function declaration for a function which returns the arithmetic average of an array of integers:

```
int average(int numbers[], int how_many);
```

See 14.3.1 for more information on function declarations.

D.5 Operators.

In this section, each of the C operators are presented, grouped by the operation they perform. Within the tables, is a precedence class for each operator, numbered from 1 to 18. Operator within lower numbered classes have higher precedence than ones within higher numbered ones. Within the same precedence class, operators associate left-to-right or right-to left, as indicated by the associativity column. For example, the addition operator + and subtraction operator – are in the same class (7) and are grouped left-to-right. So, for the expression

```
x - y + z
```

the subtraction is performed first.

Also included for each operator is a reference to the text where a description of the operation it performs and the types of values it expects can be found.

D.5.1   Assignment operator.

Operator symbol	Operation	Example usage	Precedence	Associativity	Ref
=	assignment	x = y	18	r-to-l	12.2.2

Table D.2: The assignment operator.

D.5.2 Arithmetic operators.

Operator symbol	Operation	Example usage	Precedence	Associativity	Ref
+	positive	+x	4	r-to-l	12.2.3
-	negative	-x	4	r-to-l	12.2.3
+	addition	x + y	7	l-to-r	12.2.3
-	subtraction	x - y	7	l-to-r	12.2.3
*	multiplication	x * y	6	l-to-r	12.2.3
/	division	x / y	6	l-to-r	12.2.3
%	modulus	x % y	6	l-to-r	12.2.3

Table D.3: Arithmetic operators in C.

D.5.3 Bitwise operators.

Operator symbol	Operation	Example usage	Precedence	Associativity	Ref
&	bitwise AND	x & y	11	l-to-r	12.2.5
|	bitwise OR	x | y	13	l-to-r	12.2.5
~	bitwise NOT	~x	4	r-to-l	12.2.5
^	bitwise XOR	x ^ y	12	l-to-r	12.2.5
<<	left shift	x << y	8	l-to-r	12.2.5
>>	right shift	x >> y	8	l-to-r	12.2.5

Table D.4: Bitwise operators in C.

D.5.4 Logical operators.

Operator symbol	Operation	Example usage	Precedence	Associativity	Ref
&&	logical AND	x && y	14	l-to-r	12.2.6
||	logical OR	x || y	15	l-to-r	12.2.6
!	logical NOT	!x	4	r-to-l	12.2.6

Table D.5: Logical operators in C.

D.5.5   Relational operators.

Operator symbol	Operation	Example usage	Precedence	Associativity	Ref
==	equal	x == y	10	l-to-r	12.2.7
!=	not equal	x != y	10	l-to-r	12.2.7
>	greater than	x > y	9	l-to-r	12.2.7
>=	greater than or equal	x >= y	9	l-to-r	12.2.7
<	less than	x < y	9	l-to-r	12.2.7
<=	less than or equal	x <= y	9	l-to-r	12.2.7

Table D.6: Relational operators in C.

D.5.6   Special operators.

Operator symbol	Operation	Example usage	Precedence	Associativity	Ref
++	increment (prefix)	++x	3	r-to-l	12.2.8
++	increment (postfix)	x++	2	r-to-l	12.2.8
++	decrement (prefix)	--x	3	r-to-l	12.2.8
++	decrement (postfix)	x--	2	r-to-l	12.2.8
+=	add and assign	x += y	18	l-to-r	12.2.8
-=	subtract and assign	x -= y	18	l-to-r	12.2.8
*=	multiply and assign	x *= y	18	l-to-r	12.2.8
/=	divide and assign	x /= y	18	l-to-r	12.2.8
%=	modulus and assign	x %= y	18	l-to-r	12.2.8
&=	and and assign	x &= y	18	l-to-r	12.2.8
|=	or and assign	x |= y	18	l-to-r	12.2.8
^=	xor and assign	x ^= y	18	l-to-r	12.2.8
<<=	left shift and assign	x <<= y	18	l-to-r	12.2.8
>>=	right shift and assign	x >>= y	18	l-to-r	12.2.8

Table D.7: Special operators in C.

D.5.7   Conditional expression.

Operator symbol	Operation	Example usage	Precedence	Associativity	Ref
? :	conditional expression	x ? y : z	17	l-to-r	12.2.8

Table D.8: Conditional expressions in C.

D.5.8   Pointer, array, structure operators.

Operator symbol	Operation	Example usage	Precedence	Associativity	Ref
*	dereference	*x	4	r-to-l	17.2.2
&	address of	&x	4	r-to-l	17.2.2
[]	array reference	x[i]	1	l-to-r	17.3.1
.	structure member operator	x.y	1	l-to-r	19.2.1
->	structure pointer operator	p->y	1	l-to-r	19.2.1

Table D.9: Pointer, array, structure operators in C.

D.5.9   Miscellaneous operators.

Operator symbol	Operation	Example usage	Precedence	Associativity	Ref
sizeof	size of data item in bytes	sizeof(x)	4	r-to-l	19.3
(type_name)	cast	(int)	5	r-to-l	19.3

Table D.10: Miscellaneous operators C.

D.5.10   Precedence.

Precedence group	Associativity	Operators
1	l-to-r	*function call* () [ ] . ->
2	r-to-l	*postfix* ++ *postfix* --
3	r-to-l	*prefix* ++ *prefix* --
4	r-to-l	*dereference* * *address* &
		unary + *unary* -
		˜ ! sizeof
5	r-to-l	*cast* (type)
6	l-to-r	*multiply* * / %
7	l-to-r	+ -
8	l-to-r	<< >>
10	l-to-r	< > <= >=
11	l-to-r	== !=
12	l-to-r	&
13	l-to-r	^
14	l-to-r	|
15	l-to-r	&&
16	l-to-r	||
17	l-to-r	?:
18	r-to-l	= += -= *= etc...

Table D.11: Operator Precedence, highest to lowest.

D.6   Expressions and statements.

D.6.1   Expressions.

An expression is any legal combination of constants, variables, operators, and function calls. An expression has an associated type, which is determined according to C typing rules. If all the elements of an expression are **int** types, then the expression is of **int** type.

Below are several examples of expressions.

```
a * a + b * b
a++ - c / 3
a <= 4
q || integrate(x)
```

See 12.2 for more information on expressions.

D.6.2 Statements.

In C, simple statements are expressions terminated by a semicolon ;. Typically, statements modify a variable or have some side effect when the expression is evaluated.

```
c = a * a + b * b;     /* Two simple statements */
b = a++ - c / 3;
```

Related statements can be grouped togethered into a compound statement, or *block*, by surrounding them with curly braces { }. Syntactically, the compound statement is the same as a simple statement and they can be used interchangeably.

```
{                      /* One compound statement */
  c = a * a + b * b;
  b = a++ - c / 3;
}
```

See 12.2 for more information on statements.

D.7 Control flow.

D.7.1 if

An if statement has the format:

```
if (expression)
   statement;
```

If the *expression*, which can be of any basic (see D.3.2) or pointer type, evaluates to a non-zero value, then the *statement*, which can be a compound statement, is executed.

Example:

```
if (x < 0)
   a = b + c;     /* Only executes if the value of x is less than zero */
```

See 13.1.1 for more examples of if statements.

D.7.2 if-else

An if-else statement has the format:

```
if (expression)
   statement1;
else
   statement2;
```

If the *expression*, which can be of any basic (see D.3.2) or pointer type, evaluates to a non-zero value, then *statement1*, which can be a compound statement, is executed. Otherwise, *statement2* is executed.

Example:

```
if (x < 0)
   a = b + c;    /* Only executes if the value of x is less than zero */
else
   a = b - c;    /* otherwise, this is executed. */
```

See 13.1.2 for more examples of `if-else` statements.

D.7.3   switch

A `switch` statement has the format:

```
switch(expression) {
case const-expr1:
     statement1A;
     statement1B;
     :
     :

case const-expr2:
     statement2A;
     statement2B;
     :
     :


     :
     :
     :

case const-exprN:
     statementNA;
     statementNB;
     :
     :
```

```
}
```

A `switch` statement is composed of an *expression*, which must be of integral type (See D.3.2), followed by compound statement (though it is not required to be compound, it almost always is). Within the compound statement exist one or more `case` labels, each with an associated constant integral expression, called *const-expr1, const-expr2, const-exprN* in the example above. Within a `switch`, each `case` label must be different.

When a `switch` is encountered, the controlling *expression* is evaluated. If one of the case label matches the value of `expression`, then control jumps to the statement which follows and proceeds from there.

The special case label `default` can be used to catch the situation where none of the other case labels match. If the `default` case is not present and none of the other labels match the value of the controlling expression, then no statements within the `switch` are executes.

Example:

```
char k;

k = getchar();
switch (k) {
case '+':
  a = b + c;
  break;       /* the break statement cause control to leave the switch */

case '-':
  a = b - c;
  break;       /* the break statement cause control to leave the switch */

case '*':
  a = b * c;
  break;       /* the break statement cause control to leave the switch */

case '/':
  a = b / c;
  break;       /* the break statement cause control to leave the switch */
}
```

See 13.1.3 for more examples of `switch` statements.

D.7.4 while

A `while` statement has the format:

```
while (expression)
   statement;
```

The `while` statement is an iteration construct. If the value of *expression* evaluates to non-zero, then *statement* is executed. Control does not pass to the subsequent statement, but rather *expression* is evaluated again and the process is repeated. This continues until *expression* evaluates to 0, in which case control passes to the next statement.

Example:

```
x = 0;
while (x < 100) {
   printf("x = %d\n", x);
   x = x + 1;
}
```

See 13.2.1 for more examples of `while` statements.

D.7.5   for

A `for` statement has the format:

```
for (initializer; term-expr; re-initializer)
   statement;
```

The `for` statement is an iteration construct. The *initializer*, which is an expression, is evaluated only once, before the loop begins. The *term-expr* is an expression which is evaluated before each iteration of the loop. If the *term-expr* evaluates to non-zero, the loop progresses, otherwise the loop terminates and control passes to the next statement. Each iteration of the loop consists of the execution of the *statement* which makes up the loop body and the evaluation of the *re-initializer* expression.

Example:

```
for (x = 0; x < 100; x++) {
   printf("x = %d\n", x);
}
```

See 13.2.2 for more examples of `for` statements.

D.7.6   do-while

A `do-while` statement has the format:

```
do
  statement;
while (expression);
```

The do-while statement is an iteration construct similar to the while statement. When a do-while is first encountered, the *statement* which makes up the loop body is executed first, then the *expression* to determine whether to execute another iteration is evaluated. If it is non-zero, then another iteration is made and *statement* is executed again. In this manner, a do-while always executes its loop body at least once.

Example:

```
x = 0;
do {
    printf("x = %d\n", x);
    x = x + 1;
}
while (x < 100);
```

See 13.2.3 for more examples of do-while statements.

D.7.7   break

A break statement has the format:

```
break;
```

The break statement may only be used in an iteration statement or in a switch statement. It passes control out of the smallest statement containing it to the statement immediately following.

Typically, break is used to exit a loop before the terminating condition is encountered.

Example:

```
for (x = 0; x < 100; x++) {
  :
  :
  if (error)
    break;
  :
  :
}
```

See 13.2.4 for more examples of break statements.

D.7.8   `continue`

A `continue` statement has the format:

```
continue;
```

The `continue` statement may only be used in an iteration statement. It prematurely terminates the execution of the loop body statement of the loop, ie., it terminates the current iteration of the loop. The looping expression are evaluated to determine whether another iteration. In a `for` loop the *re-initializer* is also evaluated.

Example:

```
for (x = 0; x < 100; x++) {
  :
  :
  if (skip)
    continue;
  :
  :
}
```

See 13.2.4 for more examples of `continue` statements.

D.7.9   `return`

A `return` statement has the format:

```
return expression;
```

The `return` statement cause control to return to the current caller function, ie., the function which called the function which contains the `return` statement. The *expression* which follows the `return` is necessary for functions which return values. The value it evaluates to is returned to the caller function.

Example:

```
return x + y;
```

See 14.3.4 for more examples of `return` statements.

D.8 Standard libary functions.

D.8.1 I/O functions.

D.8.2 String functions.

D.8.3 Math functions.

Appendix E

Extending C to C++.

Appendix F

Useful Tables

F.1 Conversion Specifications for C I/O.

printf Conversions	printed as
%d, %i	signed decimal
%o	octal
%x, %X	hexadecimal (a-f or A-F)
%u	unsigned decimal
%c	single char
%s	string, terminated by \0
%f	single precision floating point in decimal notation
%e, %E	double precision floating point in decimal notation
%p	pointer

Table F.1: **printf** conversion specifications.

scanf Conversions	parameter type
%d	signed decimal
%i	decimal, octal (leading 0), hex (leading 0x or 0X)
%o	octal
%x	hexadecimal
%u	unsigned decimal
%c	char
%s	string of non-white space characters, \0 added
%f, %e	floating point number

Table F.2: **scanf** conversion specifications.

F.2   ASCII code table

Character	ASCII	Character	ASCII	Character	ASCII	Character	ASCII
nul	0	sp	32	@	64	`	96
soh	1	!	33	A	65	a	97
stx	2	"	34	B	66	b	98
etx	3	#	35	C	67	c	99
eot	4	$	36	D	68	d	100
enq	5	%	37	E	69	e	101
ack	6	&	38	F	70	f	102
bel	7	'	39	G	71	g	103
bs	8	(	40	H	72	h	104
ht	9	)	41	I	73	i	105
lf	10	*	42	J	74	j	106
vt	11	+	43	K	75	k	107
ff	12	,	44	L	76	l	108
cr	13	-	45	M	77	m	109
so	14	.	46	N	78	n	110
si	15	/	47	O	79	o	111
dle	16	0	48	P	80	p	112
dc1	17	1	49	Q	81	q	113
dc2	18	2	50	R	82	r	114
dc3	19	3	51	S	83	s	115
dc4	20	4	52	T	84	t	116
nak	21	5	53	U	85	u	117
syn	22	6	54	V	86	v	118
etb	23	7	55	W	87	w	119
can	24	8	56	X	88	x	120
em	25	9	57	Y	89	y	121
sub	26	:	58	Z	90	z	122
esc	27	;	59	[	91	{	123
fs	28	<	60	\	92	|	124
gs	29	=	61	]	93	}	125
rs	30	>	62	^	94	~	126
us	31	?	63	_	95	del	127

Table F.3: ASCII values represented in decimal.

F.3 Commonly Used Numerical Prefixes

Amount	Commonly used Base-2 approx	Prefix	Abbrev	Derived from
10^{24}	2^{80}	yotta	Y	Greek for eight *okto*
10^{21}	2^{70}	zetta	Z	Greek for seven *hepta*
10^{18}	2^{60}	exa	E	Greek for six *hexa*
10^{15}	2^{50}	peta	P	Greek for five *pente*
10^{12}	2^{40}	tera	T	Greek for monster *teras*
10^{9}	2^{30}	giga	G	Greek for giant *gigas*
10^{6}	2^{20}	mega	M	Greek for large *megas*
10^{3}	2^{10}	kilo	k	Greek for thousand *chilioi*
10^{-3}		milli	m	Latin for thousand *milli*
10^{-6}		micro	μ	Greek for small *mikros*
10^{-9}		nano	n	Greek for dwarf *nanos*
10^{-12}		pico	p	Spanish for a little *pico*
10^{-15}		femto	f	Danish and Norwegian for fifteen *femten*
10^{-18}		atto	a	Danish and Norwegian for eighteen *atten*
10^{-21}		zepto	z	Greek for seven *hepta*
10^{-24}		yocto	y	Greek for eight *okto*

Table F.4:

Index